S0-FQY-633

# The University of Mantua,
# the Gonzaga, and the Jesuits, 1584–1630

# The UNIVERSITY of MANTUA, the GONZAGA & the JESUITS, 1584–1630

PAUL F. GRENDLER

THE JOHNS HOPKINS UNIVERSITY PRESS
*Baltimore*

*This book has been brought to publication with the generous assistance of the Lila Acheson Wallace–Reader's Digest Publications Subsidy at Villa I Tatti.*

© 2009 The Johns Hopkins University Press
All rights reserved. Published 2009
Printed in the United States of America on acid-free paper
2 4 6 8 9 7 5 3 1

The Johns Hopkins University Press
2715 North Charles Street
Baltimore, Maryland 21218-4363
www.press.jhu.edu

Library of Congress Cataloging-in-Publication Data
Grendler, Paul F.
The University of Mantua, the Gonzaga, and the Jesuits, 1584–1630 /
Paul F. Grendler.
p. cm.
Includes bibliographical references and index.
ISBN 978-0-8018-9171-7 (hardcover : alk. paper)
1. University of Mantua. 2. Gonzaga family. 3. Jesuits—Education (Higher)—
Italy—History—17th century. 4. Jesuits—Education (Higher)—Italy—History—
16th century. I. Title.
LF3893.M36G74 2009
378.45'281—dc22      2008035750

A catalog record for this book is available from the British Library.

*Special discounts are available for bulk purchases of this book. For more information, please contact Special Sales at 410-516-6936 or specialsales@press.jhu.edu.*

The Johns Hopkins University Press uses environmentally friendly book materials, including recycled text paper that is composed of at least 30 percent post-consumer waste, whenever possible. All of our book papers are acid-free, and our jackets and covers are printed on paper with recycled content.

To my friends and former students

at the University of Toronto

# Contents

|  |  |
|---|---|
| List of Illustrations | xi |
| List of Tables | xiii |
| Preface | xv |
| Abbreviations | xix |
| Values of Some Coins and Monies of Account ca. 1625 | xxi |

CHAPTER 1. **The Place and the People**   1
1. The Duchy of Mantua   1
2. The Economy and the People   3
3. Monferrato   9
4. Jesuit Attempts to Enter Italian Universities   14

CHAPTER 2. **The Jesuits Come to Mantua**   24
1. The Founding of the Jesuit College   24
2. Blessed Luigi Gonzaga   41
3. Growth of the College and School   48

CHAPTER 3. **Ferdinando Gonzaga and the Jesuits Create a University**   54
1. University Dreams   54
2. Gonzaga Support of Learning   56
3. The Education of Ferdinando Gonzaga   59
4. Duke Ferdinando Gonzaga   68
5. The Jesuit Part of the University   73
6. The Public Academy of Mantua   79

CHAPTER 4. Doctor Marta     83
    1. Early Life and Works   84
    2. Ecclesiastical and Civil Jurisdiction   92
    3. A Spy for James I   101
    4. The *Supplicatio ad imperatorem . . . contra Paulum Quintum*   108
    5. Was Doctor Marta a Doctor?   114
    6. The *Compilatio totius iuris ex universi orbis*   117
    7. The Move to Mantua   122

CHAPTER 5. Fabrizio Bartoletti and Other Professors     127
    1. Fabrizio Bartoletti   128
    2. The *Encyclopaedia hermetico-dogmatica*   130
    3. The Courting of Bartoletti   140
    4. More Searches   144

CHAPTER 6. The Peaceful University of Mantua     149
    1. Final Preparations and Crises   149
    2. Finances   154
    3. The Pacifico Gymnasio Mantuano Begins   158
    4. Students   170

CHAPTER 7. Medicine, Law, and Tacitus     175
    1. Botanical Medicine   175
    2. Chemical Medicine   178
    3. Bartoletti's Research on Angina Pectoris   184
    4. Law Professors and Marta's Research   192
    5. The Tacitus Professorship   195

CHAPTER 8. The Jesuit Professorships     198
    1. The Jesuit Curriculum and Teaching   199
    2. The Career Paths of Jesuits and Lay Professors   216
    3. Two Academic Cultures   217

CHAPTER 9. The End of the University of Mantua     227
    1. The Crisis of the Mantuan Succession    227
    2. The Contenders    232
    3. War, Plague, and the Sack of Mantua    235
    4. The Imprisonment and Death of Doctor Marta    240
    5. The End of the University of Mantua    245
    6. After the Sack    246

*Appendix: Jesuit Professors at Mantua, 1624–1630*     251
*Bibliography*     255
*Index*     277

# Illustrations

## MAPS

1. The Duchy of Mantua and states ruled by cadet branches of the Gonzaga ca. 1585   2
2. Northern Italy ca. 1625   12
3. The Jesuit island and university ca. 1625   34
4. Reconstruction of Santissima Trinità ca. 1630   38

## GENEALOGICAL CHARTS

1. The Gonzaga of Mantua   8
2. The Gonzaga of Castiglione delle Stiviere   42

## FIGURES

1. Duke Guglielmo Gonzaga, Duke Vincenzo I Gonzaga, Duchess Eleonora of Austria, Duchess Eleonora de' Medici   40
2. Cardinal Ferdinando Gonzaga   64
3. Duke Ferdinando Gonzaga   70
4. Proclamation of the opening of the Jesuit Public Academy of Mantua   80
5. Giacomo Antonio Marta   85
6. Title page of Giacomo Antonio Marta, *Decisionum novissimarum almi Collegii Pisani*   90

7. Proemium from Giacomo Antonio Marta, *Tractatus de iurisdictione*   94

8. Title page of Giacomo Antonio Marta, *The New Man*   110

9. Title page of Fabrizio Bartoletti, *Encyclopaedia hermetico-dogmatica*   132

10. Proclamation of the opening of the Peaceful University of Mantua   150

11. Title page of Giacomo Antonio Marta, *De Accademiae Mantuanae institutione et praestantia oratio*   160

12. Title page of Fabrizio Bartoletti, *Methodus in dyspnoeam seu de respirationibus*   186

13. Fabrizio Bartoletti, synopsis of the symptoms of sudden death from difficult breathing   189

# Tables

1.1 Population of Mantua and the Mantovano, 1511–1625   6
3.1 Public Academy of Mantua Roll, 1624–1625   81
6.1 University of Mantua Roll, 1625–1626   163
6.2 University of Mantua Roll, 1627–1628   168

# Preface

his is a book about the University of Mantua. It began in 1999 when I saw tantalizing references to a Jesuit university in Mantua in documents in the Archivum Romanum Societatis Iesu. Then in December 2001 I found a treasure trove of material about a real and lively institution in the Archivio di Stato of Mantua. Despite the abundant records, not even specialists in university history have heard of the University of Mantua. Previous scholarship consists of a short article published in 1871 and a laureate thesis of 1969–70, which yielded another short article in 1972, plus a handful of passing references.[1] Bringing to light an unknown university proved irresistible.

The Peaceful University of Mantua, its formal name, was a joint lay and Jesuit institution. The Jesuit part began in 1624, and law and medicine were added in 1625. But the university lasted only until the autumn of 1629. The War of the Mantuan Succession and the terrible Sack of Mantua, July 18–20, 1630, sealed its fate. Mantua has no university today.

Why study a university that lasted only a few years? There are several reasons. The story of the University of Mantua offers the opportunity to follow the creation of a university *ab uovo*, as the Gonzaga and the Jesuits organized the institution, raised the money, and found professors. Another reason is that the documents provide unusually detailed information about the relationship between an Italian ruling family and a university. Previous

---

1. See Mainardi, 1871; Ardenghi, 1969–70, 1972. Despite its title, Davari, 1876, has only a fleeting comment on the university. Some recent studies, especially of the Jesuits, note that there was a university but offer no further information. Frijhoff, 1996, 87, in his comprehensive list of European universities between 1500 and 1800, writes only "Mantua (1625). Jesuit; suppressed in 1771/3. Catholic."

Gonzaga dukes had supported a variety of scholars in different fields of learning; Duke Ferdinando (1587, ruled 1613–26) extended patronage of learning to its logical conclusion by founding a university. Still another reason is that the events in Mantua display the higher education politics of the Society of Jesus. Although the Jesuits had considerable success joining and sometimes dominating established universities and creating new ones in northern Europe, they met many rebuffs in Italy. They succeeded in Mantua.

The university united a princely family and the Society of Jesus, two powerful forces shaping Italian history. The partnership produced a medium-sized Italian university with professorships in canon and civil law, the full range of medical positions, and the first professorship of chemistry in Italy. Jesuit professors taught the humanities, mathematics, philosophy, and theology. While common in northern Europe, a university with both lay professors and Jesuits was unusual for Italy.

The winds of intellectual change blew briskly through the lecture halls of the Peaceful University of Mantua. The medical faculty taught a heady mix of anatomical dissection, experimentation, Galenism, and Paracelsianism. The star professor of medicine was the first to isolate the symptoms of angina pectoris. Giacomo Antonio Marta, the leading law professor, attempted to shift the foundations of *ius commune* from traditional texts to the decisions of tribunals. He also had much to say about church-state jurisdiction, the most controversial legal issue of the day. Studying the University of Mantua opens a window into Italian intellectual history in a time of ferment. Examination of the University of Mantua also permits comparison between what Jesuits and professors in civic universities taught. Despite many similarities, Jesuits and lay professors inhabited two different academic cultures.

Colorful figures walked through the classrooms of the University of Mantua. Ferdinando Gonzaga fancied himself a scholar and dared to debate Galileo Galilei. Although the Gonzaga were better known for their exploits on the battlefield and in the bedroom, Luigi Gonzaga became a Jesuit, a saint, and the heavenly patron of the Mantuan Jesuit college. Professor Marta also loved the Jesuits. But he hated the papacy and spied for a Protestant monarch.

The setting is Mantua. Except in art and music, Mantua and the Gonzaga, whose rule began in 1328 and ended ignominiously in 1708, have not attracted much scholarly attention in recent decades. In the 1920s and 1930s Romolo Quazza produced comprehensive political and diplomatic histories about Mantua and the Gonzaga when they were at the center of European politics.[2] Then scholarly attention shifted to other regions of Italy. It is time to return to Mantua and the world of north Italian princely courts.

---

2. See Quazza, 1922, 1926, 1933. Recent studies on the War of the Mantuan Succession will be cited in the appropriate places.

# Preface

SEVERAL INSTITUTIONS AND INDIVIDUALS AIDED MY RESEARCH. A RESEARCH grant from the Social Sciences and Humanities Research Council of Canada funded a first visit to the Archivum Romanum Societatis Iesu in 1999. I made a second visit in 2001 in the weeks preceding a conference in Siena, for which Professor Maurizio Sangalli secured travel funds. I am grateful to Mark Lewis, S.J., codirector of the Jesuit Historical Institute, for his hospitality and a room at the Casa di Scrittori on both visits. Father Joseph De Cock, S.J., archivist of the Archivum Romanum, and his staff were helpful. I thank Professor Gian Paolo Brizzi and the Centro interuniversitario per la storia delle università italiane for travel funds to a conference in Parma, which made possible my first visit to Mantua. A Franklin Research Grant from the American Philosophical Society supported a return visit to Mantua in 2003 and side trips to Turin and Bologna. Dott.a Daniela Ferrari, director of the Archivio di Stato of Mantua, and her staff facilitated my research. Because the Mantuan state archive is located in the building where Jesuits and students lived and studied centuries ago, the past was very present during the archival phase of the research. The Lila Acheson Wallace–Reader's Digest Publications Subsidy at Villa I Tatti generously provided a publication grant. I am grateful to Director Joseph Connors and the Publications Committee for their support.

I found the books of Mantuan professors and secondary literature in the libraries of the University of North Carolina at Chapel Hill, Duke University, Duke Divinity School, the History of Medicine Division of the National Library of Medicine in Bethesda, Maryland, the British Library, and elsewhere. I thank all them. I am particularly grateful to the staff of the Interlibrary Borrowing Office of the Library of the University of North Carolina at Chapel Hill. Elizabeth Bernhardt, Nelson Minnich, Nicholas Terpstra, and William A. Wallace, O.P., generously answered questions. An anonymous reviewer for the press made useful comments and Melanie Mallon carefully edited the manuscript. Chapter 4 expands on material first published as "Giacomo Antonio Marta: Antipapal Lawyer and English Spy, 1609–1618," in *The Catholic Historical Review* 93 (2007), 789–814.

This book is dedicated to my friends and former students at the University of Toronto, another idiosyncratic university.

# Abbreviations

### ARCHIVAL AND LIBRARY

| | |
|---|---|
| ARSI | Archivum Romanum Societatis Iesu |
| ASB | Archivio di Stato di Bologna |
| ASCT | Archivio Storico della Città di Torino |
| ASM | Archivio di Stato di Mantova |
| AG | Archivio Gonzaga |
| ASMc | Archivio di Stato di Macerata |
| AST | Archivio di Stato di Torino |
| NLM | National Library of Medicine, Bethesda, Maryland, History of Medicine Division |

### PRINTED WORKS

| | |
|---|---|
| AHSI | *Archivum Historicum Societatis Iesu* |
| CE | *The Catholic Encyclopedia*, edited by Charles G. Herbermann et al. 16 vols. New York, 1907; reprint New York, 1913. |
| DBI | *Dizionario biografico degli italiani*. Rome, 1960–. |
| DHCJ | *Diccionario Histórico de la Compañía de Jesús. Biográfico-temático*, edited by Charles E. O'Neill, S.J., and Joaquín M. Domíngues, S.J. 4 vols. Rome and Madrid, 2001. |
| DSB | *Dictionary of Scientific Biography*, edited by Charles C. Gillispie et al. 18 vols. New York, 1970–80; second printing, New York, 1981. |
| *Gesuiti e università* | *Gesuiti e università in Europe (secoli XVI–XVIII)*. Atti del Convegno di studi, Parma, 13–15 dicembre 2001. Edited by Gian Paolo Brizzi and Roberto Greci. Bologna, 2002. |

| | |
|---|---|
| *The Jesuits* | *The Jesuits: Cultures, Sciences, and the Arts 1540–1773*, edited by John W. O'Malley, S.J., Gauvin Alexander Bailey, Steven J. Harris, and T. Frank Kennedy, S.J. Toronto, Buffalo, and London, 1999. |
| *Mantova e i Gonzaga* | *Mantova e i Gonzaga nella civiltà del Rinascimento*. Atti del convegno organizzato dall'Accademia Nazionale dei Lincei e dall'Accademia Virgiliana con la collaborazione della città di Mantova sotto l'altro patronato del Presidente della Repubblica Italiana Giovanni Leone. Segrate, 1978. |
| *The Mercurian Project* | *The Mercurian Project: Forming Jesuit Culture 1573–1580*, edited by Thomas M. McCoog, S.J. Rome and St. Louis, 2004. |
| *L'Università di Pisa* | *Storia dell'Università di Pisa*. Vol. 1 in 2 parts: 1343–1737. Pisa, 1993. |
| | |
| Bu. | busta |
| F. | filza |
| f. | folio |
| ff. | folios |
| sig. | signature(s) |
| A, B | When a page has two columns of text, A refers to the first column and B to the second. |

# Values of Some Coins and Monies of Account ca. 1625

12 denari (pennies) = 1 soldo

20 soldi = 1 lira

1 Mantuan scudo = 5 lire or 6 lire. Sometimes a value in lire was specified and sometimes not.[1] Scudo was also used generically to indicate money without indicating which money of account or coin was meant.

1 Mantuan thaler = about 7 lire

1 sesino (a small copper coin used in Mantua and Milan) = 6 denari

1 parpaglioia (Milanese coin) = 1.5 soldi or 18 denari

1 Milanese ducatone = 115 soldi (5.75 imperial lire);[2] however, "ducat" and "ducatone" were often used indiscriminately, making it impossible to determine which was meant.

1 trono (Venetian coin) = 1 lira

1 Venetian ducat = 6 lire 4 soldi (124 soldi)

A master mason earned about 30 soldi per day in Pavia and about 40 soldi in Milan in 1625. A pound of bread cost 4 soldi in Milan in 1625.[3]

1. But see also Simonsohn, 1977, 742–44, with some different values.
2. Sella, 1968, 67–68.
3. Sella, 1968, 98, 117, 138.

# The University of Mantua,
the Gonzaga, and the Jesuits, 1584–1630

CHAPTER 1

# The Place and the People

Three developments in the sixteenth century prepared the way for a university in Mantua in the seventeenth. The Gonzaga family arranged a dynastic marriage that doubled the size of their state. The clever and adaptable merchants and people of Mantua and the Mantovano created a prosperous economic base. And Jesuit failures to enter or create universities elsewhere in Italy left them searching for other opportunities.

## 1. THE DUCHY OF MANTUA

In 1328 Luigi Gonzaga seized control of the government of Mantua and made it into an hereditary principality. The Gonzaga quickly expanded their authority over the surrounding territory, called the Mantovano, thus creating a small state in north central/northeastern Italy. In 1433 Emperor Sigismund I of Luxemburg raised it to a marquisate and a fief of the Holy Roman Empire. Gonzaga rulers combined timely alliances and military prowess as mercenary captains to expand their state in the late fifteenth and early sixteenth centuries. The city of Mantua was a major asset because it was simultaneously a secure capital and a commercial center. Situated on the banks of the Mincio River where it broadens into three lakes, Mantua is surrounded on three sides by water. Canals and fortifications on the fourth side made Mantua an impregnable fortress town immune from assault by Renaissance implements of war. And in the sixteenth century Gonzaga dukes further strengthened the ducal castle near one of the lakes and added more fortifications on the land approach to the city.[1] By 1500 the marquisate of

---

1. Oresko and Parrott, 1997, 29.

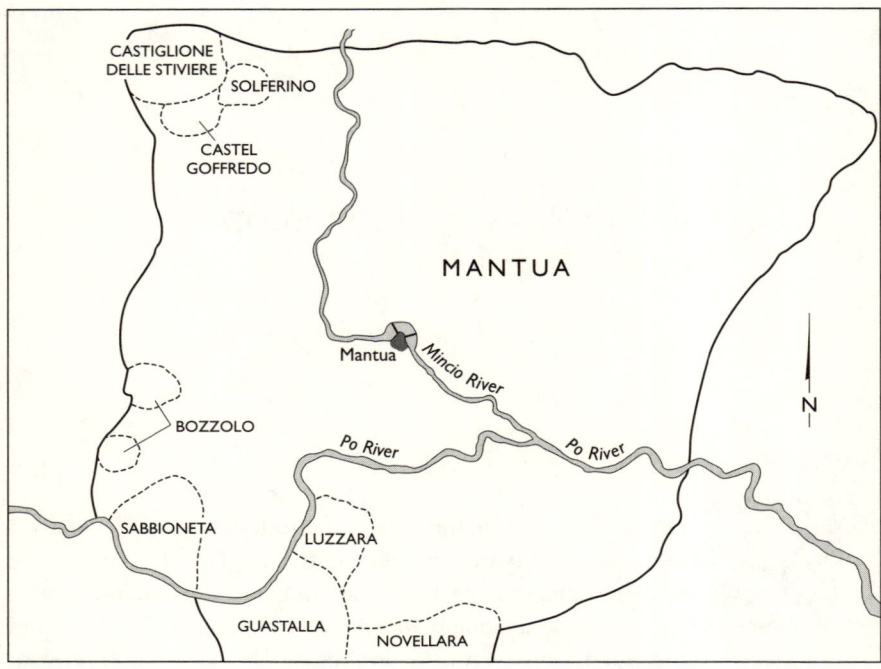

MAP 1. The Duchy of Mantua and states ruled by cadet branches of the Gonzaga ca. 1585

Mantua competed with Ferrara, Milan, Piedmont-Savoy,[2] and Venice for influence and territory.

The Gonzaga were unusual among Italian ruling families in that they had a tradition of partible male inheritance. When the ruler died, his territory was divided among all his sons, a policy that eventually created mini-states ruled by cadet branches of the family.[3] Most other Italian ruling families had eliminated the territories of cadet branches and created states that were more integrated. The Gonzaga of Mantua tried through marriages and purchases to meld the lands of cadet branches into the larger state but with limited success.

---

2. There is a question of the appropriate name for the territories ruled by the dukes of Savoy. The family name was Savoia, and the Savoia dukes ruled several territories, including Piedmont, the principality of Oneglia, and others. In 1562 Duke Emanuele Filiberto moved the capital south from French-speaking Chambéry to Italian-speaking Turin. This made Piedmont the Savoia's most important possession, and they increasingly involved themselves in Italian politics. Hence, the name Piedmont-Savoy will be used to convey the dual nature of the Savoy state and the importance of Piedmont in it.

3. Parrott, 1997a, 26–29.

# The Economy and the People

In 1588 the Venetian ambassador reported that there were eighty-five Gonzaga lords and knights of some importance, and twenty-four of them were imperial feudatories.[4]

Thus, in the sixteenth and seventeenth centuries the geographical entity called the Mantovano contained the duchy of Mantua and several tiny independent states ruled by male members of cadet branches of the Gonzaga family; see map 1. The most important would prove to be Guastalla. Emperor Charles V alienated the principality of Guastalla from his own duchy of Milan and awarded it to Ferrante Gonzaga in 1539 as a reward and payment for his military services.[5] Emperor Ferdinand II raised Guastalla to the status of duchy in 1621. The principality of Castiglione delle Stiviere and the duchy of Sabbioneta, also ruled by cadet branches of the Gonzaga, were almost as large as Guastalla. Lesser states ruled by cadet branches included the principality of Bozzolo and the county of Novellara. And finally there was the tiny imperial fief of Gazoldo, ruled by the Ippoliti family. Except Gazoldo, which was completely surrounded by the duchy of Mantua, these tiny states were located on the periphery of the Mantovano.[6]

The Gonzaga mini-states were a mixed blessing to the Gonzaga of Mantua. The male members of the cadet branches often served the Gonzaga of Mantua as soldiers, administrators, and diplomats. The economies of the tiny states were integrated into the economy of the duchy of Mantua. But the rulers of these states could pursue their own policies and marriage alliances, which were sometimes at variance with the wishes of the Gonzaga of Mantua. Above all, each ruler dreamed that if all the males of the Gonzaga of Mantua expired, his branch of the family would rule Mantua.

## 2. THE ECONOMY AND THE PEOPLE

The Gonzaga were wealthy. Part of their wealth came from the large tracts of land they owned. They also financed their state, court, armies, marriages, and patronage of art and music by numerous indirect taxes on goods, commerce, services, and transport of their subjects, the common pattern of Italian princedoms and republics.[7] Fortunately, Mantua had a thriving economy that could support the necessities and extravagances of the Gonzaga and the state as a whole. Mantua and the Mantovano lived on the textile industry. Manufac-

---

4. "Oltre il duca di Nivers, vi sono nella casa Gonzaga 85 signori e cavalieri di molta stima, tra' quali 24 feudatari." *Relazione* of Francesco Contarini, October 3, 1588, in *Relazioni*, 1912, 81.

5. Coniglio, 1967, 473–99, provides a guide to the rulers and histories of the mini-Gonzaga states.

6. Parrott, 1997a, 26–29.

7. See De Maddalena, 1961, 21–42, for a list of the taxes collected in the years between 1526 and the 1580s.

turers produced and merchants sold a variety of woolen goods as they shifted from one item to another in response to market conditions.

In the early sixteenth century Mantua concentrated on the production of woolen cloth, but then production plummeted.[8] Silk cloth initially compensated for the decline in woolen cloth, but it also began to lose to foreign competition after 1585 and remained at a low level through the 1620s. Mantua compensated by producing the berretta, a knitted woolen headpiece. The term "berretta" included the beret as well as larger woolen caps covering more of the head, somewhat like a modern ski cap. In the 1550s Mantua produced 450,000 to 500,000 woolen caps annually, four to five caps for every man, woman, and child in the city of Mantua and the Mantovano.[9] The city became famous for its caps: in 1585 Tommaso Garzoni (1549–89) wrote, "today the capmakers flourish in the highest degree in Mantua and Verona," the latter being Mantua's chief rival.[10]

Cap production fell at the end of the century, however, because tastes changed. Men preferred caps of felt and other materials more elegant than wool; the headpiece became more a fashion statement and less a utilitarian article of clothing.[11] The resourceful merchants of Mantua switched to the production of knitwear (*agucchieria*), especially knitted stockings, as well as gloves and vests. The knitted stocking, a sixteenth-century innovation not traceable to a single person or place, gripped the leg better than cloth stockings and rose to just below the knee, where colorful ribbons held it in place.[12] Because knitted hose did not need to be sewn and fitted by a tailor, they were an early example of ready-to-wear clothing. Mantua produced knitted stockings for men, women, and children in different sizes; in red, yellow, white, black, and other colors; and sometimes with elaborate decorations and embellishments.[13]

Mantua was the knitwear capital of Italy in the early seventeenth century despite strong competition from Verona and Padua. Even Mantua's Jewish community played a significant role in the knitwear industry, despite efforts of Christian merchants to exclude them.[14] Changes in the title of the major

---

8. Unless otherwise indicated, this and the following four paragraphs are based on Coniglio, 1962; De Maddalena, 1962; Belfanti, 1982, 1988, 2005, 2006.

9. De Maddalena, 1962, 617.

10. "Con questi tali vengono i Berettari, che oggidì fioriscono in Mantoa & Verona sommamente." Garzoni, 1601, discorso 102, p. 736. The punctuation has been modernized. Garzoni, a keen observer of the Italian scene, first published this book in 1585.

11. Belfanti, 2005, 25.

12. Belfanti, 2005, 12; Belfanti, 2006, 245–46.

13. See the illustrations following p. 80 in Belfanti, 2005.

14. Simonsohn, 1977, 280; Belfanti, 1988, 446–47, 451–52.

guild illustrated the importance of stocking manufacturing. The guild of capmakers (mercanti di berette) became the guild of merchants of capmakers and other knitwear (Università de mercanti de berette et altre agucchierie di Mantova) in 1587. It then became the guild of merchants of knitwear (Università dei mercanti d'agucchieria) in 1611.[15] Knitted stockings warmed the legs of Mantua's economy.

Knitwear manufacturing employed a putting-out system. Mantuan merchants acquired the raw materials, above all, woolen thread. The knitters from the countryside, some living tens of kilometers away, came to Mantua to pick up thread, needles, and instructions. They knitted in the villages and farms across the Mantovano with the aid of wooden frames and other devices. A worker could produce a pair of stockings a day.[16] So far as can be determined, men did most of the knitting; peasants knitted in the winter or all year round if they lived on farms with poor soil. The knitted stockings returned to Mantua for finishing, then were shipped to the rest of Italy and abroad by land and by the Po River, which flowed through the southern part of the Gonzaga state. Although no exact count is available, the knitwear industry employed several thousand workers from Mantua and the Mantovano.[17]

In addition to knitwear, small groups of artisans produced swords, wax, ironworks, and jewelry, a craft in which the Jews played a major role. The countryside produced wheat and several lesser cereal grains, such as barley, millet, and rye, plus beans and other vegetables. And the Mantovano had enough pasture to support a limited number of sheep.[18] Mantua also had a small but adequate printing establishment, which received support from the Gonzaga.[19] Thanks to its manufacturing base and adequate foodstuffs, the population of Mantua and the Mantovano remained stable through the sixteenth and early seventeenth centuries (table 1.1).

The population figures include only the duchy of Mantua, that is, the part of the Mantovano ruled by the Gonzaga of Mantua. They do not include the tiny states ruled by other branches of the Gonzaga family, that is, Guastalla, Castiglione delle Stiviere, Sabbioneta, Bozzolo, and Novellara. These tiny

15. Belfanti, 2005, 26.
16. Belfanti, 2005, 48.
17. Documents of the knitwear guild of 1611 and 1614 stated that there were twenty thousand workers in the industry, a number that was probably exaggerated unless it included family members of workers. Another guild document, of 1625, stated that the knitwear industry supported thirty thousand and more workers. Again, the figure may have included family members. Although both figures may have been exaggerated, the knitwear industry certainly employed a great many workers. See Coniglio, 1962, 354 (1614 document); De Maddalena, 1962, 640 (1611 document); Belfanti, 1988, 448 (1625 document); Belfanti, 2005, 29 (1614 document).
18. Coniglio, 1962, 323–36, 359–66.
19. Pescasio, 1971.

TABLE I.I
Population of Mantua and the Mantovano, 1511–1625

| Year | Mantua | Mantovano | Total |
| --- | --- | --- | --- |
| 1511 | 27,741 | — | — |
| 1559 | 36,196 | — | — |
| 1562 | 35,619 | — | — |
| 1566 | 34,931 | 80,708 | 115,639 |
| 1571 | 34,367 | — | — |
| 1574 | — | 90,251 | — |
| 1587 | 34,281 | 86,868 | 121,149 |
| 1592 | 31,422 | — | — |
| 1625 | 29,710 | — | — |

*Source:* The figures come from periodic censuses that government officials compiled to determine how much grain was needed to feed the people of the state. Several scholars have reported some or all the figures: Coniglio, 1962, 387–92; Belfanti, 1982, 116 table; Belfanti, 1988, 449–50, 452. The slight dip between 1587 and 1592 was caused by the famine of 1590–93. See Belfanti, 1982.

states probably added another twenty thousand to twenty-five thousand people to the greater Mantovano area.

Mantua's Jewish community, one of the most important in Italy by the early seventeenth century, also contributed to the economy. In 1500 Mantua had only about 150 to 200 Jews, and the Mantovano another 100. Their numbers increased to 960 in Mantua and another 200 to 250 in the Mantovano in 1587. Four years later Mantua had 1,591 Jews, and another 253 lived in the Mantovano. Most of the increase came from refugees from the Papal States, the duchy of Milan, and elsewhere.[20]

The Jews engaged in various trades and crafts, such as banking, jewelry, used clothing, the knitwear industry, and especially printing. The Mantuan Hebrew press produced a handful of works in the fifteenth century. After a pause, a few more Hebrew books were published in the second decade of the sixteenth century. Mantua's Hebrew publishers resumed publication in the middle of the sixteenth century and this time produced a small but steady stream of works annually into the seventeenth century. Sabbioneta, ruled by a cadet branch of the Gonzaga, also had a Hebrew press in the second half of the sixteenth century.[21] The lists of the books owned by Mantuan Jews at the time, and the surviving books and manuscripts, testify to an active intellectual

20. Again the figures are available because the Gonzaga government periodically required all residents to register in order to anticipate the needed food supplies. Simonsohn, 1977, 190–95.
21. Pescasio, 1971, 86–90, 202–9, 247–50; Simonsohn, 1977, 681–94.

# The Economy and the People

and religious community, which included about a dozen public and private synagogues in the early seventeenth century.[22]

The Gonzaga treated the Jewish community relatively well for the times by honoring their agreements and protecting Jewish merchants from the guilds. The latter, which excluded Jews, frequently demanded that the government impose special taxes on Jewish businesses or otherwise restrict them. The Gonzaga rebuffed the guilds. On the other hand, the Gonzaga, and especially Vincenzo I (ruled 1587–1612), periodically extorted money from the Jewish community. And while the government protected the Jews from physical violence, it could not, or would not, stop all of it. The vicious anti-Jewish preaching of a monk led to the hanging of seven Jews before the monk was driven away in 1602. In the aftermath, Duke Vincenzo I announced that a ghetto would be created, as the papacy had demanded for some time. The Jewish community did not object.[23] The ghetto was created between 1610 and 1612 by expanding an area in the center of the city where about two-thirds of the Jews already lived. The ghetto was adjacent to "the Jesuit island," the block of buildings that included the Jesuit church, residence, and school (see chapter 2 and map 3).

In 1610 Jews constituted about 7.5 percent of the population of Mantua: 480 families with a total of 2,325 individuals, of which 1,490 lived in the space set aside for the ghetto.[24] Thus, the creation of the ghetto necessitated a considerable amount of relocation, moving Jews in and Christians out, and some new construction, paid for by the Jews. The Jews of Mantua were the last large Italian community to be confined to a ghetto. On the other hand, the 500 to 700 Jews living elsewhere in the Mantovano were not required to live in ghettoes.[25]

The Gonzaga rulers were absolute rulers and often spent more than they raised in taxes. But they did not attack their neighbors, and they took up arms only to defend themselves. Their concern to feed the people and their pursuit of moderate policies toward the Jews and the population as a whole suggest

---

22. See *Libri ebraici a Mantova*, 1996–2003, which catalogues 162 manuscripts and 1,549 printed Hebrew works (333 of them sixteenth-century editions) of the Jewish community, now housed in the Biblioteca Communale of Mantua; and Baruchson-Arbib, 2001. For the synagogues, see Simonsohn, 1977, 567–72.

23. Simonsohn, 1977, 31–44, 196–236.

24. See Simonsohn, 1977, 191, for the number of Jews in 1610. The exact population of Mantua in 1610 is unknown. The nearest census was that of 1624, which counted 30,991. Belfanti, 1982, 116. Hence, 2,325 divided by 30,991 = 7.5 percent Jews. This percentage is higher than the 5 percent estimated by Simonsohn (p. 193), who overestimated the population of Mantua because he lacked the census material uncovered by Belfanti and others.

25. Simonsohn, 1977, 39–43.

CHART I

The Gonzaga of Mantua*

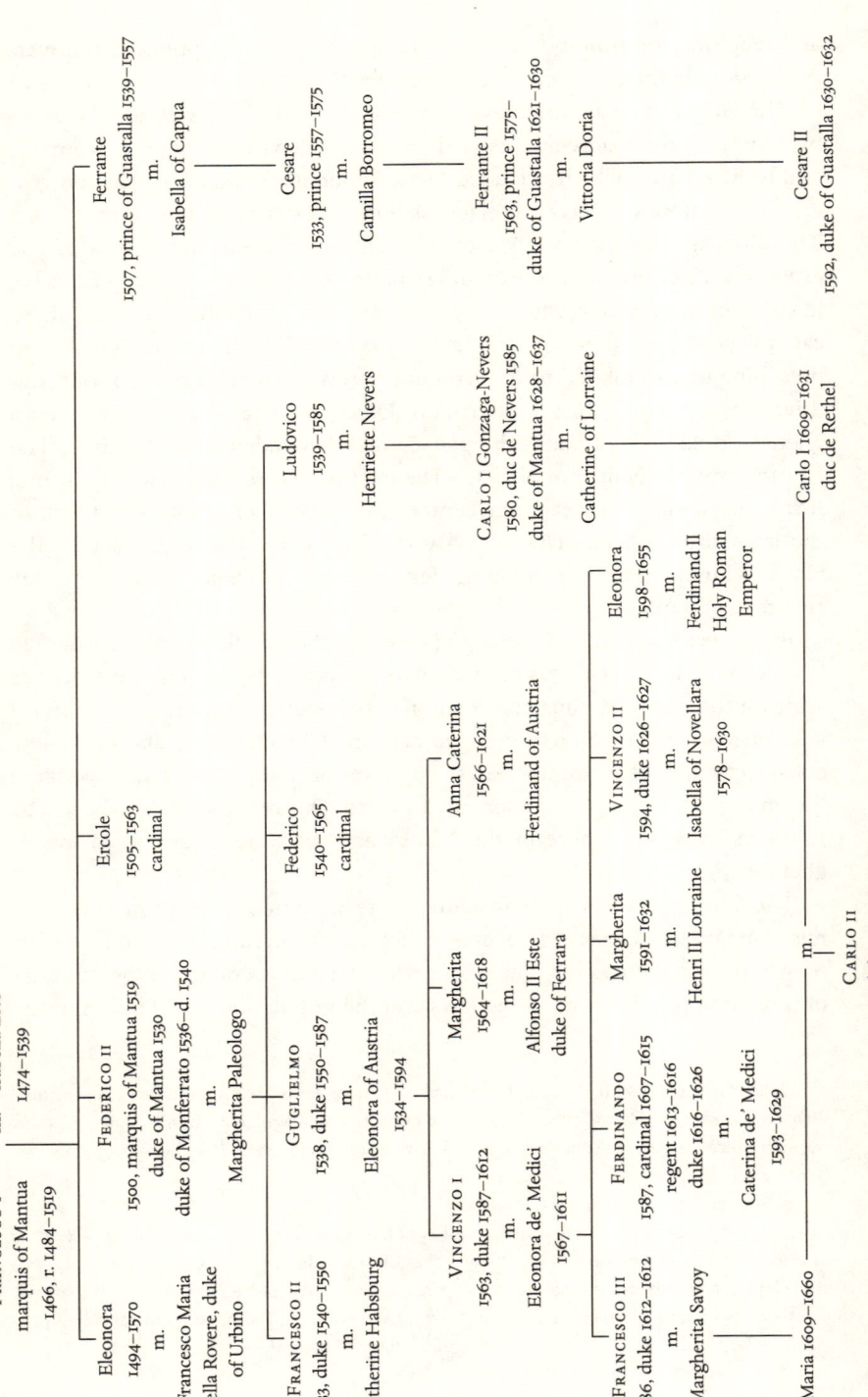

*The names of rulers are given in capital letters.

# Monferrato

that they were good rulers by the standards of the times. No opposition to the Gonzaga rose in Mantua and the Mantovano, and some of them were popular.[26]

### 3. MONFERRATO

The Gonzaga of Mantua doubled the size of their state in the middle of the sixteenth century by acquiring the marquisate of Monferrato in northwestern Italy. Monferrato came to the Gonzaga as the consequence of two well-calculated political marriages and some fortuitous deaths. Established around 1000, the marquisate of Monferrato from 1305 onward was the possession of a cadet branch of the famous Paleologus family, which ruled the Eastern Roman Empire until the last Paleologus emperor was killed at the fall of Constantinople in 1453. Unlike practically every other Italian state, the marquisate could be inherited through the female line; it was a *feudo feminino*.[27] Led by the astute and determined Isabella Este (1474–1539), duchess of Mantua, the Gonzaga dreamed and schemed to acquire Monferrato. The first step was to arrange a marriage between the two families. In 1517 Federico Gonzaga (1500–40), the son of Isabella and Francesco Gonzaga, but not yet ruler of Mantua, married Maria Paleologo (1509–30), the eldest daughter of Guglielmo IX Paleologo, marquis of Monferrato.[28] But the union was not consummated, because Maria was only eight. The marriage contract stipulated that Federico would not bring his bride to Mantua and consummate the marriage until 1524, when she would be fifteen. The Gonzaga, and especially Isabella Este, looked to the future.[29]

Then the political winds changed direction. Federico became marquis of Mantua in 1519, and Charles V raised Mantua from a marquisate to a duchy in 1530. Federico put off bringing Maria Paleologo to Mantua. With better marriage possibilities on the horizon, in 1529 he obtained from Clement VII an annulment of his unconsummated marriage with Maria. In the meantime, Federico found comfort in the arms of Isabella Buschetti, the wife of a Gonzaga from a cadet branch, who bore Federico two illegitimate children.[30]

---

26. Vincenzo I was popular according to the Venetian ambassadors Vincenzo Tron (1588) and Francesco Contarini (1608) in *Relazioni*, 1912, 79, 88. This was more the consequence of his dashing personality than his policies. To be sure, a ruler's popularity with his subjects seldom mattered.

27. The expression comes from Parrott, 1997a, 34.

28. Because the Paleologus became an Italian family ruling an Italian marquisate, "Paleologo" will be preferred to "Paleologus."

29. Quazza, 1933, 111–12; Coniglio, 1967, 239–41, 264; Benzoni, 1995, 710; Pescasio, 1997, 61.

30. Quazza, 1933, 112, 117–19; Coniglio, 1967, 269–72, 277–78; Benzoni, 1995, 713–15; Oresko and Parrott, 1997, 13–16; Pescasio, 1997, 62–69.

The political winds shifted again, as members of the Paleologo family began to die. The current marquis of Monferrato, Bonifacio (1512–30), Maria's younger brother, fell off his horse while hunting and died in June 1530. The last Paleologo male in the direct line, the old and sickly Gian Giorgio Paleologo, bishop of Monferrato and Maria's uncle, gave up his bishopric, was laicized, and became marquis of Monferrato. As the chances of a huge return looked better and better, the Gonzaga reappraised the value of a marriage with the Paleologo. Declaring that he was stricken by pangs of conscience about the hasty dissolution of his marriage to Maria, Federico asked Clement VII to reconsider his decision. The pope dutifully declared the marriage to Maria valid. But then Maria suddenly died in September 1530. There was one Paleologo left, Margherita (1510/15–65), Maria's younger sister. In October 1531 Federico, now thirty-one, an advanced age for a ruler who had not yet begat legitimate heirs, married Margherita. Marquis Gian Giorgio Paleologo tried to thwart the Gonzaga by marrying on April 21, 1533, but he died on April 30, 1533, and his widow did not produce a child. Margherita became the marquise, and Federico, her husband, would become the marquis of Monferrato in addition to being duke of Mantua.[31]

But first Federico sought the approval of Charles V. Although not required, it was always wise to secure the endorsement of the emperor, because Monferrato was an imperial fief and because the emperor was so powerful. Charles V held the Gonzaga in high regard, not least because Don Ferrante Gonzaga (1507–57), Federico's younger brother, had served Charles well as a military commander in Italy, Austria, and North Africa, and was currently viceroy of Sicily (appointed in 1535).[32] In addition, Charles did not want Monferrato to fall into the hands of the Savoia, who were friendly to France. After further negotiation and a financial payment to Gian Giorgio's widow, Charles gave his blessing. Federico Gonzaga was proclaimed marquis of Monferrato through the female line, his wife's inheritance, on November 29, 1536.[33] However, neither Federico nor his immediate successor could take possession of Monferrato, because French troops moved into Monferrato in 1536 and did not leave until after the Peace of Cateau-Cambrésis of 1559. The treaty confirmed Gonzaga rule over Monferrato, and the Gonzaga finally took active possession at this time.

The marquisate of Monferrato had two parts connected by a narrow strip of land (see map 2). It was a little larger than the Mantovano and had more

---

31. Quazza, 1933, 119–21; Coniglio, 1967, 278–83; Benzoni, 1995, 715–16; Oresko and Parrott, 1997, 17–18; Pescasio, 1997, 70–73.

32. Brunelli, 2001b, 734–36.

33. Quazza, 1933, 119–21; Coniglio, 1967, 278–84; Benzoni, 1995, 715–16; Oresko and Parrott, 1997, 19–20; Pescasio, 1997, 70–73.

people (e.g., 171,000 in the 1580s). Casale Monferrato, the capital, had 8,200 souls, while several smaller towns had 2,400 to 4,300, at that time.[34] Casale Monferrato was located about 180 kilometers directly west of Mantua as the crow flies, but the distance between the two was far longer by land. The marquisate of Monferrato had a long and convoluted western border with Piedmont; indeed, a few Monferrato towns were only about fifteen kilometers east of Turin. Monferrato bordered the duchy of Milan, part of the Spanish Empire, on the east, and the Republic of Genoa on the south. The major product of the hilly countryside of Monferrato was wine—today it produces the well-known Barbera vintage—followed by wheat and other cereals. A small textile industry existed as well as limited glass making. Its geographical location put Monferrato on several trade routes, such as from the sea to the mountains, between Lombardy and Turin, and to France.

In the eyes of the rulers of Piedmont-Savoy, Lombardy, France, and Spain, Monferrato's political and military importance dwarfed other considerations. The northern part of Monferrato was the natural route for any military invader from the northwest (meaning France) into the plains of Lombardy. From the other direction, it was the military route by which Spain might march from Milan into Piedmont and, eventually, France. No army from either direction could avoid Casale Monferrato on the upper Po River, a natural military position made stronger by fortifications.

The acquisition of Monferrato not only doubled the size of the Gonzaga state, it greatly expanded the family's importance. As the ruler of two substantial states, the Gonzaga of Mantua had more political visibility and as much or more prestige than any other family in the northern half of Italy. When Emperor Rudolf II raised Monferrato to a duchy in 1575, Guglielmo Gonzaga became duke of Mantua and duke of Monferrato. Rudolf II also bestowed on Guglielmo and his successors the right to be addressed as "La Sua Altezza" (Your Highness) instead of the lesser "La Sua Eccellenza" (Your Excellency).[35]

Acquiring Monferrato took only a marriage and imperial approval; ruling it was harder. The dukes of Piedmont-Savoy had coveted Monferrato for centuries and had matrimonial ties with the Paleologo, albeit more distant than those of the Gonzaga. They encouraged dissent in Monferrato. And the nobility of Monferrato had many kinship and other connections with the court of Piedmont-Savoy, but few initial ties to the Gonzaga.

Like every other Italian prince in the second half of the sixteenth century,

---

34. The exact figure, as found in an undated census from the 1580s, was 171,228. Raviola, 2003, 128 (for the populations of the towns as well). On the other hand, the Venetian ambassador, Francesco Contarini, gave the population of Monferrato as 200,000 in 1588. *Relazioni*, 1912, 82.

35. Parrott, 1997a, 30–31 and note 1 on p. 31.

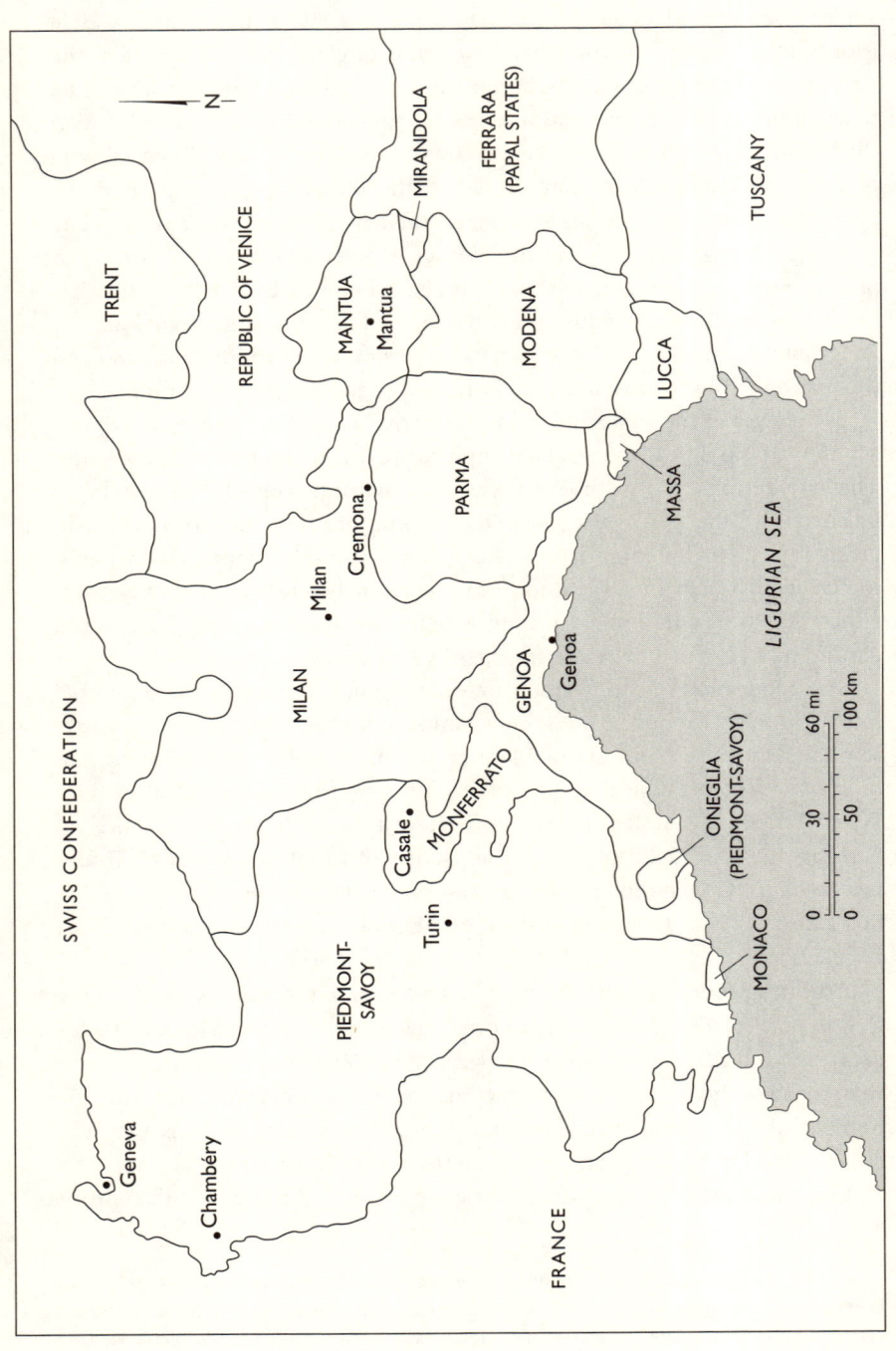

MAP 2. Northern Italy ca. 1625

Duke Guglielmo Gonzaga (ruled 1550–87) sought to enhance his personal rule by restricting the powers of nobles and traditional councils, and by eliminating historical prerogatives. And he levied new taxes. He encountered no opposition in the Mantovano, but did in Monferrato, which had a different history and traditions. The nobility of Casale Monferrato were accustomed to a certain amount of independence and privileges under the Paleologo and objected to the reduction of their powers and to the new taxes. Encouraged by Duke Emanuele Filiberto of Piedmont-Savoy (1528, ruled 1553–80), they resisted. Duke Guglielmo quashed the opposition, executed some leaders in 1567 and 1568, and eliminated the special privileges of the nobles and the town of Casale Monferrato in 1569.[36]

Once opposition was crushed, his successor, Vincenzo I, adopted different tactics to integrate Monferrato into the Gonzaga state and to win the loyalty of the nobility. He appointed several members of cadet branches of the Gonzaga as governors and administrators in Monferrato. At the same time, he reorganized Monferrato's institutions in a less oppressive way and co-opted some of the nobles. Vincenzo I created many new fiefs with castles, which he awarded to favorites from Monferrato and elsewhere, a classic example of the refeudalization of an Italian state. And beginning in 1590 he constructed at enormous expense a citadel at Casale Monferrato.[37] Over time the nobles and people of Monferrato became loyal subjects and contributed significantly to the Gonzaga treasury. Monferrato produced annual income of 15,000 to 20,000 ducats in the first decades of Gonzaga rule. This grew to 120,000 ducats annually during the rule of Guglielmo (1550–87). By 1615 Monferrato produced 230,000 ducats, which was more than what the Gonzaga harvested in taxes from the Mantovano.[38]

The Gonzaga gained a great deal of territory and money, and higher rank among Europe's rulers, through the acquisition of Monferrato. Mixing their blood with the Paleologo meant something in an age that lamented the disappearance of the Byzantine Empire and longed for a crusade against the Turks.[39] The duchy of Monferrato also brought new dangers. Because of Monferrato's military significance, its ruler mattered in European geopolitics. Should the Gonzaga exhibit any weakness, Piedmont-Savoy would pounce on

---

36. Quazza, 1933, 129–32; Coniglio, 1967, 319–35; Belfanti and Romani, 1987, 123, 130–32; Mozzarelli, 1987, 85; Raviola, 2003, 74–80.

37. Quazza, 1933, 143; Belfanti and Romani, 1987, 132–36; Carpeggiani, 1997; Oresko and Parrott, 1997, 23–35; Raviola, 2003, 80–92. In 1681 the Gonzaga were forced to cede Casale Monferrato to Louis XIV, after which the French demolished the citadel.

38. According to the Venetian ambassador Giovanni Da Mula, Monferrato produced 230,000 ducats annually and the Mantovano about 200,000 ducats. *Relazioni*, 1912, 137. See also, Belfanti and Romani, 1987, 116–17.

39. This point is made by Parrott, 1997b, 161–63.

Monferrato. On the other hand, France, Spain, and the Empire would resist any territorial or political changes weakening their influence in northern Italy. Hence, every move of the Gonzaga would attract the attention of the great powers, and any war between them would drag in Monferrato and Mantua.

In the meantime, the Gonzaga of Mantua lived in a manner befitting their status. Three marriages with members of the imperial Habsburgs in seventy-three years demonstrated to all their importance. In 1549 Francesco Gonzaga (1533–50), duke of Mantua since 1540 under a regency, married Catherine Habsburg of Austria, daughter of Duke Ferdinand I. In 1561 Duke Guglielmo Gonzaga married Eleonora Habsburg (1534–94), another daughter of Ferdinand I, now Holy Roman Emperor. Then in 1621 her granddaughter, also named Eleonora (1598–1655), married Holy Roman Emperor Ferdinand II. Marriages, coronations (the Gonzaga as well as emperors), the visits of dignitaries, and other events were the occasion for splendid festivals, triumphal entries, pageantry, fireworks, music, theater, and dance.[40] The Gonzaga were generous patrons of the arts, especially music. The years of Claudio Monteverdi (1567–1643) at the Gonzaga court (1590–1612) were of immense importance in the history of music.

The size and magnificence of the court inspired awed comment. The ducal palace, on high ground looking out on two of the lakes of Mantua, was the Gonzaga residence and the seat of government. Begun in 1290 and expanded in succeeding centuries, it reached a size of more than five hundred rooms and fifteen interior courtyards and gardens. The palace had ample room for the eight hundred people of the court in the later years of Vincenzo I's reign.[41] Courtiers, ladies-in-waiting, advisers, soldiers, musicians, masters of the stables, and everyone else received stipends from the Gonzaga, who worried little about expenses. Visitors marveled at the ducal collection of Renaissance paintings, the music and theater that entertained the court, and the hundreds of fine horses in the Gonzaga stables. Life was good for the Gonzaga of Mantua.

## 4. JESUIT ATTEMPTS TO ENTER ITALIAN UNIVERSITIES

The Jesuits had little interest in the ducal art gallery or Mantuan stockings. But they wished to develop university-level schools to train their own members and to expand their educational ministry. These imperatives drove the Jesuits to try to become university teachers, either in established universities or in universities that they would found.

---

40. See *Mantova: Le lettere*, 1962, 568–612, for an overview; Parisi, 1989, for musical events and Gonzaga musical patronage; and *I Gonzaga e l'Impero*, 2005, for Gonzaga-Habsburg celebrations. There is much more bibliography, especially about music at the Gonzaga court.

41. Relazione of Venetian ambassador Pietro Gritti of 1612 in *Relazioni*, 1912, 118.

## Jesuit Attempts to Enter Italian Universities

The Jesuits were almost predestined to become university professors. The Society was born in a university, as Loyola and the original Jesuits, all of them students, joined hands at the University of Paris. Even before the Society was approved in 1540, two of the original band of Jesuits taught at the University of Rome. In November 1537 Pope Paul III appointed Pierre Favre (1506–46) and Diego Laínez (1512–65) to teach theology at the Studium Urbis. They taught for two academic years but never returned to university teaching.[42]

Within a few years the Jesuits established themselves in northern universities. In 1549 they began to teach in the University of Ingolstadt and, after overcoming resistance by some faculty members, dominated the faculties of arts and theology by 1585.[43] Young prince Ferdinando Gonzaga would study there in the academic year 1601–02. The Jesuits became professors at the universities of Cologne, Trier, and Mainz in the 1550s and 1560s, and at other universities in German-speaking lands later.[44]

The Jesuit *Constitutions* of 1558, mostly written by Ignatius Loyola, declared the university goals of the Jesuits.[45] The Jesuits wanted to teach the humanities, ancient languages, logic, natural philosophy, metaphysics, moral philosophy, mathematics, Scripture, and especially theology, but would not teach law or medicine.[46] The *Constitutions* looked to Paris and universities in German-speaking lands as models. Northern European universities mostly taught arts to teenage boys studying for bachelor of arts degrees and theology to current and future clergymen. The majority of the boys lived in residential colleges presided over by members of religious orders who taught them Latin and supervised their moral and spiritual lives. Because the Jesuits focused on teaching grammar and rhetoric to boys and theology to future clergymen, and developing the spiritual potential of both, they fitted easily into northern European universities.

Italian universities were different. They concentrated on law and medicine and paid little attention to theology. Most professors were married laymen expert in their disciplines. The students were older and sought doctorates in law and medicine. They did not live in supervised residences and, in the view

---

42. Although no faculty rolls survive for these years, several Jesuit primary and secondary sources mentioned their teaching at the University of Rome. Salmerón, 1972, 735; *Fontes narrativi*, 1943, 122–23; Tacchi Venturi, 1950, 93, 102; Schurhammer, 1973, 411.

43. See Mobley, 2004, and the bibliography therein.

44. Hengst, 1981, is the basic guide. See the useful list of Jesuit higher schools and universities, plus established universities with Jesuit professors and faculties, in Müller, 2002, 104–6, especially note 35.

45. *Constitutions*, 1996, part 4, chs. 11–17, paragraphs 440–509, pp. 177–90.

46. "The study of medicine and laws, being more remote from our Institute, will not be treated in the universities of the Society, or at least the Society will not undertake this teaching through its own members." *Constitutions*, 1996, part 4, ch. 12, paragraph 452, p. 180.

of many townspeople, were unfamiliar with the Ten Commandments. Above all, Italian universities had strong traditions of civic leadership by prince or commune (the generic name for Italian city governments) and centuries of experience in doing things their own way. Nevertheless, the Jesuits tried to enter established universities or to found new universities in Italy. They suffered a string of failures and had only one success.

They tried first in Messina. When the Society established its first European school in Messina in 1548, both the Jesuits and the commune of Messina saw this as an opportunity to create a university. The Society obtained a papal bull authorizing the creation of a university with the right to grant degrees in all subjects. The Jesuits and the commune of Messina agreed in 1549 that the university would have two parts. The commune would appoint and pay professors of law and medicine. The Society would provide Jesuits to teach philosophy, theology, humanities, and possibly mathematics, with salaries to be paid by the commune. All that remained to be settled were details of governance and finances.[47]

But the parties never reached agreement. In June 1550 the commune of Messina promulgated statutes giving it authority over all appointments, including the Jesuits, and complete control over the proposed university. The Jesuits insisted on control of their half of the university. And the commune did not offer enough money for their proposed teaching, in the view of the Jesuits.[48] Negotiations dragged on for years. In the meantime the Jesuits had their own upper school in which they taught logic, natural philosophy, metaphysics, theology, cases of conscience, and even Hebrew, but not law and medicine.[49] The commune of Messina eventually established a full university without any Jesuit participation in 1596.[50]

The Jesuits next tried to enter the existing University of Turin. Like most small Italian universities, Turin had only one or two professors of humanities (usually called "grammar and poetry" or "grammar and rhetoric"), who lectured on the classics of ancient Rome and Greece. Sometimes one professor taught the Latin classics and the other taught Greek classics. The University of Turin had a well-known and much-published Latin humanities professor, Giovanni Battista Giraldi Cinzio of Ferrara (1504–73). But when his contract came up for renewal in 1568, Duke Emanuele Filiberto dismissed him and decreed that the Jesuit school in Turin would teach the humanities to

47. For the origins and development of the University of Messina, start with the studies in *CCC anniversario*, 1900; then see Scaduto, 1948; Moschea, 1991; Romano, 1992, 2002; and Novarese, 1994. For a brief summary, see Grendler, 2002, 121–26.

48. Scaduto, 1948, 105–13; Novarese, 1994, 28–90.

49. Scaduto, 1948, 113–39; Novarese, 1994, 91–125.

50. Moschea, 1991; Novarese, 1994, 125–26, 136–63.

university students. Beginning in the academic year 1567–68, the Jesuit school taught this class for a payment of 200 scudi annually, half of what Giraldi Cinzio had been paid.[51]

Quite satisfied with the humanities instruction of the Jesuits, the duke now wanted Jesuit university professors. Or perhaps he wished to save more money. By January 1572 he and the rector of the Jesuit college, Father Achille Gagliardi (1539–1607), had worked out an agreement. The Jesuits would provide professors for nine daily lectures: single lectures in logic, natural philosophy, metaphysics, mathematics, and Sacred Scripture, plus two in scholastic theology, and two in Latin and Greek humanities. Moreover, the Jesuits would be allowed to correct the students according to part 4 of their *Constitutions*, which may have meant that the Jesuit professors would be permitted to teach Christian values and exhort the students to attend Mass and frequent the sacraments.[52] In addition, the Jesuits would be authorized to award degrees to their own students without involvement or interference by other divisions of the university. This meant that the Jesuits would have the right to award degrees in theology and arts at their own discretion, thus bypassing the colleges of doctors of arts and doctors of theology who normally examined candidates for degrees.[53]

However, the University of Turin already had professors for all the subjects that the Jesuits would teach. What should be done with the incumbents, and how would the Jesuits be inserted into the university? Duke Emanuele Filiberto had a plan: the Jesuits would be appointed singly as the contracts of incumbent professors expired. The duke would take advantage of Italian university professorial contracts (*condotte*), whose normal duration was one or two years. In practice, contracts were usually renewed year after year, making them lifetime appointments. In short, the duke intended to overturn a university tradition for his own purposes. The duke and Father Gagliardi also hatched a scheme to win public approval for incoming Jesuit professors. In the spring the potential Jesuit professor would participate in a public disputation in which he would perform brilliantly and win the admiration of the students. Then in the fall the contract of the incumbent professor in his subject would not be renewed, and the brilliant Jesuit would take his place. As each new Jesuit professor entered the university, the duke would assign 100

---

51. Chiaudano, 1972, 77–78, 90, 93–95 and note 5, 97, 99.

52. See *Constitutions*, 1996, part 4, ch. 16, paragraphs 481–87, pp. 185–86. How Gagliardi expected Jesuit professors to persuade university students to hear Mass daily, confess monthly, and attend sermons, as the *Constitutions* urged, is not clear. University students were not subject to their authority outside the classroom.

53. Achille Gagliardi to Father General Francisco Borja, January 9, 1572, Turin, in ARSI, Mediolanensis 76 I, Historia 1554–1603, ff. 15r–18r. It is printed in Grendler, 2006a, 18–21.

scudi to the local Jesuit college until the figure reached nine Jesuits and 900 scudi, which would be less than the nine incumbents were paid.[54]

Word of the plan leaked, and the commune of Turin objected. Because it contributed 1,000 scudi annually toward university expenses, it had a major stake in its fortunes. On March 7, 1572, the commune made four requests of the duke. It insisted that two of the three Riformatori dello Studio, the magistracy that oversaw the university, should continue to come from the communal council, that is, the city government. This would ensure that the commune's views would be heard. Second, it asked the duke to command the Riformatori to maintain a full complement of professors so that the University of Turin would "remain whole like all other universities," including those in the Papal States. Third, the commune asked that the Jesuits not give lectures in the university nor dispute with the professors in public. Finally, the commune asked the duke to confirm that the rules for admission into the colleges of doctors of law and medicine would not be changed. This may have been an indirect rejection of Father Gagliardi's expectation that the Jesuits would award degrees on their own authority. Duke Emanuele Filiberto agreed to the three main points, above all that the university would have a full complement of professors, but made no comment about the Jesuits teaching in the university and disputing with the professors.[55] Also in 1572, officials of the city government sent a delegation to the Jesuits asking them not to offer any philosophical courses at their school, because the university and the city would suffer unspecified grave harm.[56]

The result was victory for the commune: the Jesuits did not become professors in the University of Turin. Instead, in August 1572 Francisco Borja, the Jesuit father general in Rome, ordered Gagliardi transferred to the Jesuit Brera College in Milan, despite the objections of the duke. Gagliardi left Turin at the beginning of 1573.[57] Borja probably decided that the scheme was raising so much opposition that it would erode the good will on which the Jesuits depended in order to carry out other ministries and generate financial support. And without the Jesuits, Duke Emanuele Filiberto could not proceed with his plan. In 1574 the ducal government ceased making annual payments

---

54. Grendler, 2006a, 9–10, 20–21 (Gagliardi's letter).

55. "[C]he l'università resti sempre compita del numero dei lettori legenti attualmente nelle scuole publiche . . . affinché l'università resti intiera come in tutti gli altri studij, si nel Stato della Chiesa." Memorial of the commune to Duke Emanuele Filiberto of March 7, 1572, plus the duke's responses, in ASCT, carte sciolte no. 97, 7 marzo 1572, no pag. These are official copies made in 1840 of the original documents. Vallauri, 1875, 201 note 1, quotes some of this.

56. Grosso and Mellano, 1957, 88 note 76.

57. See the two letters of Father Juan Alfonso de Polanco, S.J., to Cardinal Carlo Borromeo and to Duke Emanuele Filiberto, December 13, 1572, Rome, in Polanco, 1969, 161–62, 163–64; plus Rurale, 1992, 139–40.

# Jesuit Attempts to Enter Italian Universities

of 200 scudi to the Jesuit college for teaching the humanities to university students. At the same time, the University of Turin reappointed the incumbent professor of Greek and appointed a lay professor of Latin humanities in 1575, after a hiatus of eight years.[58]

The Jesuits made another attempt in 1593, this time to have the teaching of philosophy and theology transferred to the Jesuit college, but the commune and the college of doctors of arts strongly objected, and the proposal was set aside.[59] Instead of becoming university professors, the Turin Jesuits developed a college for noble boys, with considerable success.[60] They also intensified their preaching and catechetical instruction in the countryside of Piedmont and Savoy.[61]

The Jesuits tried also to enter the University of Catania in Sicily. The Society established a college (residence and center of Jesuit activities) in Catania, the capital of Sicily, in 1556. It had a lower school (grammar, humanities, and rhetoric), for which the commune of Catania provided a small subsidy, but no higher school, because Messina was the center for Jesuit higher studies in Sicily.[62]

But then plague struck Messina in 1575, and many Jesuit teachers and students moved from Messina to Catania, where they opened an upper school with four classes, probably logic, natural philosophy, metaphysics, and theology.[63] In December 1575 the Jesuits asked the commune of Catania for an increase in its subsidy to pay for higher living expenses and more teaching, plus funds with which to acquire a second house for the expanded community of Jesuits.[64] The request ignited an animated debate in the city council. One university professor strongly opposed the request on the grounds that the Jesuits wished to create "a university" (*uno studio*), even though the University

---

58. Chiaudano, 1972, 110, 112.

59. AST, Istruzione Pubblica, Regia Università, mazzo 1, n. 72, "Ragioni, colle quali si dimostra il danno, che risultarebbe al Pubblico qualora le lezioni di tutte le parti della Filosofia, e della Teologia si separassero dalle pubbliche Scuole di Torino, e si leggessero nel Collegio de' Padri Gesuiti," October 8, 1593, no pag. See also Vallauri, 1875, 258–61.

60. See, for example, *Monumenta Paedagogica*, 1965–92, 4:348, document of 1580 reporting that the boarding school had ninety to one hundred noble boys from all over Piedmont.

61. For example, in 1596 the college at Turin had only three teachers, while there were eight Jesuit missionaries preaching in the mountain valleys of the state. ARSI, Mediolanensis 47, Catalogi triennales & breves 1589–1614, f. 86r et passim. There are numerous letters about the missions in Piedmont-Savoy between 1575 and 1600 in ARSI.

62. Scaduto, 1974, 354–56.

63. Letters of Father Giovanni Battista Carminata, October 17, 1575, Messina, and Father Jerónimo Doménech, October 19 and November 18, 1575, Catania, in ARSI, Epistolae Italiae 149, ff. 24r, 28r–v, 129r–v; and the letters of Father Juan Alfonso de Polanco, October 5–8 and October 30, 1575, Catania, in Polanco, 1969, 368–69, 387.

64. For what follows, see Catalano, 1917, 64–67, 86–90.

of Catania already offered lectures in logic, philosophy, and theology. He believed that a Jesuit upper school would threaten the small and fragile University of Catania, which had only about a dozen professors and perhaps two hundred to three hundred students.[65] The Jesuits had argued that their upper school would benefit the university by attracting more foreigners (anyone not from Catania and its surrounding territory) who would also study at the University of Catania. The professor rejected this idea: foreign students come to hear distinguished professors of medicine, which Catania lacked because the stipends were so low. Instead of giving the Jesuits more money, the commune should give the money to the university so that it could increase the salaries of the professors of medicine and hire another professor of philosophy.

In the end the commune voted to give the Jesuits more money.[66] But it was never paid. Instead, in June 1576 the plague arrived in Catania, killing at least one young Jesuit. The Society abandoned its efforts to establish an upper school at Catania and returned to Messina.[67] The Jesuits then made one final attempt to teach in Catania. In 1579 they asked that some professorships of the University of Catania be given to them. Viceroy Marc'Antonio Colonna, who governed Sicily for Spain and resided in Catania, refused. But Colonna did permanently suspend the university professorship of Latin grammar and poetry. The viceroy and the Jesuits signed an agreement that the Jesuit college would provide instruction in humanistic studies to university students seeking it.[68] Thus, the Jesuits taught humanities to university students but did not become university professors.

In contrast with their rebuffs in Messina, Turin, and Catania, a handful of Jesuits taught briefly in the University of Macerata, a small regional university founded in 1540–41. The town of Macerata, located in the Papal States about sixty-five kilometers inland from coastal Ancona, is best known in Jesuit history as the birth place of Matteo Ricci (1552–1610). The Jesuits established a college and lower school in Macerata in 1561, and two Jesuits taught humanistic studies at the university from 1561 to 1563. There were objections, and the commune expressed the view that the Jesuits should devote themselves to religious duties rather than university teaching. So the Jesuits stopped teaching in the university.[69] However, the commune then suppressed the human-

---

65. For the number of professors and students at the University of Catania, see Grendler, 2002, 107.

66. Catalano, 1917, 67, 90.

67. See the letters of Polanco, January 12, 17, Catania; March 21, Palermo; May 19, Catania; and June 15, 20, 1576, Siracusa, in Polanco, 1969, 441, 500, 518–19, 524–25, 529–33.

68. Catalano, 1917, 70–71; Catalano, 1934, 88–91.

69. Scaduto, 1974, 392–96. For the rolls of 1561–62 and 1562–63 listing the two Jesuits, see ASMc, Archivio Priorale 794, ff. 79v–80r, 83v. See also Marongiu, 1948, 39 notes 1 and 2 (for the objections to the Jesuits), 56–57 (the two rolls).

ities professorship and in 1567 charged the Jesuits with teaching humanities to university students. As at Catania and Turin, university students desiring humanities instruction would have to go to the Jesuit school.[70] The Jesuits later returned to the university in a small way, as four different Jesuits filled the professorship of logic between 1613 and 1625.[71] This seems to have been a temporary measure. So far as is known, the Jesuits of Macerata did not try to expand their presence in this modest regional university.

The best-known episode of university-Jesuit friction occurred in Padua, where the Jesuits never tried to enter the university.[72] The Jesuits had a flourishing upper school in Padua, which critics charged was a rival university. After some anti-Jesuit actions by rowdy students, a delegation of professors and student leaders went to the Venetian Senate in December 1591. Cesare Cremonini (1550–1631), the second-place ordinary professor of natural philosophy, delivered a fiery oration attacking the Jesuits for conducting an *antistudio,* that is, an illicit rival university. He charged that the Jesuit upper school in Padua was deliberately attempting to draw students away from the University of Padua. Despite Jesuit denials, the senate accepted this view and on December 23, 1591, ordered the Jesuit school not to accept any non-Jesuit students. The senate declared that this was necessary to restore peace and order and to protect the university. Instead, the father general of the Society decided to close the Padua school completely and to deploy the Society's resources elsewhere.

While the fear of competition was probably genuine, several personnel changes, grievances, and irritants fanned the flames of anti-Jesuit hostility.[73] Some friends of the Jesuits in the university and in the town died and were replaced by enemies. For example, Giacomo Zabarella (1533–89), a distinguished professor of natural philosophy, native of Padua, and firm friend of the Jesuits, died and was replaced by Cremonini, who differed with the Jesuits over major philosophical questions. Arts professors who taught privately for extra income saw that income shrink as their private students went to the free Jesuit school. Legal disputes over lands bequeathed to the Jesuits generated ill

---

70. Scaduto, 1992, 211.

71. ASMc, Archivio Priorale, Camerlenghi, filza 206, f. 44r; filza 209, f. 53v; filza 212, f. 46r; filza 214, f. 44r; filza 216, f. 44r; filza 217, f. 45r. There is also a brief notice in the Macerata Jesuit annual letter for 1613: "Quest'anno è eletto uno di nostri per leggere logica nello studio publico con tanto applauso universale della città." ARSI, Roma 130 II, f. 457r.

72. This story has been much studied. For what follows, see Favaro, 1877–78, 1911; Cessi, 1921–22; Donnelly, 1982; and Sangalli, 1999, 187–275.

73. Part of what follows is based on Sangalli, 1999, 187–275, and part of it is my speculation. Incidentally, Sangalli, 1999, 215–21, doubts that the anti-Jesuit disorders of the students in July 1591 led to Cremonini's oration and the senate's action of December. He points out that student misbehavior was common and directed at many targets.

will. Some Venetian patricians saw the Jesuits as Spanish agents, a Venetian prejudice for which no evidence has been uncovered. Finally, one wonders if Paduan professors knew of the attempts of the Jesuits to enter the universities of Turin and Catania and suspected that they would try to do the same at Padua.[74] Whatever the relative importance of these factors, the episode revealed that the presence of a Jesuit upper school could provoke suspicion and anger in a university community.

These experiences made it clear to the Jesuits that existing universities did not want them. Professors opposed the Jesuits because they feared losing positions. Since most academics came from prominent families of the host city or the surrounding territory, communal councils dominated by men from local families heeded their protests. Nor did universities want competition from Jesuit schools; that the Jesuits sometimes called their higher schools "universities" probably did not help.[75] In short, the Jesuits were seen as outsiders who would not add prestige to the university or income to the town.

The quest of the Jesuits to enter existing universities also foundered on governance. Differing views on this prevented the commune and Society from creating a university at Messina, and the issue was even more divisive in established universities. Beginning with Bologna in the late years of the thirteenth century, communes and princes ruled Italian universities. Colleges of doctors of law and doctors of medicine and arts examined degree candidates, while local bishops conferred degrees. All these bodies would lose some authority if the Jesuits joined universities. After three hundred years, civil governments and professors did not want to share their universities with anyone, let alone an upstart religious order. They were satisfied with the status quo.

The Jesuits would have to create their own universities. They needed help because they would not teach law and medicine, but they could join hands with a friendly prince who wished to create a new university. This happened in Parma. In 1599 Duke Ranuccio I Farnese (1569, ruled 1592–1622) approached the Society of Jesus with a proposition. The Jesuits already had a lower school in Parma. The duke proposed the creation of a university that would include the Jesuits. After some bargaining, agreement was reached: the Society provided professors for logic, natural philosophy, mathematics, and theology in return for an annual payment of 2,000 ducatoni.[76] The duke and his gov-

74. This is a surmise, because the documentation concerning the Paduan dispute does not include references to other universities.

75. For example, see Juan Alfonso de Polanco, S.J., to Cardinal Carlo Borromeo and Duke Emanuele Filiberto, December 13, 1572, Rome, in Polanco, 1969, 161 ("nella nova università di Milano"), 163 ("università di nostra Compagnia in Milano"). He referred to the Brera college both times.

76. Parma ducatoni were large ducats of account worth 7 lire 6 soldi instead of the Venetian

# Jesuit Attempts to Enter Italian Universities 23

ernment would choose and pay the professors of law and medicine. Duke Ranuccio I obtained a papal charter for a university empowered to award degrees, and some medical and law professors began teaching in the academic year 1600–01. The full university began in the autumn of 1601. The University of Parma continued through the seventeenth century and beyond.[77]

The Jesuits wanted a university, and the Gonzaga of Mantua and Monferrato ruled a large and prosperous state. It remained for them to come together.

---

ducat of account worth 6 lire 4 soldi. For the University of Parma see Berti, 1967, 23–39; D'Alessandro, 1980; Brizzi, 1980; and the brief summary with some university rolls in Grendler, 2002, 126–37.

77. The small universities of Cagliari and Sassari in Sardinia, founded in the 1620s and 1630s, were also joint Jesuit and civic universities. They will not be discussed here, because they began after Mantua. In addition, Sardinia, a province of the Spanish crown, looked to Madrid in educational matters. The bibliography starts with Zanetti, 1982, and Turtas, 1988, 1995.

CHAPTER 2

# The Jesuits Come to Mantua

lthough a Gonzaga cardinal established close rapport with the superior general of the Jesuits in the middle of the sixteenth century, it took many years before the Gonzaga invited the Jesuits to Mantua. Once the Society's college was founded, Luigi (Aloysius) Gonzaga—a Jesuit, a Gonzaga, and a saint—sealed the bond between the Jesuits and the family. The Jesuit college in Mantua then grew in size and importance.

## 1. THE FOUNDING OF THE JESUIT COLLEGE

Cardinal Ercole Gonzaga (1505–63) asked the Society of Jesus to establish a college in Mantua. De facto ruler of Mantua as regent for two underage dukes (Francesco and Guglielmo) and, later, papal legate to the Council of Trent, Ercole was a major ecclesiastical and political figure who wanted the best for his native city.

On April 16, 1559, Cardinal Ercole wrote to Diego Laínez (1512–65), superior general of the Society of Jesus, asking the Jesuits to establish a college in Mantua. Ercole wanted to provide better religious instruction for the laity in Mantua than could be done by means of catechetical schools, which had not been very successful.[1] But the Jesuits hesitated because of doubts about Ercole's orthodoxy that circulated as a consequence of his friendship in the 1540s with two prominent Italian apostates and association with others suspected of heresy.[2] Nevertheless, the two remained in touch, especially at the

---

1. Scaduto, 1974, 204–5; Rurale, 1997, 39–40 note 1; Murphy, 2007, 105–7.
2. Ercole welcomed to Mantua Bernardino Ochino (1487–1564) and Pier Paolo Vergerio

# The Founding of the Jesuit College

last session (1562–63) of the Council of Trent, which Ercole chaired as a papal legate and Laínez attended as a theologian. Ercole offered to purchase a house in Mantua for the Jesuits and suggested that Laínez visit the city. Laínez agreed. He and fellow Jesuit Juan Alfonso de Polanco (1517–76) went to Mantua in the middle of February 1563, where they met with Margherita Paleologo, mother of the young Duke Guglielmo; clergymen; and others. They inspected buildings that might serve the Jesuits as a residence. Satisfied, Laínez returned to Trent and met with Cardinal Ercole on February 23. Everything seemed ready for the Jesuits to establish a college in Mantua.[3]

But the following day Ercole fell ill with a high fever and rapidly declined. Laínez gave him the last rites, and Ercole died on the night of March 2, 1563. Although he did not live to see the Jesuits established in Mantua, Ercole left 4,000 scudi for the college: 2,000 to purchase a house, the rest to furnish it and to provide some income. He also bequeathed properties that would provide an annual income of 300 scudi to support the Jesuits. His will obligated his three heirs, the young Duke Guglielmo Gonzaga; Guglielmo's brother Ludovico, who became duke of Nevers; and Ercole's brother Ferrante, or their heirs, with implementing the will.[4] But nothing happened at this time. In December 1563 Laínez wrote to Cardinal Federico Gonzaga (1540–65), the next Gonzaga cardinal, that the Society could not establish a college in Mantua because it had its hands full with those already in existence and had many prior requests for new colleges. He hoped that the project could be realized in the future.[5] The future did not come for twenty-one years.

Nevertheless, a cadet branch of the Gonzaga did welcome the Jesuits into the Mantovano. In 1571 Camillo Gonzaga and Barbara Borromeo, sister of Cardinal Federico Borromeo, count and countess of Novellara, one of the independent states ruled by a cadet branch on the edge of the duchy of Mantua, helped the Jesuits establish a house of probation, that is, a house for training novices. It was located in the small town of Novellara, about forty kilometers south of Mantua across the Po River (see map 1). By the academic year 1579–80, the Jesuits had added a Latin grammar class, enrolling thirty

---

(1498–1565), two prominent future apostates. Ochino fled Italy in 1542, and in 1546 Gonzaga broke with Vergerio, who left Italy in 1549. Ercole also had a longtime friendship with cardinals Giovanni Morone and Reginald Pole; the first was tried for heresy during the pontificate of Paul IV (1555–59) but was exonerated after the pope's death, while Pole might have been arrested had he lived longer. Ercole owned works of Luther, Melanchthon, and Zwingli because he wished to understand their beliefs. Although never remotely a Protestant, he maintained an open mind and treated dissenters gently. Scaduto, 1974, 63; Murphy, 2007, 28–29, 115–57.

3. Scaduto, 1974, 204–7; Rurale, 1997, 13–15.
4. Scaduto, 1974, 205–6; Gorzoni, 1997, 59.
5. Rurale, 1997, 15.

boys.⁶ But this was the extent of Gonzaga family support for the Jesuits at this time.

A Habsburg princess revived the idea of bringing the Jesuits to Mantua. In April 1561 Duke Guglielmo Gonzaga (1538, reigned 1550 to d. 1587) married Princess Eleonora Habsburg (1534–94), the eighth of fifteen children of Emperor Ferdinand I (1503, ruled 1558–64) and Anne of Bohemia.⁷ Able, devout, and determined, Eleonora had wished to become a nun. She rejected two proposed husbands because they were Protestants. Now twenty-seven, she yielded to the wishes of her father and married Guglielmo, even though he was hunchbacked. Eleonora of Austria, as the documents call her, was a pious woman.⁸ After guaranteeing the succession by producing a son and two daughters, she and Duke Guglielmo, also a religious man, agreed in 1568 to a chaste marriage. As duchess she initiated several projects of practical charity. In the late 1570s she established a school for poor girls, paying for teachers, books, cloth for sewing, and wood for the fires. It eventually enrolled about a hundred poor girls aged seven to twelve. She also supported catechism schools for girls, an orphanage, and a refuge for sick pilgrims. She took an active role in all these enterprises and exhorted noblewomen to help.⁹

Soon after arriving in Mantua, Eleonora of Austria began to urge her husband to implement the will of Cardinal Ercole. According to her confessor and biographer, she was following Habsburg family tradition, as her father had invited the Jesuits to Vienna and Prague, and brothers and sisters had established Jesuit colleges in their realms.¹⁰ In Italy Eleonora's sisters Bar-

---

6. Scaduto, 1992, 93–94, 345. In addition, every Sunday Countess Barbara taught in Schools of Christian Doctrine (catechism schools) for girls. Carbone, 1596, 132. For some details and the Latin grammar class of 1579–80 at Novellara, see the annual letter of the Jesuit provincial, Mario Beringucci, January 1, 1580, in ARSI, Veneta 105/I, f. 63r–v. The Latin grammar class at Novellara was inadvertently omitted in Grendler, 2004, 495 table 3.

7. The many children of Ferdinand and Anne of Bohemia offered useful instruments for extending Habsburg influence. In Italy alone, Barbara (1543–65) became duchess of Ferrara, Eleonora duchess of Mantua, and Giovanna (or Joanna, d. 1578) grand duchess of Tuscany.

8. She will be called Eleonora of Austria throughout this book because she appears that way in the documents and to avoid confusion with her future daughter-in-law, Eleonora de' Medici (1567–1611).

9. The sources differ on the details of the school for girls. Pellizzer, 1992, 420 (and 421 for Eleonora's other charitable works), sees the school beginning in 1575 or 1576. Possevino, 1594, 49–50, gives the foundation date as 1588. Folcario, 1598, 157–65, 432–35 (the most detailed account), gives an enrollment of 113 girls and the rules of the school, and saw it beginning after the Jesuits were established. Carbone, 1596, 132, gives no foundation date, but states that the school enrolled ninety girls.

10. According to Folcario, 1598, 138–39, Eleonora's brother Archduke Ferdinand founded the Jesuit college in Graz, and brother Archduke Charles did the same in Innsbruck, while her sisters Maddalena, Margherita, Elena, Elisabeth (the wife of Sigismond of Poland), and Anna (married to Duke Albrecht of Bavaria) did the same in other lands.

bara, married to Duke Alfonso II Este of Ferrara, and Giovanna, married to Francesco I de' Medici, grand duke of Tuscany, strongly supported the Jesuit colleges in Ferrara and Florence respectively. The two sisters also shared a German-speaking Jesuit confessor.[11]

Despite Eleonora's urging, Duke Guglielmo did nothing for many years for several possible reasons. He had differences with Pope Pius V (1566–72), who revoked the duke's right of presentation (the right to name the bishop) to the bishopric of Casale Monferrato, which the previous pope had granted him. This irritated Duke Guglielmo when he was putting down a rebellion there. He also clashed with Pius V over what he saw as the overly zealous prosecution of prominent Mantuan citizens by the Mantuan inquisition, run by Dominicans, Pius V's order.[12] While his conflicts with Pius V should not have prejudiced him against the Jesuits, who had their own difficulties with the imperious pope, contemporaries viewed the Jesuits as strong proponents of papal authority. Duke Guglielmo, like many other sovereigns, wished to rule his state in both civil and ecclesiastical matters without acknowledging great differences between the two. It is also possible that a young Paolo Sarpi (1552–1623) influenced him. The Venetian-born Sarpi joined the Servants of Mary, which assigned him to a monastery in Mantua about 1567. The brilliant Sarpi taught cases of conscience at the cathedral and came to the attention of Duke Guglielmo, who made him his personal theologian until Sarpi's order transferred him to Milan in 1574.[13] Finally, Duke Guglielmo, who was pretty tight fisted for a Gonzaga ruler, may not have implemented Cardinal Ercole's will because he did not want to disburse the money. Nor did the Jesuits pursue the matter. They were stretched to the limit to staff their existing colleges in Italy during the generalcies of Francisco Borja (1565–72) and Everard Mercurian (1573–80). The Society strove to strengthen their existing colleges rather than found new ones.

Then in the late 1570s the duke and duchess had a more pressing issue to resolve, the marriage of their eldest son and heir, Vincenzo (1562–1612). His bride was expected to come from one of the four other leading princely families of northern Italy, the Medici of Florence, the Farnese of Parma, the Este of Ferrara, or the Savoia of Piedmont-Savoy. Although the Gonzaga might net a Spanish or Austrian Habsburg as a bride, and one of their daugh-

---

11. Folcario, 1598, 138–39, somewhat grandly credited Barbara Habsburg with founding the Jesuit college in Ferrara, and Giovanna, the Jesuit college in Florence. The colleges were already in existence, but both strongly supported the Jesuits, and Barbara persuaded her husband, and Giovanna shamed hers, to do the same. Scaduto, 1992, 214–15, 217–18, 300–305, 351–52.

12. Pastor, 1891–1953, 17:321–25. For additional speculation on the reasons for Duke Guglielmo's inaction, see Bazzotti, 1977, 28–29, and Rurale, 1997, 13–16.

13. Gaetano and Luisa Cozzi, "La formazione culturale e religiosa. 1552–1605," in Sarpi, 1969, 4–6.

ters occasionally marry a Habsburg or Valois, their sons and daughters normally married within the four dynasties. Since the Medici were grand dukes and had marital connections with the Valois of France, the Habsburgs of Spain, and the Habsburgs of the Holy Roman Empire, and the Gonzaga ruled two duchies and had also married into the Habsburgs of the Holy Roman Empire, they probably considered themselves to be a little better than the other families. Hence, Grand Duke Francesco I de' Medici offered his daughter Eleonora as wife to Vincenzo in 1579. The fact that Eleonora and Vincenzo were first cousins, because their mothers were sisters, did not deter anyone, because a papal dispensation could be obtained.

But moral indignation and family honor trumped dynastic politics this time. Guglielmo and Eleonora rejected the Medici offer, primarily because of Eleonora's hostility toward Bianca Capello, the new wife of Francesco I de' Medici. For years Grand Duke Francesco had lived openly with Bianca, who was already married, thus humiliating his legal wife, Giovanna, sister of Eleonora of Austria, until Giovanna died in 1578.[14] Having rejected the Medici marriage, Vincenzo married Margherita Farnese (1567–1643), daughter of Alessandro Farnese, governor of the Low Countries, in April 1581. This linked the Gonzaga with the ruling family of Parma.

But Vincenzo's marriage to fourteen-year-old Margherita Farnese could not be consummated, probably because of a physical defect of the bride, and was annulled in October 1583.[15] Guglielmo and Eleonora had to swallow their pride and beg the Medici for the union that they had earlier spurned. Francesco I de' Medici and Bianca Capello accepted their offer, but first they wished to humiliate the Gonzaga. Because malicious tongues wagged that the failure to consummate the marriage with Margherita Farnese was Vincenzo's fault, Francesco I and Bianca demanded that Vincenzo prove his virility, even though he was already known for his amorous exploits. They insisted that he have intercourse before witnesses with a woman selected for the purpose. The

---

14. Pellizzer, 1992, 421; Tamalio and Besutti, 2003, 3–4.

15. According to the reports, Vincenzo's attempted penetration caused Margherita great pain and she screamed loudly. Shocked by her distress, Vincenzo was unable to perform his role. It seems likely that Margherita had an anatomical malformation, possibly an occlusion by a membrane very resistant to being broken and close to a nerve. Medical scholars, including the famous Girolamo Fabrici d'Acquapendente, professor of anatomy at the University of Padua, offered divergent advice, including surgery to cut the membrane, while Cardinal Carlo Borromeo advised on the moral issues. Some believed that surgery would put Margherita's life at risk, because it could produce infection, for which there was no antidote. If she consented to the operation and died, she might be considered to have committed suicide, and the surgeon be viewed a murderer. In the end the decision was taken out of her hands. Surgery was not attempted, the marriage was annulled by Pope Gregory XIII, and Margherita entered a convent. See the medical analysis of Pazzini, 1978, 324–27. For a colorful and somewhat imaginative account, see Bellonci, 1963, 39–77; repeated in Bellonci, 1956, 34–70.

## The Founding of the Jesuit College

*prova* (test or proof) attracted wide attention at the time, and with historians and voyeurs subsequently. It even became the subject of a film. Vincenzo passed the test and married Eleonora de' Medici in April 1584.[16]

With the marriage negotiations proceeding satisfactorily, Duke Guglielmo began to consider bringing the Jesuits to Mantua. Two Jesuits were invited to preach in Mantua, obviously to be evaluated.[17] And he asked his councillors for advice. Some told him that the Jesuits would bring great benefit to the city. They would provide excellent education for Mantuan boys, schooling that would draw them out of their homes and the soft care of their mothers and bind them to their peers. Other councillors were opposed. They argued that the Jesuits would put their noses into public affairs and private matters; under the guise of piety, they would intrude themselves into the secrets of princes. They would gain the confidence of women who would then manipulate their husbands and relatives in order to further Jesuit interests. Avid for rich patrimonies, the Jesuits would impoverish families by drawing the richest, and most noble and spirited, sons into the Society. In rebuttal, the councillors favoring the Jesuits pointed out that the latter were not begging to come to Mantua, nor would the duke be doing them a favor. He would simply be honoring his uncle's memory by disbursing the money left for this purpose.[18] In short, the duke's councillors saw the Jesuits as schoolmasters or busybodies. Neither group mentioned the other ministries to which the Jesuits devoted much energy and resources.

Duchess Eleonora of Austria attempted to ease her husband's concerns by telling him that it was true that clergymen sometimes intervened in private and public matters when the common good was involved, but they did so rarely and only on request.[19] Reassured but still cautious, Duke Guglielmo decided to talk to the Jesuits. The Society authorized its most famous diplomat, Antonio Possevino (1533–1611), a native of Mantua who had served Cardinal Ercole as a secretary and had tutored two Gonzaga princelings before becoming a Jesuit in 1559, to discuss the matter with the duke.[20] Possevino

---

16. Bellonci, 1963, 78–99, repeated in Bellonci, 1956, 71–88, again provides a colorful account. *Una vergine,* 1965, reprints portions of the Gonzaga-Medici correspondence concerning the test and provides color pictures from the 1965 film *Una Vergine per il Principe,* directed by Pasquale Festa Campanile. Vittorio Gassman played Vincenzo Gonzaga, and the beautiful Virna Lisi played Giulia, the woman chosen for the test. For brief but more sober summaries of the marriage diplomacy and test, see Pellizzer, 1992, 421; and Tamalio and Besutti, 2003, 3–4.

17. Schizzerotto, 1979, 19–20.

18. Gorzoni, 1997, 60. In addition to the notes that follow, see Rurale, 1997, 13–18, 39–42, for a good account of the founding of the Jesuit college.

19. Gorzoni, 1997, 60–61.

20. Scaduto, 2001, 3201; Brunelli, 2001a, 717. In addition to his diplomatic missions and other duties, Possevino represented the Society in several discussions with northern Italian princes, most notably in Parma in 1599, when Ranuccio I Farnese was founding the University of Parma.

told the duke that it was a prince's duty to ensure the security of his state by providing for the cultivation and good education of youths, since they were so easily attracted to vice.[21] Here Possevino animadverted on a Renaissance humanistic commonplace that educating well the sons of the town would secure the future of the state, thus bringing forth the civic goal of Jesuit schools.[22] He added a princely spin: uneducated youths were more likely to become tumultuous and seditious, which would unsettle the state and Gonzaga rule.[23] Possevino added that many devout families in the city felt the same way and hoped that the duke would establish a Jesuit school. He assured the duke that the Society did not actively seek legacies and would not interfere in civil matters.[24]

With the approval of the duke, Duchess Eleonora took the first concrete step. She divided her jewelry into four equal parts, three parts for her three children, and then she sold the fourth, which yielded 7,500 gold scudi.[25] She offered the Jesuits the money. The 7,500 gold scudi could be invested in "secure properties" in the Mantovano that would yield 600 scudi (at 6 lire = 1 scudo) in annual income. The income was to be used to support in perpetuity "three lettered persons who would teach humane letters to the poor citizens of Mantua," that is, a Jesuit school with three teachers. She would do this for "the public good of the city of Mantua."[26] In her offer the duchess initially

---

21. "A questo dire del duca [Guglielmo] rispose il Possevino essere proprio d'un prencipe il provedere alla sicurezza dei suoi stati con la coltura e buona educatione della gioventù, tanto facile a' vitii." Gorzoni, 1997, 61.

22. See Grendler, 1989, 13–14, for other appearances of this commonplace. O'Malley, 2004, 513–16, points out the civic and cultural mission of Jesuit schools.

23. Using an early seventeenth-century history of the Gonzaga, Schizzerotto, 1979, 24–25, presents a slightly more reason-of-state interpretation of Possevino's words. Gorzoni had Possevino putting greater emphasis on the moral and religious value of a Jesuit education.

24. Gorzoni, 1997, 62–63.

25. The story about raising the money through sale of her jewels is not found in the offer to the Jesuits cited in the next note but appears in the biography of Eleonora of Austria written by Antonio Folcario and repeated in other accounts. Folcario, 1598, 141–42, described the amount raised as "several thousand scudi" (*alcune migliarà di scudi*). There is no reason to doubt Folcario's word on the jewelry sale, since he knew the duchess and other members of the Gonzaga family very well. Folcario (1544–1601), from Santo Stefano (Mondovì) but of German origin, was a Jesuit priest who served in several colleges in northern Italy until coming to Mantua before or in 1590. He taught in the lower school, later taught cases of conscience, and died in Mantua. He was Eleonora's confessor in her later years, perhaps because he spoke German. After her death in 1594, he became the confessor of Duke Vincenzo I and his sons Francesco and Ferdinando. Scaduto, 1968, 58; Schizzerotto, 1979, 31; Gorzoni, 1997, 100–101.

26. "[E]t mantenere tre persone letterate le quali insegnino lettere d'humanità à cittadini poveri di Mantoa" and "beneficio publico della città di Mantua." Statement of the offer, undated but probably late 1583 or early 1584, in ASM, AG, Bu. 3366, f. 354r–v (quotes 354r and 354v). See also Gorzoni, 1997, 66, who uses nearly the exact words as in the first quote.

mentioned her desire to provide education for the poor boys of Mantua, then named the Jesuits as the potential providers, which suggests that the latter were a means to an end.

This was the beginning of negotiations, which also involved a church, other buildings, additional money, guarantees from the Jesuits, and the Jewish community. Cardinal Agostino Valier, bishop of Verona and an experienced mediator, was summoned to help.[27] The duke, the duchess, and the Jesuits came to agreement in principle in March 1584, and a final document delineating the commitments of the Jesuits and the duke and duchess was signed in December 1584.[28] The Jesuits agreed to maintain a school that would teach Latin grammar, humanities, rhetoric, and Greek, plus hear confessions, preach, and provide catechetical instruction. They promised to recognize the duke and duchess and their heirs as the founders of the college and would say Masses and pray for them and their posterity in perpetuity. If the Jesuits abandoned their college, the church and other buildings would revert to the duke or his heirs, who might use them for other pious works. There were proportional penalties if the Jesuits reduced their commitment. This part of the agreement demonstrated the influence of Cardinal Valier, because it referred to Jesuit arrangements in Verona, where they had established a college and school in 1579 and 1580. The duke wanted the Jesuits to maintain a community that would include a minimum of six Jesuit priests and three teachers, but the agreement did not stipulate a minimum number of Jesuits.

The most difficult issue was finding a church for the Jesuits. The duke, the bishop of Mantua, and the Jesuits eventually settled on the parish church of San Salvatore with its benefice and adjoining house. The pastor was persuaded to renounce his right to the church, house, and benefice worth 80 scudi annually to the papacy. The papacy, in turn, assigned them to the Jesuits, who agreed to pay the priest 100 scudi annually for the duration of his life, which lasted until 1612. Cardinal Valier also promised to try to obtain from the papacy a second benefice for the priest but was unsuccessful.[29] Responsibility for the care of the parishioners' souls was transferred to other parishes, thus

---

27. See the three autograph letters of Valier to Duke Guglielmo, March 21, 22, 27, 1584, Verona, obviously written shortly after a verbal agreement had been reached, in ASM, AG, Bu. 3366, ff. 14r, 16r, 18r.

28. There is a fair copy of the agreement in ASM, AG, Bu. 3366, ff. 399r–400r. The obligations of the Jesuits are on f. 399r–v. Although undated and unsigned, the agreement matches Gorzoni's description of the terms of the agreement; indeed, at times the wording is identical. And Gorzoni, 1997, 62–66, adds detailed information about its implementation. There are at least three other manuscript copies of the agreement. Schizzerotto, 1979, 20–22, cites two from ASM and one from ARSI, and quotes almost the entire offer from ASM, AG, Bu. 3309, ff. 445–48. It is practically identical with the version in ASM, AG, Bu. 3366, ff. 399r–400r, which is used here.

29. Gorzoni, 1997, 62–64; and ASM, AG, Bu. 3366, f. 400r.

freeing the Jesuits of parish duties. The duke also promised to give the Jesuits, as part of the legacy of Cardinal Ercole Gonzaga, 2,000 scudi to be used to purchase buildings contiguous to the church for living quarters and classrooms. The money would also help purchase furniture and books for the school, bedding, and household goods. The Jesuits took possession of San Salvatore in September 1584.

Overall, the duke and duchess were very generous.[30] As mentioned earlier, the duchess provided 7,500 scudi to be used to purchase Mantovano lands yielding 600 scudi annually in income for the Jesuits. Because the agreement did not indicate who would choose the lands to be purchased, it is likely that Gonzaga agents did it. Finally, the 1584 agreement promised that Ludovico Gonzaga, who had moved to France and become duke of Nevers, would give the Jesuits 2,000 scudi, and Ferrante II Gonzaga (1563–1630), duke of Guastalla and grandson of the original heir, Ferrante Gonzaga, would give them 1,000 scudi for the college. These provisions completed implementation of Cardinal Ercole's will.[31] The payments also demonstrated that familial obligations continued to bind together members of the far-flung Gonzaga clan. In the end the Jesuits realized far more than the 4,000 scudi and annual income of 300 scudi bequeathed by Cardinal Ercole. On the other hand, the investments in land did not yield income immediately. Hence, the Jesuits had to live on alms at first, while Duchess Eleonora and ladies of the court sewed table and kitchen linens for them.[32]

The Jesuit college formally opened on November 21, 1584, and the Jesuits inaugurated their school of three classes. The duke ordered the pages at his court to attend the school, and by 1590 it was "full of nobles and distinguished people," in the words of the Jesuit chronicler Giuseppe Gorzoni.[33] The three classes probably enrolled about 150 boys.[34] The Jesuits added a class in cases of conscience for priests in or about 1586.[35]

---

30. See ASM, AG, Bu. 3366, f. 400r, for the commitments of the Gonzaga. Although comparing the amounts of money and land set aside by various northern Italian rulers in the last third of the sixteenth century for Jesuit colleges would be difficult, it appears that the Gonzaga were more generous and haggled less than most.

31. For the promise of money from Ludovico and Ferrante II Gonzaga, see the undated agreement in ASM, AG, Bu. 3366, f. 400r. See Gorzoni, 1997, 59, for the terms of Ercole's will.

32. Gorzoni, 1997, 70.

33. "Tre scuole, cioè grammatica, humanità e retorica erano aperte, ma piene di nobiltà e di gente qualificata. Sin dal primo dì che s'apersero volle sua altezza che venissero per iscuolari li suoi medesimi paggi, con obligarli alle più rigorose leggi delle scuole." Gorzoni, 1997, 79.

34. No enrollment figures for the early years have been located. The estimate comes from enrollment figures of Jesuit colleges with the three classes of the lower school in other colleges, such as Bologna, Brescia, and Verona, in the Jesuit Province of Venice. See Grendler, 2004, 495–96.

35. Rurale, 1997, 18, gives a date of 1586. Gorzoni, 1997, 70, indicates that it was sometime after the foundation in 1584 ("qualche tempo anche i casi di conscienza").

## The Founding of the Jesuit College 33

The Mantuan printing press took advantage of the opening of the Jesuit school. In 1585 Francesco Osanna, the leading Mantuan publisher, issued an edition of the *De arte rhetorica libri tres* of Cypriano Soares, S.J. (1524–93), a rhetoric manual often used in Jesuit schools.[36] In 1588 Duke Vincenzo I named Francesco Osanna the ducal printer and gave him exclusive rights to publish elementary and secondary school textbooks, catechisms, and "all the humanity works that the Reverend Jesuit Fathers have adopted and will adopt in the future for their schools in this city."[37] In the next years, Osanna issued editions of Virgil's poetry and Martial's epigrams whose title pages carried emblems involving a cross, IHS (Jesus), and a heart with three arrows, common Jesuit symbols.[38] Virgil's poetry was a curriculum text in Jesuit schools, while Martial's epigrams were occasionally taught. In addition, Osanna issued seven works of the prolific Antonio Possevino, S.J., between 1585 and 1604.[39]

As Jesuits did elsewhere, the Mantuan Jesuits organized fraternal societies called congregations for different groups in the community. The congregation of merchants and artisans met on Sunday morning, the congregation of clergymen on Wednesday, the cavaliers (nobles) met on Friday morning, and the penitents on Friday evening. Male members of the Gonzaga family enrolled in the congregation of cavaliers and participated in its religious exercises.[40] The teachers and pupils of the free school for girls founded by Eleonora of Austria came to the Jesuit church for devotions.[41] The Jesuits also preached, heard confessions, organized and taught in catechetical schools for children, worked at peacemaking, and helped fallen women live virtuous lives.

The Jesuits soon found the church of San Salvatore inadequate for their needs and wished to build a new one. The Jewish community of Mantua was equally unhappy, because San Salvatore and its contiguous houses were inside the Jewish quarter (not yet a ghetto) and close to the most important synagogue of the city (see map 3). The Jews, realizing that the Jesuits planned to expand, feared further encroachment on their quarter and synagogue. So, leaders of the Jewish community told the duke that they would pay half the cost of acquiring some other property farther away for the Jesuits. The duke and the Jesuits accepted. In a series of complicated payments and promises that adjusted the agreement of 1584, the duke gave 2,500 scudi. The Jews contributed 1,100 scudi immediately and promised another 2,200 scudi over

---

36. Pescasio, 1971, 213, item 31.
37. "[E] tutte l'opere d'humanità che i Reverendi Padri Gesuiti adoprano et per l'avenire adopreranno nelle scuole loro di questa città." Quoted in Coniglio, 1962, 361.
38. Schizzerotto, 1979, 27–29 and figures 1, 2, 3; Pescasio, 1971, 215, items 73, 78.
39. Pescasio, 1971, 213–19, items 26, 115, 129, 130, 133, 135, 149.
40. Gorzoni, 1997, 121–22, 130.
41. Gorzoni, 1997, 100.

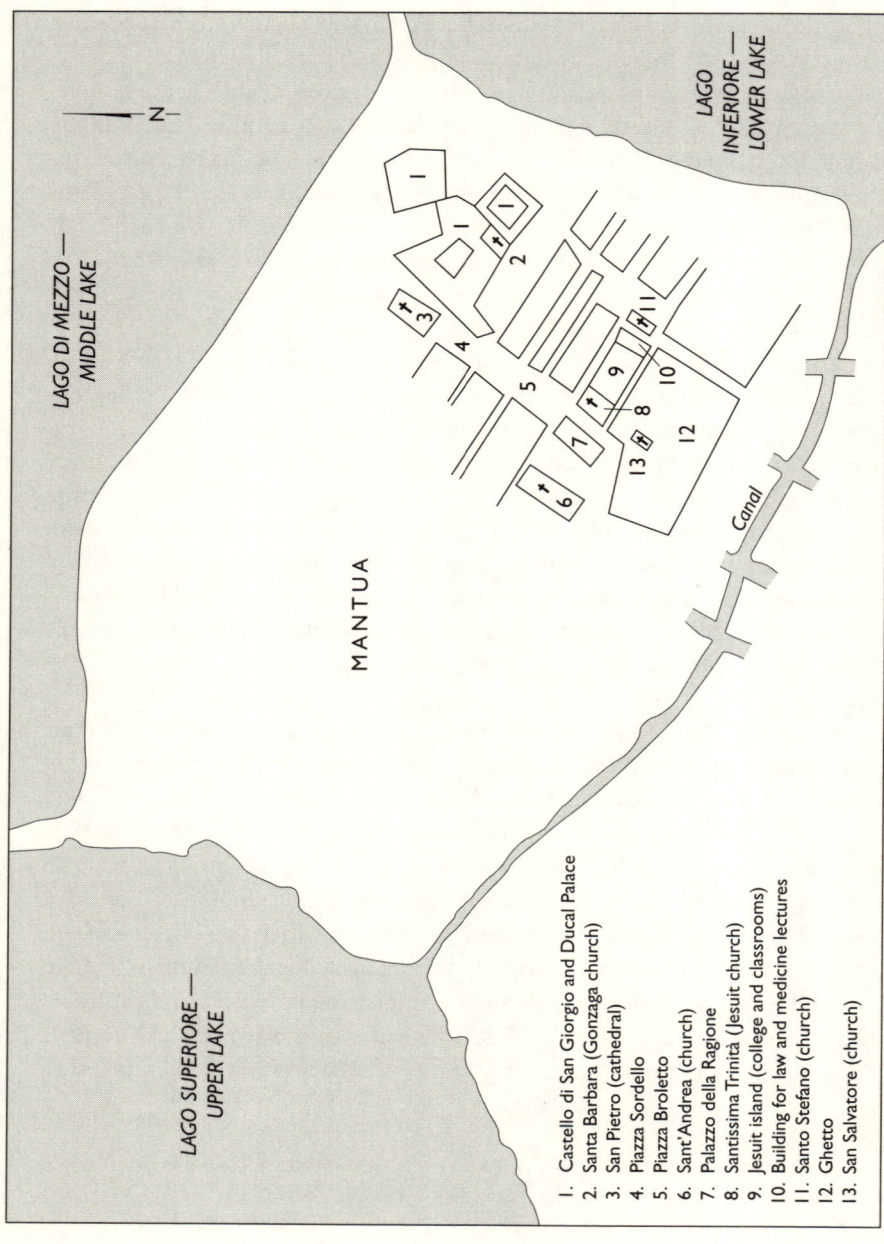

MAP 3. The Jesuit island and university ca. 1625

# The Founding of the Jesuit College

time, making the eventual price of new land and buildings 5,800 scudi. In return the Jews asked the Jesuits to close off a small street that led directly to the synagogue, and the Jesuits did so by erecting a large door.[42] The newly purchased houses and the future church would become the nucleus of an expanding contiguous area of urban Mantua that people began to call the Jesuit "island" (see map 3).[43]

The announcement that the Jesuits would build a church stimulated an outpouring of donations from the duke, the duchess, members of cadet branches of the Gonzaga, and many Mantuans. The close association of the Gonzaga with the Jesuits obviously encouraged others to contribute. It is also likely that townspeople appreciated the educational, spiritual, and charitable ministries of the Jesuits. The gifts and legacies included houses, properties, and large and small monetary bequests, some immediate and others postponed until the donor died. Inevitably, some legacies generated bitter and extended litigation, as disappointed family members challenged testaments.[44] Duke Guglielmo deeded to the Jesuits a small street offering some open space that might be used for a church, while the financial support enabled them to buy additional houses and parts of houses, and to level them. Construction of the new church began in 1587.

Although the duke offered the services of court architects for the new church, the Jesuits had their own ideas. Even though the Jesuits did not have a single style of architecture,[45] many Jesuit churches built in Italy in the late sixteenth century resembled each other, because the same Jesuits designed and constructed multiple churches, and because the general in Rome reviewed church plans. Giovanni Tristano (1515–75) and his Jesuit assistants and followers had some common ideas, which partly rose from practical con-

---

42. Gorzoni, 1997, 66–67, 72; Simonsohn, 1977, 27–28. Relying on Jewish sources, Simonsohn offers a slightly different interpretation: "Most probably the church [San Salvatore] was given over to their use not by chance but with the clear intention of extorting money from the Jews to finance the housing of the Jesuits" (27). And he writes that the Jews paid 3,500 scudi. Although Simonsohn may be correct, because the Gonzaga did extort money from the Jewish community from time to time, no additional evidence of this motivation for initially choosing San Salvatore has been located.

43. Gorzoni, 1997, 87, was happy to report that in 1602 the Jesuits purchased the last part of the last house in "our island," so that it was "completely ours." "Era questa casa unica che restasse nella nostra isola di mezzo e che non fosse acquistata da noi"; "e finalmente del 1602, tutta la casa fu nostra e nostra tutta fu la sopradetta isola." The maps, diagrams, and photographs in *Il palazzo degli studi*, 1998, 20–29, especially 20, show the development of the Jesuit island.

44. Gorzoni, 1997, 67–69. Here and elsewhere Gorzoni described the complicated bequests, property purchases, financial arrangements, and negotiations involving many parties that were necessary to create and expand the Jesuit college.

45. See Bailey, 1999, 45–46, 64–65; Robertson, 1999, 142–44.

cerns.⁴⁶ They preferred a Latin cross design. With a wide nave and no interior columns, the Latin cross plan created a large, open, even theatrical central space. The major altar located at the center of the cross under a high vaulted ceiling was the focal point of the church. A raised pulpit toward the middle of the nave enabled a preacher to speak directly to the congregation and the latter to hear him. The straight nave without curves and columns further promoted good acoustics. Shallow chapel arches could fit into both walls of the nave, while round windows on the high walls of the second story let in light. The simple design left ample space for much interior decoration, including the spectacular frescoed vaults found in some Italian Jesuit churches. A relatively plain neoclassical façade without statuary, but with some rosettes and flanking wings terminating in scrolls, completed the design. This was basically the form of the Jesuit church in Mantua.⁴⁷

The college designs prepared by Tristano and his disciples tended to be functional.⁴⁸ Classrooms around a courtyard, plus an atrium and vestibule, accommodated the school. Another part of the college held living quarters for members of the Society, which had to be distinct from the school. Individual cells, a refectory, and other rooms encircled another courtyard square with a garden and well. Finally, church and college were expected to be contiguous so that Jesuits living in the college and students from the school would have easy indoor access to the church, while the public entered the main door.

In July 1587 the Mantuan Jesuits prepared a design for their church, obviously with the aid of an architect unless one of the local Jesuits had such expertise, and sent it to Rome for approval. General Claudio Aquaviva showed it to Father Giovanni De Rosis (1538–1610), who designed or helped build Jesuit churches throughout Italy and had inherited Tristano's mantle as the chief architect of the Society.⁴⁹ Over the next months and years, the Mantuan Jesuits sent many plans and queries to Rome, and Aquaviva sent back the advice of Father De Rosis to Mantua, which meant that the latter's comments

---

46. Pirri, 1955, and more succinctly Pirri and Di Rosa, 1975, 4. There is much more bibliography. Father Giuseppe Valeriano (1542–96) from Aquila was another Jesuit architect whose churches in Italy and Spain resemble those built by Tristano and that of Mantua. See the illustrations in *L'Università dell'Aquila*, 2000, 604, 612, 626, 650, 656, 676. Although Valeriano proposed to the father general that he draft a common design for Jesuit churches and colleges, it did not happen. Pirri, 1955, 41.

47. This statement is advanced cautiously with the aid of the illustrations in *Il palazzo degli studi*, 1998, 30–35, which attempt to reconstruct the original design.

48. Pirri and Di Rosa, 1975, 5.

49. The following account of the building of the Jesuit church in Mantua is based on Pirri and Di Rosa, 1975, 37–39, 96–99; and Schizzerotto, 1979, 32–40, 52–56. On De Rosis, see Pirri, 1955, ab indice; Pirri and Di Rosa, 1975; and Di Rosa, 2001.

# The Founding of the Jesuit College 37

had the force of commands. The Mantuan Jesuits and General Aquaviva wanted a church of balanced proportions that would be large enough to accommodate the public functions rising from the ministries of the Society. Aquaviva, following the advice of De Rosis, informed the Mantuan Jesuits that if the size of the school had to be reduced to enlarge the church, this could be done, because there would still be enough room for classrooms.[50] Father Aquaviva also assured Eleonora of Austria that the Jesuits would not sacrifice the beauty of the church to the need for space.[51]

Most recommendations were practical rather than aesthetic. They dealt with the size of the three major chapels, technical problems with the transept, making sure that the floor of the church was on the same level as the adjoining college, and that visitor accommodations in the college were separate from the living quarters of the Jesuits.[52] General Aquaviva came to Mantua in the late summer or early fall of 1592 to check on the progress of the church. And he sent Giorgio Soldati (1533–1609) to help. A temporal coadjutor in the Society of Jesus as well as an experienced architect and engineer, Soldati helped design and build Jesuit churches and colleges in Forlì, Imola, Mantua, Modena, Novellara, Parma, Piacenza, and Cracow, where he died.[53] He made several visits to Mantua between 1592 and 1597 to oversee the remaining construction.

The Jesuits gave Duke Guglielmo the honor of naming the church, and he chose Most Holy Trinity (Santissima Trinità, or SS. Trinità), because there had once been a shrine to the Holy Trinity at that location.[54] Although Duke Guglielmo died on August 14, 1587, Duke Vincenzo I continued to support the construction of the church. And because Eleonora of Austria wanted it, Aquaviva in 1590 agreed that the Gonzaga coat of arms might be affixed to the façade of the church.[55] Enough of the church was built and roofed so that the first Mass could be celebrated there on June 9, 1591, the Feast of the Most Holy Trinity.[56] On Christmas Day 1594 the major chapel of the church was completed, and the church as a whole was finished just before Christmas 1596.[57]

When part of the church was available, it became the center of liturgical

---

50. See the observations of De Rosis on the Mantuan plans forwarded by Aquaviva to Prospero Malavolta, rector of the Mantuan college, on August 8, 1587, Rome, in Pirri and Di Rosa, 1975, 97.

51. Schizzerotto, 1979, 39.

52. Pirri and Di Rosa, 1975, 37–39, 96–99; Schizzerotto, 1979, 32–40, 53–56.

53. On Soldati, see Pirri, 1955, ab indice; Pirri and Di Rosa, 1975, 23, 36, 95; Schizzerotto, 1979, 34–35, 54–55; and Strobel, 2001.

54. Bazzotti, 1977, 29; Schizzerotto, 1979, 53 note 50; Il palazzo degli studi, 1998, 30.

55. Aquaviva to the Jesuit rector in Mantua, June 9, 1590, Rome, quoted in Schizzerotto, 1979, 55 note 60. The Gonzaga coat of arms is no longer there.

56. Schizzerotto, 1979, 34; Gorzoni, 1997, 80.

57. Schizzerotto, 1979, 43. For diagrams and pictures partly reconstructing how the church once was, see Bazzotti, 1977, 31–33; and Il palazzo degli studi, 1998, 30–35.

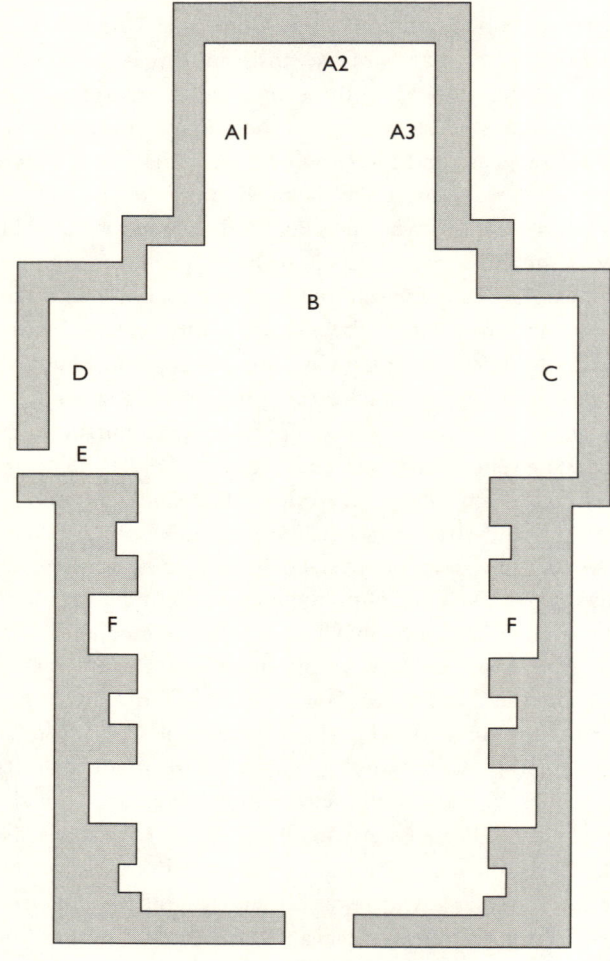

A1 Rubens, *The Baptism of Christ*
A2 Rubens, *The Gonzaga Family in Adoration of the Most Holy Trinity*
A3 Rubens, *The Transfiguration of Christ*
B  Tomb of Eleonora of Austria under the floor in front of the high altar
C  Possible location of the chapel of St. Ignatius Loyola with the tomb of Giacomo Antonio Marta under the first step of the altar
D  Possible location of the chapel of St. Francis Xavier
E  Possible location of the entrance from the college
F  Possible locations for the chapel of Blessed (later Saint) Luigi Gonzaga

MAP 4. Reconstruction of Santissima Trinità ca. 1630

# The Founding of the Jesuit College 39

celebrations. For example, in 1592, the first year in which Lenten observances were held in the new church, Duke Vincenzo I and members of the confraternity to which he belonged attended. Dressed in sackcloth, the duke carried the crucifix in the Holy Thursday procession, a practice that continued in subsequent years.[58] When Eleonora of Austria died on August 5, 1594, Father Antonio Possevino came from Padua to deliver the funeral oration. She was buried under the floor near the high altar (see map 4).[59] The Jesuits were enormously grateful for all her help, including a final bequest with her most appreciated gift: her villa located two or three miles beyond the city, along with its land, peasants, cattle, and fat pigs. The Jesuits used it as a place of recreation.[60]

After Duke Guglielmo and Duchess Eleonora of Austria were gone, Duke Vincenzo I continued to support the Jesuits in various ways. In May 1590 he granted the Society several tax exemptions. The Jesuits did not have to pay taxes on legal documents recording contracts, donations, and testaments, nor did they have to pay the taxes imposed on goods brought into the state. They were relieved of city imposts and the tax on grinding grain. He also arranged for the Jesuits to receive salt sufficient for all the members of the college, which was still being delivered in the early eighteenth century.[61] His consort, Duchess Eleonora de' Medici, also supported the Jesuits with gifts.

Duke Vincenzo's greatest contribution came later: he commissioned Peter Paul Rubens (1577–1640) to paint a very large triptych for the three walls of the major chapel behind the high altar. Rubens began in 1602, spent most of 1603 elsewhere, then returned to the paintings in 1604, and finished in late May 1605. His masterworks were solemnly unveiled on June 5, 1605. The painting on the left wall (facing the major chapel) depicted the *Baptism of Christ,* and the one on the right wall *The Transfiguration of Christ.* The center wall held the most important panel: *The Gonzaga Family in Adoration of the Most Holy Trinity.* It had two levels: above were God the Father, the Son, and the Holy Spirit; below were Duke Guglielmo and Duchess Eleonora of Austria, and Duke Vincenzo I and Duchess Eleonora de' Medici, kneeling or standing in adoration. Members of the Gonzaga family, notably the four children of Vincenzo I and Eleonora de' Medici, and other figures appeared in various peripheral areas in the very large painting.[62] The triptych as a whole, and especially *The*

---

58. Gorzoni, 1997, 85.
59. Gorzoni, 1997, 87, 89. Possevino's lengthy oration was quickly published: Possevino, 1594.
60. Gorzoni, 1997, 80–81, 88, 90–91.
61. Gorzoni, 1997, 78–79, 81.
62. The past tense is used because the paintings are no longer found in the church or together. However, the illustrations in *Rubens a Mantova,* 1977, 34–47, give some idea of the original arrangement, beauty, and power of the paintings. For further analysis of the triptych and the sojourn of Rubens in Mantua, see the studies in *Rubens a Mantova,* 1977, especially Bazzotti, 1977,

FIG. 1. Portraits of dukes Guglielmo and Vincenzo I Gonzaga and duchesses Eleonora of Austria and Eleonora de' Medici from Peter Paul Rubens, *The Gonzaga Family in Adoration of the Trinity*. Mantua, Museo del Palazzo Ducale. *Photo: Scala / Art Resource, NY*

*Gonzaga Family in Adoration,* may have been the most important work that Rubens did in Italy.[300] Vincenzo I paid Rubens 1,300 scudi for his masterpieces and another 1,000 scudi for the frescoes decorating the vault of the major chapel.[63] The Jesuit chronicler opined that one of the three paintings alone was worth far more than what Vincenzo paid and noted that people came from afar to see them.[64]

## 2. BLESSED LUIGI GONZAGA

The Gonzaga, a family with many sinners, produced a Jesuit saint. The short, holy life of Luigi Gonzaga tied family and Society together as little else could have. Luigi (Aloysius in English) Gonzaga (1568–91) came from the cadet branch of the Gonzaga that ruled Castiglione delle Stiviere, a little town about thirty-five kilometers northwest of Mantua.[65] The town with its castle (*rocca*) occupied a natural fortified position guarding the southern end of Lake Garda. His father, Ferrante Gonzaga (1544–86), was the signore and later marquis of Castiglione delle Stiviere, as well as a prince of the empire from 1574. Castiglione delle Stiviere, Castel Goffredo, and Solferino were three tiny contiguous territories on the northwest periphery of the duchy of Mantua (see map 1). Three brothers ruled the three towns (see genealogical chart 2). All had been under the tutelage of Cardinal Ercole Gonzaga, who assigned them their lands. The tiny signorie were imperial fiefs, which meant that the Habsburg emperor had a voice in succession matters.

Luigi's mother was Marta Tana di Sàntera (1544?–1605), daughter of a notable of Chieri in Piedmont-Savoy.[66] Despite her modest lineage and birthplace, she had lived for many years in two of the most important courts of Europe. At the age of thirteen she left her family to go to Paris to become a lady-in-waiting to Elizabeth Valois (d. 1568), daughter of King Henry II and Catherine de' Medici. When Elizabeth went to Spain to become the third wife

---

and Schizzerotto, 1979. For the story of the deconsecration of the church and the dismemberment of *The Gonzaga Family in Adoration,* see chapter 9, section 6.

63. Bazzotti, 1977, 34.

64. Gorzoni, 1997, 103–4, who gave the fee as 1,300 doubloons.

65. The following life of Luigi Gonzaga is based on Ferri, 1991; Vigna, 1991; Giachi, 2001; and Giordano, 2006, without further references. There are no significant differences in the accounts, partly because they all rely on Virgilio Cepari, *Vita del Beato Luigi Gonzaga,* first published in Rome, 1606. Incidentally, Ferrante Gonzaga of Castiglione delle Stiviere (see Tamalio, 2001a) should not be confused with Ferrante I or Ferrante II of the Gonzaga of Guastalla.

66. It has not been possible to establish her date of birth. Ferri, 1991, 13, writes that she was eighteen years of age when Luigi was born. On the other hand, Vigna, 1991, 21, states that she was one year younger than Ferrante. Other evidence suggests, but does not prove, that she was the same age as her husband.

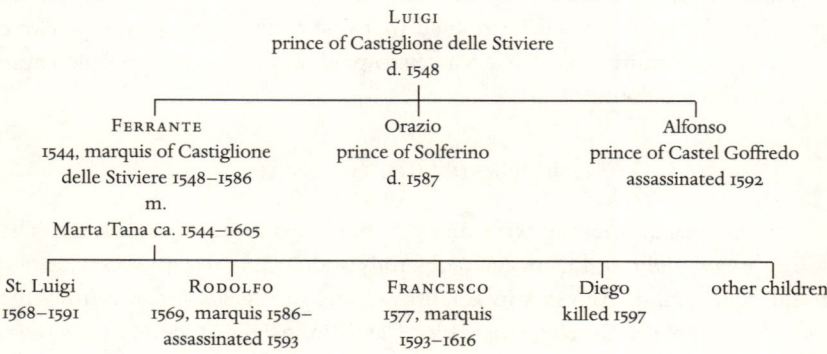

CHART 2
The Gonzaga of Castiglione delle Stiviere*

*The names of rulers are given in capital letters.

of Philip II in 1560, Marta Tana accompanied her. Ferrante Gonzaga was also at the court in Madrid, where he enjoyed the confidence of the king. He and Marta were married there on June 24, 1566. Philip II gave them lands in Lombardy and the Kingdom of Naples and a pension of 1,000 scudi as wedding gifts.

The couple left Madrid for the rocca of Castiglione delle Stiviere. There Marta gave birth to Luigi on March 9, 1568. Duke Guglielmo Gonzaga of Mantua, third cousin to Ferrante, was Luigi's godfather, although he was not present at the christening. Even though little Luigi came from a cadet branch of the Gonzaga, he was still the first born of the signore of Castiglione delle Stiviere, and his parents were in good odor with the most powerful monarch of Europe. He was raised accordingly.

His father introduced him to soldiering. Ferrante Gonzaga, a professional soldier, fought for the king of Spain against Protestants in Flanders and for a short time governed Monferrato for the duke of Mantua. In 1573 Philip II charged Ferrante with training three thousand men for a campaign against the Moors in North Africa. Ferrante brought little Luigi to the military camp in Casale Monferrato to give him a taste of military life before Ferrante went off to fight in North Africa.

Luigi also learned the ways of courts more important than his own. When he was nine, his parents sent him and his brother Rodolfo (b. 1569) to the Medici court of Florence, where they lived from November 1577 to November 1579. The two boys, along with two teachers and a priest, lived in a house rented to them by the grand duke and attended the Medici court at the Pitti Palace. They dressed in court finery and played with the Medici children, including Eleonora de' Medici, a year older than Luigi, who would become duchess of Mantua, and little Maria, who would become Queen Marie de Médicis (1573–1642) of France.

But Luigi preferred the company of God. He pledged himself to God at the age of seven and offered him the gift of his chastity at the age of ten. But he said nothing publicly and was often ill. Upon his return to Castiglione delle Stiviere, he prayed, fasted, and catechized children. He read a small book of meditations of Peter Canisius, the great Dutch-born Jesuit, which may have first stimulated his interest in the Jesuits.

In the summer of 1581 the family made an extended visit to the court of Madrid, because Empress Maria Habsburg, the widow of Emperor Maximilian II and sister of Philip II, desired their company. Thirteen-year-old Luigi lived in the royal palace and served as a page to Don Diego, the first-born son of Philip II. On March 29, 1583, Luigi, with the aid of court teachers, prepared a Latin oration that he recited in the presence of the king, who was impressed. Luigi also pursued a challenging program of studies and attended a disputation at the University of Alcalá de Henares. In the summer of 1583 he decided to join a religious order. He had became acquainted with several Jesuits at Philip's court and chose the Society of Jesus for four reasons: (1) it was a young and vigorous order; (2) the Jesuits had many schools and sodalities devoted to youth; (3) the Jesuits refused high church offices; and (4) they were missionaries. Like many other devout young men, Luigi longed to convert the pagans of the Indies, Japan, and America.[67]

The family returned to Castiglione delle Stiviere in July or August 1584, where he informed his father of his wish to renounce his right to the succession and become a Jesuit. His mother supported him, but Ferrante was disbelieving and furious for several reasons. The able and pious youth was loved by everyone; Ferrante believed that he would make a superb ruler of Castiglione delle Stiviere. Moreover, because Ferrante's two brothers had no male heirs, it was understood that Luigi would eventually become the ruler of Castel Goffredo and Solferino as well. This would greatly increase the size of the state and the prestige of the Gonzaga of Castiglione delle Stiviere. Finally, if Luigi renounced his claim, Rodolfo would become the heir, and Ferrante and Marta had grave doubts about his judgment and capacity to rule. Consequently, Ferrante refused to give his consent and brought in prominent clergymen and others to test his son's resolve. This went on for more than a year. However, Luigi remained firm, and Ferrante finally gave his consent.

But it was not as simple as that. Because Castiglione delle Stiviere was an imperial fief, and maintaining friendly relations with the Habsburgs was essential, Ferrante and Luigi had to obtain the permission of Emperor Rudolf II

---

67. Vigna, 1991, 77–78.

for Luigi to renounce his claim in favor of Rodolfo. And the senate of Milan also had to approve. Lawyers drafted a petition, which Ferrante sent, along with a substantial financial gift, to the emperor in Prague. They waited for an answer.

Meanwhile, Luigi was still a Gonzaga prince and a talented young man. While all waited for imperial assent, he went to Milan to negotiate some matters for Duke Guglielmo Gonzaga of Mantua. He also attended classes in philosophy and mathematics at the Brera College, the Jesuit school in Milan. And in July 1585 Luigi, not yet a Jesuit, went to Mantua, where he undertook Loyola's Spiritual Exercises while living in a little room in the Jesuit college. When he ventured outside, members of the Gonzaga of Mantua kissed his clothes, so he retreated to his room. Finally, imperial permission arrived. On November 2, 1585, members of the Gonzaga of Castiglione delle Stiviere and the Gonzaga of Mantua met in Mantua for the formal act of renunciation by Luigi in favor of Rodolfo. His father wanted him to do his novitiate at the provincial novice house in nearby Novellara, ruled by another branch of the Gonzaga. But Luigi preferred Rome. On November 4, 1585, he left for Rome, accompanied by a Jesuit who acted as his spiritual guide on the journey.

Still a Gonzaga, he stopped at the courts of Ferrara and Florence, where the Gonzaga of Mantua had relatives and strong political connections. He made a detour to Loreto to visit the famous Holy House, the house where Jesus, Mary, and Joseph lived in Nazareth, which had been miraculously transported to Loreto. When on November 20, 1585, he arrived in Rome, he went first to the Jesuit general, Claudio Aquaviva, who joined him in prayer at the tomb of Ignatius Loyola. He also had an audience with the pope and called on Este, Farnese, and Medici cardinals. Although this was not the usual way to enter a religious order, Luigi Gonzaga was not an ordinary recruit. Finally, on November 25, 1585, at the age of seventeen years, eight months, and eleven days, he entered the Jesuit novice house at Sant'Andrea al Quirinale.

He shed his princely robes, which the Jesuits evaluated as worth 48 scudi, about the annual earnings of a laborer, and donned the black habit of a novice. After completing his novitiate, he lived and studied in the Collegio Romano, while dedicating himself to prayer and performing humble duties. He also taught the catechism to children and visited the sick in hospitals. Robert Bellarmine, not yet a cardinal, was his spiritual adviser. Luigi spent the next six months studying natural philosophy in Naples; upon his return, he disputed in the presence of three cardinals. On November 25, 1587, Luigi took minor orders and swore vows of poverty, chastity, and obedience. He was on his way to becoming a priest, and his superiors probably expected great things from him.

Meanwhile, matters deteriorated in Castiglione delle Stiviere. Ferrante Gonzaga died on February 13, 1586, probably of cancer. Rodolfo Gonzaga succeeded him as marquis of Castiglione delle Stiviere and promptly realized his parents' worst fears: he lacked judgment and was hot tempered and prone to violence.[68] By contrast, Luigi was intelligent and pious. Hence, many still saw him as the head of the family and sought his advice, even though he had renounced worldly titles.

In 1589 Marta Tana Gonzaga, mother of Luigi and Rodolfo, and Duchess Eleonora of Austria, the mother of Vincenzo I Gonzaga, together begged Luigi to return in order to resolve a fierce quarrel between his brother Rodolfo and Vincenzo I. It had begun when Orazio Gonzaga, ruler of Solferino, died on January 14, 1587, without male heirs. Although it had been expected that Rodolfo would succeed him, Orazio named Vincenzo I as his heir. Marta went to Prague to plead for Rodolfo's right to Solferino, and the emperor eventually supported her, which angered Vincenzo. War between Rodolfo and Duke Vincenzo I, which would have been a catastrophe for the Gonzaga of Castiglione delle Stiviere, was a possibility. Because peacemaking was a major Jesuit ministry, General Aquaviva ordered Luigi to go to Castiglione delle Stiviere and Mantua to do that. Luigi spent nearly eight months, from September 14, 1589, to May 1590, mediating the dispute. He went back and forth between Castiglione delle Stiviere, where, although only in minor orders, he preached, and Mantua, where he lived in the Jesuit college. He finally brought the cousins to agreement. He also persuaded Rodolfo to make public his secret marriage to a commoner whom he had allegedly originally abducted. This solution legitimized the union and the birth of their daughter, and mollified his mother, even though it was hardly the marriage expected of even a cadet branch Gonzaga. For these peacemaking accomplishments and Luigi's piety, many more in Castiglione delle Stiviere and Mantua viewed him as a holy man.

Luigi returned in May 1590 to a Rome suffering from an outbreak of typhus. General Aquaviva organized a hospital, where Luigi visited the sick. Despite his poor health and weak constitution, he devoted himself to caring for and comforting the ill, while continuing his regimen of intense prayer and fasting. Members of the Jesuit community in Rome increasingly saw him as a saint, and two of them secretly wrote down his words and deeds.[69] Luigi became ill on March 3, 1591, and slowly declined. He died on June 21, 1591, at the age of twenty-three years and three months. When she heard of his death, Eleonora of Austria declared that Luigi would be the first saint of the Gonzaga family.[70]

---

68. Tamalio, 2001b.

69. Vigna, 1991, 154–55. A recently discovered autograph letter of Luigi Gonzaga dated December 12, 1590, offers information about his conversations with other Jesuits. Munitiz, 2007.

70. Vigna, 1991, 151.

After Luigi's death, matters went from bad to much worse in Castiglione delle Stiviere. Eight men, probably hired by Rodolfo, assassinated Alfonso Gonzaga, ruler of Castel Goffredo and uncle of Rodolfo. They immediately informed Rodolfo of Alfonso's death, and he took possession of Castel Goffredo. The emperor wanted an investigation of the murder, while Duke Vincenzo I opposed Rodolfo's assumption of power in Castel Goffredo on the grounds that he had arranged the assassination. In addition, Pope Clement VIII excommunicated Rodolfo for minting counterfeit papal coinage. On January 3, 1593, a revolt broke out in Castel Goffredo, during which a servant of the murdered Alfonso Gonzaga killed Rodolfo. Duke Vincenzo I of Mantua, who was widely suspected of having armed the rebels, then seized Castel Goffredo. Francesco Gonzaga (1577–1616), the third son (of four) of Ferrante and Marta Gonzaga, became marquis of Castiglione delle Stiviere. More violence followed, possibly instigated by Duke Vincenzo I. In one incident Marta Gonzaga and her last son, Diego, were stabbed. Marta recovered, but Diego died. Marquis Francesco Gonzaga then captured and hanged the murderers in 1598. After years of conflict, the Gonzaga of Castiglione delle Stiviere lost control of their little state, and in 1706 a French army demolished the castle in which Luigi had been born.[71] The contrast between Luigi and other Gonzaga males must have made him seem all the more saintly.

A cult of Luigi sprang up among the Jesuits in Rome immediately after his death, as people began to see him in visions. Father Stanislaus Oborski, a Polish Jesuit who had been a novice with Luigi, had a vision in which he saw Ignatius Loyola; Stanislaus Kostka (1550–68), a Polish Jesuit viewed as a saint; and Luigi Gonzaga together.[72] When Luigi's mother fell gravely ill after the assassination of Rodolfo, Luigi appeared to her and she recovered. Miracles followed: a blind man saw, a deaf man heard, and a Florentine nun recovered from a cancer thanks to devotion to Luigi Gonzaga and a bone from his finger. Others in Castiglione delle Stiviere, Florence, and even Poland reported miracles and visions. Father Virgilio Cepari (1564–1630), who had lived with Luigi in the Collegio Romano and written down his words and deeds before Luigi died, began to collect materials in support of canonization.[73] Requests for beatification and canonization arose spontaneously in several places.

The road to beatification and canonization was not the orderly and methodical pathway that it would become in future centuries. Local dioceses could authorize public veneration of those considered blessed.[74] And once a

---

71. For the unedifying last chapters of the Gonzaga delle Stiviere, see Ferri, 1991, 224–36.
72. Vigna, 1991, 153.
73. Vigna, 1991, 154–55. On Cepari, see Pignatelli, 2001.
74. Only in 1634 did Pope Urban VIII reserve to the papacy the right to declare a person

cult spread beyond local veneration, the papacy could issue decrees, each of them a step toward beatification and canonization. In addition to spontaneous outpourings of devotion, enthusiastic proponents tirelessly petitioned for beatification. Moreover, each small step on the road to canonization offered the opportunity for another religious celebration and more expressions of piety.

Beginning in 1600, ecclesiastical authorities in Castiglione delle Stiviere, Mantua, Florence, Piacenza, Rome, and other towns established commissions to gather information and testimony about Luigi's holy deeds and the miracles attributed to his intercession. On May 12, 1604, the ecclesiastical synod of Mantua proclaimed Luigi "blessed." His overjoyed mother was present at the first Mass sung in his honor.[75] A 1604 portrait of Luigi showing rays of light over his head called him "Beatus Aloysius Gonzaga Societatis Iesu."

However, the Gonzaga wanted papal endorsement. The bishop of Mantua, Francesco Gonzaga, Duke Vincenzo I, and Marquis Francesco Gonzaga, Luigi's brother, who had been appointed imperial ambassador to Rome in 1603, petitioned the pope.[76] So did various Jesuits, a German cardinal, and some princes. The papacy responded with a series of actions. On June 21, 1605, the anniversary of Luigi's death, Paul V proclaimed him "blessed," which probably meant that the papacy authorized public worship in Rome, Gonzaga states, and some other Italian towns, but not universally. Paul V followed with a breve of October 19, 1605, which again proclaimed Luigi blessed.[77] And he authorized Virgilio Cepari to call him blessed in his *Vita del Beato Luigi Gonzaga*, published in 1606.[78] The cumulative effect was papal approval of beatification. Luigi Gonzaga was only the second Jesuit so honored. Stanislaus Kostka was declared blessed by Pope Clement VIII in 1602 and by Paul V in 1605.[79] By contrast, Ignatius Loyola had to wait until 1609. In the following

---

"blessed" and worthy of veneration. Moreover, the cult of the blessed person was limited to specific localities or members of religious orders. Canonization, by contrast, meant that the person was to be honored and worshiped as a saint everywhere. See Beccari, 1913a, esp. 366; and Beccari, 1913b.

75. Ferri, 1991, 235.

76. For the diplomatic posts of Francesco Gonzaga, see *Le istruzioni generali di Paolo V*, 2003, 1:449 note 25.

77. Pastor, 1891–1953, 25:265–67, narrates the steps by which Paul V beatified Luigi Gonzaga. But not until April 30, 1618, did he permit the celebration of Masses in honor of Luigi, and then only in Jesuit houses in Rome. See also Vigna, 1991, 163, and Giachi, 2001.

78. Sommervogel, 1890–1932, 2: cols. 957–60. Many other editions plus translations into German, English, French, Spanish, and other languages followed.

79. Stanislaus Kostka's life was similar to that of Luigi Gonzaga. A young Pole of noble birth, he studied at the Jesuit college in Vienna and then decided, over his father's objections, to become a Jesuit. He arrived in Rome and entered the novice house of Sant'Andrea al Quirinale in

decades, members of the Gonzaga extended family pressed the papacy to proceed with canonization, which finally occurred on December 31, 1726.

Papal approval of the beatification of Luigi Gonzaga produced great joy among the Jesuits in Mantua. They celebrated his beatification in 1606 and again with a solemn Mass and panegyric by a Jesuit orator on June 21, 1607. All the principal members of the Gonzaga family from Mantua and beyond attended, as well as a crowd of nobles and townspeople. The Jesuits set aside what they called "the bedroom and room of Blessed Luigi" as a shrine to him and a place of prayerful reflection for members of the college.[80] A benefactor was so moved by "this new devotion of the city and people toward Luigi Gonzaga" that he gave the Jesuits a jeweled monstrance (an ornate holder for the consecrated host) worth 130 scudi. Luigi Gonzaga became the patron of the Mantuan college.[81]

Luigi Gonzaga's life and the aftermath bound the Jesuits and the Gonzaga to an extraordinary degree. Members of the Gonzaga family, even those who lived lives very different from the example that Blessed Luigi set, were proud that their house had produced a saint. The Jesuits were equally proud that this holy aristocratic youth was "one of ours." And they felt a special bond with and gratitude toward the family that had produced the Society's second *beato* and offered so much support. That this holy youth appeared so soon after the introduction of the Jesuits into Mantua must have seemed a sign of God's approval. Blessed Luigi cemented the union between Jesuits and Gonzaga so firmly that people must have seen them as an indissoluble unit. No other Italian princely family had such strong public and spiritual links with the Society of Jesus.

## 3. GROWTH OF THE COLLEGE AND SCHOOL

The number of Jesuits at Mantua grew slowly but steadily. The Mantuan college had fourteen Jesuits in 1584, sixteen in 1590, seventeen in 1593, twenty (ten of them priests) in 1600, and twenty-seven in 1622.[82] Forty to fifty percent

---

1567, devoted himself to prayer, but contracted malaria and died on August 15, 1568. He was immediately seen as a saint. He and Luigi Gonzaga were canonized on the same day, December 31, 1726. Majkowski and O'Donoghue, 2001.

80. "[S]antificò quelle camere in cui egli habitò, chiamate pur hoggi 'la camera e la sala del beato Luigi,' tenuta perciò in veneratione da' nostri." Gorzoni, 1997, 69. The date at which the Jesuits set aside the two rooms of Blessed Luigi is not clear. It may have happened before he was beatified.

81. "Non è fuor di credenza che questa commune novella divotione della città e popolo al beato Luigi risvegliasse la divotione d'un particolare a far un degno e nobile donativo alla nostra chiesa." Gorzoni, 1997, 107.

82. Rurale, 1997, 18; also Gorzoni, 1997, 79 (sixteen Jesuits in 1590).

## Growth of the College and School

were priests; the rest were scholastics (students) and temporal coadjutors (also called brothers). And the Jesuit school expanded its offerings. In the academic year 1595–96 the Jesuits added a class in logic because Duke Vincenzo I wanted it.[83] At this time the school included three lower classes plus logic and cases of conscience.

The Mantuan Jesuit academic year began in early November and lasted through August.[84] Jesuit schools normally met Monday through Saturday except for the numerous religious holidays, which yielded a whole day or a half day free of classes in practically every week. And if the week had no religious holiday, teachers were encouraged to give the students a "break day" free of ordinary classes but sometimes with special activities.[85]

Like other Italian schools and universities, the Mantuan Jesuit school followed the traditional sunset to sunset clock by dividing the day into twenty-four one-hour segments beginning at sunset. Thus, sunset was hour zero, hour I was one hour after sunset, and so on. To convert the timetable into modern hours, it should be assumed that sunset occurred at 6 p.m. in Mantua in early November. Hence, hour XV was 9 a.m. and hour XXII½ was 4:30 p.m. In early June, when sunset occurred at about 8 p.m., hour XV was at 11 a.m. and hour XXII½ was at 6:30 p.m.

The three lower school classes in Mantua in the academic year 1595–96 were named (in descending order) humanities, higher grammar, and lower grammar. Each had a carefully planned academic day of four and one-half to five hours of instruction. Although the Society had already produced two versions of its *Ratio studiorum* in 1586 and 1591, it had not yet drafted and promulgated the final version of 1599. Hence, the texts taught in the Mantua school reflected a Jesuit curriculum still in flux.[86]

---

83. "Sed quando nunc ab ipso Ser.mo Duce Vincentio postulatur a nobis, ut hoc anno logicae usu(m) ac praecepta doceamus." ASM, AG, Bu. 3366, f. 22. Entitled "Civibus Mantuanis Collegium Societatis Jesu," this is a large handwritten folio page listing the courses but not the names of the teachers of the Jesuit school for the academic year 1595–96. It presents in considerable detail the daily schedule and the texts taught for the lower school. It does not mention the separate cases of conscience lectureship, for whom the logical audience consisted of priests and future priests. Rurale, 1997, 18, states that the logic class began in 1594–95 but does not provide a reference.

84. ASM, AG, Bu. 3366, f. 22, "Civibus Mantuanis Collegium Societatis Jesu."

85. Although the 1595–96 "Civibus Mantuanis Collegium Societatis Jesu" did not list the holidays, the school probably generally followed the academic calendar and honored break days as described in the 1599 *Ratio studiorum*. See *Ratio Studiorum*, 2005, paragraphs 58, 60–70, 93, pp. 25–29, 36.

86. The Jesuits produced three versions of the *Ratio studiorum:* a draft of 1586, which summarized current pedagogy; the 1591 version, which was binding on the schools but not final pending receipt of comments; and the definitive version of 1599. For three recent studies of the development of the *Ratio studiorum*, see Ladislaus Lukács, "Introductio generalis," in *Monumenta*

At hour XVI (about 10 a.m. in November) the humanities class studied Cicero's oration "Pro Lex. Roscio," either his *Pro Roscio Amerino* or *Pro Roscio Comoedo,* two little known legal orations of Cicero, which none of the three versions of the *Ratio studiorum* mentioned. On Thursdays and Saturdays they read Caesar's *De bello gallico.* After Easter the class on alternate days studied the "Compendium" of Cypriano, that is, *De arte rhetorica libri tres,* a comprehensive rhetoric manual of the Spanish Jesuit Cypriano Soares first published in 1562, and with at least 135 printings, including one in Mantua in 1585.[87] The 1586 version of the *Ratio studiorum* mentioned Soares' Latin grammar; the 1591 version ignored it; and the 1599 version recommended it.[88] Hence, the Mantuan Jesuits anticipated the final decision on the preferred grammar manual.

At hour XVII (11 a.m.) the humanities class studied "ars metrica," meaning Latin poetic meters, that is, long and short syllables and set patterns. At hour XXI (3 p.m.) the class studied Virgil's *Aeneid,* book 6. All three versions of the *Ratio studiorum* directed Jesuit schools to teach the *Aeneid.* This lesson may have lasted an hour and a half, because the next scheduled lesson began at hour XXII½ (4:30 p.m.) and was devoted to Greek grammar review and Isocrates' oration *To Demonicus,* which dealt with the duties of kings. Again, all three versions of the *Ratio studiorum* endorsed the orations of Isocrates, which were standard fare in Italian Renaissance Latin schools generally. Since it would have been difficult to teach both Greek grammar and an oration of Isocrates in thirty minutes, this lesson must have lasted an hour or more, making a school day of four and one-half to five hours.

The upper-level grammar class followed a similar schedule but devoted more time to learning Latin and Greek grammar and less to reading texts.[89] For Latin grammar, it concentrated on the grammar manuals of the Portuguese Jesuit Manuel Álvares (1526–83), who published *De institutione grammaticae libri tres* in 1572 and an abridged version in 1583. Both the 1586 and 1591 versions of the *Ratio studiorum* recommended Álvares' grammar, while the 1599 version mentioned it only in passing.[90] For Latin prose, the class studied

---

*Paedagogica* 1965–92, 5:1*–36*; and its English translation in Lukács and Cosentino, 1999, 17–46; Mancia, 2000; and Padberg, 2000. For the comparisons that follow, see the relevant sections of the versions of 1586 and 1591 in *Monumenta Paedagogica,* 1965–92, 5:100, 145, 192–200, 279–80, 286–308 passim. For the corresponding sections in the 1599 *Ratio studiorum* see *Ratio Studiorum,* 2005, pp. 101–3, 118, 140–41, 166–69, 172–75, 179–81 et passim. Appendices 3 and 4 at pp. 226–35 summarizing the academic day for the Latin and Greek classes are particularly useful.

87. On Soares, see Escalera, 2001.

88. *Monumenta Paedagogica,* 1965–92, 5:138, 153, 191 (all references to the 1586 version); *Ratio Studiorum,* 2005, paragraphs 395–96, 402, pp. 166–68, 172.

89. ASM, AG, Bu. 3366, f. 22, "Civibus Mantuanis Collegium Societatis Jesu."

90. *Monumenta Paedagogica,* 1965–92, 5:121–24, 187–88, 238; *Ratio Studiorum,* 2005, paragraph 46, p. 22. On Álvares, see Vaz de Carvalho, 2001a.

Cicero's letters to Brutus, a section of twenty-six letters (seventeen by Cicero, nine by Brutus) from the *Familiar Letters,* plus Sallust's *Bellum Iugurthinum* on Thursdays and Saturdays, and Cicero's *De senectute* (On Old Age) after Easter. For Latin poetry, the class studied the *Aeneid,* book 5. Cicero's prose and Virgil's poetry had been the heart of the Italian Renaissance humanistic school curriculum since the middle of the fifteenth century, and all three versions of the *Ratio studiorum* required that they be taught. Sallust was less important to the Jesuits but not excluded.

For Greek grammar, the Mantuan upper grammar class studied the grammar manual of Nicolaas Cleynaerts (Clenardus, 1495–1542); his *Institutiones in linguam Graecam,* which first appeared in 1530, had at least three hundred printings and was widely used in both Catholic and Protestant schools across Europe. However, none of the three versions of the *Ratio studiorum* recommended a specific Greek grammar manual. The lower grammar class studied letters from Cicero's *Familiar Letters* for Latin prose, the Latin grammar manual of Álvares, and Ovid's *Tristia* (Sorrows) for Latin poetry. The 1586 version of the *Ratio studiorum* authorized the teaching of the last work, and the 1591 version continued to endorse Ovid without mentioning this title. However, the more cautious 1599 version insisted that some of Ovid's elegies and letters should be taught only in expurgated form.[91] The students also studied Greek nouns and spent considerable time doing Latin grammar and writing exercises.

The students in the logic class at Mantua studied universals, then *Categories, On Interpretation, Prior Analytics,* and *Posterior Analytics,* that is, four parts of Aristotle's *Organon*.[92] Logic was the first part of the Society's upper-school philosophical cycle of logic in the first year, natural philosophy in the second year, and metaphysics in the third year. However, the Mantuan Jesuits did not add the other two courses at this time. The documents do not indicate the hour at which the logic class met, nor any information about the class in cases of conscience.

The Mantuan college and school became more important to the Society as a result of events in Venice. After a series of disputes, in April 1606 Pope Paul V laid the Republic of Venice under interdict, thus forbidding clergymen to exercise almost all sacerdotal functions, including celebrating Mass and administering the sacraments. The Venetian government ordered all clergymen in the state to ignore the interdict under penalty of death, and most obeyed. But the Jesuits refused, so the Venetian government ordered the Jesuits out of Venice and the rest of the Venetian state on May 8 and 10, 1606.[93] The Jesuits

---

91. *Monumenta Paedagogica,* 1965–92, 5:148, 149, 197, 303; *Ratio Studiorum,* 2005, paragraphs 405, 415, pp. 173–74, 179–80.
92. ASM, AG, Bu. 3366, f. 22, "Civibus Mantuanis Collegium Societatis Jesu."
93. See Pirri, 1955, 19–30.

had to abandon their professed house in Venice and their colleges and schools in Padua, which were limited to Jesuit students, plus those in Brescia and Verona, which were open to all students.

The Society distributed the displaced Jesuits among other colleges in the Jesuit Province of Venice, which was not coterminous with the Republic of Venice but included Emilia Romagna (with colleges at Bologna, Ferrara, and Forlì) and parts of eastern Lombardy (colleges at Mantua and Modena, and a novice house at Novellara). Because Mantua for a short time had fifteen more Jesuits, Duke Vincenzo I and the father provincial allocated funds with which to pay the additional expenses. However, when two of the new Jesuits preached against the Republic of Venice, the duke asked the pair to leave.[94] Some of the expelled Jesuits undertook a new mission: they went to towns along the border between the duchy of Mantua and the Venetian state and preached to and delivered the sacraments to Venetian subjects who crossed the border. Venice reacted by forbidding its subjects all communication with the Jesuits, even by letter.[95] Although the papacy lifted the interdict on April 21, 1607, the republic did not allow the Jesuits to return. Hence, the border missions may have continued. Not until 1657 were the Jesuits permitted to re-enter the Venetian state.

The expulsion led to expansion of the Mantuan school. At this time, each of the five Jesuit provinces in Italy had one or two colleges whose schools taught higher subjects, meaning the three-year philosophical cycle of logic, natural philosophy, and metaphysics, plus sometimes mathematics and theology. Although primarily intended for Jesuit scholastics, they were open to laymen and other clergymen. After the expulsion, which closed the school at Padua, the part-Jesuit, part-civic University of Parma took up most of the slack. But the Mantuan college helped by inaugurating a philosophy class in 1607, which quickly had two hundred students and was praised throughout the city.[96] The Mantuan college now had a flourishing lower school and part of an upper school consisting of logic, philosophy, and cases of conscience.[97]

---

94. Putelli, 1911, 237–39, 241–45, 254–59.

95. Gorzoni, 1997, 106–7.

96. Gorzoni, 1997, 108, who called it "this new class in philosophy" (questa novella scuola di filosofia). Because Gorzoni did not mention metaphysics, it is assumed that the course was natural philosophy. Of course, it could have combined elements of both natural philosophy and metaphysics.

97. In 1622 the Mantua school had 140 students in its grammar class, 70 in its humanity class, 40 in the rhetoric class, and 30 in the cases of conscience class, making its lower school second in size only to the Parma school, whose enrollment was boosted by the local boarding school for nobles, in the Province of Venice. But, curiously, the ARSI document with the enrollments did not list a logic or philosophy class at Mantua. Ferri and Giberti, 1997, 1:109 note 401.

# Growth of the College and School

In 1610 Duke Vincenzo I told the father provincial that the Mantuan school should become a university.[98]

The Jesuit college and school had come a long way since 1584. Invited to Mantua after much hesitation by Duke Guglielmo, the Jesuits now enjoyed the full confidence and support of the Gonzaga ruler and his extended family. Blessed Luigi Gonzaga cemented the bond, while the school now included some university-level courses.

98. Rurale, 1997, 48 note 77, referring to an ARSI document dated September 8, 1610.

CHAPTER 3

# Ferdinando Gonzaga and the Jesuits Create a University

The people and rulers of Mantua had wanted a university for some time. Although better known for their patronage of music and literature, dukes Guglielmo and Vincenzo I supported scholars and their research. Then Duke Ferdinando, who studied at a university and loved learning, decided to collaborate with the Jesuits to create a *studium*. The first fruit of their collaboration was the Public Academy of Mantua, the Jesuit part of the University of Mantua.

## 1. UNIVERSITY DREAMS

The rulers and leading citizens of Mantua had long desired a university. The first step was to obtain a charter authorizing prince or commune to create an institution with all the privileges of established universities, including the authority to confer degrees recognized throughout Christendom. Legal tradition and common consent recognized emperors and popes as the supranational authorities who might charter universities.

Marquis Gian Francesco Gonzaga (1395, ruled 1407–44) asked Emperor Sigismund I of Luxemburg (ruled 1410–37) for a university charter when the emperor visited Mantua, and the emperor responded with a university charter on September 27, 1433.[1] Emperor Albert II (ruled 1438–39) confirmed the privileges of a possible Mantuan *studium generale* on January 1, 1439. So did Emperor Frederick III (ruled 1440–93) on December 21, 1442, and again on August 27, 1455. During a visit to Mantua, Emperor Charles V (ruled 1519–56) on November 24, 1531, conferred on the priors of the Augustinian monastery

---

1. Summaries and quotes from the various charters for university privileges are found in ASM, AG, Bu. 3366, ff. 4r–11r. See also ARSI, Veneta 115, f. 191r; Mainardi, 1871, 3–4; and Davari, 1876, 5.

# University Dreams

of Sant'Agnese of Mantua count palatine authority to award bachelor, licentiate, and doctoral degrees in all subjects. This was not a university charter but authority to award degrees outside a formal university structure.[2]

A title and authority that originated in the early Middle Ages, a count palatine initially was someone delegated to act for the emperor, and later the pope, in two major legal areas, appointing notaries and legitimizing bastards. Moreover, once a man was appointed a count palatine, his direct legitimate male heirs inherited the office in perpetuity. By the fourteenth century, counts palatine were also awarding academic degrees. After the power of awarding academic degrees became part of a count palatine's authority, emperors and popes increasingly made professors and quasi-academic bodies, such as colleges of doctors of law or medicine, counts palatine, especially in the sixteenth century. Like individuals, organizations also possessed count palatine authority in perpetuity.[3] However, the monastery of Sant' Agnere seldom, if ever, used its power to award degrees.

There was more to come. On January 1, 1539, Charles V issued another charter for a University of Mantua that would have the same privileges of conferring degrees and other rights as the universities of Paris, Bologna, Orleans, and Montpellier. A more unusual charter followed. In 1562 Cesare Gonzaga (1533, prince of Guastalla 1557–75) and a group of men from Mantua founded the Accademia degli Invaghiti. Like other academies of the time, it consisted of a group of local men, leavened by one or two scholars, who met periodically to discuss literary and philosophical ideas and to enjoy each other's company. Then Duke Guglielmo Gonzaga in 1564 procured from Pope Pius IV the right of the academy to confer degrees in canon and civil law, medicine, and poetry, so long as professors found the candidates qualified.[4] Although it was exceptional for a literary academy to enjoy the privilege of awarding degrees, it does not appear that it actually did so.

University charters and count palatine authority to award degrees signaled that prince and people would like to have a university, but they did not act. Creating a functioning university by recruiting professors to teach, finding the money to pay them, and attracting students was much more difficult. No Gonzaga marquis or duke attempted to create a university in the fifteenth and sixteenth centuries.

---

2. The decree further explained that degree recipients might enjoy the same rights and privileges as degree recipients of the universities of Paris, Pavia, Bologna, and Vienna. In addition, the priors might also create notaries and legitimize bastards. See the copy of the decree in ARSI, Veneta 115, ff. 181r–82v. Davari, 1876, 18–19, exaggerates its significance.

3. For a short history and bibliography on counts palatine, see Grendler, 2002, 183–86, 484–86. A good recent study of the role that counts palatine played in conferring degrees is Martellozzo Forin, 1999.

4. Davari, 1876, 21.

## 2. GONZAGA SUPPORT OF LEARNING

Gonzaga dukes and princes warmly supported learning, a prelude to an eventual university. This and their extensive personal contacts with professors have been somewhat overlooked amidst their much better-known musical and literary patronage. Gonzaga assistance to scholars and scholarship expanded in the late sixteenth and early seventeenth centuries under Vincenzo I, an unexpected candidate for the role of patron of learning.

It began with humanistic schooling. In 1425 Marquis Gian Francesco Gonzaga brought the famous humanist pedagogue Vittorino Rambaldoni da Feltre (1373 or 1378–1446 / 47) to Mantua to teach his children and other court children, plus some poor students whom Vittorino sheltered. After Vittorino died, a succession of humanist pedagogues taught at the court school, or taught Gonzaga children, or did both.[5] This was the pattern for young princes across Italy.

A change occurred at the end of the fifteenth century, when some rulers chose university professors as tutors for their sons. These scholars combined tutoring with university lecturing, or they accepted tutorial positions before and between university teaching stints. For example, the Bentivoglio rulers of Bologna hired three distinguished humanists then teaching at the University of Bologna to tutor their sons, and possibly daughters, in the late fifteenth and early sixteenth centuries. Lorenzo il Magnifico de' Medici selected Angelo Poliziano to tutor his sons; Poliziano soon became a professor of rhetoric at the University of Florence.[6]

The Gonzaga did the same. In 1576 Duke Guglielmo Gonzaga arranged for Giuseppe Moletti of Messina (1531–88), an innovative mathematician who taught at the University of Padua from 1577 until his death, to tutor his son, Vincenzo. Moletti combined teaching at Padua and tutoring Vincenzo until 1582.[7] Duke Guglielmo also hired the medical scholar and philosopher Gian Paolo Branca to tutor young Vincenzo. When Branca left in 1578 to become a professor of medicine at the University of Padua, Marcello Donato (1538–1602), medical scholar, philosopher, and humanist, came to teach Vincenzo in 1578 and settled in Mantua for the rest of his life. After he became duke, Vincenzo I hired Giovanni Antonio Magini, longtime professor of mathematics at the University of Bologna, to teach his sons Francesco and Ferdinando (see section 3 below). Friendships as boys with university professors meant that Gonzaga rulers felt comfortable as adults in professors'

---

5. Davari, 1876, 4–23.
6. Grendler, 2002, 224, with further bibliography.
7. For Moletti's position as tutor to Vincenzo see Davari, 1876, 22–23; for his professorship at the University of Padua, see Tomasini, 1986, 339, 424, and Facciolati, 1978, part 3, 321–22.

## Gonzaga Support of Learning

company and were more appreciative of, and sympathetic to, university learning than might be expected from princes with many patronage and pleasure options.

Gonzaga rulers had contacts with the most famous scholars of the day. During a visit to Padua, Duke Vincenzo I heard Galileo Galilei explain the use of a military compass and was given one.[8] Galilei also sent Duke Vincenzo I one of his telescopes and instructions for its use. In return, the duke gave Galilei a chain with a medallion bearing the image of Vincenzo, which Galilei assessed as worth 900 lire.[9] Galilei also made at least two trips to Mantua. In a visit of April or May 1604 Vincenzo invited him to become his military architect at a salary of 300 ducats and expenses for himself and one servant. Galilei asked for 500 ducats and expenses for three persons, which price the duke declined to meet.[10]

Another beneficiary of the generosity of Vincenzo I was Gaspare Tagliacozzi (1545–99), professor of surgery and anatomy at the University of Bologna and a pioneering plastic surgeon. He dedicated his 1597 book, the first major work on plastic surgery, to Vincenzo I with comments about the latter's generosity. Tagliacozzi also praised the Gonzaga as brave warriors who inflicted the kinds of wounds that he could heal with plastic surgery.[11]

Self-interest inspired some of the patronage of Vincenzo I. Because he spent lavishly and always needed more money, he supported a stable of alchemists who promised that they would produce gold for him. Not everyone approved. Duchess Eleonora de' Medici tartly observed that if the duke would get rid of the alchemists, it would be good for his pocketbook and even better for his reputation.[12] Vincenzo I supported several people at his court who claimed expertise in poisons and cures because he feared that the Farnese would poison him in revenge for the annulment of his marriage to Margherita Farnese.[13] And he listened too eagerly to mountebanks. At one point he asked Galilei's advice about a man who claimed to understand every secret of medicine and astrology. Rather than criticize the duke's credulity directly, Galilei responded with another tall tale. He knew of a man who had invented

---

8. Favaro, 1966, 1:158, 177. Vincenzo's Paduan host was Giovanni Battista Del Monte (1541–1614), who fought for Spain and France and helped liberate Malta from the Turks, before serving the Venetian republic. Galilei, 1964–66, 20:488.

9. Galilei, 1964–66, 2:370, 534; 19:155, 607.

10. Galilei to Duke Vincenzo I, May 22, 1604, Padova, and Vincenzo's reply, May 26, 1604, Mantua, in Galilei, 1964–66, 10:107, 109.

11. Pazzini, 1978, 337–38; Franchini et al., 1979, 122–27.

12. This was in 1606. Pazzini, 1978, 304. After Vincenzo I died, his successor, Duke Francesco III, immediately dismissed all the alchemists. Relazione of Pietro Gritti of 1612, in *Relazioni*, 1912, 188. But Duke Ferdinando brought some of them back.

13. Pazzini, 1978, 305.

a pill that would keep one healthy and vigorous for a whole month without food or drink![14]

The Gonzaga nourished a surprisingly active Mantuan press willing and able to publish works of learning and literature. After it languished in the first forty years of the sixteenth century, the Gonzaga brought the Mantuan press back to life. Cardinal Ercole Gonzaga used tax concessions to entice a Venetian publisher, Venturino Ruffinelli, to come to Mantua in 1543. The results were instant and dramatic: from 1544 through 1630 Mantuan publishers produced at least 381 editions, an average of 4.4 editions per year, an impressive number for a small city.[15] In 1588 Duke Vincenzo I named Francesco Osanna of Mantua, Ruffinelli's major successor, as ducal printer and gave him further benefits. Osanna's heirs continued to hold this title in the seventeenth century.

The Mantuan presses produced some works of great significance. After Duke Vincenzo secured the release of Torquato Tasso (1544–95) from a Ferrara prison, the restless poet lived intermittently in Mantua from 1586 until 1591. Francesco Osanna issued twenty-two editions of the poet's works between 1581 and 1591, including the highly praised 1584 edition of *Gerusalemme Liberata*.[16] Mantuan publishers also published at least ten medical works, all but one in the first thirty years of the seventeenth century.[17] A press capable of publishing complex scholarly works in Latin was a desirable part of the infrastructure that might support a university.

Vincenzo I was not a philosopher-prince. A Venetian ambassador observed that he still looked youthful at forty-six because he had never given up the dissolute pleasures of youth.[18] He loved hunting, he fathered bastards, and he killed a Scot in a street brawl in July 1582.[19] Vincenzo I longed for military glory, as his three expeditions against the Turks in Hungary in 1595, 1597, and 1601 demonstrated. Despite all this, he continued the Gonzaga tradition of

14. Galilei to Duke Vincenzo I, May 22, 1604, Padua, in Galilei, 1964–66, 10:106.

15. This and the following paragraph are based on Pescasio, 1971; see also Franchini et al., 1979, 217. The count is based on surviving editions. How many editions have disappeared (that is, not one copy of a print run has survived) is impossible to know.

16. There is a convenient list of Osanna's Tasso editions in Pescasio, 1971, 234–35; see also pp. 227–28.

17. In addition to Pescasio, 1971, passim, see Zanca and Galassi, 1978.

18. Relazione of Francesco Morosini of June 21, 1608, in *Relazioni*, 1912, 88.

19. The victim was James Crichton (1560–82), known for his learning and a favorite of Duke Guglielmo. The two got into a fight, perhaps provoked by Vincenzo or his low-life companion, and Vincenzo killed him with a sword on the night of July 3, 1582. Franchini et al., 1979, 30–33. For Vincenzo's love of hunting and his love affairs, see the relazioni of Francesco Contarini of October 3, 1588, and Francesco Morosini of June 12, 1608, in *Relazioni*, 1912, 79, 89, 91. Morosini identified three bastards and rumors of more. Coniglio, 1967, genealogical table 2, no pag., lists four illegitimate children.

supporting musicians, poets, artists, and scholars, patronage that helped prepare the way for a university.

## 3. THE EDUCATION OF FERDINANDO GONZAGA

If ever there was an Italian prince at ease in the university world, it was Ferdinando Gonzaga, the most intellectually gifted Italian ruler since Lorenzo de' Medici (1449–94). Early association with the Jesuits and a tutor enthusiastic about astrology and alchemy helped form Ferdinando, while his studies at the universities of Ingolstadt and Pisa completed his education.

The future duke was born on April 26, 1587, the second son of Duke Vincenzo I and Eleonora de' Medici.[20] Ferdinando became well acquainted with the Mantuan Jesuits as a boy, because he and his brother Francesco, born a year earlier, often visited the Jesuit college. Ferdinando went to a Jesuit to make his first confession and, after preparing himself with the aid of Loyola's *Spiritual Exercises*, made his first communion at about the age of nine. He and Francesco were pleased to receive holy pictures from the Jesuit fathers.[21]

Because he was the second son, his destiny was to serve his family in the church; because he was a Gonzaga, he would be a cardinal. So he needed to be educated appropriately. One early teacher was a local abbot; a more important one was Giovanni Antonio Magini (1555–1617). A university professor, Magini had a significant intellectual influence on Ferdinando over many years.

Born in Padua, Magini obtained a doctorate in arts at the University of Bologna in 1579, and in 1588 he won one of the two afternoon ordinary professorships of mathematics there, a position that the younger Galileo Galilei unsuccessfully sought. Magini held the position, in which he taught mathematics and astronomy, until his death.[22] In his long and productive career, he corresponded with Johann Kepler and Tycho Brahe, and was both a friend and critic of Galilei. He published *Novae coelestium orbium theoricae congruentes cum observationibus Nicolai Copernici* (New theories of the celestial orbs agreeing with the observations of Copernicus) in 1589. Magini argued that Copernicus had devised hypotheses that fitted the positions of the stars and the planets very well. He praised Copernicus and wanted others to accept this part of the Copernican system. But he rejected heliocentrism as false and upsetting, and he feared that others would reject the good matter of Coper-

---

20. Unless otherwise indicated, the following biography of Ferdinando Gonzaga is based on Chambers, 1987, and Benzoni, 1996. Benzoni did not use Chambers; hence, Benzoni has some small inaccuracies concerning Ferdinando's education.

21. Gorzoni, 1997, 94.

22. The basic biography is Baldini, 2006. For Magini's Bolognese teaching, see *I rotuli dello Studio Bolognese*, 1888–1924, 2:231–331 passim, and Galilei, 1964–66, 20:472.

nicus for this reason. So, he constructed his own heavenly system, which mixed together a good deal of Ptolemy, some Copernican elements, and his own complicated ideas. In short, Magini was well versed in the new astronomy of Copernicus and Galilei and accepted part of what they wrote but leaned toward a more conservative astronomy. His work was esteemed, possibly because it was a compromise. Magini also published several ephemerides (astronomical tables predicting the future positions of planets and stars), horoscopes, works on judicial astrology and medical astrology (using astrology to determine when medicines should be administered), and a commentary on the *Geography* of Ptolemy.[23]

Magini had a long and close association with the Gonzaga. In 1589 he visited Mantua and the library of Vincenzo I, which was rich in scientific works and instruments. In 1592 he dedicated a book on trigonometry to Duke Vincenzo I. From that date onward, Magini spent every summer in Mantua, where he constructed scientific instruments and procured books in natural magic and medical alchemy for the duke. He also calculated through astrology the right moments for actions and offered prognostications. In 1605 he wrote for Duke Vincenzo I a little treatise on metroposcopy, divination of the character and destiny of a person on the basis of the wrinkles in his face and forehead. In 1608 he dedicated to Prince Francesco Gonzaga a summary of sixty regional maps of Italy, part of a large project to map all of Italy that he never finished.[24]

Beginning in 1599, Magini taught mathematics to Ferdinando and Francesco, who were twelve and thirteen respectively, for about two years. He concentrated on the pseudo-Aristotelian *Mechanics*, a treatise on the practical use of mathematics, which was taught in universities.[25] Magini continued to guide Ferdinando; for example, he advised Ferdinando on alchemical experiments when the latter set up a laboratory in Rome a few years later.

Magini was a cautious Baroque polymath. While respectful of the new astronomy of Copernicus and Galilei, he tried to preserve much of Ptolemy. He followed Aristotle, and he limited himself, publicly at least, to the astrology that the Council of Trent authorized. Ferdinando's eclectic interests and tendencies echoed Magini's combination of versatility, boldness, and conservatism. Ferdinando as an amateur scholar liked to think of himself as multitalented and open to new ideas, while retaining a conservative core similar to that of the Jesuits.

Duke Vincenzo I next sent young Ferdinando to the University of In-

---

23. Thorndike, 1923–1958, 5:250–51; 6:55–59, 64, 122 note 63, 164–65; Biagioli, 1993, 96 note 296; and Baldini, 2006.

24. Baldini, 2006, 414–16.

25. Chambers, 1987, 115–16; Baldini, 2006, 414.

## The Education of Ferdinando Gonzaga

golstadt in Bavaria for the academic year 1601–02, because he wanted him to learn German. Ingolstadt at that time was a part-Jesuit university: Jesuits dominated arts and theology, while lay professors taught law and medicine. In particular, the Jesuits did the teaching in the *paedagogium,* the secondary school that prepared students for university studies. There students studied advanced Latin literature, Greek, poetry, and some dialectic and rhetoric.[26] Ferdinando studied in the paedagogium, although he may have attended some university-level lectures as well. About 17.5 percent of the students at the university were nobles; Ferdinando was one of them, albeit more privileged and protected.[27] He lived in a household with tutors and eight priests, received private instruction, and was expected to speak Latin there, while the rector of the Jesuit college at Ingolstadt heard his confessions. Nevertheless, he found time to play ball games and go sightseeing in Munich.[28]

After one year at Ingolstadt, Ferdinando returned to Mantua for the latter half of 1602 and much of 1603, where he received more tutoring from Magini and probably others. In the fall of 1603 Ferdinando enrolled in the University of Pisa. He arrived at the age of sixteen and one-half, twelve to eighteen months younger than the average entering student, and remained through the first half of 1607. Very few princes in Italian ruling families enrolled in universities. Those who did were usually second sons intended for the church with the necessary intellectual capacity, which exactly described Ferdinando. But he did have one illustrious ancestor who was a university student and serious about learning. Ercole Gonzaga, already a bishop but not yet a cardinal, had attended the University of Bologna for two and one-half years, December 1522 through May 1525, leaving without a degree when his mentor and friend, the eminent philosopher Pietro Pomponazzi, died.[29] After leaving Bologna, Ercole became a lifelong student who employed tutors and read widely, especially in humanistic studies, Scripture, and theology.[30]

Ferdinando wanted to study natural philosophy at Pisa.[31] But his great-uncle Grand Duke Ferdinando I de' Medici (1549, ruled 1587–1609), who oversaw his university career, insisted that he study law. It was conventional

26. Mobley, 2004, 215–16 especially note 7.
27. Mobley, 2004, 244.
28. Ferdinando to his brother Francesco, November 7, 1601, Ingolstadt, as quoted in Chambers, 1987, 117 note 26. The expression that Ferdinando used was "giocho da palla." A *palla* was a small ball made of leather and either relatively hard or with a hard exterior and an empty interior. The player hit the ball with his fist, which made the game resemble modern handball. Grendler, "Fencing, Playing Ball."
29. Murphy, 2007, 5–13.
30. Murphy, 2007, 13–14, 18–42.
31. Chambers, 1987, 118–19. For the University of Pisa, see the articles in *L'Università di Pisa,* 1993.

advice for a future prince of the church, because the vast majority of Italian popes, cardinals, papal diplomats, and bishops studied law rather than theology, if they attended a university. Grand Duke Ferdinando knew this because he had been a cardinal until his older brother died without male issue. He was then obliged to shed his cardinal's robes, become ruler of Florence, and marry. Ferdinando Gonzaga bowed to the wishes of his great-uncle and studied law. But he also read natural philosophy as time allowed.

Like most students, Ferdinando took the course in logic early in his university career, because it was considered necessary preparation for studies in both law and philosophy. He also attended lectures on the *Institutes,* the introductory course in civil law. Professor Giacomo Angeli di Barga (sometimes called Barga or Bargeo, d. 1609) taught him *Institutes* in 1603–04 and canon law in the academic year 1606–07, and possibly was Ferdinando's legal mentor.[32] Angeli approached jurisprudence humanistically to some extent, an approach that may have appealed to Ferdinando.

Like other highborn and wealthy students, Ferdinando along with his tutors and minders organized a little academy for study, lectures, and informal disputations. Usually hosted by wealthy students, academies were limited to invited students, professors, and guests, and were a part of the network of private instruction that weakened the public lecture system of Italian universities at this time.[33] Ferdinando's academy met twice a week in his house.

On February 19, 1605, Ferdinando participated in an informal disputation in his house in the presence of Grand Duke Ferdinando I de' Medici. For two hours he put forward twenty-two "ingenious" arguments in the process of defending six legal and six philosophical propositions against two other students and nine *dottori.*[34] Ferdinando's minders sent back to Duke Vincenzo I glowing accounts of his intellectual prowess and his fabulous memory. Naturally they were inclined to see the best in him. But other observers not in the employ of the Gonzaga made similar observations about Ferdinando's intel-

---

32. Chambers, 1987, 119, 122, which refer to "Giacomo Barta" or "dottor Barga." See Barsanti, 1993, 506, for fuller identification. Barta is a town in the Tuscan Alps northeast of Lucca. Giacomo Angeli di Barga began teaching in 1562 and was ordinary professor of civil law at the University of Pisa from 1592 until 1609, when he probably died. See also Cascio Pratilli, 1975, 72 note 196 and index.

33. Although Ferdinando's academy was informal and transitory, several of the academies at the University of Pisa had names and formal structures and continued for decades. Volpi Rosselli, 1993, 450–58. Critics complained that some professors spent more energy teaching privileged students in these academies, plus private tutoring, than on their public university lectures.

34. Chambers, 1987, 120–21. The Medici court usually spent the season of Lent in Pisa. Hence, Grand Duke Ferdinando did not have to travel far to hear the young man perform. Still, he did come.

lect. And he continued to demonstrate wide-ranging curiosity. He applied to the Holy Office in Rome for permission to read Paracelsus (Theophrastus Philippus Aureolus Bombastus von Hohenheim, ca. 1493–1541), whose works were prohibited by the 1596 Index of Prohibited Books. The Holy Office denied his request in May 1606.[35]

The young prince did not spend all his time studying. Ferdinando hunted and fished. He was made a knight of St. John and was thrilled to take a short voyage on a warship. In the summer of 1606 he traveled to France to attend the wedding of his sister Margherita (1591–1632) to Henry, Duke of Lorraine. He spent the hot summers with his Medici relatives in Florence or visiting monasteries in cool rustic settings. And he developed a strong interest in the musical performances at the Florentine court. Ferdinando had enough musical and literary ability to compose music and verse for a ballet and a pastoral comedy, plus write occasional poetry.[36] Music remained a lifelong passion, which he indulged by supporting musical performances at Mantua and writing some musical compositions after he became duke.

Ferdinando wanted a doctoral degree, but his advisers urged him not to get one for two reasons. First, it would be expensive. A new doctor was obliged to pay substantial fees to the members of the college of doctors who examined him, professors, university officials, and witnesses, as well as host a lavish banquet. As a prince, Ferdinando would have had to be very generous. Second and most important, it would be politically inappropriate. The 1544 statutes of the University of Pisa required all recipients of doctoral degrees to swear an oath of allegiance to the grand duke of Tuscany. While this oath probably meant little to most non-Tuscans, the son of the duke of Mantua could not swear fealty to the ruler of another state, even his friendly great uncle.[37] Ferdinando did not get a doctorate.

Ferdinando returned to Mantua in June 1607, and Pope Paul V named him a cardinal on December 10, 1607, when Ferdinando was twenty years and seven months old. He was made a cardinal because the Gonzaga, like the Medici, the Este, and other ruling families of Italy, were so politically important that the papacy felt obliged to give them representation in the college of cardinals.[38] However, rather than moving to Rome, Ferdinando remained in

---

35. Baldini, 2001, 175 note 14. The enthusiasm for Paracelsianism at the University of Mantua will be discussed in chapters 5 and 7.

36. Chambers, 1987, 122–24.

37. See Lelio Arrigoni to Duke Vincenzo I, March 31, 1607, Pisa, quoted in Chambers, 1987, 122 note 63. Arrigoni estimated that the cost of the degree would be 4,000 piastre (Spanish dollars). On the oath, see Cascio Pratilli, 1975, 140, 142–43, Mango Tomei, 1976, 38–39.

38. See Chambers, 1987, 125, 135. From the elevation of Ercole Gonzaga in 1526 through Vincenzo (the future Duke Vincenzo II) Gonzaga's resignation in 1616, the Gonzaga had seven cardinals, three from cadet branches. Only Ercole was a churchman of distinction.

FIG. 2. Portrait of Cardinal Ferdinando Gonzaga by Domenico Domenichino. Pinocoteca Nazionale, Bologna. *Photo: Scala/Ministero per i Beni e le Attività Culturali/Art Resource, NY.*

## The Education of Ferdinando Gonzaga 65

Mantua for the next two years, studying botany, composing madrigals, and organizing musical and dramatic events.

The Mantuan Jesuits marked his elevation by inviting him to their college for a celebration. As he entered the building, he found the atrium festooned with posters, *imprese* (iconographic illustrations), inscriptions, and compositions alluding to his merit and virtue. A Jesuit or a student recited a Latin oration in his praise. After Ferdinando dined in the college, some of the students from the school presented a drama, which Cardinal Ferdinando applauded.[39] His respect and affection for the Jesuits was genuine. At some point in his youth, he had vowed to become a Jesuit, but his father obtained a release from the vow from the Sacred Penitentiary in Rome.[40]

Ferdinando finally took up residence in Rome in early 1610. The pope appointed him to the Congregation of Rites, which dealt with the liturgy and evaluated candidates for beatification and canonization. It was not the most important congregation in the Vatican, but it gave him the opportunity to urge the canonization of Blessed Luigi Gonzaga. He took the four minor orders, which did not involve the obligation of celibacy, and considered taking major orders (subdiaconate, diaconate, and priesthood), which did.[41]

Most important, in Rome he had ample opportunity to pursue his many intellectual and artistic interests. He created a laboratory where he engaged in alchemical experiments under the guidance of Magini. He haunted the Vatican Library and spent hours in discussions with the scholars and notables who gathered there. Even after he became duke he continued to visit the Vatican Library when in Rome.[42] He bought books and main-

---

39. Gorzoni, 1997, 113. The celebration honoring Ferdinando's cardinalate occurred sometime in 1608. See Gorzoni, 1997, 101–2, for praise of Ferdinando's intellect.

40. Chambers, 1987, 126–27, including note 103, with Ferdinando's letter to his father, September 10, 1611, referring to the vow and release. One suspects that the vow was more than a pledge to himself if it caused Vincenzo I to apply to the Sacred Penitentiary for release.

41. See Ferdinando to Duke Vincenzo I, September 10, 1611, Rome, quoted in Chambers, 1987, 127 note 103. I thank Nelson Minnich for explaining the four minor orders, which no longer exist in the Catholic Church. Although a cardinal, Ferdinando could not take major orders until he reached canonical age, which the Council of Trent had specified as twenty-two for the subdiaconate, twenty-three for the diaconate, and twenty-five for the priesthood. In addition, Trent had decreed thirty as the minimum canonical age for cardinals, although Sixtus V (1585–90) had lowered it to twenty-two, provided that the cardinal became a deacon within a year. Of course, dispensations were granted, as in Ferdinando's case. See Rock, 1913, 207.

42. "[E]t per memoria, che io tengo di quel giorno, nel quale V(ostra) A(ltezza) desceso per suo diporto dalle stanze pontificie in questa (Vaticana) Biblioteca, honorò il loco con la dimora di molte hore in dottissimi ragionamenti, de' quali con tutti i precipi et dotti che capitano qui, che ne capitano ogni giorno." Nicolo Alemanni to Duke Ferdinando, July 20, 1624, Rome, in ASM, AG, Bu. 1028, Diversi, no pag. Alemanni was one of Ferdinand's agents in Rome. See also Alemanni to Duke Ferdinando, July 12, 1625, Rome, in ASM, AG, Bu. 1029, no pag., when he

tained an interest in natural philosophy. In 1610 he obtained a papal pardon for the painter Caravaggio, who had killed a man in Rome in 1606.[43] He composed more music and lyrics, and he persuaded Andreana Basile (ca. 1580–after 1639), a famous Neapolitan contralto, to move to Mantua to join the other musicians there.[44] All of this cost money. Even though he enjoyed an annual income estimated at 60,000 to 80,000 ducats, he spent all of it and more.[45] He asked his father for additional funds to purchase a palace in Rome, but Duke Vincenzo I, a prodigious spendthrift in his own right, said no. So Ferdinando retreated to Mantua in early 1611, partly to avoid his creditors. Nevertheless, he purchased an unfinished villa in Frascati in 1612.

Ferdinando kept abreast of contemporary scientific matters. In May 1611 the Jesuits of the Province of Venice held a congregation (general meeting) in Mantua. Along with the congregation, the Mantua Jesuits organized some scholarly presentations. Two Jesuits came from Parma for a theological disputation, a famous Jesuit orator preached, and Cardinal Ferdinando arranged for a mathematical presentation by a "bravo" mathematician.[46]

The "bravo" mathematician was the Jesuit Giuseppe Biancani (1566–1624), the ablest mathematician and astronomer in the Venetian province, then teaching at the University of Parma. At Mantua he discussed the height of the mountains on the moon based on telescopic observations and mathematical calculations. Before long an anonymous summary of his presentation appeared: "De lunarium montium altitudine problema mathematicum ter habitum Mantuae, in templo Sanctissimae Trinitatis, in nostra aula coram serenissimo duce et in cubiculo coram illustrissimo Cardinali Gonzaga" (Mathematical problem of the height of the mountains of the moon presented at Mantua three times, in the church of the Most Holy Trinity, in our hall in the presence of the most serene duke, and in the bedroom [or private room] in the presence of the most illustrious Cardinal Gonzaga.).[47] The pri-

---

referred to "the last time" that he was in Rome and in the Vatican Library: "L'ultima volta, che V(ostra) A(tezza) fu in Roma et nella Biblioteca Vaticana."

43. Gash, 1996, 715B.

44. Chambers, 1987, 128–33; Pannella, 1965; Benzoni, 1996, 243–44.

45. See the relazione of Francesco Morosini of June 21, 1608, which estimated his income as 75,000 to 80,000 ducats, and that of Pietro Gritti of 1612, which estimated it as 60,000 ducats, in *Relazioni*, 1912, 89, 121.

46. See the description of the meeting, including the phrase "Fecero venire un bravo matematico a far un problema," in Gorzoni, 1997, 118; and in Baldini, 1992, 241 note 1, who concludes that Ferdinando arranged for the presentation.

47. The treatise, sometimes called "il problema mantovano," is printed in Galilei, 1964–66, vol. 3, part 1, pp. 302–7. It is not clear if it circulated in manuscript or in print.

vate session for Ferdinando demonstrated, once again, Ferdinando's keen interest in current scientific matters. The anonymous summary criticized Galilei, who responded with an angry rebuttal.[48]

Later that year Ferdinando participated in an informal disputation with Galilei and two others. During a visit to Grand Duke Cosimo II de' Medici in Florence in the fall of 1611, he engaged in a luncheon dispute about the buoyancy of bodies in water. On one side of the table sat, figuratively and maybe physically, Galileo Galilei and Cardinal Maffeo Barberini (b. 1568), the future Urban VIII (1623–44). On the other side were Cardinal Ferdinando and the Aristotelian natural philosopher Flaminio Pappazoni (ca. 1550–1613), who had just been appointed ordinary professor of natural philosophy at the University of Pisa after teaching at the universities of Bologna and Pavia.[49] Pappazoni and Ferdinando defended Aristotelian views, which Galilei and Barberini rejected. Given Ferdinando's Jesuit schooling and university study, it was to be expected that he would be an Aristotelian and differ from Galilei. In 1612 Galilei published his views on the subject: *Discorso . . . intorno alle cose che stanno in su l'acqua* (Discourse on bodies on or in water). He looked at buoyancy somewhat in Archimedian terms and as a function of dynamics and mechanics. And he attacked unnamed Aristotelians.[50] Galilei sent a copy to Ferdinando, who graciously thanked him.[51]

To participate in the luncheon debate, Ferdinando had to have specialized knowledge and be agile enough verbally to dispute the immensely learned and sharp-tongued Galilei. Ferdinando was an unusual amateur scholar to contemplate such a test, even if Galilei treated him gently. The presentation of a mathematical-astronomical problem and the informal disputation were typical university events. Ferdinando was still a student at heart.

48. Christoph Grienberger, a Jesuit and friend of Galilei then teaching mathematics and astronomy at the Collegio Romano in Rome, conveyed Galilei's displeasure to Biancani and asked for an explanation. The latter, who fundamentally endorsed Galilei's astronomical discoveries, hastened to write that he had expressed only praise and admiration for Galilei at the Mantuan meeting, and that the duke, Cardinal Ferdinando, and the Jesuits present at Mantua could vouch for this. Moreover, he was not really the author of the treatise; he had only helped revise it. Although temporarily mollified, Galilei later wrote a rebuttal that criticized Biancani. See Galilei, 1964–66, 11:126–27, 130–31, 178–203 (Galilei's rebuttal); Grillo, 1968, 33; and Baldini, 1992, 217–50, some of which is recapitulated in Blackwell, 1991, 148–53.

49. See Galilei, 1964–66, 11:304, 325–26, 338–39, 496. See also Biagioli, 1993, 75, 167, 181–82, who does not identify Cardinal Gonzaga. For information on Pappazoni, see Galilei, 1964–66, 20:503, and Camerota, 1997.

50. See the analysis of the work in Biagioli, 1993, 183–209. For an expanded English version of the work, which adds fictional material, see Drake, 1981.

51. See Galilei to Ferdinando, June 15, 1612, Florence, and Ferdinando's reply, June 23, 1612, Rome, in Galilei, 1964–66, 11:325–26, 338–39.

## 4. DUKE FERDINANDO GONZAGA

On February 18, 1612, Duke Vincenzo I Gonzaga died and was succeeded by Ferdinando's older brother, who became Duke Francesco III Gonzaga (b. 1586).[52] This had little impact on Ferdinando. But when Francesco suddenly died on December 22, 1612, apparently of smallpox,[53] Ferdinando's life changed decisively. Since Duke Francesco III had left only one living child, a daughter, Maria, born July 29, 1609, Ferdinando was next in line to become duke of Mantua and Monferrato. At first it was believed that Francesco's widow, Margherita Savoia (1589–1655), the daughter of Duke Carlo Emanuele I (1562, ruled 1580–1630), of Piedmont-Savoy, was pregnant. Were she to produce a son, the infant would be the next ruler, and a regency would have to be organized. Carlo Emanuele demanded that Margherita return to Turin with Maria, an obvious ploy to become de facto regent of Mantua and Monferrato should Margherita produce a son. In any case, since Monferrato could be inherited through the female line, he intended to claim Monferrato on behalf of Maria. Ferdinando refused to let mother and daughter leave. When it became apparent that Margherita was not pregnant, Ferdinando permitted her to depart but kept little Maria, who was sent to an Ursuline convent in Mantua.[54]

Undeterred, Carlo Emanuele I claimed Monferrato on behalf of his three-year-old granddaughter. Finding little diplomatic support for his claim, Carlo Emanuele I invaded Monferrato on April 23, 1613. He quickly took control of extensive parts of the duchy of Monferrato but not Casale Monferrato, as Gonzaga troops gamely fought back. But it was difficult for Ferdinando to send more troops to Monferrato, because they had to march more than 200 kilometers through Spanish-controlled Lombardy, crossing the Oglio, Adda, Ticino, and Po rivers, to reach Casale Monferrato. Fortunately, most other states condemned or failed to support Carlo Emanuele's claims, while the Spanish attacked Piedmont-Savoy. The fighting petered out, as the military struggle became a diplomatic campaign. It was resolved in 1617, with further adjustments later, with the Gonzaga still ruling Monferrato.[55]

---

52. Benzoni, 1997.
53. Pazzini, 1978, 307.
54. Benzoni, 1996, 244. All of this was carefully calculated, as Holy Roman Emperor Matthias endorsed this disposition of Maria. Her great-aunt Margherita Gonzaga (1564–1618), widow of Duke Alfonso II Este, oversaw her education, which included music lessons from Claudio Monteverdi. She remained with the Ursulines until 1627, then married Carlo Gonzaga, Duc de Rethel. See chapter 9, section 1.
55. A few bits of territory went to Piedmont-Savoy, and Ferdinando promised to give Carlo Emanuele I a large sum of money in lieu of an unpaid dowry of decades earlier. Quazza, 1933, 164–65; Castronovo, 1977, 335–36.

## Duke Ferdinando Gonzaga

Although Ferdinando, still a cardinal, was ruling Mantua in his own name and Monferrato as de facto regent for his niece Maria, his position was precarious. Emperor Matthias helped considerably by recognizing him as ruler of Mantua and Monferrato on October 21, 1613. Ferdinando then successfully petitioned the papacy for permission to renounce his cardinalate and to be allowed to marry. Because Ferdinando had not taken higher orders, the path was clear. He formally renounced his cardinalate on November 16, 1615. For good measure, the pope created his younger brother Vincenzo (1594–1627) a cardinal in his place on December 2, 1615, ensuring that a rich harvest of benefice income stayed in the family. Ferdinando was formally crowned duke of Mantua and duke of Monferrato on January 6, 1616.[56]

Now Ferdinando had to marry well, which he made more difficult through his ill-considered actions. In or about 1613, in the midst of war and negotiations with the papacy, Ferdinando fell in love with a lady-in-waiting, Camilla Faà (ca. 1600–62), the daughter of a Monferrato count, and secretly married her on February 18, 1616. This was neither an appropriate nor a politically useful marriage for a Gonzaga duke. So, Ferdinando repudiated the marriage as feigned, and it was declared invalid.[57] Camilla was banished to Casale Monferrato, where on December 4, 1616, she gave birth to a son, Giacinto. She was eventually moved to a convent in Ferrara, while little Giacinto was later brought to the court. With Camilla Faà out of the way, Ferdinando married his second cousin Caterina de' Medici (1593–1629) on February 5, 1617, in Florence. She was the sister of the reigning Grand Duke Cosimo II de' Medici and the daughter of Ferdinando's great-uncle Grand Duke Ferdinando I de' Medici. The marriage renewed the alliance with the Medici.

After overcoming the threat of dismemberment of his state, Ferdinando settled into the business of government and diplomacy.[58] Like other Italian rulers, Ferdinando had to make sure that his diplomacy did not arouse the disapproval of the great powers, a task that he found exhausting. Maintaining

---

56. Pastor, 1891–1953, 25:336; Benzoni, 1996, 245.

57. Ferdinando did seem to have been in love with Camilla, but historians differ on whether he deliberately deceived her or was simply heedless of the political stakes. Quazza, 1933, 166; and Chambers, 1987, 137, see it as a love marriage that Ferdinando was forced to repudiate for reasons of state. Coniglio, 1967, 415–16; Benzoni, 1996, 247; Oresko and Parrott, 1997, 42; and Malacarne, 2007, 239–40, 242–44, 351–56, see Ferdinando as deliberately deceiving Camilla with a fictitious marriage, which the poor girl thought was true, in order to gratify his passion. In any case the marriage apparently did not satisfy all the canons of Trent, which included public proclamation of the banns, so it could be declared invalid.

58. Carlo Emanuele I's invasion of Monferrato in 1613 in order to take it away from the Gonzaga was unusual. Since the Peace of Cateau-Cambrésis of 1559, Italian rulers had managed to settle their disputes peacefully.

Fig. 3. Portrait of Duke Ferdinando Gonzaga by an unknown artist. Private collection. *Reproduced with permission of the owner, of Roberto Bini who made the photograph, and of Il Bulino edizioni d'arte, Modena.*

## Duke Ferdinando Gonzaga

good relations with Spain, which ruled Lombardy, was a high priority because of the widely separated parts of the Gonzaga state.

The possibility of a land swap to make the Gonzaga state contiguous and compact arose. Ferdinando would deed the duchy of Monferrato to Lombardy (meaning Spain) in exchange for the Cremonese (the territory of Cremona excluding the city, which did not want to be ruled by Mantua) and some minor territories. Although the Cremonese was smaller than Monferrato, it was contiguous with the duchy of Mantua on the east and would have given the Gonzaga a geographically unified state. The swap would also have strengthened the Spanish presence in northwestern Italy, which would not have pleased Piedmont-Savoy or France. There were two significant disadvantages for Ferdinando. The Cremonese would not have yielded nearly as much income as Monferrato, and the Gonzaga would no longer rule two duchies, with a consequent loss of prestige.[59] In the end, nothing happened.

Despite his difficulties, Ferdinando had many advantages. He presided over a peaceful and absolutist realm, which meant that he was not answerable to council, commune, or any other body representing the people. The state, including his consort, councillors, and courtiers, revolved around him. He lived in a huge palace housing an extraordinary art collection, a natural history museum, a collection of antiquities, and much else. He presided over a brilliant court graced by talented artists and musicians.

The Venetian ambassador painted a glowing word picture of Ferdinando as duke. Ferdinando spoke Italian, Latin, German, French, and Spanish, and could read Hebrew and Greek. He needed little sleep, preferring to write music and poetry at night. Upon rising in the morning he always had something witty to say, which sometimes discomfited members of his retinue. He never forgot anything that he read. He loved both ancient and modern poetry and had written a good deal of verse. He had also written much on philosophy and theology and was so skilled in law that he had no need of legal experts.[60]

Ferdinando loved listening to and composing music; it was his refuge in

---

59. See the relazioni of Venetian ambassadors Pietro Gritti of 1612 and Giovanni da Mula of 1615, in *Relazioni*, 1912, 117–18, 153–56. See also Quazza, 1922, 25–26, 222–23; Belfanti and Romani, 1987, 121–23 especially note 35, 138–39; and Parrott, 1997a, 35–36. Gaspare Scioppio (Gaspar Schoppe, 1576–1649), scholar, busybody, and Ferdinando's friend, conducted negotiations with the Spanish about the swap on behalf of Ferdinando from 1619 through early 1621. D'Addio, 1962, 151–53. In return, Ferdinando financially supported Scioppio, who also provided historical documentation for Gonzaga dynastic claims. See Scioppio to Ferdinando, March 13 and June 1, 1624, and November 1, 1625, always Rome, in ASM, AG, Bu. 1028, Diversi (first two letters), no pag., and Bu. 1029, Diversi, no pag.

60. Relazione of Giovanni da Mula of (October) 1615 in *Relazioni*, 1912, 137–41. Chambers, 1987, 138, provides some translated passages.

time of troubles. Hence, he supported a chorus of singers attached to the ducal chapel of Santa Barbara plus female soloists, at a cost of 30,000 ducats annually, a figure that may be exaggerated. Although dazzled by Ferdinando's taste and intellect, the pragmatic ambassador also pointed out that the duke had inherited a debt of some 800,000 ducats from Duke Vincenzo I, and that the annual income of the state was only about 430,000 ducats in time of peace. Ferdinando spent as much as he took in.[61]

Ferdinando manifested the intellectual and religious sensibilities of the Baroque age. He had a wide-ranging intellectual curiosity and told his agents abroad to keep an eye out for new books that might interest him.[62] He shared in the age's optimism that alchemy and astrology would reveal the hidden secrets of nature. For example, in 1624 he ordered an agent to search for books on astrology in Venice, Padua, and elsewhere. In due course, the agent found a treasure trove of books in ancient, medieval, and Renaissance astrology, divination, prognostication, and geomancy.[63]

Ferdinando admired and supported the new poets of the Baroque, such as Gabriello Chiabrera (1552–1638) and Giambattisto Marino (1569–1625). He liked opera, the musical form created by Baroque composers. And he embraced flamboyant religious devotions. Late sixteenth- and early seventeenth-century men and women were particularly fascinated with Christian antiquities and saw them as means for deepening their devotion. Ferdinando shared

---

61. Relazione of Giovanni da Mula of (October) 1615 in *Relazioni*, 1912, 137. The figure for the debt of 800,000 ducats accumulated by Duke Vincenzo I comes from the relazione of Pietro Gritti of (August) 1612, in *Relazioni*, 1912, 119. Duke Francesco III had begun to reduce expenses but did not live long enough to accomplish much. Ferdinando made no effort to curb expenses.

62. For two examples in which his agent in Rome forwarded new books to Ferdinando, see Nicolo Alemanni to Ferdinando, July 20, 1624, and July 12, 1625, Rome, in ASM, AG, Bu. 1028 no pag., and Bu. 1029, no pag. In the first case, the book that Alemanni forwarded to Ferdinando was certainly new and interesting. It was "un libro della Vita di Giustiniano Imperatore scritta da Procopio suo consigliere di stato." This was probably the *Secret History* of Justinian I (Roman emperor 527–565), written by Procopius (ca. 500–after 544), a member of Justinian's court and eyewitness to many events. Discovered in the Vatican Library in the early seventeenth century, the *Secret History* was an invective denouncing Justinian, his wife, Theodora, and his most successful general, Belisarius, and his wife.

63. Faustino Tedeschi to Duke Ferdinando, September 29, 1624, Verona, in ASM, AG, Bu. 1556, ff. 401–2. Folio 402 lists the books that Tedeschi found, with their prices. They included major works on astrology of Francesco Giuntini (1523–90), Luca Guarico (flourished 1552), Luca Ballanti (d. 1498), and Girolamo Cardano (1501–76). The Cardano texts included *De restitutione temporum et motuum coelestium, Supplementum Almanach, Somniorum synesiorum omnis generis insomnia explicantes libri IIII*, and a commentary on Ptolemy's *Tetrabiblos*. Tedeschi also listed astrological works of three Arabs: Artemidorus Daldianus (second century), Haly Heben Rodan (dates unknown), and Albumasar (d. 886), whose book was on casting birth horoscopes. There was an edition of Ptolemy's *Tetrabiblos* and a manuscript that promised to be "a copious compendium of geomancy" collected from many authors.

# The Jesuit Part of the University 73

this attitude and demonstrated it by constructing a replica of the Scala Sancta (Holy Stairs) of Jerusalem.

According to tradition, the Scala Sancta were the twenty-eight steps of the staircase leading up to the palace of Pontius Pilate that Jesus ascended and descended before and after his appearance before Pilate. St. Helena, mother of Constantine the Great, brought them to Rome about 326 and installed them in the Lateran Palace, adjacent to the Basilica of St. John Lateran, which later became the papal residence. Medieval builders added two other staircases on either side of the Scala Sancta. The Scala Sancta then fell into disuse as a pilgrim destination because of the general disrepair of the Lateran Palace, and because the popes moved to the Vatican in the fifteenth century. In 1589 Pope Sixtus V had the old palace torn down and a new one built in its place. He had the Scala Sancta moved to its present location next to a private chapel called the Sancta Sanctorum (Holy of Holies) in the rebuilt Lateran Palace, and he added two more staircases for common use. The Scala Sancta again became a popular pilgrim destination, especially during Holy Week devotions, as the devout ascended the stairs on their knees by torchlight, singing hymns. Those who did so received plenary indulgences. Several popes are reported to have made the ascent on their knees, including Pius IX in September 1870 just before the army of the Kingdom of Italy entered Rome.[64]

Ferdinando had a replica of the Scala Sancta flanked by two other staircases, plus a chapel called the Sancta Sanctorum, built in an older wing of the ducal palace between the summer of 1614 and the spring of 1615. For good measure he added some catacombs. Then on the night of April 5, 1615, Cardinal Ferdinando (he had not yet renounced his ecclesiastical office) carried a reliquary holding a thorn from the Crown of Thorns of Jesus from the church of Santa Barbara, the court church next to the palace, to the new Sancta Sanctorum. On the night of April 15, Cardinal Ferdinando, accompanied by cavaliers and nobles in a torchlight procession, carried a tabernacle that held another reliquary containing a vial of some of the blood of Jesus to the Sancta Sanctorum. He probably obtained from Pope Paul V indulgences for those who ascended the steps of the Mantuan Scala Sancta on their knees.[65]

## 5. THE JESUIT PART OF THE UNIVERSITY

Duke Ferdinando enjoyed the company of the Jesuits. In the words of the Jesuit chronicler of the Mantuan college, Ferdinando came at any hour and became "a familiar presence in our house." To make his visits easier and more

---

64. Oliger, 1913; Pastor, 1891–1953, 22:277–78.
65. Franchini et al., 1979, 178–84, with diagrams and documents. Unfortunately, the ducal palace has been so altered subsequently that the Scala Sancta and Sancta Sanctorum no longer exist.

private, Ferdinando had built an elevated wooden passageway from his palace to the houses next to the Jesuit island. Once inside the college, he donned the informal dress that Jesuits wore at home and participated in their recreations and exhortations. He made the Spiritual Exercises of St. Ignatius.[66] Ferdinando also became the leader of the congregation of nobles organized by the Jesuits.

There was more. In 1618 Blessed Luigi Gonzaga was declared the protector of the city of Mantua, an event celebrated in grand style on his feast day, June 21. Ferdinando obtained permission from Rome for the reading of the Office (prayers that priests, monks, and nuns were obliged to recite daily) and Mass of Blessed Luigi in all the Gonzaga states.[67] He sent artisans to modify the Jesuit college and ducal musicians to play at the religious and civic celebration, which included religious exercises, the fanfare of trumpets, the tattoo of drums, the firing of artillery pieces, and much else. Ferdinando announced that he had placed himself, his family, and all his subjects under the protection of Blessed Luigi.[68]

Ferdinando had even larger plans that would include the Jesuits. In or about 1622 he told others about his resolve to found a university in Mantua.[69] Although a momentous decision, he never explained his reasons beyond two passing comments. In the summer of 1624 he wrote that the university was for the public benefit.[70] And he wanted the Jesuit part of the university to begin in November so that the city would quickly enjoy the benefit of the university.[71]

---

66. "S'era egli [Ferdinando] fatta famigliare la nostra casa, dove egli per strade private segretamente ad ogni hora veniva. Fece egli perciò far un passaggio o corridore di legno in aria che, partendo dal suo palazzo, attraversava la strada detta del Zuccaro ed inoltrandosi per quelle case immediate arrivava copertamente fin al nostro collegio. Suo gusto era intervenire alle nostre ricreationi, alle nostre fonzioni di casa, alle nostre essortationi. Anzi, egli stesso, vestendo una nostra vesta da camera che noi chiamiamo vesta grossa, così faceva a' padri dotte e spiritu[ali] essortationi et a' suoi, et anzi facea gl'essercitii spirituali di sant'Ignatio." Gorzoni, 1997, 120.

67. That is, the prayers of the Office and Mass were modified slightly to include references to Blessed Luigi Gonzaga.

68. Gorzoni, 1997, 128–33; Parisi, 1989, 310–11. The Jesuits in Rome held similar celebrations honoring Blessed Luigi.

69. "Li riccorda V. S. Ill.ma che gl'anni passati a Perto quando l'Altezza Serenissima di Madama [Duchess Caterina de' Medici] era ivi convalescente, si trattò con risolutioni di principiare lo studio." Fabrizio Bartoletti to Ferdinando, July 9, 1625, Bologna, in ASM, AG, Bu. 1173, f. 651v. Other letters document that Bartoletti and Ferdinando were in contact as early as 1622; see chapter 5, section 3. "Perto," which has not been further identified, may have been a spa.

70. "[A] beneficio publico." Duke Ferdinando to his brother Vincenzo, June 10, 1624, Florence, in ASM, AG, Bu. 2176, Lettere originali dei Gonzaga 1624 e 1625, f. 52r.

71. "Potrà V(ostra) I(llustrissima) far intimare à i Padri Gesuiti che debbano principiare lo studio à quatro novembre, acciò quanto più presto la città possa godere del beneficio." Duke Ferdinando to his brother Vincenzo, July 9, 1624, Florence, in ASM, AG, Bu. 2176, Lettere originali dei Gonzaga 1624 e 1625, f. 109r.

Ferdinando undoubtedly believed that the coming university would benefit his subjects and the city of Mantua. By "public benefit," he may have meant the training of civil servants, physicians, and lawyers for the state, the reasons often suggested by historians for founding universities. But it is not likely that this was the most important reason. The Gonzaga government did not need many highly trained civil servants because it lacked the many magistracies, councils, and offices of republics. Moreover, his subjects in the Mantovano could easily attend the nearby universities of Parma, Pavia, Ferrara, Bologna, or Padua to obtain legal and medical degrees, while those living in Monferrato could attend the University of Turin, which was even closer. If the Jesuits pressed him to create a university, they did so informally, because no documents have come to light.

It is most likely that he decided to found a university because he loved learning. Ferdinando was a prince-savant and perpetual student who reveled in the university environment. He had studied the humanities in the pre-university paedagogium at the University of Ingolstadt and law at the University of Pisa. He had a keen interest in several university subjects, notably natural philosophy and astronomy. As a cardinal, he had done alchemical experiments in his laboratory. Ferdinando also followed developments in two fashionable subjects of the day, astrology and Paracelsian chemical medicine. He clearly enjoyed participating in university-style events, such as Biancani's elucidation of an astronomical-mathematical problem and the disputation with Galilei. As duke he was comfortable in the presence of scholars. No other Italian ruler for a century before or after Ferdinando had such a keen interest in learning or greater familiarity with universities and scholars.

The Gonzaga tradition of strong support for learning also probably moved him toward creating a university. Guglielmo, Vincenzo I, and Ferdinando supported scholarship in botany, pharmacy, medicine, and alchemy, thus building a foundation for the medical teaching of the university. Ferdinando would fulfill the long-held Gonzaga desire for a studium generale, which would add more prestige to a family that already ruled two duchies.

Ferdinando's close association with and respect for the Jesuits meant that the Society would be part of his university. He looked to Ingolstadt and Parma as models and began to create a joint Jesuit-civic university. He proceeded on parallel tracks. On one he negotiated with the Jesuits concerning their part of the university. On the other he recruited professors of law and medicine and considered taxation schemes to pay their salaries. He started with the Jesuits. Ferdinando sought a formal agreement with the Society and money with which to expand the Jesuit school into the arts and theology part of the university.

Duke Ferdinando initially tried to get the money from an ecclesiastical benefice. In January 1623 one of the duke's agents reported on his efforts to secure from Pope Gregory XV (Alessandro Ludovisi, 1554, elected pope 1621, d. July 8, 1623) permission to use income from a prosperous abbey to support the Jesuits and the new university. The abbey in question was the Cistercian monastery of Santa Maria di Lucedio, usually just called Lucedio in the documents.

Probably founded in 1123, Lucedio was of one the wealthiest monastic houses in Italy, because it owned and managed a considerable amount of land near the tiny village of Lucedio, located about twenty kilometers west-northwest of Casale Monferrato. Emperor Charles V originally possessed the right to confer the abbey on whomever he chose, and he chose the Gonzaga. However, Pope Paul III (ruled 1534–49) attempted to seize the abbey for his grandson, Cardinal Alessandro Farnese, and a long, nasty fight developed. Cardinal Ercole and the Gonzaga dukes finally secured Lucedio and its *ius patronatus,* that is, the right to bestow it on whomever they chose and to select abbots and administrators, even though they had to share some of the income with Farnese cardinals for many years.[72] Lucedio became a money stream on which Gonzaga cardinals floated.

As cardinal, Ferdinando had enjoyed benefice income of 25,000 to 30,000 ducats, of which the Lucedio abbey and a priory were the two chief sources.[73] Although no longer a cardinal, Duke Ferdinando probably still had some influence over Lucedio.[74] On the other hand, the pope had ultimate authority over all benefices and the disposition of their revenues. So in January 1623 Ferdinando's agent asked Pope Gregory XV to allow a pension (a diversion of part of the annual income of the abbey to a third party for religious or pious reasons) of 4,000 ducatoni for the support of an expanded Jesuit community in Mantua, which would be part of the planned University of Mantua.[75] There was precedent for the request, because earlier popes had permitted the diversion of ecclesiastical benefice income to the support of universities.[76]

Gregory XV resisted. He objected that the money would be used for houses and furnishings rather than for learning. He doubted that the duke

72. See the relazione of the Venetian ambassador Bernardo Navagero of 1540 in *Relazioni,* 1912, 55; Hallman, 1985, 39; Raviola, 2003, 381–90; and Murphy, 2007, 176–81.

73. See the relazioni of Francesco Morosini of 1608 and Pietro Gritti of 1612 in *Relazioni,* 1912, 89, 121. Since the total amount of benefice income was estimated as 25,000 to 30,000 ducats in 1608, and 30,000 ducats in 1612, and Lucedio and the priory of Barletto were the only two benefices named, they must have provided a significant part of the total, possibly 10,000 ducats or more.

74. See Raviola, 2003, 386–90. Although Raviola does not deal with the destination of the income from Lucedio, it likely went wherever Ferdinando wanted it to go.

75. Fabrizio Aragona to Duke Ferdinando, January 28, 1623, Rome, in ASM, AG, Bu. 1027, no pag. For an explanation of ecclesiastical pensions, see Fanning, 1913.

76. For example, in 1516 Leo X diverted 3,000 ducats from Tuscan ecclesiastical revenues toward the support of the University of Pisa and raised it to 5,000 ducats in 1521. Del Gratta, 1993, 42.

## The Jesuit Part of the University

could actually create a university, in which case the money would only end up financing the expansion of the Jesuit college. And he thought that the university should be financed through other means, offering the example of Bologna, where a gabelle, a tax on goods coming into the city to be sold, financed the university. He did not like income from a religious institution to be diverted to non-ecclesiastical purposes.[77]

Ferdinando's agent responded with the plea that the duke could not raise such a large sum in any other way. He assured the pope that the proposed university would be a great success and become one of the best universities of Italy. Not only would it draw students from the Gonzaga state, it would attract many students from parts of Germany with which the duke had connections.[78] He argued that because the income of the abbey was intended to provide for members of religious orders, supporting the Jesuits and the university was a legitimate use. Although nothing was decided, Ferdinando's agent believed that the pope was favorably inclined. The agent then met with the Jesuit father general, Muzio Vitelleschi, who promised to do all that he could to further the enterprise.

But the pope did not change his mind and, even worse, died in July 1623. Things did not go better with his successor, Urban VIII. By early March 1624, the duke's agent was less optimistic about a pension from the Lucedio abbey, after which the matter disappeared from the correspondence.[79] Ferdinando would have to find the money for the Jesuits from his own resources.

So he did. By late March 1624, Alessandro Striggi, his chief minister who spoke for Ferdinando, had offered the Jesuits 1,000 scudi.[80] By June Ferdinando had raised the bid to 2,000 ducatoni plus some land, while the Jesuits were willing to start teaching in the autumn. By July they reached agreement in principle, and in August the two sides were discussing the details of money, land, and a building. On December 4, 1624, Ferdinando instructed Duchess Caterina to approve some new unspecified articles and to give the Jesuits what she and the duke's ministers thought right.[81]

---

77. Fabrizio Aragona to Duke Ferdinando, January 28, 1623, in ASM, AG, Bu. 1027, Lettere di diversi, no pag. On the *grossa gabella* that financed the University of Bologna, see Grendler, 2002, 14.

78. "[B]uona copia di studenti dalla parte di Germania collegata con l'A(ltezza) V(ostra)," i.e., Duke Ferdinand. Fabrizio Aragona to Duke Ferdinando, January 28, 1623, Rome, ASM, AG, Bu. 1027, Lettere di diversi, no pag.

79. Fabrizio Aragona, March 4, 1623, Rome, in ASM, AG, Bu. 1027, no pag.

80. See the letter of Alessandro Striggi, March 26, 1624, in ASM, AG, Bu. 3366, f. 23r.

81. Although the negotiations cannot be followed in detail, one can get a rough idea of their development from the correspondence in ASM, AG, Bu. 2176, Lettere originali dei Gonzaga 1624 e 1625, Ferdinando to Vincenzo Gonzaga, June 10, 18, July 9, and August 6, 1624, Florence, at ff. 52r–v, 74v, 108r–09v, 139r–40v; Ferdinando to Striggi, June 13, 18, and July 23, 30, 1624, Florence, at ff. 62r–63r, 77r, 112r–v, 120r–v; Ferdinando to Caterina de' Medici, December 4, 1624, Casale Monferrato, ff. 166r–67r; and Caterina to Ferdinando, June 4, 14, July 5, and November 29, 1624,

The Gonzaga and the Jesuits signed an agreement on December 19, 1624, after the Jesuit university had already begun.[82] To support the Jesuit professors, Ferdinando deeded to the Society seven properties belonging to the Villa Fabrico (probably located near the modern village of Fabbrico) in the territory of Correggio in the extreme southern part of the Mantuan state. The agreement stated that these properties were worth a little less than 60,000 scudi, calculated at 6 Mantuan lire equals 1 scudo. To bring the value of the endowment up to 60,000 scudi, the duke added an annuity *(censo)* of 2,045 scudi, on which Ludovico Gonzaga (not further identified) would make annual payments of 5 percent. The combined annual income from the properties and annuity was expected to be 1,500 scudi.[83]

The contract stated that this amount was enough to support twenty-five Jesuits, professors and students, each at the rate of 60 scudi per annum. In addition, the duke gave the Jesuits a house contiguous to their college for classrooms and pledged to renovate it. For their part, the rector of the Mantuan college and the father general agreed that from the beginning of November 1624 onward the Jesuits would provide professors to teach scholastic theology, cases of conscience, natural philosophy, mathematics, rhetoric, and the humanities at the university. In addition, they agreed that they would maintain in perpetuity a minimum of twenty-five Jesuits, divided between professors and students, in the Mantuan college. Father Orazio Ferrari, the rector of the Mantuan college, signed for the Jesuits, and Duchess Caterina de' Medici, procurator general for her absent husband, signed for the duke.[84]

Although Duke Ferdinando was quite generous toward the Society, the Jesuits did not realize as much income from the land at Fabrico as they had anticipated. Even though they immediately arranged for crops to be planted

---

Mantua, at ff. 236r–38v, 387r–v, 431r, 347r–50r (the letters are not in strict chronological order). See also Father Orazio Ferrari, the rector of the Jesuit college, to Duke Ferdinando, July 9, 15, 1624, Mantua, in ASM, AG, Bu. 2767, ff. 355r, 380r–380bis recto. The last are letters of gratitude, indicating that the father provincial and the father general of the Jesuits had agreed to the terms, and that the Jesuits would begin teaching in November. Muzio Vitelleschi, the general of the Society, added his formal thanks and approval in a letter to Ferdinando, February 8, 1625, Rome, in ASM, AG, Bu. 1029, Diversi, no pag. Incidentally, in Ferdinando's frequent absences from Mantua, he usually made Caterina his regent. She capably presided over the council of advisers and reported their deliberations to Ferdinando, who made the final decisions.

82. It is very likely that the Public Academy of the Jesuits began with an inaugural lecture and other ceremonies on Monday, November 4, 1624. See below and Duke Ferdinando's letter to his brother Vincenzo, July 9, 1624, Florence, in ASM, AG, Bu. 2176, Lettere originali dei Gonzaga 1624 e 1625, f. 109r.

83. A copy of the agreement is found in ASM, AG, Bu. 3366, ff. 28r–37v. For a summary and comments on the agreement from the Jesuits, see ARSI, Veneta 115, ff. 191r–93r. Gorzoni, 1997, 144–45, also summarizes the agreement.

84. See the references in note 83.

# The Public Academy of Mantua

and buildings to be improved, the properties never produced the expected income for several reasons. The land was not very fertile and was subject to flooding. It was quite far from Mantua, which made transferring the proceeds to Mantua time consuming and expensive. And the Jesuits lost some of the land to local people as a result of monetary and legal disputes that Ferdinando had left unresolved. By 1628 the Jesuits wanted to exchange the Fabrico properties for others. But the plague, the war, and the devastation of the countryside by soldiers in 1629 and 1630 made this impossible. They were stuck with the Fabrico land, which over time yielded an average income of 2.5 to 3 percent, rather than the expected 5 percent.[85]

## 6. THE PUBLIC ACADEMY OF MANTUA

The land endowment and other arrangements made the Jesuit part of the university, called the Public Academy of Mantua for the time being, possible. On October 25, 1624, Ferdinando issued a printed proclamation announcing "a new university" (*un nuovo Studio*) in Mantua in which the Jesuit fathers would teach rhetoric, mathematics, logic, philosophy, and theology. He invited his subjects to attend. He prohibited those desiring instruction in these disciplines from going outside the state, and he ordered all those studying these subjects abroad to return within three months under pain of his displeasure (see figure 4).[86] The terms of the proclamation were customary, as Italian governments routinely ordered their subjects to study in the university of the state and were routinely ignored.

A printed poster announced the "Public Academy of Mantua [Publica Academia Mantuana] of Ferdinando Gonzaga, sixth duke of Mantua and fourth duke of Monferrato." It included a roll (rotulus): a schedule of professors and lectures that would begin in November 1624. The roll listed twelve daily lectures to be delivered by nine Jesuits along with the texts that they would teach.

In addition to listing the courses, the printed roll attempted to bring the Jesuit university to the attention of potential students. Copies were posted throughout the city and sent to other towns and abroad. The roll mentioned a public oration "in Templo" (probably the Jesuit church), with the date and the hour to be filled in by hand. This was probably an oration formally opening the Public Academy. The Jesuits also promised that disputations on philosophical and theological questions would be held nearly daily and weekly,

---

85. ARSI, Veneta 115, f. 192v; Gorzoni, 1997, 148–49; and Rurale, 1997, 25, 45 note 55. The Mantuan Jesuits frequently discovered that bequests and land gifts did not yield the expected income or entangled them in lengthy legal disputes.

86. A copy of the printed proclamation is found in ASM, AG, Bu. 3366, f. 43.

## FERDINANDO PER LA GRATIA DI DIO
### Duca di Mantoua, & di Monferrato, &c.

ER il desiderio, c'habbiamo del bene de i nostri Popoli essendo stato eretto da Noi vn nuouo Studio in questa Città, nel quale da i molto Reuerendi Padri Gesuiti si leggerà publicamente delle infrascritte scienze, cioè Retorica, Matematica, Logica, Filosofia, e Theologia; ordiniamo con la presente publica grida à tutti i nostri Sudditi dell'vno, e dell'altro Stato, che volendo studiare in alcuna delle sudette professioni, debbano farlo ne i nostri Stati, con prohibire à ciascuno l'andar altroue per il sopradetto effetto, sotto pena à chiunque cõtrafarà, della disgratia nostra, e d'altra reale, & personale à nostro arbitrio. Et se alcun nostro suddito già si trouasse in alieni Stati per la sopradetta occasione, vogliamo sotto la medesima pena, che tutti se ne vengano in quà, dando loro tempo vn mese dopò la publicatione di questa se saranno in Italia, e tre mesi se si troueranno in altre Prouincie più remote. Auuertisca dunque ogn'vno di non contrauenire à questa nostra volontà, altrimente non fuggiranno i contrafacienti la pena come sopra comminata.

Di Mantoua li 25. d'Ottobre 1624.

FERDINANDO.

V.<sup>t</sup> Striggius.

R.

Luogo del Suggello.

*Franciscus Cominus Cancell. mand. Serenijs. Domino. rel.*
*D. Herculis Marliani eius Celf. a Secretis Status, subscr.*

Marlianus.

FIG. 4. Proclamation of the opening of the Jesuit Public Academy of Mantua. ASM, AG, Bu. 3366, f. 43. *With permission of the Ministero per i Beni e le Attività Culturali, Archivio di Stato di Mantova.*

TABLE 3.1
Public Academy of Mantua Roll, 1624–1625

| Hour | Lecture and Texts | Jesuit Professor |
|---|---|---|
| | Morning | |
| XV | Rhetoric: Cicero, *Partitiones oratoriae* and *Pro Milone* | Giacomo Accarisi of Bologna |
| XVI | Theology: quaestiones de Incarnatione Verbi Divini and Sacramentis in genere | Francesco Rossano of Forlì |
| XVI | Natural Philosophy and Metaphysics: *De generatione*, bk. 2; *De anima*; and *Metaphysics* | Vincenzo Serugo of Forlì |
| XVI | Logic: Porphyry, *Isagoge*; Aristotle, *Categories, On interpretation,* and *Analytics* | Antonio Morando of Piacenza |
| XVII | Moral Philosophy: Aristotle, *Nicomachean Ethics* | Matteo Torto of Verona |
| | Afternoon | |
| XX½ | Poetry: Aristotle, *Poetics*; Virgil, *Aeneid,* bk. 12; and Seneca, *Medea*, in alternation | Giacomo Accarisi of Bologna |
| XX½ | Cases of Conscience: Ten Commandments | Emilio Zucchi of Parma |
| XX½ | Mathematics: Euclid, *Elements*; Clavius, *Sphaera*; & sundials* | Cesare Moscatelli of Bologna |
| XXI½ | Theology: questions on angels, blessedness, & human actions | Giacomo Filippo Trezzi of Innsbruck |
| XXI½ | Natural Philosophy & Metaphysics: same texts as taught in hour XVI | Vincenzo Serugo of Forlì |
| XXI½ | Logic: same texts as taught in hour XVI | Antonio Morando of Piacenza |
| XXII½ | Scripture: Gospel parables | Giovanni Battista Noceto of Genoa |

*Source: Ad Maiorem Dei Gloriam. Catalogus Patrum Societatis Iesu, qui in Publica Academia Mantuana a Serenissimo Ferdinando Gonzaga Duce Mantuae VI Montisq. Ferrati IV liberaliter erecta docebunt à mense Novembri Anno Domini MDCXXIV & MDCXXV.* ACM, AG, Bu. 3366, f. 103. This is a large printed sheet, 36 x 50 cm. The table conveys the information of the roll but is not a translation. Latin personal and place names have been rendered into Italian according to the best available information. Further explanation of the teaching and texts is found in chapter 8. See Appendix: Jesuit Professors at Mantua, 1624–1630, for more information about the Jesuits.

*The Latin is "docebit ELEMENTA EUCLIDIS, & SPHAERAM, & DE HOROLOGIIS SCIOTERICIS." Capitalization in the original. It is likely that "docebit . . . SPHAERAM" meant that he taught *In Sphaeram Ioannis de Sacro Bosco commentarius* (1581 with many reprints) of the eminent Jesuit mathematician and astronomer Cristoph Clavius (1537–1612) at the Collegio Romano. The *De sphaera* (written ca. 1220) by Johannes de Sacrobosco (John of Holywood, d. 1244 or 1256) was the most used and commented on astronomical work in medieval and Renaissance universities. The commentary of Clavius rejected Copernicus' heliocentric system as physically wrong. Teaching "DE HOROLOGIIS SCIOTERICIS" meant teaching about sundials, possibly how to construct and use them. Sundials did a better job of measuring time than other instruments in use at this time. I am grateful to William A. Wallace, O.P., for much of the information in this note.

with more solemn disputations on a monthly schedule and on the afternoons of feast days.[87]

Thus, the Jesuit part of the university began. It taught an expanded Jesuit higher studies curriculum of rhetoric, poetry, logic, natural philosophy and metaphysics, moral philosophy, mathematics, casuistry, Scripture, and theology, just like the program of studies of the Jesuit half of the University of Parma and perhaps the University of Ingolstadt. The professor of natural philosophy and metaphysics taught the same texts in both the morning and the afternoon, although it is likely that he lectured on different parts of the texts rather than repeating his lecture. The logician also taught the same texts in morning and afternoon, either presenting different material or repeating his lecture for different students. The humanist taught rhetoric in the morning and poetry in the afternoon. The other six Jesuits lectured once a day.

The arts and theology part of the University of Mantua was launched. Duke Ferdinando now had to create the law and medicine part of the university.

---

87. "Disputationes de questionibus Philosophicis, ac Theologicis praeter quotidianas fere, atque hebdomadarias singulis Mensibus solemniores, & Academicis diebus festis pomeridianae dabuntur." ASM, AG, Bu. 3366, f. 103, roll of the Jesuit Public Academy of Mantua of 1624–25.

CHAPTER 4

# Doctor Marta

ith the Jesuit part of the university established, Duke Ferdinando moved to complete the university with professors of law and medicine. The recruitment of these scholars began three to four years before the full university opened its doors. Duke Ferdinando and Chancellor Alessandro Striggi instructed the duke's agents and representatives to look for potential faculty members in other universities. The agents sent back reports on the abilities, ages, current positions, and possible salary demands of likely candidates. Duke Ferdinando may have played an active role in some searches, and he approved appointments.

Above all, the new university had to have two star professors, one in civil law and the other in medicine. These two men would proclaim the scholarly distinction of the university and attract students. Hence, princes and communes pursued men viewed as stars, paid them huge salaries, and endured their antics. Their presence, in turn, made it easier to attract other faculty. Ferdinando knew that if he could appoint a star civilian (expert in civil law) and a star professor of medicine, his new university would have instant credibility.

The star professor of civil law came first. From the mid-fourteenth century onward, the most important person in an Italian university was the leading professor of traditional Italian civil jurisprudence. He held the first-position ordinary professorship of civil law, teaching at a popular hour. He was more important than the professors who lectured on specialized topics in civil law or taught canon law. Indeed, he might range over the whole of the *Corpus juris civilis* and write on what he chose, including the most controversial and important legal issues of the day. Although universities might want several distinguished professors in civil law and medicine, they usually limited themselves to one star for law and one for medicine, because of their high salaries, and because university culture permitted stars to behave in ways that made it difficult for two eminences in the same subject to coexist.

Duke Ferdinando chose Giacomo Antonio Marta to be the star civil law professor. It was an excellent choice. Marta was an innovative and highly productive scholar at the forefront of the legal scholarship of his times. The topics and contents of his many legal works open a wide window into the research and teaching of law in the early seventeenth century, especially on the rights of civil rulers, something that Duke Ferdinando surely noticed. Marta published a major work on church-state jurisdiction, the most prominent and contentious legal issue of the day. He sought to overcome what he saw as a crisis in contemporary jurisprudence by trying to build a new foundation for ius commune. He taught at Italy's leading universities before coming to Mantua. But he was also quarrelsome, had spied for a foreign monarch, and had written a stinging antipapal pamphlet.

## I. EARLY LIFE AND WORKS

Giacomo Antonio Marta was born in Naples in 1557 or 1558, perhaps of affluent parents.[1] In his will Marta stated that the Jesuits raised him from the age of ten and that he had come under the protection of Father Alfonso Salmerón (1515–85), one of the original Jesuits and the leader of the Jesuit Province of Naples from 1558 to 1575.[2] In other words, Marta was probably orphaned, and Salmerón looked after the little boy. In these circumstances it is very likely that he attended a Jesuit lower school. At the age of twelve he began legal studies; he later called one Girolamo Gabriello his teacher.[3] In 1578 he published his first work, an *Apologia de immortalitate animae,* in which he defended the view that the human soul is immortal and that this can be demonstrated philosophically. He published his treatise as part of an edition of some short works of the Neapolitan Aristotelian philosopher Simone Porzio. A professor of natural philosophy at the universities of Pisa and Naples, Porzio (1496–1554) agreed with Pietro Pomponazzi (1462–1525), who argued that according to reason the soul was mortal and corruptible with the

---

1. On February 20, 1618, Marta referred to himself as being sixty years of age. Marta, 1621, sig. ):( 2 verso, dedicatory letter. In October 1621 he wrote that he was sixty-three. De Paola, 1984, 10. An agent for Duke Ferdinando Gonzaga wrote in June 1625 that Marta was sixty-seven years of age. See section 7 and note 124 below. The death notice from a Mantuan archival document stated that he died on September 22, 1629, at the age of seventy-two, which would make his birth date 1557. Paglia, 1886, 6.

2. Paglia, 1886, 8, for the text of Marta's will of 1628. There is no reference to Marta in Salmerón's published correspondence.

3. Giustiniani, 1787–88, 2:233. I have been unable to identify Gabriello. He was not a professor at the University of Naples.

FIG. 5. Portrait of Giacomo Antonio Marta by an unknown artist. Reproduced from Enrico Paglia, *Il Dottor Jacopo Antonio Marta giureconsulto napolenato giusta i documenti inediti mantovani* (Mantua, 1886). Copy of Paul F. Grendler.

body. Marta, by contrast, argued that the human soul was immortal and created in God's image; man's soul was God's partner in reason and capable of goodness. Marta used a wide variety of authors, including Cicero, Lactantius, Boethius, St. Augustine, and St. Thomas Aquinas, as well as Aristotle, Avicenna, and Averroes, to refute Porzio, Pomponazzi, and Tommaso de Vio Cajetan (1469–1534).[4]

In 1587 Marta published in Rome a defense of Aristotle against the natural philosophy of Bernardino Telesio (1509–88) of Cosenza, who lived much of his life in Naples.[5] The anti-Aristotelian Telesio rejected the Aristotelian linkage of metaphysics and physics; he emphasized sensation as the basis for understanding physical reality and developed a new philosophy of nature. Marta's work became a footnote to history, because it provoked Tommaso Campanella (1568–1639) to write his first book. In 1588 Campanella, a young Dominican monk, discovered and greatly admired Telesio's philosophy of nature. But then he came upon Marta's *Apologia;* Campanella immediately wrote a refutation, which became his first work, *Philosophia sensibus demonstrata,* written in 1589 and published in 1591. Campanella poured scorn on Marta, defended Telesio, and laid the foundations for his own philosophy of nature.[6] Marta's agreement with the Jesuits on these issues suggests that he may have attended the Society's upper-school philosophical courses at the Jesuit college in Naples.

In or about 1583 Marta went to Rome, where Cardinal Luigi Este (1538–86), a philo-French cardinal, initially supported him. Marta probably spent most of the years between 1583 and 1597 in Rome. He may also have taught civil law privately in Naples for a short time in the vain hope of getting a professorship at the University of Naples. Another report has him teaching law to applause and a high stipend at a new university in Benevento.[7] Although Benevento had no university, towns lacking one sometimes hired a legist to teach a course in *Institutes,* the introductory course in legal studies, for the benefit of

---

4. *Opuscula Simonis Portii . . . cum Jacobi Antonii Marthae . . . Apologia de immortalitate animae adversus opusculum Simonis Portii de mente humana.* Naples: Horatium Salvianum, 1578. Not seen nor located in a library catalog. But see Giustiniani, 1787–88, 2:236; Di Napoli, 1963, 374–76, who provides a short summary of Marta's *Apologia;* Garin, 1966, 2:543, 576; and Lohr, 1980, 667. For a discussion of Porzio's views, see Saitta, 1961, 355–80.

5. *Pugnaculum Aristotelis adversus principia Berardini [sic] Telesii, Iacobi Antonii Martae.* Rome: Typis Bartholomaei Bonfadini, 1587. The Indiana University Library has a copy. See also Giustiniani, 1787–88, 2:236; repeated in De Paola, 1984, 13–14; and Ascarelli, 1972, 167. Giustiniani, 1787–88, 2:237, also reports that Marta published another work in 1587: *Memoria localis. Romae anno 1587, apud Barthol. Bonfadium* in 12. No further information has come to light.

6. Bonansea, 1969, 25–26, 311 note 34.

7. Giustiniani, 1787–88, 2:234; De Paola, 1984, 15.

local youths intending to go to a university elsewhere and anyone else interested. When, where, and if he acquired a doctorate of law is not known.

Marta published two more works in Rome in 1589, one legal and the other a brief description of the Roman Curia (Curia Romana).[8] In one of them Marta stated that he was currently teaching law at the University of Rome.[9] Years later, when some at Padua questioned whether he had a doctorate, Marta again stated that he taught civil law at the University of Rome beginning in 1589.[10] His claim cannot be confirmed or denied, because rolls for the years 1588 through 1592 are missing. He does not appear on the University of Rome rolls after 1592.

At this time and later Marta called himself an "advocate [i.e., lawyer] at the Roman curia" (*in Romana curia advocati*).[11] But he never gave more precise information about his legal position or what he did. Because some of the agencies that made up the curia functioned as courts to decide disputes involving assignment of clerical offices and benefices, taxes, forgiveness of

---

8. *Tractatus de tribunalibus urbis et eorum praeventionibus . . . Doctoris Martae Neapolitam in Romana curia advocati*. Rome: Apud Marcum Antonium Morettum, 1589. Copy in the Harvard Law Library. *Epistola qua ordo theatri Curiae Romanae explicatur et virorum illustrium totius orbis terrarum notitia habeatur: quorum historiae ibidem nunc scribuntur Romae a Doctore Marta Neapolitano in eadem Curia advocato*. Rome: Apud Iacobum Ruffinellum, 1589. Copy in Yale Law Library. A third work of 1589 is sometimes listed as edited by Marta: *Decisiones R. P. D. Marcelli Crescenti Rotae Auditoris postea S. R. E. cardinalis. Doctoris Martae Neapolitani in Romana Curia advocati*. Rome: Apud Marcum Antonium Morettum, 1589. Copy in Columbia Law Library. An expert in canon law, Cardinal Marcello Crescenzi (ca. 1500–52) was an auditor of the Sacred Rota, then papal legate to the Council of Trent at Bologna, 1551–52. However, the most recent biography states that his nephew and namesake edited the volume of his opinions. Poverini Fosi, 1984, 641. Moreover, neither Giustiniani, 1787–88, nor Ascarelli, 1972, 79, list it as a work in which Marta had a hand.

9. On the basis of Marta's own words, Giuseppe Carafa, the first historian of the University of Rome, stated that Marta taught at the University of Rome in 1589. "Jacobus Antonius Marta Neapolitanus, anno MDLXXXIX. Jura in Gymnasio profitebatur, ut ipsemet asserit in epistola ad Laurentium Blanchettum, qua ei nuncupat Tractaum de Tribunalibus Urbis." Carafa, 1971 (first published in 1752), 2:417. Giustiniani, 1787–88, 2:234; and Renazzi, 1971 (first published in 1803–06), 3:37, followed Carafa.

10. Marta made this claim in his undated letter (but June 1613) to the Riformatori dello Studio di Padova in De Paola, 1984, 140 (see next note for quote). However, Marta's name does not appear in the surviving faculty rolls for the academic years 1587–88, 1592 through 1596, and 1599–1600. *I maestri di Roma*, 1991, 1:124–51.

11. For example, in 1613 he asserted that he had been both a professor at the University of Rome and an advocate at the Roman Curia: "sino del 1589 hebbi la lettura civile nello studio di Roma, e che in quell'anno stampai un trattato *de preventionib.* come Avocato di quella corte e lettore in quello studio che fù stampato in Roma dal Morelo." Marta to the Riformatori dello Studio di Padova, no date, but probably July 1613, from Padua, in De Paola, 1984, 140. He also claimed to be an advocate of the Roman Curia in the title page of Marta, 1608.

sins, marriages, dowries, the granting of favors, and much else, petitioners needed lawyers to represent them.[12] It is likely that Marta was accredited to serve clients who had cases before the curia. And he may have seen at close hand papal actions that caused him to assume antipapal positions in the future. Marta wrote some sycophantic letters claiming relationships with prominent figures. For example, in 1608 he dedicated his first major legal work to Francisco Peña (Pegna, ca. 1540–1612), at the time dean of the Apostolic Sacred Rota. Peña was the senior *auditore* (judge) in the most important court in Catholicism as well as a distinguished canon lawyer best known for his editorial scholarship on the revised edition of the *Corpus juris canonici* published in 1582. In his dedicatory letter, Marta wrote that he had been devotedly attached to Peña for twenty-five years.[13] But the nature of the attachment is unknown.

Marta left Rome in 1597 to become ordinary professor of civil law at the University of Pisa.[14] While at Pisa he published three legal works that appear to have been products of his teaching.[15] Marta left the University of Pisa in 1603, possibly because of differences with senior colleagues.[16] He probably returned to Rome as a practicing lawyer, but not as a professor at the univer-

---

12. For brief descriptions of the organization and functions of the Curia Romana, see Ojetti, 1913, and D'Amico, 1983, 19–35.

13. "[A]bhinc vigintiquinque annis devinctissimum Martam aplecti," in the dedicatory letter to "Domino Francisco Pegnae Sacrae Rotae Apostolicae Decano. Doctor Marta. S. D.," February 1, 1608, in Marta, 1608, sig. a2 recto.

14. Barsanti, 1993, 524, 547. However, Marta stated in 1613 that he became ordinary afternoon professor of civil law at the University of Pisa in 1595. Undated letter of Marta to the Riformatori dello Studio di Padova in De Paola, 1984, 140.

15. *Doctoris Martae Neapol. J. C. praeclaris. Et in almo studio Pisano juris Caesarii professoris dignissimi, hors vespertinis repetitiones in rubricam et in L. I D. solut. matrimonio.* Florentiae, apud Georgium Marescotum, 1599, as cited in Giustiniani, 1787–88, 2:237; and *Doctoris Martae J. C. praeclaris. Repetitiones in rubric. et in1. 1ff. de novi operis nunciatione.* Florentiae, apud Georgium Marescotum, 1600, copy in Harvard Law Library and listed in Giustiniani, 1787–88, 2:237; *Disputationes Doctoris Martae, quas in Circulis Pisanis anno 1599. A Mense Novemb. cum excell. collegis arguendo, et defendendo digessit.* No printer or place; Giustiniani, 1787–88, 2:237, with the first two repeated in De Paola, 1984, 15 note 26. The first two works appear to be Marta's discussions of specific passages in the *Corpus juris civilis,* and the third is probably a written version of Marta's participation in circular disputations at the University of Pisa in November 1599. At Pisa and other universities, professors and students were required to dispute with one another informally outside the classroom. See Grendler, 2002, 156. The title of the third work suggests that these particular circular disputations may have involved other members of the Pisan college of legists besides Marta.

16. Spagnesi, 1993, 247, writes that Marta battled with two senior professors, Alessandro da Rho and Girolamo Papponi, in the circular disputations, and that this was the reason for his departure. Marta, 1608, reveals that Marta often differed with his colleagues, especially with Rho. De Paola, 1984, 15–16, incorrectly states that Marta taught at the University of Pisa until 1609, then taught at the University of Rome.

## Early Life and Works

sity.[17] He suffered a financial reverse that forced him in 1608 to sell possessions and properties in Naples for 8,000 scudi to pay his creditors. But he reserved the right to buy them back when he could.[18]

Marta published his first major legal work in 1608: *Decisionum novissimarum almi Collegii Pisani, causarum delegatarum vel ad consilium sapientis transmissarum vota Doctoris Martae iurisconsulti Neapolitani in Romana Curia Advocati*, published in Venice.[19] A second, expanded edition appeared in Venice in 1614 and possibly again in 1615. The volume collected and published the opinions (decisones) of members of the college of doctors of law of the University of Pisa on which he served when he was a professor there. It was an innovative work that set the direction for one of the two major themes of his legal scholarship.

Every university town, and some non-university towns, had a college of doctors of law, either a single college for doctors of both civil and canon law or, less often, separate colleges for doctors of canon law and doctors of civil law. Each college comprised a group of men, typically ten to twenty-four in the sixteenth century but tending to increase in size, drawn from the more senior law professors from the local university and some prominent local men with doctorates in law, usually obtained at the city's university.[20] At Pisa professors of civil law, canon law, and *Institutes*, plus some local lawyers considered exceptionally meritorious, were members of the college.[21] The best-known activity of colleges was to examine candidates for doctorates in law.

Colleges of doctors of law also delivered advisory opinions on cases submitted to them by governments, courts, and individuals. At least from the reign of Duke Cosimo I de' Medici (ruled 1537–74) onward, the Medici government of Tuscany sought the views of the Pisan college on cases pending at non-Tuscan courts in which the government had an interest. It also asked the college to review sentences pronounced by Florentine courts.[22] The government viewed the Pisan college of doctors of law as a prestigious source of legal knowledge. Even though university professors held their appointments

---

17. Giustiniani, 1787–88, 2:235, states on the basis of some references to Rome in Marta, 1628, that Marta taught at the University of Rome "again." However, the surviving university rolls of this period (1603–04, 1605–07, and 1609–10) do not list Marta. *I maestri di Roma*, 1991, 1:156–71.

18. Marta's will of 1628, printed in Paglia, 1886, 9.

19. The full title gives a good description of the work. See figure 6. The Library of Congress copy has been used. It is a folio-sized volume with 338 double-columned pages plus indexes. The second edition is *Decisionum novissimarum almi Collegii Pisani, causarum delegatarum vel ad consilium sapientis transmissarum vota. Secondo impressa quibus addita sunt quiquaginta non ad huc publicata*. Venetiis: Jacobum de Franciscis, 1614. Copy in Harvard Law Library. Although Ascheri, 1989, 220, states that it was reprinted in 1615 as well, this edition has not been located.

20. Grendler, 2002, 174–75, for more information and bibliography.

21. Cascio Pratilli, 1975, 132 note 57.

22. Cascio Pratilli, 1975, 132–33.

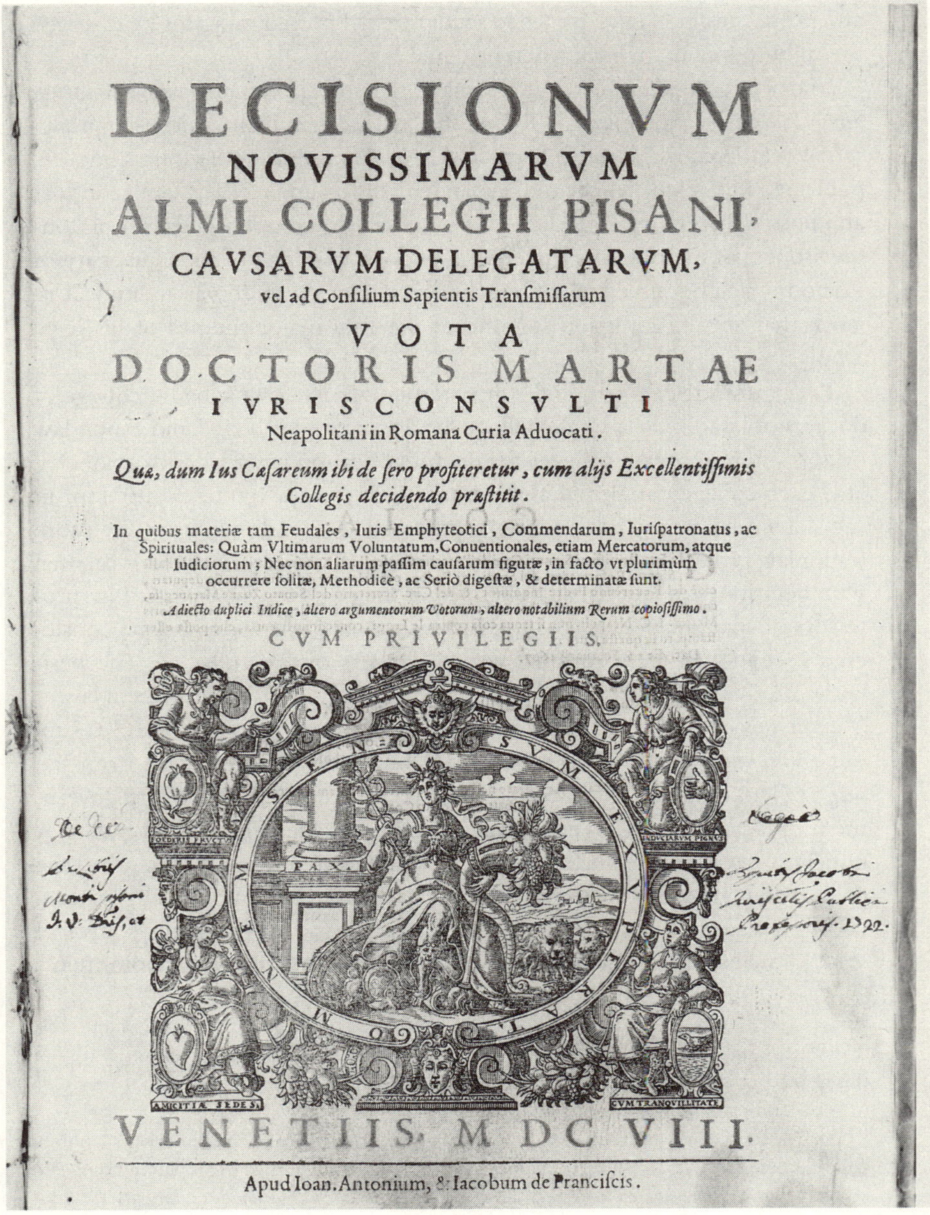

# DECISIONVM
## NOVISSIMARVM
## ALMI COLLEGII PISANI,
CAVSARVM DELEGATARVM,
vel ad Consilium Sapientis Transmissarum
## VOTA
# D O C T O R I S   M A R T A E
## IVRISCONSVLTI
Neapolitani in Romana Curia Aduocati.

*Quæ, dum Ius Cæsareum ibi de sero profiteretur, cum alijs Excellentissimis Collegis decidendo præstitit.*

In quibus materiæ tam Feudales, Iuris Emphyteotici, Commendarum, Iurispatronatus, ac Spirituales: Quàm Vltimarum Voluntatum, Conuentionales, etiam Mercatorum, atque Iudiciorum; Nec non aliarum passim causarum figuræ, in facto vt plurimùm occurrere solitæ, Methodicè, ac Seriò digestæ, & determinatæ sunt.

*Adiecto duplici Indice, altero argumentorum Votorum, altero notabilium Rerum copiosissimo.*

## CVM PRIVILEGIIS.

## VENETIIS. MDCVIII.
Apud Ioan. Antonium, & Iacobum de Franciscis.

FIG. 6. Title page of Giacomo Antonio Marta, *Decisionum novissimarum almi Collegii Pisani*. Venetiis, 1608. Apud Ioan.Antonium & Iacobum de Franciscis. *Courtesy of the Law Library of the Library of Congress.*

at the pleasure of the government, the Pisan college was also probably as objective a legal body as could be found in a hierarchical age. In the years in which Marta taught at Pisa, the college included two well-established professors of law with Italy-wide reputations, Alessandro da Rho (1548–1632) and Andrea Fachinei or Fachineo (d. 1607), plus the more junior Marta.

As the title announced, the book offered college members' opinions on legal cases presented to the college.[23] It was a legal reference work organized into 203 *vota*, that is, individual cases with the advisory opinions by members of the college concerning the relevant legal issues, with cases of similar subject matter grouped together. Each *votum* title was the legal issue or principle involved, not the individual case. Next came a summary of the legal issues listed in numbered sentences. A subsequent paragraph presented a brief summary of the case, sometimes with names and occasionally an explanatory sentence or two in Italian. But neither the agency nor the person who requested the opinion was given, nor were the opinions dated. The opinions of members of the college presented in numbered paragraphs corresponding to the sentences in the summary followed.

The cases included feudal claims and fiefs, plus emphyteusis contracts, which were long-term leases of property in which the lessee harvested crops in exchange for a small annual fee to the owner. There were *commenda* disputes: cases in which the income from a position, such as an ecclesiastical benefice, was assigned temporarily to someone other than the holder of the position. In practice, holders of positions *in commendam* often treated the income as permanent, which led to lawsuits. Other cases involved *iurispatronatus* issues (patrons and their rights and powers), wills and testaments, dowry disputes, arguments over property given to religious orders, the rights of fief holders, a small number of commercial disputes between merchants, and a few criminal cases. For example, votum 138 had as its title the legal principle that a member of a religious order accused of a crime may not be condemned by the testimony of laymen who are participants in the crime. The case concerned a clergyman who allegedly sodomized adolescent boys.[24] Votum 144 discussed whether a layperson might appeal to the pope in a fief dispute. Marta argued that the subject of a lay prince may not appeal to the pope and presented various precedents and cases to support his views.[25]

The college did not have the power to decide guilt or innocence, or to grant victory to a disputant over his rival, because it was not a court. Individuals did not appear before the college to argue their cases; nor is it clear that

---

23. The following analysis is based on Marta, 1608.

24. "Religiosus non potest condemnari ex depositionibus laicorum qui fuerunt participes criminis." Marta, 1608, pp. 123r–24r, quote on 124r. Only the recto side of a folio is numbered.

25. Marta, 1608, 139r–40r.

members of the college engaged in oral arguments with each other. Rather, it appears that the members wrote their views in response to written summaries of the cases presented to them. Finally, the college did not deliver a collective opinion endorsed by all. Instead, individual members of the college, most often Marta, Rho, and Fachinei, rendered opinions on the issues involved, garnishing their opinions with references to the works of distinguished legal scholars. In short, each votum focused high-powered legal opinion on a contentious issue.

Marta was not reticent about presenting his views. He often summarized the works of other members of the college, while presenting his opinions in more detail. His first-person singular expressions appeared throughout the work: ego credo, nec me movit, sed respondebam, dubiam, sum igitur, confirmabam in casu. Marta also made it clear when he differed with other members of the college, and he often disagreed with Alessandro da Rho.[26]

Publications of the opinions of doctoral colleges were not new, but they appeared more frequently in the early seventeenth century and had greater weight than before.[27] Even though a prince or a court rendered decisions, the advisory opinions of colleges of doctors of law might help determine the precise contents, scope, and limits of decisions. They offered a broader and deeper understanding of laws and legal principles affecting or rising from a case. Collections of opinions had more weight if the legal body was respected or represented a major state. For example, the Catholic legal world accorded considerable respect to the decisions and opinions of the Sacred Rota in Rome on ecclesiastical and other matters. The publication of the opinions of members of colleges of doctors of law may have helped to make the application of legal principles more uniform across political boundaries and different jurisdictions. At the minimum, such volumes poured more legal water into the sea of legal opinions in which lawyers, judges, and professors of law so enjoyed swimming. The book undoubtedly enhanced Marta's reputation. Indeed, this kind of publication became a signature part of his legal scholarship.

## 2. ECCLESIASTICAL AND CIVIL JURISDICTION

Marta's next work was a very large treatise on ecclesiastical and civil jurisdiction: *Tractatus de iurisdictione per et inter iudicem ecclesiasticum et secularem exercenda, in omni foro et principum consistoriis versantibus maxime neces-*

---

26. "Sed mihi, & D. Alexandro contrarium videbatur: & ideo ego respondebam, non obstare, que in eadem quantitate temporis." Marta, 1608, 11v. For the first-person singular expressions listed and others, see 2r, 2v, 3r, 4v, 17r, 21r, et passim.

27. For what follows, see Ascheri, 1989, 89–137, 148–49, 195–96, 218–23. For comments on Marta, see ibid., 91, 135, 196, 219–20, 222, 248; and Spagnesi, 1993, 247–48.

*sarius Doctoris Martae, iurisconsulti Neapolitani, in alma urbe Advocato* (Treatise concerning the exercise of jurisdiction through and between the ecclesiastical and secular judge, in every forum and especially necessary for princely consistories so occupied, by Doctor Marta, Neapolitan juriconsult and advocate in the holy city), published in Mainz in 1609. It was reprinted in Cologne, 1616; Turin, 1620; Mainz 1620; Avignon, 1620; Avignon, 1669; and Avignon, 1709.[28] It is a folio-sized book of about 775 double-columned pages, including indices and front matter, divided internally into two volumes with separate pagination. Marta dedicated volume 1 to Pope Paul V and volume 2 to Cardinal Ottavio Pallavicino.

Anything written about ecclesiastical and civil jurisdiction was guaranteed to attract considerable attention in Italy and Europe after the bitter struggle over the Venetian Interdict of 1606 and 1607.[29] In December 1605 Pope Paul V issued an ultimatum: if the Republic of Venice would not hand over for trial in a church court two clergymen accused of crimes, whom the republic intended to try in civil courts, and revoke a law asserting secular jurisdiction over clergymen accused of crimes, he would excommunicate the Venetian Senate and impose an interdict on the republic. The pope also demanded that the republic repeal laws sharply limiting the rights of church organizations to receive land bequests, to build churches, and to regain control of lands leased to laymen. Venice refused, and the pope acted on his threat in April 1606. Both sides made ostentatious preparations for war before cooler heads prevailed. In February 1607 the Venetians accepted mediation by a French cardinal, and on April 21, 1607, the pope lifted the interdict. A compromise favoring Venice was

---

28. The title page also includes the title of volume one, as follows: *Volumen primum eiusque pars prior. In quo singulorum principum iurisdictiones, e dominia tractantum, et quomodo in casibus mixtae iurisdictionis, procedendum sit, atque mandata Principum exequenda, & de Praeventionibus atque Inhibitionibus, ac Excommunicationibus ferendis, ob ipsam iurisdictionem. Discutiuntur etiam omnes artiali legum, statutorum, atque Editorum Principum secularium, an comprehendant ecclesiasticos, & eorumbone: Tractaturque de omnibus casibus iudiciorum civilium, & criminalium, inquibus subiatatur, an seculares iudices procedant contro ecclesiasticos. Cum gratia & privilegio summi Pontificis.* Volume 2 has a separate title page. It repeats *Tractatus de iurisditione* . . . as in the beginning, then adds *Pars quarta. In qua per duas Centurias casuum, discutiuntur omnes articali legum Imperialium, Statutorum, Constitutionum, & Edictorum Principum secularium, an comprehendant ecclesiastica, & eorum bona, in omnibus casibus Iudicorum civilium, & criminalium* . . . Moguntiae Ex Typographia Albini, 1609. The British Library copy is used. The list of subsequent editions comes from Giustiniani, 1787–88, 2:237; Paglia, 1886, 12; De Paola, 1984, 14–15 note 20, 243 note 1; and library catalogs. There are copies of the Turin, 1620, edition in the libraries of the Catholic University of America, University of Michigan, and Yale Law Library, plus copies of the Avignon, 1669, edition in the Harvard Law Library, Yale Law Library, and the Robbins Collection of the University of California at Berkeley Law Library.

29. There is an extensive bibliography on the Venetian Interdict and the debate over jurisdiction. Start with Pastor, 1891–1953, 25:111–83; Cozzi, 1958, 93–147; Bouwsma, 1968, 339–482; and Cozzi, Knapton, and Scarabello, 1992, 87–91, 192–93.

## *DOCTORIS MARTÆ*
# IVRISCONSVLTI
## NEAPOLITANI, ET IN
### ROMANA CVRIA
Aduocati,

## TRACTATVS

*DE IVRISDICTIONE INTER IVDICEM ECCLE-*
*siasticum, & Laicum exercenda.*

### PROOEMIVM.

Em non nouam, neque insolitam aggredimur, sed antiquis etiam Iurisconsultis placitam, Tractatum omnium practicarum quæstionum iurisdictionis inter vtrumq; iudicem, omnibus quidem exoptatum, sed quem interea nullus integrè ad effectum ducere ausus est.

    Arduum sanè opus, quod non leuiter, & perfunctoriè, vt plurimi fecerunt, sed accuratè, &, vt rei dignitas, & difficultas exigit, pertractandum est.

    Quantis enim difficultatibus inuoluta sint iurisdictionis monumenta, est explicatu difficillimum, quod quidem minimè mirandum est, nam sunt prius multa cognitione comprehendenda, sine quibus haud facile quisq; poterit ad illarum scientiam peruenire. Primū sunt omnes leges atque iudicia mente complectenda, item historiæ cognitio & totius antiquitatis memoria, quæ non solùm ex sanctis literis, verùm etiam ex Græcis & Latinis scriptoribus est diligentissimè repetenda; Nec interim disserendi facultas negligenda est, vt implicita definiendo explicari valeant, & ambigua distingui, & argumentum ratione concludi, vera denique à falsis internosci, ne videlicet veritatis locum vanitas fucata, inani q    dam specie veritatis, obtineat.

    Deinde opus est arte latius & vberius disserendi, vt facilius intelligi possit, quantis difficultatibus, & contradictionibus plena sint scripta antiquiorum Doctorum, etiam iuris canonici, qui hanc materiam sparsim aliquando tetigerunt.

    Tanta est igitur huius operis magnitudo, vt quò plura diffinias, eò maiora semper occurrant, habet enim fructuum innumerosam congeriem, vt veluti ex pingui agro, solo hærentibus seminibus, omni collecta fruge, post metentium terga spicas legere, ac ex grandi vindemia racemos carpere semper supersit, sicuti ex magno flumine noui semper riuuli renascuntur.

    Quare non est dissimulandum iis, qui vel doctrina culti, vel rerum vsu exerciti sunt, inprimis arduum, & fortè ex omni humano opere longè difficillimum fore.

    Ego Iacobus Antonius Marta, ingenio, ac doctrina me aliis inferiorem agnoscens, qui neque illius acumine, neque literarum scientia sum cum doctissimis, & eloquentissimis vllo modo comparandus, tanti operis prouinciam tentare non audebam.

    Sed quia mirantur omnes, quid est, quod pro iurisdictionis ecclesiasticæ dignitate nequaquam satis multi ingenio, & excelsa naturæ vi præstantes viri, iam inde ab initio sunt inuenti, qui vice publica commoti, eius propugnationem fortem aduersus eos suscipere voluerunt, quorum libidinoso sceleris furore, & effrenata audacia ius dicendi ecclesiæ vsurpantium, omnia diuina, humanaq; iura & Principum priuilegia insolenter violata, corrupta, atq; euersa videntur.

    Vt alios mei ordinis professores elicerem, hanc inaccessam, & præruptis viis asperam viam, primus ipse volui periclitari, ac me prætentare, atq; hominum iudiciis credere, saltem aliis ad sequendum viam aperiam: Nam si turpe est in huiusmodi causis vel inimicis negare patrocinium, quantò magis iurisdictioni ecclesiæ, & veritati?

                                    A          Lau-

FIG. 7. Proemium from Giacomo Antonio Marta, *Tractatus de iurisdictione*. Moguntiae. Typis Ioannis Albini sumptibus vero Hulderici Rewall, 1609, Sig Ar. *Copyright British Library Board. All rights reserved.*

reached. The Venetians handed over to the French king the clergymen sought by Rome but retained the laws restricting the rights of the church.

Outside Venice and Rome, the church-state issues debated by polemicists and scholars across Europe were more important than the interdict itself. They articulated with heat and in detail the complicated questions of the competing jurisdictional claims of church and state. The reasons were obvious: governments everywhere, Catholic and Protestant, were seeking to expand their control over the subjects and institutions in their states, while churchmen saw their traditional rights and liberties revoked or threatened.

Marta's treatise was not a pamphlet arguing the case of either side. Indeed, Marta never mentioned the Venetian Interdict or the conflict between the papacy and the republic; his only reference to Venice was a short chapter on Venice-imperial jurisdiction. Instead, he produced a huge legal work discussing jurisdictional issues in the broadest legal and historical context and in hundreds of theoretical legal situations.

The book had four parts. The first nineteen chapters presented Marta's historical and theoretical views on jurisdiction.[30] Marta began by recognizing the pope as God's vicar on earth and the source of all jurisdiction. He defined jurisdiction as dominion over temporal things. Because God conceded jurisdiction to Adam and then to men, it followed that God was the master of all temporal things and the source of all authority. Dominion over earthly things came from God, and no king has power over temporal things without the will of God. Marta made considerable use of the Old Testament, especially the books of Judges and Samuel in which God granted jurisdiction to priests, who then denounced or chose rulers. God wanted his people to be governed by priests, such as the prophet Elias. Marta noted that the Israelite judge Samuel, a ruler over temporal things, was a priest first. From these and other examples it followed that the church approved the Holy Roman Emperor, who was a feudatory of the church.

But then Marta narrowed jurisdiction by dividing it into the office of jurisdiction and the authority of jurisdiction. The former meant the faculty or means of administering justice and ensuring equity. The second form of jurisdiction was the power of governing the people by right and with laws. This was subdivided into spiritual jurisdiction, which he further defined as ecclesiastical jurisdiction, and temporal jurisdiction. Both came from God. Ecclesiastical jurisdiction meant the divine power delegated to Moses and ordinarily guided by Christ for the purpose of governing the faithful according to the Gospel in supernatural things and, when necessary, in temporal

---

30. Marta explained the organization of the book in his "Proemium," in Marta, 1609, vol. 1, sig. A recto-verso. The first nineteen chapters are found in vol. 1, pp. 1–39. De Paola, 1984, 17–20, 246–50, provides a useful summary.

matters. Secular jurisdiction was the divine power conceded to Moses the priest to enable men to live well according to natural precepts. It was also given to usurpers and confirmed in their successors according to the natural laws of peoples.

Because God conceded also to usurpers the faculty of legislating, it followed that one must obey unfaithful princes, because they also draw their power from God. Insofar as he discussed political philosophy, Marta endorsed the divine right of kings, probably the dominant position of his day, and rejected constitutionalism. Since the ruler's power came from God or from the church, rather than from the original consent of the people, no argument to limit or depose the ruler could be made. Subjects must obey even a bad ruler because his power came from God. The most important principle espoused in the treatise may have been that the power of temporal princes came directly and immediately from God.[31] In particular, Marta seemed almost eager, if legal writing ever can be described as eager, to affirm the rights and importance of the Holy Roman Emperor. The empire was a transmitter of divine power; the emperor was the father of all.

The pope and the emperor were the ordinary judges of men, because God delegated to them power, and they had the consent of provinces and peoples. Such power eliminated dissent and violence. Marta then passed in review authorities such as St. Augustine, who argued that there were two authorities governing the world. He noted that the pope's temporal jurisdiction in Italy was founded on the Donation of Constantine, and he cited it as a reminder that the world was ruled by two powers, king and priest.[32]

Having established that there were two authorities on earth, pope and emperor, Marta separated their spheres in ways that sharply limited the authority of the pope and church in temporal matters. He cited St. Ambrose's dictum that emperors have competence over palaces, and priests over churches. He introduced the juridical principle that if the pope were superior in all temporal jurisdiction, the law would give him authority in the appeal of sentences, which was not the case. Marta cited popes Alexander III (1159–81) and Clement V (1305–14) to support the principle that popes did not have jurisdiction beyond the Papal States and might not participate in appeals from civil judges. He noted that St. Peter ordered Christians to obey kings, even the pagan kings of those times (1 Peter 2:13–14). There cannot be two conjoined masters. Consequently, the emperor, not the pope, was master of the world.

31. De Paola, 1984, 18, makes this point.
32. That Marta accepted the Donation of Constantine is not surprising. Many legists did, partly because it offered an explanation for papal rule over the Papal State, which was a reality. For them questions about temporal power and papal jurisdiction transcended the debate concerning whether the Donation of Constantine was authentic. Antonazzi, 1985, 148–49, 167 et passim.

## Ecclesiastical and Civil Jurisdiction

Marta adduced a long series of authorities from the Old Testament, the New Testament, and the Middle Ages in support of the separation of the two and the temporal power of the emperor. Because the spiritual monarchy and the temporal monarchy were two distinct functions, they could not be combined in one person. In spiritual matters Marta noted with approval that Cardinal Tommaso de Vio Cajetan argued that the pope had the most ample authority over every temporal jurisdiction and could use it when necessary for supernatural ends. He had the power to create new princes, to remove others, and to divide empires. But then Marta added that Cardinal Robert Bellarmine had argued that the pope was not the master of all the world, but only of his own sheep, which Peter had entrusted to him. Infidels were not the pope's sheep.

Despite the complexities, to this point Marta basically argued for separation of ecclesiastical and civil jurisdiction, and he tended to deny to the church the authority to intervene in temporal matters. But then in the next chapters, Marta reversed direction to argue that popes had jurisdiction in temporal matters, citing in support a vast number of mostly medieval authorities.

However, the book was fundamentally a legal reference work, not a theoretical treatise. The rest of the huge tome dealt with precise legal questions. Some fifty-five chapters discussed mixed church and state jurisdiction.[33] On the whole, Marta favored the rights of the church more often than the state in these examples. Next came a section on the legal aspects of excommunication and interdicts, including the warnings that should be issued before they are exercised, and when they should be lifted. This was neutral legal advice. Marta defended interdicts and excommunication but set limits to their use. As noted earlier, he never referred to the recent papal-Venetian conflict. The fourth part of the book, which constituted volume two, consisted of some two hundred chapters dealing with every possible kind of civil and criminal case in which civil judges presumed they had jurisdiction over ecclesiastics, as Marta summarized it.[34] Unlike the format of the *Decisionum Collegii Pisani*, actual cases were not discussed. Instead, Marta presented one theoretical example after another to indicate the legal paths to be taken in every possible permutation of the question about whether lay courts might try clergymen. While it is difficult to generalize from theoretical examples, most of the time Marta insisted on ecclesiastical jurisdiction over clergymen. But under some

---

33. Marta, 1609, 1:156–292; the material on excommunication and interdict is found in 1:295–344.

34. "In quarta parte per duas centurias casuum discutiuntur omnes articuli legum Imperialium, Statutorum, Constitutionum, edictorumque Principum secularium, an comprehendant Ecclesiasticos & eorum bona, atque disputatur de omnibus casibus iudiciorum civilium & criminalium in quibus seculares iudices putant habere iurisdictionem in ecclesiasticos." Marta, 1609, vol. 1, Proemium, sig. A verso.

circumstances he permitted civil courts to try clergymen, a principle that Paul V rejected. In one example he argued that the secular court might punish a clergyman who committed murder if the ecclesiastical court first passed sentence.[35] To some extent he restricted the actions of clergymen in the civil sphere. Because Marta was a legal scholar rather than a political theorist, it should not be expected that the book would be internally consistent. Overall, perhaps the strongest message of the book was to narrow the practical applicability of ecclesiastical jurisdiction.

Like the learned jurisconsult that he was, Marta drew fine distinctions, took note of different legal circumstances, and demonstrated his comprehensive knowledge of biblical, canonical, historical, theological, and legal precedents and sources. He heaped up citations. As a master of the literature, Marta probably enjoyed giving references and examples supporting both sides of the issue, a tradition stemming from the *sic et non* nature of scholastic legal reasoning. Legal scholars and political theorists probably found the book a storehouse of distinctions and references that could be used to support either civil or ecclesiastical jurisdiction, depending on the particular dispute. This was one reason for writing the book; the other was to boost Marta's reputation. The four additional printings of the work that appeared between 1616 and 1620 suggest that he succeeded in reaching both goals.

Despite dedications to the pope and a cardinal, and many pages supporting ecclesiastical jurisdiction, the papacy was not happy with the book. On April 2, 1610, the Congregation of the Index placed the book on the Index of Prohibited Books for its "many errors" in matters of faith.[36] Possibly Marta's argument that a ruler's temporal authority came directly from God was what

---

35. Marta, 1609, vol. 2, casus 129, pp. 222–23. See also cases 126 and 127, pp. 218–20. In addition, Marta argued that lay courts might try clergymen in a minority of the cases numbered 150 through 200, pp. 184–314.

36. See *Index,* 2002, 592, for the date of the decree, but without the text of the decree, which has not been located. The prohibition was reaffirmed on July 3, 1623, and repeated in subsequent indices including the revised *Index* of 1758. See *Index,* 1758, 173. Hence, some scholars have mistakenly concluded that 1623 was the date of condemnation. However, the letter of Cardinal Scipione Borghese, the papal secretary of state, to Berlinghiero Gessi, the papal nuncio to Venice, September 20, 1614, Rome, confirmed that the Congregation of the Index condemned the book at the earlier date and gave as a reason the "many errors in matters of faith": "Della causa dello sdegno, et malignità del Marta, qui si crede, che V. S. sia stata altre volte informata. Tuttavia a cautela se le dice di nuovo, che costui stampò un libro a favore della giurisdittione ecclesiastica, qual libro essendo stato visto, et censurato dalli Cardinali della Congregatione sopra l'Indice, et trovato in esso molti errori etiam in cose di fede, fu dalla medesima Congregatione prohibito per editto publico, di che lui sdegnato, et vedendosi caduto dalle speranze di premio, che pretendeva per detto libro, ritiratosi a Padova, dove è stato condotto a leggere, ha prorotto in queste sue essorbitanze, et dato *in reprobum sensum.*" Quoted from Savio, 1955, 63 note 2.

the Congregation of the Index found objectionable. But it is not clear that Marta viewed his book as challenging papal jurisdiction; he may have seen himself as presenting a nonpartisan scholarly analysis of complicated legal issues. As a scholar Marta resolutely followed arguments to their logical conclusions without necessarily realizing how readers in the real world might react to his words.

After the publication of the *Tractatus de iurisdictione*, Marta turned sharp critic of Rome. Evidence of Marta's new attitude appeared in August 1611, when he wrote an unflattering assessment of Pope Paul V and eleven new cardinals created on August 17, 1611, for the English ambassador to Venice, Sir Dudley Carleton (1573–1642), who forwarded it to London.[37] Marta may have been in Venice at this time. When the papacy became aware of Marta's antipapal views, it concluded that the reason was disappointment. Papal authorities believed that Marta had hoped for a Roman reward, perhaps a university professorship, for his book, and when it was not forthcoming, they concluded that he turned against the papacy and sought patronage elsewhere.[38] The charge of pique over thwarted ambition cannot be rejected out of hand, but Marta may also have become increasingly angry and disenchanted with papal jurisdictional and political policies, plus Roman nepotism and simony.

What the papacy found objectionable in *Tractatus de iurisdictione*, the Republic of Venice welcomed. Marta came to the attention of Paolo Sarpi, the intellectual leader of the antipapal group of senators and others in Venice. It is likely that they met at about this time. Even though Sarpi did not cite Marta's *Tractatus de iurisdictione*, he must have known it. On April 12, 1612, Sarpi wrote a *consulta* (a brief combining historical, legal, and political matters in support of a course of action) for the Venetian Senate defending Venetian dominion over the Adriatic Sea, a perennial point of contention with the papacy, because the Papal State also bordered the Adriatic. Sarpi defended Venetian rights over the Adriatic on the basis of concessions that Pope Alexander III allegedly granted to Venice in 1177, but which the papacy viewed as legendary, plus imperial privileges given to Venice. Sarpi mentioned Marta as a legal authority who counseled the republic to use the imperial concession to defend its jurisdiction over the Adriatic.[39] Although Sarpi did not cite any works of Marta, in a short section of the *Tractatus de iurisdictione* Marta wrote that Venice was free of imperial jurisdiction and that the Venetians had dominion

---

37. The document is printed in De Paola, 1984, 55–57; see also 22–23.

38. Savio, 1955, 63 note 2.

39. "Anzi il dottor Marta consiglia la Republica a guardarsi dal dire di dominar il mare per altro titolo che per privilegio imperiale, perché ogn'altro sarebbe usurpativo e tanto peggiore quanto più antico." Sarpi, "Scrittura seconda che tratta del titolo del legitimo dominio sopra il mar Adriatico. 1612, 12 april," in Sarpi, 1969, 627.

over the Adriatic Sea.[40] Sarpi also listed Marta as one of twenty-three living and dead jurisconsults, including the revered Bartolo da Sassoferrato (1313/14–57) and Baldo degli Ubaldi (1327?–1400), who supported Venetian claims.[41] This was high praise by association.

Thanks to the *Tractatus de iurisdictione* and Venetian support, Marta obtained a professorship at the University of Padua, a prize in the Italian academic world. In 1611 Sebastiano Montecchio, who had filled the position of first afternoon professor of canon law at the University of Padua since 1582, died.[42] For his replacement, the Venetian government wanted someone who would interpret canon law and deal with jurisdictional issues in ways compatible with the stand taken by the government during the interdict. This mattered, because many young Venetian nobles, the future rulers of the republic, plus men from the Venetian state, Germany, and elsewhere, studied in Padua. The two major candidates were Marco Antonio Pellegrino (1530–1616) of Padua, holder of the first morning professorship of canon law since 1603, and Marta. Sarpi and several influential Venetian patricians with fervent antipapal views did not believe that Pellegrino supported civil jurisdiction strongly enough. Indeed, he had clashed with Sarpi on a point of canon law.[43] By contrast, they saw Marta as a learned scholar with the right views. They prevailed, and the Venetian Senate chose him in the fall of 1611.[44] Marta

---

40. After presenting a short history of Venice based on ancient works, the history of Venice by Marco Antonio Sabellico, and the *Supplementum chronicarum* of Jacopo Filippo Foresti, Marta wrote, "Venetias liberas dicunt ab Imperiali iurisdictione." A little later he wrote, "Veneti sunt etiam Domini maris Hadriatici." Marta, 1609, part 1, chapter 33, pp. 96A, 97B. The same can be found in Marta, 1669, same pagination.

41. Sarpi, 1969, 630.

42. For what follows, see Tomasini, 1986, 240, 246; Facciolati, 1978, part 3, 82–83, 94; Savio, 1955, 62; and Cozzi, 1958, 130–32; Reinhard, 1969, 213–14; and De Paola, 1984, 21–22.

43. Pellegrino served as a legal consultant to the Venetian government during the interdict and after. He and Sarpi clashed when advising the collegio, the executive committee that acted as the cabinet for the senate. Pellegrino reportedly said that the relevant canon made it very clear that the church had jurisdiction in the matter at issue and that he, at the age of eighty-one, would be endangering his soul if he told them differently. The collegio rejected his advice and relieved him of his position as consultant. Since Pellegrino, born in 1530, said that he was eighty-one at the time, the clash occurred in or about 1611, after the interdict. See the letter of Nuncio Berlinghiero Gessi, August 3, 1613, Venice, quoted in Savio, 1955, 62 note 6. Although the issue on which they differed is unknown, it must have been of some importance. Otherwise, the senate, which respected age, might have appointed Pellegrino, with the expectation that he would soon die.

44. Two of the three Riformatori dello Studio di Padova, the magistracy of Venetian senators who oversaw the university and recommended the appointment of Marta to the Venetian Senate, were strongly antipapal. They were Nicolò di Zuanne Donà and Agostino di Zorzi Nani. For a brief biography of Donà, see Grendler, 1979, 336; for Nani, see Grendler, 1990, 83–84. The views of the third riformatore, Francesco Contarini, are unknown. For the senate action, including the names of the Riformatori appointing Marta, see Cozzi, 1958, 131 note 2 and 132 note 1; see

received a four-year contract at a salary of 650 Paduan florins, the same as his predecessor. It was a good salary, but far from the highest among the professors of law.

### 3. A SPY FOR JAMES I

At the same time that he taught law at the University of Padua, Marta began a second career as a spy. He secretly gathered information and passed it on to Sir Dudley Carleton, English ambassador to the Republic of Venice.[45] Marta also communicated directly with James I, king of England and Scotland.

On June 19, 1612, Marta wrote to both James I and Carleton, offering to inform them regularly about what was happening at the papal court. He promised to provide information on papal policies, its correspondence with other nations, and its aggressive plans.[46] James I accepted Marta's offer because it would fill a need. England, a Protestant state, had no diplomatic ties with the papacy or any other Italian state except for Venice. Hence, Carleton had to gather information for all of Italy. Marta would be a big help.

From June 1612 through May 28, 1615, Marta's correspondence with the English came to 120 letters: 81 from Marta to Carleton and 1 to Carleton's secretary, 7 from Marta to James I, 5 from Marta to the secretary of James I, 22 from Carleton to Marta, and 4 letters of Marta and Carleton to other parties.[47] The vast majority of letters, including those of Carlton to Marta, were written in Italian; a few were written in Latin, and some parts of some letters used a simple code in which a two-digit number represented an individual. The surviving documentation does not include *consulti* that Marta may have written at Carleton's request. Carleton's gondolier and sometimes his secretary carried the letters back and forth between Padua and Venice. Because poling a gondola between Venice and Padua through the Brenta Canal would have been very slow, the gondolier probably rode a horse.

James I paid Marta good money for information about the papacy because he wanted to create an alliance of Protestant and Catholic states against Spain and the pope, whom he considered an ally of Spain. Ambassador Carleton was an orthodox predestinarian Calvinist who labored tirelessly on behalf of

---

also Reinhard, 1969, 213–14. The vote was overwhelming: seventy-nine in favor of Marta, two opposed, and nine abstentions. Of course, most recommendations from the Riformatori dello Studio di Padova for professorial appointments passed by wide margins.

45. For Carleton, see Reeve, 2004. The on-line version is at www.oxforddnb.com.libproxy.lib.unc.edu/view/article/4670.

46. Marta to James I and Carleton, June 19, 1612, Padua, in De Paola, 1984, 58–60.

47. The correspondence from the Public Record Office in London is printed in De Paola, 1984, 58–215.

James' scheme. So did Paolo Sarpi, who collaborated with Carleton in an effort to persuade the Venetians to join an anti-Spanish alliance.[48]

Because he lived in Padua, Marta could not personally gather information in Rome or anywhere else. So he organized, directed, and paid people who lived in Rome and elsewhere to gather information. Marta evaluated the intelligence, then gave Carleton a summary with commentary. The only informant whom Marta ever named was his "secret correspondent" in Rome, one Francesco Visdomini, described as a most noble Milanese gentleman.[49] According to Marta, Visdomini was an old Vatican hand. He first served as secretary to the cardinal of Como, Taddeo Galli (1526–1607), a prominent cardinal since the 1560s. He then served as secretary to Cardinal Michelangelo Tonti (named cardinal 1608; died 1622), who held an important office under Paul V until 1611, when he had a falling out with Cardinal Scipione Borghese and left Rome. Marta wrote in April 1614 that Visdomini currently lacked a position but was courting Cardinal Scipione Borghese (1578–1633). As Paul V's nephew and secretary of state, Borghese was the second most important person in Rome, and Visdomini was trying to attach himself to his *familia*, the laymen and clerics who assisted a cardinal in his political, religious, ceremonial, and cultural duties. In addition, Visdomini had a cousin who was *maggiordomo* (head servant) to a member of the Aldrobrandini family, which included Cardinal Pietro Aldrobrandini (1571–1621), cardinal nephew and secretary of state for Pope Clement VIII (ruled 1592–1605), and still a powerful figure in Rome.[50] Marta also had contacts in Milan, ruled by Spain, who provided intelligence from that city.[51] And on one occasion a Paduan priest who spent time in Mantua passed on information from Mantua and Casale Monferrato.[52] Others may also have worked for Marta.

The English crown thought highly enough of Marta's information to pay

---

48. See the correspondence between Sarpi and Carleton, August 12, 1612, through October 1615, along with the excellent notes of Gaetano and Luisa Cozzi, in Sarpi, 1969, 635–719.

49. "Io scrissi in Rome per haver un corrispondente secreto, e con 400 scudi l'anno, quanti Vostra Eccellenza mi disse, s'haveria il Secretario Visdomini, gentilhuom nobilissimo Milanese, il quale fù secretario del Cardinale di Como, e poi è stato secretario del cardinal Tonto, e poi ch'il cardinale Tonto fù disgratiato, esso si licentiò della sua servitù, et hor non stà con nissuno, ma corteggia il card.le Borghese." Marta to Carleton, April 6, 1614, Padua, in De Paola, 1984, 170. In a letter of April 18, 1614, no place, Marta gave Visdomini's first name as "Francesco." De Paola, 1984, 173. For another reference to Visdomini's information, see Marta to Sir Ralph Winwood, July 11, 1614, Padua, in De Paola, 1984, 183.

50. "Questo Visdomini hà un suo cugino, ch'è maggiordomo dell'abbate Aldobrandino qui, e per mezzo suo hò tentato questo trattato." Marta to Carleton, April 18, 1614, no place. De Paola, 1984, 173.

51. "Io hò inteso per letter d'amici di Milano." And "Di Milano anco si scrive." Marta to Carleton, May 8, 1613, Padua, in De Paola, 1984, 114, 115.

52. Marta to Carleton, May 10, 1613, Padua, in De Paola, 1984, 116.

him handsomely: 50 ducats per month, a total of 1,200 ducats for the period October 1, 1612, through September 30, 1614.[53] And the payments probably continued into the first few months of 1615. This was 14 percent more than his academic salary, and law professors were paid well.[54] But Marta may not have realized much profit, because he had to pay his informants. He paid Visdomini 400 scudi (a scudo was worth about the same as a ducat) per year, some of which Visdomini may have dispersed to others.[55] In other words, two-thirds or more of what Marta received from the English crown went to members of his network.

The first major issue about which Marta provided intelligence was the attitude of the papacy toward the proposed marriage between Prince Henry (February 19, 1594–November 6, 1612),[56] the oldest son of James I, and Caterina de' Medici, sister of Cosimo II de' Medici, grand duke of Tuscany. For some time James had been seeking a marriage alliance with a major Catholic ruling family, and the Medici were such a family, not least because Marie de Médicis was the queen of France. Such a marriage would be a large step toward his dream of becoming the mediator between Protestant and Catholic Europe and would provide a large dowry for the king, who was always short of funds. The marriage would harvest more prestige and money than marriage to a daughter of the king of Sweden or Denmark or a daughter of a German Lutheran prince. Most important, it had the potential to change the religious and political map of Europe, because in the normal course of events Henry Stuart and Caterina de' Medici would become king and queen of England and produce children. Such a marriage had the potential of being the first step toward bringing England back into the Catholic fold, a goal for which the papacy and many in England and the continent hoped. Fearing such an outcome, Protestants, including Carleton, opposed the marriage. But Caterina would have to get papal permission to marry a Protestant; would the papacy approve, and under what conditions?

53. For the letters concerning payments, see Marta to Carleton, January 8, 1613, Padua, which established the payment as 600 ducats per annum; Marta to James I, January 15, 1613, Padua; a note by Carleton concerning payments to Marta, no date, but probably early 1614, no place; and Marta to Carleton, September 14, 1614, Venice, in De Paola, 1984, 87, 92, 175–76, and 188–89. Although Marta wrote "scudi" in the first letter, all the other letters refer to ducats.

54. Marta received 650 Paduan florins annually for teaching, because University of Padua professors were paid in Paduan florins rather than Venetian ducats. See Grendler, 2002, 22 note 55. The Venetian ducat of account was worth 6 lire 4 soldi (20 soldi = 1 lira), while the Paduan florin was worth only 5 lire. Thus, Marta's academic salary yielded 3,250 lire (650 × 5) annually, while spying for the English earned 3,720 lire (600 × 6.2), which was 14 percent more. To be sure, law professors could earn additional income through private tutoring, examining degree candidates as members of colleges of doctors of law, and writing *consilia* for clients.

55. Marta to Carleton, April 6, 1615, Padua, in De Paola, 1984, 170.

56. The birth and death dates of Henry come from De Paola, 1984, 73 note 6.

On July 15, 1612, Marta assessed papal opinion for Carleton. He reported that the cardinals were divided. Some favored the marriage, believing that the Medici princess might be permitted to remain Catholic in such a union. But canon law prohibited marriage between spouses of different religions, and Cardinal Bellarmine had written against such unions. And there was the question of the religion of their children. In Marta's opinion, the majority of the cardinals did not think that Paul V would grant the necessary papal dispensation for the marriage to take place.[57] In the end, no decision was needed, because Prince Henry, never strong, suddenly died on November 6, 1612. Caterina de' Medici married Ferdinando Gonzaga on February 5, 1617.

The most important issue on which Marta reported directly involved Mantua. When Carlo Emanuele I, duke of Piedmont-Savoy, invaded Monferrato on April 23, 1613, Spain objected to the aggression, because if Casale Monferrato fell, the door would be open for the French to invade Spanish-held Lombardy. So, Spain attacked Piedmont-Savoy. Carlo Emanuele I responded by loudly proclaiming a war of Italian liberation against the Spanish tyrant. Soon France and Venice became diplomatically involved, and everyone sought the support of the papacy.[58] The struggle soon became more diplomatic than military, and Rome was a good listening post.

From May 1, 1613, through May 1615, Marta sent the English ambassador letter after letter with information about the actions and stances of the parties involved based on his sources in Rome, Milan, and Mantua.[59] He had agreed to send two letters per month, and he often sent more. Marta reported that the papacy wished to remain neutral, that the governor of Milan would not let Mantuan troops pass through Lombardy to attack Piedmont-Savoy without permission from Spain, and that Ferdinando Gonzaga lacked money. Marta frequently reported on the number of troops available to the various parties and presented other information, sometimes in code. The Mantua-Piedmont-Savoy-Spanish war was the most important event about which Marta gathered and passed on information.

Not only did Marta provide information, he gave James I advice. In a letter to the king of June 6, 1613, Marta combined information with strategic counsel. He began by announcing that the war offered the opportunity for an

---

57. Marta to Carleton, July 15, 1612, Padua, in De Paola, 1984, 67–68. See also Pastor, 1891–1953, 26:190–91.

58. For a good military and political account, see Quazza, 1950, 408–19. For papal policy during the War of Monferrato, see Pastor, 1891–1953, 25:420–22.

59. See Marta to Carleton, May 1, 8, 10, 12, 21, 28, and July 20, 1613; January 27, March 8, September 2, 9, 21, November 21, December 12, 1614; January 25, 26, 29, February 19, April 9 (two), May 3 and 28, 1615, in De Paola, 1984, 111–12, 114–16, 118, 129–30, 139–40, 155–56, 168, 191–93, 196, 197, 200, 203–12, 214. It appears from some of Carleton's letters to Marta that there were other letters from Marta that have not been located.

# A Spy for James I

alliance of all Christians, Catholics and Protestants alike, against the barbarous tyrants and perverse and vicious ecclesiastics. The barbarous tyrants were the Spanish, and the perverse and vicious ecclesiastics were the pope and cardinals. Marta saw Spain and the papacy working hand in glove, an assessment not shared by modern scholars. Marta described nefarious deals that the Spaniards and the pope allegedly had made. He assured James that to escape Spanish rule, the people of Naples, Marta's native city, would happily become subjects of the English king.[60] Above all, he urged James to assist the duke of Piedmont-Savoy. Then with the king's help, a council with authority over the pope could be called to deal with the Roman thieves. The barbarous tyrants would be extirpated, he concluded.[61]

Marta advised what the king desired. James I sought to forge a grand anti-Spanish alliance consisting of England, the United Provinces of the Netherlands, the German Protestant Union of Halle, three Protestant Swiss cantons, and the Catholic states of Piedmont-Savoy and Venice. But it did not come to pass. All that James I could produce for Piedmont-Savoy was a little money. After a while Carlo Emanuele I could no longer afford to keep troops in the field, and the war sputtered on at a reduced level, as the sides engaged in protracted peace negotiations.

As a legal scholar, Marta had hoped to profit from the dispute over Monferrato in another way. Kings and princes laying claim to disputed territories sought legal support. In January 1613 Carlo Emanuele I sent an emissary to Marta asking him to write a *consilium* in support of his claim to Monferrato. It was a complex case. The duke claimed Monferrato for his three-year-old granddaughter, Maria Gonzaga, based on an investiture originally conferred by Holy Roman Emperor Otto II (ruled 967–983) and renewed by other emperors. The consilium would have to be a legal and historical brief following a legal thread through a tapestry of centuries, the kind of research that Marta loved. But he needed permission of the University of Padua college of doctors of law to undertake the commission, and the college, following orders from Venice, said no. The reason was political. If the college or individual professors offered legal advice concerning disputes involving other states, the Venetian government feared that this would be viewed as reflecting the republic's views and compromising its neutrality. Marta had to forego a fee of 100 ducats.[62]

In addition to the war, Marta provided information to James I on other

---

60. The idea was not as far fetched as it sounds. In their anti-Spanish revolt of 1647 the Neapolitans declared Naples a free republic under a Frenchman, Henry of Lorraine, Duke of Guise. Quazza, 1950, 505, 507–11.

61. Marta to James I, June 6, 1613, Venice, in De Paola, 1984, 131–34.

62. Marta to Carleton, January 8, 1613, Padua, in De Paola, 1984, 87–88.

matters. He reported what he heard about the pope's diplomatic leanings and rumors about elevations to the college of cardinals. He faithfully reported every illness or rumor of illness of Paul V.[63] On January 31, 1615, the father general of the Society of Jesus died. Marta reported that France wanted the Jesuits to choose a Frenchman as successor, and Spain wanted a Spaniard.[64] The astute Jesuits elected an Italian, Muzio Vitelleschi. In addition to the military information, which was obviously important, much of what Marta reported consisted of opinions and rumors about the actions and intentions of governments; the health and inclinations of rulers; the comings and goings of diplomats; and rumors of future appointments. Some of the information was clearly significant and useful; other tidbits did not rise above gossip.

At a time when many individuals in courts across Europe passed on information to foreign diplomats, the distinction between espionage and the lesser but still culpable act of acquiring and selling information to a foreign ruler was not always obvious. It depended greatly on the relationship between the states involved and the attitudes of governments toward those who clandestinely gathered and passed on information.

Marta's actions should be seen as espionage for several reasons.[65] He secretly gathered information about the papacy and passed it on to England, which was hostile to the papacy. Although not at war with each other, England and the papacy adhered to opposed, and sometimes warring, diplomatic alliances. Above all, they were on opposite sides of the religious fence. James I persecuted English Catholics at various times in his reign and barred them from communicating with the pope. For these reasons, the papacy viewed Marta's spying as a hostile act. In addition, Marta's actions were unlawful in the eyes of the Venetian government. It punished even senators for passing on information to foreign powers or engaging in unauthorized contacts with the agents of foreign rulers.[66] If the Venetian government had discovered Marta's activities, it would have punished him. At the minimum, it would have forced him to stop. Finally, Marta relayed to James I military information in a time of war. Governments then and now take a dim view of the delivery to foreign governments of information about the numbers and movements of troops, even if the troops are those of another power.

Marta provided intelligence to Carleton at the rate of three to six letters per month through January 1615. But Carleton cooled toward Marta. In June

63. See, for example, Marta to Carleton, May 28, 1615, in De Paola, 1984, 213.
64. Marta to Carleton, February 19, 1615, Padua, in De Paola, 1984, 208.
65. For a succinct description of Renaissance espionage, see Jensen, 1999.
66. The Venetian government imposed fines, exclusion from offices for several years, exile for years or permanently, imprisonment, and in at least one case death on those caught passing information to foreign governments. Grendler, 1979, 322–23 note 58; and Queller, 1986, 194–95, 212–24.

# A Spy for James I

1614 he complained to Marta that while much of his information from Rome was "good and authentic," some of it was simply "talk and inventions," of which he already had an abundance in Venice. Moreover, Carleton did not like Marta writing directly to the king and his minister in London, and he had become weary of Marta's battles with his academic colleagues.[67] Carleton left it to his secretary to reply to Marta from June 1614 onward. In late January 1615, James I ordered Carleton to go to Turin to try to negotiate peace between Piedmont-Savoy and the Spanish governor of Milan, and he left in February.[68] Marta continued to write to Carleton, but the letters dwindled: one in February, two in April, and two more in May, the last on May 28, 1615.[69]

Marta's spy career continued with the next ambassador, Sir Henry Wotton (1568–1639), famous for his pun, "An ambassador is an honest man sent to lie abroad for the good of his country."[70] He arrived in Venice on June 9, 1616. Marta went to Wotton with a new scheme. He had a plan for a council of Greek bishops, and he wished Wotton to meet two Greeks, one a bishop in the Greek Orthodox Church. The proposed council of Greek bishops would transfer much papal authority to the patriarch of Constantinople. It would also reexamine canon law, the decisions of the councils of Florence (1438–45) and Trent (1545–63), "where the suffrages [votes] were not free," and papal claims that it had the power to depose kings. In other words, it would be a church council that would revisit the decisions of Florence and Trent and sharply restrict papal authority. Marta gave Wotton a list of more than a hundred Greek bishops who were prepared to attend such a council.[71] Wotton told Marta that he would have to consult with the king. Instead, he talked to Sarpi and his follower Fulgenzio Micanzio (1570–1654). They were skepti-

---

67. "Quanto a gli avisi di Roma sono sicurissimo per molti argomenti, che Ella me ne fara parte quando sono buoni et autentichi. Però s'ella gli indica più tosto discorsi et inventionj che cose sode e realij, fa meglio assai di non mandarli, perche di robba cosi fatta non ci è mai carestia in Venetia." Carleton to Marta, June 8, 1614, Venice, in De Paola, 1984, 177. See also Carleton to Lord Somerset, June 24, 1614, Venice, in De Paola, 1984, 178–79.

68. One may follow Carleton's movements in the notes to the Sarpi-Carleton correspondence in Sarpi, 1969, 691–94.

69. De Paola, 1984, pp. 207–15.

70. Wotton's famous quip was a pun because "lie" at that time had two meanings: to reside and to tell a falsehood. Indeed, Wotton often used "lie," meaning "reside," in his correspondence. For an example see Smith, 1907, 2:98. But in 1604 he wrote it for a friend in Latin, in which the pun disappears: "Legatus est vir bonus peregre missus ad mentiendum rei publicae causa." "Mentior" has only one meaning, to tell a falsehood. When Wotton's quip (in Latin) was relayed to James I, the king was not amused, and Wotton's career suffered a temporary halt. Loomie, 2004, 379–80. Also on Wotton, see Curzon, 2003. This was Wotton's second posting to Venice; he had been ambassador to Venice from 1604 to 1610.

71. Wotton to James I, August 9, 1616, Venice, in Smith, 1907, 2:98. The Old Style date, which was ten days behind, has been converted to New Style.

cal, and Wotton relayed their doubts to James I.[72] The proposed council of Greek bishops did not happen.

Although he dismissed the idea of a council of Greek bishops, Wotton told the king that he expected to be able to use Marta "in some things" and would keep him on the payroll. Since Wotton paid Marta 300 ducats in September 1616, and more money in June 1618, it is likely that Marta continued to spy for England, at least until Wotton left Venice in May 1619.[73]

### 4. THE *SUPPLICATIO AD IMPERATOREM* . . . *CONTRA PAULUM QUINTUM*

In addition to spying for the English, Marta published a virulent anonymous attack against the papacy. In October 1612 Marta wrote to James I about a new book by an unknown author that argued for calling a general council of the Catholic Church. It was his own work. In December he gave the manuscript to Carleton, who forwarded it to London, where James read it. The king was very pleased with the work and instructed Carleton to put Marta under his protection. In April 1613 Marta was happy to learn that the book had been published in London.[74] The book was *Supplicatio ad imperatorem, reges, principes, super causis generalis concilij convocandi. Contra Paulum Quintum* (Supplication to the emperor, kings, and princes, concerning the reasons for calling a general council. Against Paul V), published in London, 1613. It is a small octavo of thirty pages of text plus introductory matter.[75] The dedicatory letter to James I was signed by "Novus Homo," who was Marta.

The expanded title of the English translation of 1622 gives a better idea of the contents of the work: *The New Man, or a supplication from an unknown Person, a Roman Catholicke unto James, the Monarch of Great Brittaine, and from him to the Emperour, Kings, and Princes of the Christian World. Touching the causes and reasons that will argue a necessity of a Generall Councell to be forthwith assembled against him that now usurps the papall Chaire under the name of Paul the fifth. Wherein are discovered more of the secret Iniquities of the Chaire and Court, then hitherto their friends feared, or their very adversaries did suspect. Translated*

---

72. Wotton to James I, August 9, 1616, Venice, in Smith, 1907, 2:99.

73. Wotton to James I, September 2, 9, 1616, and June 11, 1618, in Smith, 1907, 2:101, 104, 141.

74. Marta to James I, October 1, 1612, Padua, and no date (but December 1612), no place; Carleton to Marta, January 5, 1613, Venice, informing Marta of the king's approval; and Marta to James I, April 24, 1613, Padua, in De Paola, 1984, 71, 83, 84, 109.

75. The copy examined is in the Rare Book Room of the Library of Congress. De Paola, 1984, 215–42, also provides the complete text. Some library catalogs attribute the book to other authors, such as Martinus Becanus (1563–1624). Incidentally, while Pastor, 1891–1953, 25:69 note 3, did not know the name of the author of the *Supplicatio*, he shrewdly guessed that it came from "Sarpi's milieu."

into English by William Crashaw, Batchelour in Divinity, according to the Latin Copy, sent from Rome into England, published in London, 1622.[76]

In the dedicatory letter, Marta, in the guise of Novus Homo, addressed the king, saying that it was now clear that the Church of Rome suffered greatly from simony and other crimes of the current pope, and no one in Rome was willing to rectify matters. Hence, God had stirred up the New Man to write down all the reasons why a general council of the church should be summoned to purge the Church of Rome. Novus Homo was sending the king this supplication, which he should give to the emperor and the other kings and princes of Europe.[77]

The sweeping argument of the pamphlet was that Sixtus V, Clement VIII, and Paul V, who ruled from 1585 through 1613, were not true popes because they were fraudulently elected. (Marta did not discuss four short-lived popes, Urban VII, Gregory XIV, and Innocent IX, who succeeded one another from September 15, 1590, through December 30, 1591, and Leo XI, who lasted seventeen days in April 1605.) Since they were not true popes, the cardinals whom they created were not true cardinals. Moreover, Paul V had engaged in nepotism and simony on a grand scale. Only a general church council could set the church right. Because the pope and the cardinals were not legitimate, they could not summon it. But the emperor had the power and the duty to call a general council to deal with a corrupt papacy. The pamphlet combined conclave stories, detailed accusations of simony and nepotism, personal attacks against Paul V and Cardinal Scipione Borghese, conciliar history and theory, and legal arguments and citations.

Marta began with an account of the election of Sixtus V in 1585, alleging that Sixtus V (1585–90) bought the papacy with the aid of Cardinal Luigi Este, Marta's early patron, and a promise to make a key supporter a cardinal. Marta alleged that Clement VIII (1592–1605) and Paul V (1605–21) also became popes as a result of conclave misbehavior by them and their supporters. Marta argued that canon law authorities decreed that the crime of simony invalidated papal elections. Hence, Sixtus V, Clement VIII, and Paul V were not true popes and had no power to create cardinals. Marta next turned to Paul V's alleged simony and nepotism. He charged that the pope auctioned off church benefices while retaining part of the income; he described the procedures used and gave examples with monetary figures. According to Marta,

---

76. The copy used comes from the Harvard University Library and is available through Early English Books Online, STC 1705.5. Other copies can be located in various libraries. It is a small duodecimo book of sixteen pages of introductory matter, including table of contents, and forty pages of text. There were two printings of the 1622 edition with very minor differences that do not affect the content. In the discussion that follows, references are made to all three versions: the 1613 Latin edition, De Paola's reprint of the text, and the 1622 English translation.

77. Marta, 1613, sig. A3r–v; De Paola, 1984, 217–18; Marta, 1622, sig. B recto–B2 verso.

# THE
# NEVV MAN

OR,

A SVPPLICATION FROM AN
vnknowne Perſon, a Roman Catholike vnto
IAMES, *the Monarch of Great Brittaine,* and
from him to the Emperour, Kings, and Princes of the Chriſtian World.

*Touching*

The cauſes and reaſons that will argue a neceſſity
*of a Generall Councell to be forthwith aſſembled a-
gainſt him that now vſurps the papall Chaire
vnder the name of Paul the fifth.*

Wherein are diſcouered more of the ſecret Iniqui-
*ties of that Chaire and Court, then hitherto their friends
feared, or their very aduerſaries did ſuſpect.*

Tranſlated into Engliſh by *William Craſhaw,* Batchelour in Di-
uinity, according to the Latine Copy, ſent from
*Rome* into *England.*

LONDON,
Printed by *Bernard Alſop,* for *George Norton,* and are
to bee ſold in *Diſtaffe-lane,* at the ſigne of
the *Dolphin.* 1622.

FIG. 8. Title page of Giacomo Antonio Marta, *The New Man*. London: Bernard Alsop, 1622. *Courtesy of the Houghton Library, Harvard College Library. STC 1705.5.*

Paul had diverted much church income to his nephew Cardinal Scipione Borghese.[78]

Marta also criticized Paul V for failing to defend the rights of the church. He used the case of the Venetian Interdict to charge Paul V with surrendering church rights and jurisdiction to the civil power. After listing the Venetian laws that provoked Paul V to impose the interdict, Marta argued that the pope moved too slowly and in a cowardly fashion against Venice. Then he withdrew the interdict without obtaining his goal. Marta went on to say that governments in Milan, Florence, Lucca, and Naples had so encroached on the rights and immunities of the church that papal authority was as weak in Italy as it was with the heretics.[79] In other words, Paul V was weak as well as illegitimate and corrupt. Practically the only charge that Marta did not level against Paul V or any other pope was sexual immorality. He did accuse two unnamed contemporary cardinals of incest, of having sexual relations with their brothers' wives, and of sodomy, meaning homosexuality.[80]

The remedy for a corrupt papacy was to call a general council to set matters right, including deposing the pope, Marta continued. But an illegitimate and sinful pope and his cardinals could not judge themselves. Because the power of the people resided in the emperor, he could and must convoke a council. Marta offered examples from the early Christian era of emperors who convened church councils, beginning with Constantine the Great, who called the Council of Nicea in 325. Marta then rejected the argument that emperors did not have the authority to convene councils. A general council of the church has its power and authority immediately from God without the mediation of the pope; the council represented the whole church, whose head was Christ. Only it could make the church right, Marta concluded.[81]

Several aspects of the treatise were noteworthy. As in his letters about papal politics, Marta demonstrated an insider's knowledge of the workings of the papacy, in this case conclave politics and the personalities and techniques involved in buying and selling benefices.[82] He placed enormous importance on the rights and powers of the Holy Roman Emperor, a theme that ran through his legal writing. The emperor was the most important civil ruler, one whose authority rivaled the pope's. Finally, although the pamphlet in-

---

78. At this point the English translation added that it was a common trick for popes and cardinals to describe their own bastards as the children of a brother or sister. Marta, 1622, 27–28. This passage is not found in the original Latin version.

79. Marta, 1613, 18–19; De Paola, 1984, 232–33; Marta, 1622, 33–35.

80. Marta, 1613, 21; De Paola, 1984, 235–36; Marta, 1622, 40.

81. Marta, 1613, 26–30; De Paola, 1984, 239–42; Marta, 1622, 51–56.

82. Comparison of the accounts of the conclaves of 1585, 1592, and 1605, in Marta, 1613, and Pastor, 21:8–22; 23:6–18; 25:28–37, demonstrates that Marta had a good knowledge of some of the major events in these conclaves. Of course, his interpretation was different from Pastor's.

cluded personal attacks, it was mostly a legal treatise full of legal citations and references to previous councils. Marta the polemicist remained Marta the legal scholar.

The call for a general council was not new. The most recent ruler to do so was James I, who, through emissaries, proposed a general council to Pope Clement VIII in 1603 and spoke of it publicly in 1604. However, James wanted to invite representatives from the magisterial Protestant churches, and his goal was religious union between Catholics and Protestants under the diminished authority of the pope. Pope Clement VIII imposed conditions that James would not accept, while James played a double game of paying respectful homage to the pope, while denouncing him elsewhere and continuing to harass and persecute English Catholics. Nothing came of the king's call for a council.[83]

Marta had different aims. He never raised the issues of restoring Christian unity or inviting Protestants to attend. Marta was not sympathetic to, or very interested in, Protestantism at any time in his writings. Rather, he saw a general council as a means of deposing a corrupt pope and purifying the leadership of the Catholic Church, a goal that was closer to the goals of fifteenth-century conciliarists. Marta's *Supplicatio* gave evidence of the continuing importance of conciliar ideas in the works of antipapal writers of the early seventeenth century.[84]

But calling on the emperor to convene a general council to deal with papal corruption was unrealistic. Emperor Matthias (1557, ruled 1612–19) had more pressing matters as Europe lurched toward the Thirty Years' War. Most important, a church council would have been enormously divisive within Catholicism when it had recovered the initiative in the battle against Protestantism. Marta's plea that the emperor must and could convene a church council manifested nostalgia for a bygone era.

Marta's reasons for writing the *Supplicatio* were probably mixed and not always lofty. A whiff of opportunism rises from the book, because Marta wrote something of which James I approved, even though the king's idea of the council's purpose was different. Marta certainly was angry with Paul V, possibly because of the condemnation of his *Tractatus de iurisdictione*, perhaps for other reasons stemming from his years in Rome. He expressed himself in hyperbole and overstatement, which was common in contemporary polemics. Nevertheless, it is also likely that he was genuinely outraged by the grand-

---

83. Pastor, 1891–1953, 24:54–62, 70–80, esp. 78; Willson, 1956, 219–22; Patterson, 1997, 35–43.

84. Oakley, 2003, 141–81, demonstrates that supporters of the English Oath of Allegiance, defenders of Venice in the interdict crisis, and French Gallicans used conciliar ideas as they promoted civil jurisdiction and attacked the papacy.

scale nepotism and simony of Paul V and Cardinal Borghese, by the conclave bargaining that produced popes, and perhaps by other papal maneuvers.[85] His passion for the law and its observance led him to criticize popes when, in his opinion, they violated the law.[86]

The book's strong criticism of the papacy found appreciative readers in northern Europe. In late 1613 and early 1614 a Jesuit in Mainz wrote to Cardinal Bellarmine in Rome that the *Supplicatio* was widely read.[87] An expanded French translation appeared in Leyden at the end of 1613, and reprints of the Latin edition appeared in Augsburg and Heidelberg in 1614.[88] The papacy tried to stop its circulation by writing to inquisitors in Italy and papal nuncios in Venice, Graz, Luzerne, Paris, Cologne, Vienna, and Spain, ordering them to get the work banned. The results were not very satisfactory. Then the nuncio to Cologne had an agent buy all available copies on sale at the Frankfurt book fair, and he managed to get about 650 copies of the various editions.[89]

By June 1614 the papacy had concluded that Marta was the author of the *Supplicatio* and that he was spying on the papacy for the English, although it could not determine the identity of his Roman informant(s). The papacy responded with a carrot. Cardinal Scipione Borghese, whom Marta had criticized so strongly, thought that disappointment become rage had motivated Marta to attack the papacy. He had expected a reward for publishing the *Tractatus de iurisdictione,* but the Congregation of the Index had prohibited the book. So Borghese told the nuncio to Venice to drop hints to Marta that major honors and rewards, such as a professorship at the University of Rome, might be his if he would return to Rome. The nuncio doubted that Marta

---

85. For a detailed study of nepotism and papal financial practices during the pontificate of Paul V, see Reinhard, 1974. See also Pastor, 1891–1953, 25:59–72.

86. The *Supplicatio* was not Marta's only projected polemical writing at this time. In 1613 and 1614 he told Carleton and James I that he had begun to write two works, one in Latin, the other in Italian, defending the Oath of Allegiance that James I had imposed on English Catholics in 1606 in the wake of the Gunpowder Plot. Marta to Carleton, March 27, Padua, to James I, April 24, 1613, Padua, and to Carleton, March 2, 1614, Padua, in De Paola, 1984, 45, 107, 109–10, 166. But nothing more is known of them, which suggests that Marta did not finish them.

87. Reinhard, 1969, 207–08.

88. Nicolas de Marbais, who rejected Catholicism to become a Protestant, produced the expanded French translation, which added more alleged crimes of the popes and cardinals and criticized papal temporal pretensions. See Patterson, 1997, 120, and Reinhard, 1969, 206 note 108. For the Augsburg, 1614, Latin edition, see Reinhard, 1969, 208 note 129. Marta reported that German students at the University of Padua had told him that the book had been reprinted in Heidelberg under a slightly different title, *Novus et Magnus homo per extinctione sedis apostolicae romanae.* Marta to Carleton, August 8, 1614, Padua, in De Paola, 1984, 185. Reinhard, 1969, 226 note 242, also mentions this edition but under the authorship of Adamo Multei at Heidelberg. Neither Reinhard nor I have been able to examine any of these editions.

89. For the full story, see Reinhard, 1969, 190–210.

would come, and he was right.[90] As time passed, the papacy instructed the nuncio to keep it informed of Marta's movements, especially if he decided to leave Padua for another Italian state or Germany. The papacy may have hoped to arrest him if he ventured into a state where it had influence.[91]

Spying for a Protestant monarch and attacking the papacy raise the questions, was Marta a secret Protestant? Was he angling for a handsome offer from James to come to England, where he would change religion in return for a court appointment or a professorship at Oxford or Cambridge? The answers are "no" and "very unlikely." Denouncing papal corruption and policies did not make Marta a Protestant. Nor did his opponents and associates think that he was. Papal representatives did not believe that Marta was a secret Protestant and only briefly entertained the idea that he would move to Germany or England.[92] Other negative evidence comes from the fact that the strongly Calvinist Carleton and Marta never discussed apostasy, religious matters, or a move to England in their correspondence.[93] It was strictly politics. Marta reveled in his roles as spy and self-appointed counselor to the king; he avidly sought the king's favor and took his penny. But why would he want to move to England? What role could he play at the English court, far from Rome and Italy? Nor would a regius professorship attract him, because continental scholars looked down on Oxford and Cambridge as minor provincial universities. A professorship in England did not begin to compare with one at Padua. There is no sign that Marta was an apostate-in-waiting.

It is more likely that Marta dreamed of a purged papacy through the agency of emperor and council. His knowledge of the medieval legal tradition and respect for the rights of the emperor suggest nostalgia for the Middle Ages, a time in which emperor and pope shared authority in such complicated ways that only a brilliant legal scholar such as Marta could give guidance. Marta showed himself to be a learned, combative, self-confident, and opportunistic legist pursuing a dream.

## 5. WAS DOCTOR MARTA A DOCTOR?

While Marta played a role in international politics by spying and writing against the papacy, his professorship was threatened at home. Members of the University of Padua college of doctors of law charged that Doctor Marta, as he always signed himself, did not have a doctorate. Hence, they argued, he

---

90. Savio, 1955, 63 note 2, with a quotation from a letter of Cardinal Scipione Borghese, September 20, 1614, Rome.

91. Savio, 1955, 63–65, 73–74 note 3; Reinhard, 1969, 214, 217–18, 221, 225, 228, 235.

92. Reinhard, 1969, 220.

93. By contrast, James I invited Sarpi to come to England. Sarpi, 1969, 637–38, including note 5.

had obtained his professorship under false pretenses and should be deprived of it, as well as expelled from the college. A fellow Neapolitan, Jacopo Gallo (1544–1617), led the attack. Gallo taught at the University of Naples from 1563 to 1591, then practiced law in Rome, was a professor at the University of Messina in 1596, argued a case in Rome in 1602, and then was appointed first-position afternoon ordinary professor of civil law, the most important law professorship, at the University of Padua in 1602.[94] He probably knew Marta in Naples or Rome and may have been in a position to investigate whether Marta had a doctorate. In December 1612 Marta's critics took their case to several authorities: the college of doctors of law, the Riformatori dello Studio di Padova, and the Venetian governors of Padua, who often weighed in on university matters. Marta asked Carleton for help, and Carleton instructed his secretary to speak to the Riformatori on Marta's behalf.[95]

Shortly thereafter the Venetian government issued a ducal letter stating that Marta was to be considered a doctor because he had taught civil law at the University of Rome from 1589 onward. Moreover, the Riformatori declared that Marta had been an advocate at the Curia Romana and had published a legal treatise at that time.[96] In other words, the Riformatori avoided a categorical affirmation that he had a doctorate but did state that other legal organizations had recognized him as a doctor of law, and therefore the Paduan college of doctors should as well. This was pretty strong support.

Nevertheless, the persecution, as Marta saw it, continued.[97] Marta pleaded his case to the members of the college of doctors in a speech of an hour and a half on August 14, 1613, which he briefly summarized in a letter to the Riformatori dello Studio di Padova. Marta claimed that evidence of his doctorate could not be located because the documents of Rome's college of doctors of law were scattered among various notaries.[98] In other words, he implied that

---

94. Gallo received a salary of 1,400 Paduan florins, more than twice Marta's. Facciolati, 1978, part 3, 136; and Grendler, 2002, 124–25. Unfortunately, the *Dizionario biografico degli italiani* does not offer a biography of this important legal scholar.

95. Carleton to Marta, December 8, 1612, Venice, and Marta to Carleton, December 12, 1612, Padua, in De Paola, 1984, 74–76.

96. Marta to the Riformatori, no date, but ca. August 1, 1613, in De Paola, 1984, 140–43. While Marta did publish the work that he mentioned, *Tractatus de tribunalibus urbis et eorum praeventionibus*, 1589, as noted in section 1, no documents have been located to confirm or disprove that he taught at the University of Rome. Nevertheless, it is important that the Venetian government cared enough about Marta to support him. Sarpi and the antipapal senators probably rallied to Marta's defense.

97. The inventory of his goods after his death included a folder of manuscripts entitled "Persecutio Patavina." Paglia, 1886, 24.

98. "E perche nè anco di questo si contentavano et volevano fede del mio Dottorato che per esser de tanti anni non si trovava nota nello Collegio di Roma (perche quelle scritture sono state solite maneggiarsi da diversi Notari)." And "la quale dice che fatta diligenza nelle scritture dello

he received a doctorate in Rome. Moreover, he continued, the University of Pisa, which appointed him in 1595 (the correct date was 1597), plus the Pisan college of doctors of law and Ferdinando I de' Medici, grand duke of Tuscany, had all recognized him as a doctor. His numerous publications testified that he had a doctorate, and most Italian princes with whom he had negotiated addressed him as Doctor Marta. Marta concluded that he had been recognized as a doctor for twenty-eight years. Thus, if Marta's assertion is true and his chronology accurate, he received his doctorate or recognition of the same in 1585 at the age of twenty-eight.

Either Marta persuaded the Paduan college, or it bowed to pressure from the Venetian government, because it declared his claim of a doctorate to be valid and ordered his adversaries to be silent. Moreover, the *podestà* of Padua, one of the two Venetian governors of the city, threatened to imprison any students who harassed Marta. Marta credited Carleton for the podestà's intervention.[99]

But the question remains: did Doctor Marta possess a doctorate? Some of his omissions and statements suggest that he did not. If Marta did earn a doctorate whose record could not be located, one would think that he would have a copy or it or a document from a notary attesting that he had a degree with relevant data. And, so far as is known, Marta did not provide any information about the date, place, examiners, promoters, or witnesses of his doctoral examination and conferral of the degree, in his correspondence or in his books. Moreover, a close reading of his letters reveals that he claimed that notice of his doctorate could not be located in the notarial records of Rome's college of doctors of law. This was not the same as claiming that the University of Rome acting through the Roman college of doctors of law had conferred the degree. He may have meant that he acquired it elsewhere. If so, where? So far as can be determined, he never referred to any other university. Nor did he name any professors as his teachers, which was unusual reticence at a time when men were eager to claim connections with famous legists.[100]

Of course, he might have received his doctorate from a count palatine. Count palatine doctorates cost considerably less and had less prestige than doctorates conferred by a university college of doctors. But they were recognized.[101] However, Marta did not say that he had a count palatine doctorate

---

Collegio di Roma non se ritrova nota del mio Dottorato." Marta's undated letter to the Riformatori dello Studio di Padova in De Paola, 1984, 140–43, quotes on 141 and 142.

99. Marta's letter to the Riformatori, no date, and four letters to Carleton: no date, August 14, September 7, 1613, and no date, all from Padua and Venice, in De Paola, 1984, 140–48. See also Reinhard, 1969, 216.

100. The only teacher to whom Marta referred was Girolamo Gabriello, possibly from Naples, who has not been identified. Giustiniani, 1787–88, 2:233.

101. For count palatine doctorates and other alternate paths to the doctorate, see Grendler, 2002, 180–86.

The *Compilatio totius iuris ex universi orbis* 117

either. In short, there is the strong possibility that Marta had no doctorate. He may have believed that his legal practice in Rome, his prodigious legal scholarship, and his professorships more than justified calling himself a doctor of law even if he lacked the degree. Indeed, Marta always signed his books and letters Doctor Marta, rather than Giacomo Antonio Marta or Marta.

Marta continued to enjoy the favor of the Venetian government. In 1615 the senate raised his salary from 650 florins to 800. When Gallo, his enemy, died in the spring of 1617, Marta was appointed second-position afternoon ordinary professor of civil law at 800 Paduan florins beginning in the autumn of 1617. Even though his salary remained the same, this was a promotion, because civil law ranked higher than canon law. Moreover, Marta had no concurrent (someone who lectured at the same hour on the same texts).[102] He was the de facto leading civil law professor at Padua until the eminent Giulio Pace (1550–1635) was appointed to Gallo's first position in 1620.

## 6. THE *COMPILATIO TOTIUS IURIS EX UNIVERSI ORBIS*

Even as he spied for England, attacked the pope, battled the college of doctors of law, and wrote consilia,[103] Marta published prodigious amounts of legal scholarship. In 1614, he published *Tractatus de clausulis,* a treatise on the construction and interpretation of legal clauses in canon law, Roman law, and feudal law.[104] It was reprinted in 1615, 1616, 1618, and 1638. Marta dedicated the book to Nicolò di Zan Gabriel Contarini (1553–1631), a strongly antipapal Venetian senator with ties to Sarpi, who was elected a Riformatore dello Studio di Padova in 1614 and eventually became doge. Contarini had helped Marta get his professorship in 1611 and may have supported Marta in the battle

---

102. The various appointment notices are found in Facciolati, 1978, part 3, 94, 136, 142; and Tomasini, 1986, 246, 256, 258. The information is not always consistent.

103. There are several consilia in which Padua and the college of doctors of law of Padua are mentioned in Marta, 1628, 155r–v, 158v, and 166r–v.

104. The Venice edition of 1615 clearly states that it is the second edition: *Tractatus de clausulis: de quibus in omnibus tribunalibus hucusque disputatum est . . . cum plurimis additionibus primum impressus, nunc secundo editus cum novis atque omnibus clausulis ad feuda & ultimas testantium voluntates pertienentibus . . . a Doctore Marta.* Venice: Apud Iacobum de Franciscus, 1615. It is a folio-sized volume with a red and black title page and 364 double-columned pages. The copy used is in the Robbins Collection of the University of California, Berkeley, Law Library. Although Giustiniani, 1787–88, 2:237, stated that the first edition appeared in Venice in 1612, no copy has been located. It is far more likely that the first edition appeared in Venice in 1614, or possibly early 1615. This is because Marta referred to a disputation by students in his home in 1614: "Ideo hoc anno 1614 . . . disputavi Quaestionem . . . dominis scholaribus domi meae dicta vi." Marta, 1615, 86A. Other reprints of the work are Rome: Andrea Phaei, 1616, copy in Harvard Law Library; Cologne: Petrum & Iacobum Chovet, 1618, copy in Harvard Law Library; and perhaps Bracciano: A. Phaei, 1638. Giustiniani, 1787–1788, 2:237.

against his enemies in the college of doctors of law. The dedication letter added more evidence that Marta had the support of influential antipapal circles in Venice and Padua. Marta praised Cesare Cremonini, professor of natural philosophy at the University of Padua, and Santorio Santorio (1561–1636), an innovative medical scholar who was appointed first ordinary professor of medical theory on the same day as Marta was appointed to his position. Santorio was a Sarpi intimate and supported some measures that the papacy opposed; Cremonini, while ferociously antipapal, was not a close associate of Sarpi.[105]

Marta's *Tractatus de clausulis* discussed the definitions and uses of legal phrases following the order of the *New Digest*, books 39 to 50 of the *Digest* of the *Corpus juris civilis*. In each case, Marta listed the legal clause followed by a definition, then explanation about how and where it had been used. Many examples with references to numerous past and present legists and a limited number of judicial bodies, including the Roman Rota, followed. Most examples were dated and ranged from 1575 to 1609. Marta discussed the use of legal clauses in emphyteusis contracts involving church lands, inheritances through legitimate marriages, fief issues, and so on. He devoted a large section to *plenitudo potestatis* (the fullness of power), perhaps the most famous phrase in the *New Digest*. Marta provided a definition, then noted that the prince possessed plenitudo potestatis, allowing him to take away a fief from its holder for the public good and so on. Many uses, meanings, and variations followed. Several indexes helped make it a useful reference volume.

Then in 1620 Marta published his largest, and most innovative and important, legal work: *Compilatio totius iuris controversi ex omnibus decisionibus universi orbis, quae hucusque extant impressae a Doctore Marta Neapolitano*, published in Venice in six folio-sized volumes of about 1,828 pages.[106] The title of its reprint of Frankfurt, 1621, gives a better idea of the ambition and scope of the work: *Totius iuris controversi scientiae, ex omnibus decisionibus universi orbis, quae*

---

105. Undated dedicatory letter of Marta to Nicolò Contarini in Marta, 1615, sig. 2r–v. On Contarini's career, see Cozzi, 1958, with his support of Marta and election as a Riformatore dello Studio di Padova on p. 132. Favaro, 1966, 2:308 confirms his election as a riformatore on September 6, 1614. For relations between Sarpi and Contarini, and Sarpi and Santorio, see Sarpi, 1969, ab indice. For more information on Santorio and his medical research, see Grmek, 1981, and Siraisi, 1987, ab indice.

106. The title is taken from the edition published in Venice by the Giunta Press (Apud Iuntas) in 1620, and described in Camerini, 1962–63, part 2, number 1228, pp. 334, 336. However, the title given by Camerini does not appear to be complete, nor does he give much more bibliographical information. Some scholars following Giustiniani, 1787–88, 2:237, mention a first edition published in Venice in 1611. Spagnesi, 1993, 248, is an example. However, Marta's preface, "Ad lectores, iuris studiosos," is dated February 20, 1618, Padua. See Marta, 1621 (the Frankfurt edition), at sig. ):( 2 verso. Moreover, Marta did not mention the *Compilatio* in his correspondence with Carleton and others between 1611 and 1615.

*hucusque impressae fueret: a Doct. MARTA NEAPOLITANO iureconsulto veridico summo pratico, ad instar Digestorum Imperialium nova methoda compilata, sex tomis distincta. Quorum Primus Iudiciorum Civilium, Secundus Criminalium, Tertius Contractuum, Quartus Feudorum, Quintus Ultimarum Voluntatum, Sextus Beneficialium, & Spiritualium materias continent, atque totam legalem scientiam complectuntur.*[107] It was reprinted again in Frankfurt in 1680 and 1681.

This massive and original work was one of the first efforts to surmount what some jurists saw as a crisis in ius commune, which might also be called university law.[108] Irnerius (ca. 1055–ca. 1130), Bartolo, Baldo, and many others developed ius commune. The term meant an accepted group of legal principles, practices, and procedures derived primarily from ancient Roman law and supplemented by material from canon and feudal law. It gave lawyers and judges the tools to find their way through the thickets of different kinds of local law (statutory, communal, monarchical, ecclesiastical, and customary) found in European states and other entities as they litigated or adjudicated cases and issues. Because legal scholars and practitioners considered ius commune to be universally applicable, universities across Europe taught it from the late Middle Ages through the seventeenth century. Over time ius commune became more important than local law, whatever its form. It enabled Europe to develop a common legal culture.

But some legists, including Marta, believed that ius commune was in a state of crisis as the seventeenth century began. From the late Middle Ages onward, legal scholars had been interpreting the meaning of legal doctrines in their consilia, monographs, and collections of *opiniones* (interpretations of legal axioms and principles in specific circumstances). The vast amount of legal scholarship produced more confusion than agreement, in the view of Marta and others, because it clouded the meaning of principles, the very thing that ius commune sought to overcome. Lawyers and jurists needed more certainty.

One way to achieve certainty and order was to let the sovereign, that is, the ruler and occasionally the legislature, resolve controversial legal questions. Some favored this approach in an age of absolutism.[109] Another way was to look to major tribunals.[110] To restore certainty, some scholars partially turned

---

107. The British Library copy is used. For the third printing, not seen, see Ascheri, 1989, 222.

108. Bellomo, 1995, is a stimulating treatment of ius commune; as is Fasolt, 2007, 115–22, who uses the term "university law." Each has much additional bibliography. Ius commune based on ancient Roman law was quite different from English common law, which asserted that all Englishmen, and especially the House of Commons that represented them, inherited some common rights and privileges from the historic past.

109. Birocchi, 2002, 271; Fasolt, 2007, 126–28.

110. Most of what follows is based on the long chapter about collections of tribunal decisions in the seventeenth and eighteenth centuries in Ascheri, 1989, 85–183, and the comments of Birocchi, 2002, 269–71.

away from doctrinal law—law taught as ideal principles—in favor of studying the decisions and opiniones of judges. The way that high civil courts understood and applied legal principles might offer a disinterested application of ius commune. This jurisprudence might provide a common understanding of disputed legal principles, because courts and judges were expected to apply legal principles impartially over a broad spectrum of cases. Moreover, because the state had expanded its control over the lives of its inhabitants so much, its courts had considerable practical authority.[111] The Roman Rota, the highest court in the Catholic Church, played the same role in ecclesiastical matters. The views of judges on tribunals offered hope of getting beyond what Marta and others saw as confusion in ius commune. So a few legal scholars collected and published the opinions of judges and tribunals. The practice was not completely new but was done more often and with keener purpose in the early seventeenth century.

Marta's *Compilatio* must have been the largest and may have been the most important collection of the opiniones of tribunal jurists. After Marta's introductory chapters, the six volumes presented thousands of short statements, sometimes maxims of legal principles, found in the decisions and opiniones rendered by jurists in tribunals across Europe.[112] Marta did not publish entire legal decisions of the tribunals or present the opinions of several jurists about the same case, as he did in the volume of *Decisiones* of the College of Pisa. Rather, he presented short statements of forty-nine legists who served on thirty-six European tribunals, plus some found in the anonymous collective decisions of legal bodies such as the Roman Rota. Many of the legists quoted were jurists who served on tribunals outside Italy. These included the Imperial Camera; judicial bodies from the kingdoms of Aragon, Catalonia, Corsica, Portugal, and Lithuania; and others from the cities of Bordeaux, Grenoble, Leipzig, and Toulouse. Legists from tribunals and the occasional legislative body in Piedmont, Genoa, Venice, Mantua, Bologna, the Marches, Florence, the Roman Rota, Naples, and Sicily provided Italian representation. The volumes quoted a few famous Italian names, such as Alessandro da Rho, Antonio Tesauro (1526–93), and "Doctor Marta of the College of Pisa."[113]

Significantly absent from the list of jurists quoted were famous past and present professors of law. For a long time Renaissance legists had quoted the legal treatises and consilia of the great Italian teachers of *mos italicus,* from Bartolo da Sassoferrato and Baldo degli Ubaldi of the fourteenth century through Carlo Ruini (ca. 1456–1530), Filippo Decio (1454–1536), and Andrea

---

111. See the comments of Brockliss, 1996, 605–6.
112. The following discussion is based on Marta, 1621. See also Ascheri, 1989, 91–93, 135, 218–19, 222, and Birocchi, 2002, 271–74.
113. "Doctoris Martae, ex Collegio Pisano." Marta, 1621, sig. ):( recto.

## The *Compilatio totius iuris ex universi orbis* 121

Alciato (1492–1550) of the sixteenth. Marta, by contrast, collected and edited the wisdom of jurists serving on contemporary legal bodies. It was still traditional Italian jurisprudence based on Roman law. It did not present new ideas about natural law that some legists of the late seventeenth century developed. But it took much greater account of the practice of tribunals and helped internationalize Italian jurisprudence. Moreover, Marta's approach did not concede to rulers the power to make decisions in disputed areas.

Marta also innovated by organizing the legal statements in the same general sequence as found in Justinian's *Digest*: civil law, criminal law, contracts, fiefs, testaments, and benefices and other religious matters.[114] He provided some theoretical discussion at the beginning of sections and, never modest, argued that his work presented the nucleus of a new *Digest*.[115] He stated that he had spent twenty-one years preparing the work, and that the material had been drawn from twenty thousand books of jurisprudence.[116] Even allowing for exaggeration, it was a massive work, made larger by extensive indexes. His intention was to reduce to a unitary body the jurisprudence of the *Corpus juris civilis* as corrected and reformed by contemporary tribunals. The result was a large reference work that may have approximated his goal and that certainly gave proof of Marta's large vision and great industry.

The restless Marta sought to advance his academic career by telling people he was in demand. In June 1612, after only one academic year at Padua, Marta told Carleton that he had been offered the first ordinary professorship at the University of Pavia at double his current salary.[117] But he did not move. Then when Paul V died on January 28, 1621, papal anger over the *Supplicatio* expired with him, and Marta did move. In the fall of 1621 or sometime in 1622, Marta became first-position afternoon professor of civil law at the University of Pavia at a salary of 4,800 Milanese lire, which was about 800 scudi.[118] This

---

114. Marta explained his aims in the introductory material, where he discussed the order of his "very new *Digest*" and how it compared with the original *Digest*. Marta, 1621, sig. ):( 3 v– ):( 4 r.

115. "Nomina iurisconsultorum ex quorum decisionibus compilatio Digestorum Novissimorum facta est." Marta, 1621, sig. ):( r.

116. "Iurisprudentia igitur composita, in lex partibus quanto maiori potuit facilitate perfecto in uno & viginti annis consumata"; "ex illis legibus definiri possunt, neque ex viginti mille Iurisprudentiae libris qui passim circumuoluuntur." Marta, 1621 ed., sig. ):(4 recto, columns 1 and 2. One wonders if the 20,000 "books" might be 20,000 individual opiniones.

117. Marta to Carleton, no date or place, but about June 19, 1612, in De Paola, 1984, 62.

118. See *Memorie di Pavia*, 1970, part 1, 88. A brief notation confirms his position and adds that he taught at Pavia from 1622 to 1625 "con grosso stipendio." For his salary at Pavia in 1625, see Giovanni Domenico Verasio to Duke Ferdinando, June 1, 1625, Pavia, in ASM, AG, Bu. 1756, f. 722r, and printed in Paglia, 1886, 16. (Because the archive has been reorganized since 1886, Paglia's archival references are no longer useful.) It is more likely that Marta began teaching at Pavia in late 1621 rather than in 1622, because Facciolati, 1978, part 3, 142, wrote that Marta died in 1621. Although he did not die, he must have stopped teaching at Padua at that time for Facciolati,

was a more prestigious position than he held at Padua with a slightly higher salary.[119]

While at Pavia he published two more legal works. The first was his 1622 lectures at Pavia on marriage laws.[120] The second was a comprehensive treatise on inheritance and succession, with a great deal of material on wills, legacies, and *fidecommissi* (inheritances entrusted to one party on condition that they be transferred to a third party in due course).[121] It was a folio-sized book of six hundred pages sometimes published in two volumes. Since wills and testaments were an important part of legal practice in a litigious age, the substantial size of the book was not surprising. It was reprinted in Lyon, 1627, and in Venice, 1666 and 1680–81. In addition, Marta wrote at least one consilium for the government in Milan.[122]

### 7. THE MOVE TO MANTUA

Now in his mid-sixties, Marta was a well-established and highly productive scholar who held the leading law position at an important Italian university. He had written a substantial work about the most important legal issue of the day, church-state jurisdiction. He led the attempt to establish ius commune on the more certain foundations of the opinions of tribunals. And he had published large works on legal clauses and testaments, bread-and-butter issues for the working lawyer. There were very few contemporaries with comparable scholarly records. He had also anonymously attacked the papacy and spied for a Protestant monarch, although few knew this. Marta was ambitious, volatile, secretive, and quarrelsome, traits that did not disqualify him for positions, because many other legists were no different. Duke Ferdinando

---

who was normally accurate, to make this statement. Hence, it is likely that Marta left Padua for Pavia in 1621.

119. A Paduan florin was worth 5 lire. Hence, he earned 4,000 (800 × 5) lire at Padua. For further explanation concerning the calculation of University of Padua salaries, see Grendler, 2002, 22 note 55.

120. *Praelectiones papienses perlegendae in tuto anno scholastico MDCXXII a mense novembris, super1. de divisione,1. si anti nuptias,1. fructus,1. divortio.* Pavia: publisher unknown, 1622; not seen, copy in Harvard Law Library.

121. The title is often shortened to *Summa totius successionis legalis. . . . In quibus universa materia ultimarum voluntatum, testamentorum, legatorum, fideicommissiorum, aliarumque successionum.* The edition examined is Marta, 1666, copy in the Robbins Collection of the University of California, Berkeley, Law Library. This appears to be a reprint in two volumes of the Lyon, 1627 edition. Known editions of the work are Lyon: Sumptibus Iacobi Cardon & Petri Cavellat, 1623, copy in Harvard Law Library; reprint in 2 vols. at Lyon: Iacobi Cardon & Petri Cavellat, 1627, copy in Harvard Law Library; the above Venice, 1666 edition; and 2 vols., Venice: Apud Bertanos, 1680–81, copy in Harvard Law Library.

122. See consilium 142 in Marta, 1628, 225v–26v. Unfortunately, none of the consilia is dated.

## The Move to Mantua

needed a star professor of civil law for his new university, and Marta's star shone brightly. It remained for Ferdinando to see his light.

Marta helped him. On January 1, 1621, he wrote to Duke Ferdinando from Padua to wish him a happy new year and long life. He went on to mention that he had been contacted by Annibale Chieppio, a chief minister of the duke, about several matters over the past months. He thanked the duke for honoring him in his profession and averred that he stood as ready to serve the duke as any of his natural subjects, that is, those born in the Gonzaga state. Marta also noted that a certain "Senator Alvise" passing through Padua had told the duke that Marta's writings were well regarded in Madrid.[123] Whether Chieppio and Senator Alvise were sounding out Marta about becoming a professor at the future University of Mantua or (more likely) about some other legal task is unknown. What is clear is that Ferdinando knew of Marta, and that a key ducal councillor contacted Marta more than four years before the beginning of the University of Mantua.

It is likely that Marta periodically reminded Duke Ferdinando of his existence in the next four years. As the date for the beginning of the new university approached, the duke's agents visited established universities to identify and evaluate potential faculty members. On June 1, 1625, one of Duke Ferdinando's talent scouts sent back a report about his conversation with Marta at Pavia.[124] He began by noting that Marta was a sixty-seven-year-old scholar of great ability who had published twelve volumes of legal works. He forwarded samples of Marta's scholarship to Chancellor Alessandro Striggi, now Ferdinando's chief minister, for his inspection. But wishing to hear for himself, the talent scout attended some of Marta's lectures and was impressed. He then approached Marta to see if he would be willing to come to Mantua. Marta answered that he would be happy to serve the duke of Mantua. As evidence of his esteem, he showed the duke's emissary two letters over which he had labored for two days before sending them to the duke, which suggests that he had continued to write to the duke after 1621. Marta declared that he would be happy to move to the Mantua as first-position afternoon ordinary professor of civil law, the same position that he held at Pavia, for a salary of 1,000 scudi calculated at 6 lire per scudo, plus moving expenses. He wanted to be in Mantua by August or September, which indicated eagerness to come, because classes would not begin until early November.

---

123. The letter from ASM, AG, is printed in Paglia, 1886, 14. Chieppio had particular responsibility for Monferrato. See the relazioni of Giovanni da Mula of 1615 and Alvise Donà of February 3, 1614, in *Relazioni*, 1912, 151, 268, 269.

124. Giovanni Domenico Verasio to Duke Ferdinando, June 1, 1625, Pavia, in ASM, AG, Bu. 1756, ff. 721v–22v. The Marta sections of the letter are printed in Paglia, 1886, 15–17, with minor omissions.

Marta then offered advice to the duke about his new university.[125] He wanted the other professors at the university to be excellent men (*valenthuomini*). He recommended the appointment of a legist currently teaching at the University of Padua. He urged the duke to publish in August a booklet listing the professors and their lectureships plus the privileges that students would enjoy at the new university. And he wanted the duke to erect a residence college for students on the model of the Collegio Ferdinando of Pisa. Founded in 1595, it provided free room and board for up to six years for Tuscans attending the University of Pisa who promised to swear perpetual fealty to the grand duke of Tuscany. Its purpose was to attract and train loyal civil servants.[126] Marta proposed also that Ferdinando erect a residence college for German students. In an effort to reassure the duke about the costs, he told him that a German college would not need to provide food for its residents so long as it was next to an inn. Moreover, he assured the duke that the college would not cost the duke anything, because the students of the German nation were accustomed to paying for everything themselves. Marta had great ambitions for the new university.

While Marta was willing to come, the negotiations were not over. On June 29, 1625, Marta wrote with additional demands. He expected to have precedence over all other professors. And he reminded the duke of how much he was giving up, beginning with his salary of 4,600 lire (earlier he had said that it was 4,800 lire). That was not all. Because he was currently a member of the Pavian college of doctors of law, he would be foregoing 10 scudi a month in fees for examining candidates for degrees, plus about 400 scudi per year that he earned in consultation fees on cases before the Milanese state. Moreover, at Pavia he had been promised an additional 1,200 lire to bring his salary up to 1,000 scudi next academic year. Despite all this, Marta would be happy to come to Mantua for 900 ducatoni (large ducats of account worth about 7½ lire) so long as he was the highest paid professor in the university.[127] Still, he insisted that his first contract must be for four years, the second four-year contract should be for 1,000 ducatoni, and it would then be renewed every four years.[128] Marta, already sixty-seven years of age, obviously expected to

---

125. Verasio to Duke Ferdinando, June 1, 1625, Pavia, in ASM, AG, Bu. 1756, ff. 721v–22v; and Paglia, 1886, 15–17.

126. Biagi, 1980.

127. The letter did not indicate the value in lire of the ducatone. In Milan the imperial ducatone was worth 5.75 lire. In Parma the ducatone was worth 7 lire and 6 soldi and 7 lire and 10 soldi in the early seventeenth century. Grendler, 1989, 376; Grendler, 2002, 179. To make the confusion worse, it appears that contemporaries sometimes used "ducato" (ducat) and "ducatone" (large ducat) interchangeably. In general, as prices rose in the late sixteenth and early seventeenth centuries, a ducat of account rose in nominal value even as it purchased less.

128. Short-term contracts of one or two years, but renewed indefinitely, were the norm in

# The Move to Mantua

live a long time. Finally, he asked for 150 ducatoni for the expenses of moving his goods and library. He closed by reaffirming his wish to be established in Mantua by the beginning of August.[129]

Marta probably got everything that he wanted or more.[130] At the end of July Marta wrote to the duke that he was ready to come to Mantua but needed the permission of the Milanese government to leave Pavia. So in the middle of August a representative of the duke went to Milan and secured permission for Marta to leave.[131] Marta was probably in Mantua by the first of September, ready to help launch the new university. But Marta was still irascible: once ensconced in Mantua, he strongly criticized his former colleagues at Pavia.[132]

Thus, the new university had its star civilian who was expected to attract students. Why did Duke Ferdinando and his advisers choose Marta for this most important position? The major reason was scholarship: Marta was genuinely distinguished, highly productive, and innovative. His reputation was high and based on significant accomplishment. And Italy did not have that many star legists in the early seventeenth century. Next, Marta was movable in an era of little faculty mobility. With the exception of the universities of Padua and Rome, local bottoms filled most professorial chairs. The sons of prominent citizens obtained degrees at the city's university and taught there for the rest of their lives.[133] By contrast, Marta was itinerant; born in Naples, he had taught at Pisa, Padua, Pavia, and maybe Rome. He lacked strong ties to any place. Third, Ferdinando probably liked Marta's views on church-state jurisdiction. Although Ferdinando did not clash with Rome, he was still a prince with a prince's attitude about civil jurisdiction. Fourth, it is not likely

---

Italian universities. Marta acted in an extraordinary fashion by stating his salary demands for future contracts before he began the first.

129. Autograph letter of Marta to Ottavio Pecorelli, June 29, 1625, Pavia, in ASM, AG, Bu. 1756, f. 737r–v, followed by Marta's brief autograph letter to the duke of the same date and place, but written in a more careful hand, in ibid., f. 738r.

130. There is an undated single sheet with the names and salaries of twelve law professors in ASM, AG, Bu. 3366, f. 369. It lists Marta as receiving 1,500 scudi.

131. Marta to Duke Ferdinando, July 28, 1625, Pavia, in ASM, AG, Bu. 1756, f. 748r; also quoted in Paglia, 1886, 17–18; Giovanni Domenico Verasio to Duke Ferdinando, August 18, 1625, Milan, in ASM, AG, Bu. 1756, f. 757r.

132. "[U]na lettera inaspettata del Signore Dottore Marta piena piu tosto di maledicenze contro gli lettori di Pavia." Giovanni Battista Marinoni to Duke Ferdinando, October 19, 1625, Milan, in ASM, AG, Bu. 1756, f. 765r; also quoted in Paglia, 1886, 18–19. Marinoni unsuccessfully sought a position at the new university.

133. For a short summary and more bibliography on faculty provincialism in the early seventeenth century, see Grendler, 2002, 498–500. Of course, it was a vicious cycle. When outsiders were excluded, local men were hired. Although they cost less, they were undistinguished and produced little scholarship, with a few exceptions.

that Ferdinando knew of Marta's spying for England or his pamphlet against the papacy.[134]

Why did Marta give up a position at the University of Pavia to come to a new, untried university? Undoubtedly, the Jesuits attracted him. Marta was grateful to the Jesuits for the protection of Father Salmerón when his parents died and probably for his early education. And he agreed with their philosophical views about Aristotle and the human soul. Because Ferdinando had also attended a Jesuit school and enjoyed the company of the Jesuits at Mantua, the two shared a bond. Vanity must also have played a role: Marta would be the largest fish in Mantua's university pond. He would be the most important professor and a confidant of the duke and duchess. This mattered, because Marta had a large ego, even for a law professor. Finally, he would enjoy a very high income, as much or more than at Pavia, because it is likely that he exaggerated his supplementary income there. An orphan from Naples would be the leading professor in the new University of Mantua.

134. Since even today libraries often assign Marta's pamphlet to others, it is not likely that Ferdinando was aware of Marta's authorship. And it might not have mattered if he had known.

CHAPTER 5

# Fabrizio Bartoletti and Other Professors

he second key task was to hire the star medical scholar, the person who would give the university medical distinction through his research and teaching and by attracting students. He would become the first ordinary professor of practical medicine.

The two most important medical professorships in Italian universities were theoretical medicine (or medical theory) and practical medicine (or medical practice), while surgery, anatomy, and medical botany were less prestigious. Professors of medical theory taught and researched physiology, the principles of how the body functioned. Professors of practical medicine focused on the anatomical, pathological, and therapeutic knowledge needed to cure the sick person. Of course, there was overlap. Both sought to cure patients, and both taught Hippocrates, Galen, and Avicenna's *Canon,* although they usually taught different texts of the first two and different parts of the last.

Over the course of the sixteenth century, practical medicine became more important, because of the greater emphasis on anatomical dissection to study the body and its pathologies, and the rise of clinical medicine. By 1600 the person who filled the first ordinary professorship of medical practice received the highest salary in arts and medicine, a salary that approached what the star professor of civil law received.[1] In addition to thorough familiarity with the texts to be taught, he was expected to possess anatomical expertise gained through dissections. He sought to make new discoveries about the human body and its diseases, and if he did so, he enjoyed an international reputation. The best place to find such a person was in established univer-

---

1. See Grendler, 2002, 314–52, especially 352, for more detail.

sities. Hence, Duke Ferdinando looked to Bologna for his star professor of practical medicine.

## 1. FABRIZIO BARTOLETTI

The duke chose Fabrizio Bartoletti (occasionally spelled Bertoletti). While Bartoletti did not have nearly so colorful a career as Giacomo Antonio Marta, and was much younger, he was an original and productive scholar.

Bartoletti was born in Bologna in 1587, making him the same age as Ferdinando.[2] In 1607, while still a student, he was appointed an assistant at a large Bolognese hospital located next to the university building and run by a confraternity that also comforted criminals sentenced to death. The assistantship was reserved for a medical student, and its duties were similar to those of an intern in a modern hospital.[3] Since medical scholars sometimes dissected unclaimed bodies at hospitals plus criminals sentenced to death, Bartoletti may have had an early opportunity to observe and possibly to participate in dissections and autopsies. At the university Giulio Cesare Claudini (1550/53–1618), professor of logic, natural philosophy, and medicine from 1578 until death, was one of his teachers.[4] Bartoletti received a doctorate in philosophy and medicine from the University of Bologna on March 26, 1613, and was immediately appointed to teach.[5]

Bartoletti taught logic, an introductory position, at the University of Bologna from 1613 through the academic year 1615–16. Bartoletti then became ordinary professor of surgery and anatomy, a position that he shared with four others, in the fall of 1616. For surgery he and his concurrents taught "de vulneribus" (On wounds, probably a section from Galen's *De methodo medenti*) the first year, then "de ulceribus" (On ulcers) the second year, and Galen's *De tumoribus praeter naturam* (On tumors contrary to nature) the third

---

2. There are several short bio-bibliographical works on Bartoletti: Paitoni, 1740; Mazzuchelli, 1758, 429–31; Fantuzzi, 1965, 363–67; De Renzi, 1846, 50, 156–57, 160–61, 239, 365, 442; Medici, 1857, 107–11; Busacchi, 1943 (the best); and Forni, 1948, 107. The older sources and some recent ones give Bartoletti's birth date as 1576; however, Busacchi, 1943, 58 and 71 note 2, discovered his baptismal record. Crespi, 1964, summarizes the biographical information well without resolving bibliographical issues.

3. Forni, 1948, 107, called it "ospedale della Morte." This was the hospital of the confraternity of Santa Maria della Morte. Terpstra, 1995, 10, 142–43. Crespi, 1964, 552, doubts the appointment because Bartoletti was not yet a licensed physician. However, Professor Nicholas Terpstra informs me (private communication) that the statutes of the confraternity specifically indicated that the position was to go to a medical student, and that the duties were similar to those of modern interns, that is, they were there to assist the physicians and to learn.

4. Busacchi, 1943, 58 and note 4. For Claudini, who published many medical works but is not known for any original contributions, see Bianca, 1982.

5. For his degree, see Alidosi Pasquali, 1980, 75.

year; then repeated the cycle.⁶ In addition, the professors of surgery and anatomy were responsible for the annual public anatomy, an immensely important event in the academic year, on a rotating basis: each year one of the five had the duty and honor of doing it.⁷ Whether Bartoletti's turn came up during the four years as a professor of surgery is unknown. But he did a good deal of dissecting and began to acquire a reputation as an anatomist. Despite his increased responsibilities, his salary was very low, perhaps only 50 Bolognese lire annually. In 1618 he asked for more.⁸

Bartoletti's first book dealt with anatomy. In 1619 he engaged in a public disputation on anatomy at the University of Pisa. The result was *Anatomia humani microcosmi descripto per theses disposita ex clarissimo Anphiteatro Pisano proposita a Fabritio Bartoleto, medico, et philosopho in Accademia Bononiensi publice chirugiam, et anatomiam profitente* (The anatomy of the human microcosm described through theses presented in the renowned Pisan Amphitheater published by Fabrizio Bartoletti, physician and philosopher, professor of surgery and anatomy in the University of Bologna), printed in Bologna in 1619.⁹ Dedicated to Duke Cosimo II de' Medici, it was a short work of thirty-one pages plus anatomical illustrations. It presented numbered short statements (theses) about different parts of the body and its functions (the head, the diaphragm, etc.). Bartoletti agreed with, modified, or disagreed with Galen and modern anatomical scholars including Andreas Vesalius (1514–64), who had taught at the University of Padua, and Costanzo Varoli (1543–75), who had taught at the universities of Bologna and Rome.

Why was Bartoletti in Pisa, even though the title page identified him as a professor at the University of Bologna?¹⁰ He was invited to Pisa for a disputation and anatomical dissection because the *provveditore* of the university (the government official who oversaw the university for the Medici government) hoped to recruit him for Pisa. Indeed, the provveditore assessed Bartoletti in his letters to the government. Bartoletti was thirty-two years of age, had no

---

6. *I rotuli dello Studio Bolognese*, 1888–1924, 2:330, 334, 338, 342. For identifications of the texts, see Grendler, 2002, 324.

7. Grendler, 2002, 338.

8. On August 21, 1618, the Bolognese Senate considered Bartoletti's request. He had taught logic at the university for three years, and surgery and anatomy for two, at a salary of 50 "scudi" (which probably meant lire), and he asked for more. ASB, Assunteria di Studio, Bu. 31, Requisiti dei lettori, Lettera B, vol. 2, fascicule 18. Busacchi, 1943, 58, states that in 1615 Bartoletti received 50 Bolognese lire each quarter, making it 200 lire annually, but gives no reference. While the Assunteria di Studio document does not indicate whether the "50 scudi" was the quarterly or annual salary, it was more likely the latter.

9. Bartoletti, 1619a. The NLM copy has been used.

10. Barsanti, 1993, 508, 559, lists Bartoletti as teaching anatomy at the University of Pisa in 1618–19, but qualifies this with the comment that, although nominated, he did not appear on the faculty roll.

wife, and was highly esteemed. He had published or had in press several works.[11] The provveditore hoped that Bartoletti might be persuaded to come to the University of Pisa. When approached, Bartoletti replied that he had been invited to assume the professorship of anatomy and surgery at the University of Padua but had refused because the 500 Paduan florins offered him was not enough. Whether or not he had an offer from Padua, this was not a convincing reason to decline because 500 Paduan florins was considerably more than he received at Bologna. In other words, Bartoletti rejected Pisa politely.[12] Although Bartoletti did not move to the University of Pisa, his appearance there demonstrated his rising reputation as an anatomist. And it probably also had a positive effect on his reputation at Bologna, because his salary rose to 200 Bolognese lire in 1619.[13]

## 2. THE *ENCYCLOPAEDIA HERMETICO-DOGMATICA*

Bartoletti's second book of 1619 compared traditional Galenic medical theory and the new ideas of Paracelsus. Dedicated to Ferdinando Gonzaga, the book included original research. The title was *Encyclopaedia hermetico-dogmatica sive orbis doctrinarum medicarum physiologiae, hygiinae, pathologiae, simioticae, et therepeuticae ad sereniss. Principem D. Ferdinandum Gonzagam Mantuae et Montisferrati ducem* (Hermetic and dogmatic encyclopedia or the world of medical doctrines of physiology, hygiene, pathology, symptom, and therapeutic dedicated to Ferdinando Gonzaga, duke of Mantua and Monferrato), published in Bologna.[14] Since the title page displayed the Gonzaga coat

---

11. It is difficult to determine if Bartoletti wrote more works than the three analyzed in this study (two in this chapter and the third in chapter 7). Like other scholars of his time, Bartoletti claimed to have written many works. As a result, some older sources list additional titles, which have not been located in print. Of course, there may be undiscovered manuscript works.

12. Fabroni, 1971, 2:84, first presented this assessment of Bartoletti without a source. De Rosa, 1983, 112, identifies the source as Girolamo da Sommaja (1573–after 1636), who as provveditore oversaw the University of Pisa from 1614 to 1636. Since Bartoletti was born in 1587, the date of the comment was 1619. At that time Girolamo da Sommaja was dissatisfied with the incumbent professor of anatomy. He was well informed about professors at other universities and often urged the Medici government in Florence to make new appointments.

13. A fascicule labeled "Lettori aumenti" for arts professors and dated July 4, 1619, gives Bartoletti's salary as 200 Bolognese lire. The highest figure listed was 1,200 Bolognese lire, so Bartoletti was still not that well paid. ASB, Assunteria di Studio 92, Diversorum, fascicule 6.

14. Bartoletti, 1619b. The NLM copy has been used. The undated dedication letter to Ferdinando is on sig. a2 r–v. The earliest bio-bibliographers mention editions of 1615 and 1621. Paitoni, 1740; Mazzuchelli, 1758, 431; Fantuzzi, 1965, 366; repeated by Medici, 1857, 110; and Crespi, 1964, 552. But none of them stated that they had seen editions of 1615 and 1621 or gave library locations. Busacchi, 1943, 69, wrote that there were various editions published between "1618" (possibly a typographical error for 1619) and 1633, but did not indicate the dates of publication of any editions beyond that of 1619. I have located copies of the 1619 edition in several other American

of arms and the book was dedicated to Ferdinando, the latter probably supported it in some way, perhaps with a publication subvention or a gift. In his undated dedicatory letter, Bartoletti extravagantly praised Duke Ferdinando's intellect in vague terms but offered no information about any contacts with Ferdinando.

The *Encyclopaedia hermetico-dogmatica* was a well-organized handbook of much traditional and new academic medical knowledge.[15] Part 1 dealt with physiology. The first tract offered a comprehensive view of medicine, followed by chapters on the elements, temperaments, humors, nutrition, the body's faculties, actions, and so on—the structure of Galenic medicine. Part 2 discussed diet, with sections on different foods, water, oil, condiments, salt, and so forth, as well as the passions and motions of the body. Part 3 dealt with diseases and their symptoms. Part 4 discussed semiotics, that is, the signs of diseases, including excretions, varieties of pain, pulse, urine, and systoles (contractions) of the heart. Part 5 discussed therapies.

The combination of "Hermetic" and "dogmatic" in the title signaled a dual approach to medicine. Dogmatic meant Galenic medicine, and Bartoletti was a strong Galenist. He accepted Galen's ideas about humors, his doctrine of using contraries for healing, and much else. Hermetic meant Paracelsian medicine, using some alchemical techniques. Hermetic acquired this meaning in a circuitous way. The name came from Hermes Trismegistus, the legendary author of a body of ancient philosophical works written between the fourth century B.C. and the third century A.D. A mixture of Greek, Egyptian, and Christian ideas, they offered a higher philosophy, cosmology, and theology by means of poetic metaphors.[16] Hermes Trismegistus was also called the founder of alchemy in a handful of medieval works of practical alchemy that circulated in the Renaissance and were used by some scholars, including Paracelsus.[17] Thus, "the Hermetic art" meant alchemy, and in particular, Paracelsian medicine, using distillation.[18] This was true for Bartoletti, who was both attracted to and repelled by Paracelsianism.

Paracelsus (Theophrastus Philippus Aureolus Bombastus von Hohenheim,

---

libraries, e.g., University of Chicago, University of Pennsylvania, and Yale University. But I have not located copies of editions of 1615, 1621, or any other year. Until a 1615 edition comes to light, I assume that the first edition appeared in 1619.

15. Bartoletti, 1619b. See also the comments of Busacchi, 1943, 61–62; Crespi, 1964, 552; Thorndike, 1923–58, 7:178–80; and Zanier, 1985, 640–43.

16. See *Hermetica*, 1992, and especially the introduction by Brian Copenhaver at xiii–lxi.

17. See Sadoul, 1972, 25–26; Moran, 2005, 27, 29; and Copenhaver, introduction to *Hermetica*, 1992, xxxii–xxxviii.

18. For example, Andreas Libavius (Libau) (ca. 1555–1616), a prolific German alchemist and pioneering chemist who criticized Paracelsus, earlier used the terms "dogmatists" and "Hermeticists" in the same way. Moran, 2005, 81–82.

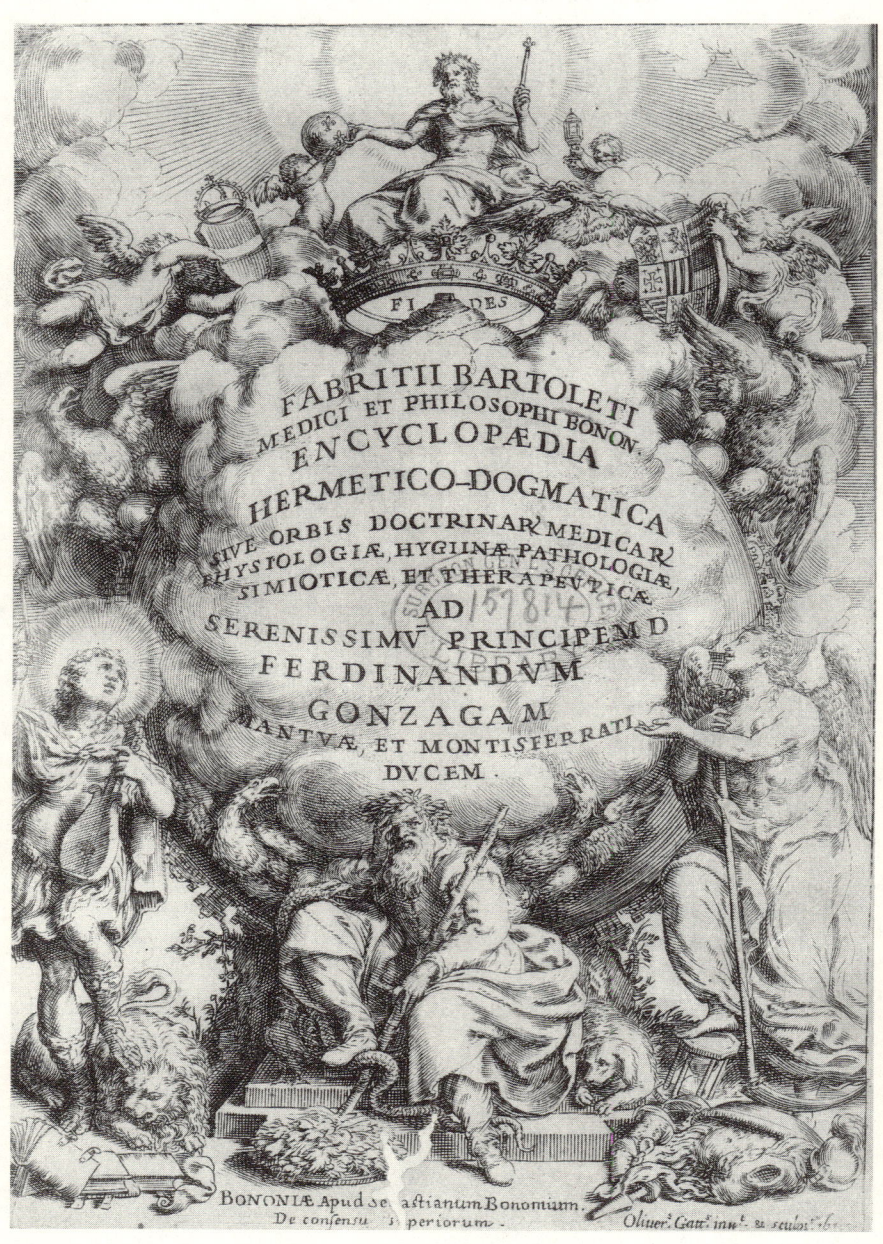

FIG. 9. Title page of Fabrizio Bartoletti, *Encyclopaedia hermetico-dogmatica*. Bononiae: Apud Sebastianum Bonomiam, 1619. *Courtesy of the National Library of Medicine.*

ca. 1493–1541) was born in Einsiedeln, Switzerland.[19] He probably studied medicine in one or more Italian universities, then held various medical positions in Switzerland and southern Germany, never staying long because of his iconoclastic views and actions. He wrote voluminously on medicine, natural philosophy, theology, astrology, and alchemy, but published little during his lifetime. After his death, others published his works, especially in the decade between 1565 and 1575.

In his medical works Paracelsus denounced traditional Galenic medicine and its humoral basis. According to Galenic theories, disease was the result of an imbalance of the four humors, blood, phlegm, yellow bile, and black bile; it caused the whole body to be ill. To restore the patient to good health, the physician had to re-create the proper balance in the four humors, often through healing by contraries, that is, removing an excess of one humor. For example, if the physician determined that the cause of the patient's ill health was too much blood, he prescribed bleeding. Galen emphasized disease, not diseases, and he sought to cure the entire body rather than one part of it.

Paracelsus had none of it. He saw diseases (plural) as local malfunctions that entered the body from outside, even from the stars, and whose cures were to be found in the chemicals existing in nature. Thus, medicine should look for local symptoms and causes. But to do this the physician had to understand the link between the microcosm (man) and the macrocosm (everything else, including the world and the heavens). The macrocosm-microcosm unity indicated a correspondence of knowledge between the two; one could learn about man by investigating nature. The job of the scholar, especially the medical scholar, was not to read the books of the ancients, nor to apply Aristotelian logic to a problem. Rather, the scholar must seek out the hidden gifts implanted in the earth (macrocosm) by God. He could acquire this knowledge through mystical experience or by observation of nature.

The heart of the Paracelsian system, if it could be called a system, consisted of complicated theories about substances and principles. Paracelsus seemed to accept the Aristotelian elements of earth, air, fire, and water, but he added what he called the three principles of salt, sulfur, and mercury, which accounted for all things. Principles were neither matter nor elements. Rather, they were "the principles within matter that condition the state in which matter can occur. There is thus in every object a principle (salt) responsible for its solid state; a principle (sulfur) responsible for its inflammable or 'fatty' state; and a third (mercury) responsible for its smoky (vaporous) or fluid

---

19. There is an enormous bibliography on Paracelsus and his influence. For the next several paragraphs, see Pagel, 1981, 1982, 1986; Debus, 1977, 1991; Zanier, 1983, 61–123; the studies in *Paracelsus*, 1998; Thorndike, 1923–58, 5:617–67 and 7:153–240; and Webster, 2008. This brief summary focuses on chemical medicine themes.

state."[20] And there was more. Mercury also referred to the highest spiritual state, and sulfur meant the soul or principle of life. Principles were means of comprehension as well. And while they could not be isolated, the scholar might be able to identify their properties in other substances. Since man the microcosm was made of the same substance as the macrocosm, if one could separate out a substance from some part of the world, that substance might be medically beneficial to man.

The way to isolate helpful substances was through iatrochemistry, a term Paracelsus coined, which included alchemy and medical chemistry. Medical scholars found this an intriguing and useful part of Paracelsus, for which his *Archidoxis,* a handbook of Paracelsian chemistry first published in 1569, was essential. Individual organs of the body had their own *archei* (spirits or life forces) that acted like internal alchemists. The organs separated useful substances from nonuseful substances. For example, the stomach acted in an alchemical way by separating the good from the bad in food; it could get the good substance from meat and reject the poison in it. Since the body acted as an alchemist, so should the scholar look for this in nature. He could seek substances in parts of the macrocosm using the theories and practices of alchemy, including gold through the transformation of other substances. But for Paracelsus, alchemy also meant using distillation and fire to understand nature and find useful substances. There was much else in Paracelsus, including a doctrine of signatures, some natural magic, and astrology. Paracelsianism was an immensely complex and confusing panoply of ideas in which real insights were embedded in a mass of speculative, superstitious, and barely comprehensible material.

The posthumous publication of his works led to considerable discussion about the usefulness of his many ideas, a debate made more contentious by the difficulty in understanding him. By the late sixteenth and early seventeenth centuries, the acrimonious debate had distilled Paracelsianism down to two substances.[21] There was pure Paracelsianism, which embraced his philosophical, occult, spiritualist, cosmological, and alchemical features as well as iatrochemistry. And there was an impure Paracelsianism, which remained after cosmology, magic, spiritualism, and the like were burnt away. This was Paracelsian chemical medicine, which meant using distillation and other techniques to obtain from animal and mineral materials chemical substances useful in medicine. Impure Paracelsianism had a great impact on medicine.

Numerous German, French, English, and Dutch scholars, especially medical men, accepted, at least in part, or attacked Paracelsian ideas. By contrast

---

20. Pagel, 1981, 309B.
21. Wear, 1995, 318–20, summarizes the situation well.

## The *Encyclopaedia hermetico-dogmatica*

Paracelsus had very little influence on medical education and research in Italian universities in the early seventeenth century, although he had a handful of fervent Italian admirers outside the universities.[22] There were several reasons.

First and foremost, Italian university medical education was committed to the traditional physiology of Galen and Hippocrates, even though scholars were beginning to notice Galen's deficiencies. Second, Italian universities strongly emphasized the anatomical research of Vesalius and his followers, the most influential medical innovation of the Renaissance. Practically every major Italian medical scholar of the late sixteenth and early seventeenth centuries, including Bartoletti, believed that anatomical investigation was a key part of medical scholarship and devoted much time to dissecting bodies. But Vesalian anatomy and Paracelsian anatomy were incompatible. Vesalius and his successors dissected the human body to catalog its parts, to determine how they functioned, and to study the differences between healthy and diseased organs. Paracelsus, by contrast, saw anatomy as chemical anatomy. Hence, anatomical study meant determining the substances that made up parts of the body and then trying to find their affinity substances outside the body.[23] This was not done by dissection.

Finally, the papal Index of Prohibited Books of 1596 banned the works of Paracelsus.[24] Although the Congregation of the Index did not give reasons, the works of Paracelsus suggest several. Neither an orthodox Catholic nor a magisterial Protestant, Paracelsus criticized established churches for what he saw as their fraudulent dogmatic rationalism and manmade views. He advocated a return to the purer, more spiritual church of early Christianity. And he endorsed the occult. The Index of Prohibited Books also banned a handful of individual titles of northern Protestant Paracelsians.[25] The index prohibitions

---

22. For Italian Paracelsians outside the universities, see Ferrari, 1982; Galluzzi, 1982; Palmer, 1985, 110–17, 309–12; and especially Zanier, 1985. Nevertheless, two or three Italian university professors were Paracelsians to some degree. Camillo Baldi (1550–1637), definitely a Paracelsian, taught logic, philosophy, and the humanities, but not medicine, at the University of Bologna for many years. Tronti, 1963; Zanier, 1985, 638–40. Zanier, 1985, 644, believes that Giulio Cesare Claudini, one of Bartoletti's teachers, was not opposed to Paracelsianism. But since he left few medical writings, it is impossible to tell. See also Bianca, 1982. Cesare Magati (1577/79–1647), a renowned surgeon who taught at the University of Ferrara from 1612 until his death and emphasized natural healing processes, may have been a follower of Paracelsus to a limited degree. Zanier, 1985, 648–49; *I maestri di Ferrara*, 1991, 242. And the University of Pisa had a Paracelsian medical scholar; see chapter 7, section 2. That was it until the founding of the University of Mantua.

23. Pagel and Rattansi, 1964.

24. *Index de Rome*, 1994, 720–21. Paracelsus' works were also listed in the local Parma Index of 1580, and the unpromulgated Roman Index of 1590. Ibid., 163, 177, 395.

25. The index banned a single title of Robert Fludd (1574–1637) in 1625, two titles of Andreas

undoubtedly hindered the circulation of works of Paracelsus and Protestant Paracelsians in Italy, and may have induced Bartoletti to substitute "Hermetic" for "Paracelsian" when discussing Paracelsian ideas. But this substitution probably did not deceive medical scholars, and many Paracelsian works written by northern European Protestants and Catholics were not prohibited and were easily obtainable in Italy.[26]

Bartoletti devoted many pages of his *Encyclopaedia hermetico-dogmatica* to discussing the views of Paracelsus and his northern followers, whom he usually called "Hermeticus" and "Hermetici." He cited Paracelsus by name at least once and often referred to his books.[27] And he mentioned northern European Paracelsians.[28] Bartoletti then criticized Paracelsian ideas, as in his discussion of Galenic physiology in which he referred to the *imposturae* (deceits) and *fraudes* (frauds) of the Hermetics.[29] He refuted their mistakes through syllogistic reasoning, but in so doing, he presented summaries of Paracelsian physiological ideas.

Bartoletti was also moderately concordist. For example, he discussed one of the imposturae of the Paracelsians in the section entitled "De facultate metallorum generatrice secundum Hermeticos" (On the means for the generation of metals according to the Hermetics). It became an eight-page trea-

---

Libavius in 1605 and 1618, and one title of Daniel Sennert (1572–1637) in 1639. *Index*, 2002, 351, 548, 828. By contrast, the index did not ban any works of Johann Rudolph Glauber (1603–1670) or Jean Baptiste van Helmont (1579–1644), two leading Protestant Paracelsians.

26. According to Wear, 1995, 319, "From the 1540s as the Catholic Counter Reformation gathered momentum Paracelsians went underground in Italy." In the light of the information on Italian Paracelsianism presented here and in chapter 7, section 2, this statement needs to be modified.

27. Bartoletti criticized Paracelsus: "Secundum modus est Paracelsi de generatione rerum lib. 2 qui cum mihi suspectus sit." Bartoletti, 1619b, 133. On other occasions Bartoletti referred to the titles (but not the author) of books of Paracelsus, sometimes to criticize. "Hermetici, qui sicut maligni sunt, ita vafri nugationes committunt, nituntur dogmaticorum temperamentum de medio tollere, ut lib. I *in Paramiro de origine morborum.*" Bartoletti, 1619b, 27 (italics in the original). The *Opus Paramirum* (Work beyond wonder) was Paracelsus' major medical treatise, in which he listed five causes of disease (astral, poison, natural, spiritual, and divine) and criticized Galen. Bartoletti, 1619b, 138, referred to "Hermetico lib. 5, Chirurgiae magnae," which is probably a reference to a Latin translation of the *Grosse Wundartzney*, the major surgical work of Paracelsus. There is also a reference to "Hermetico lib. 5 & lib. 2 chirurgiae minoris," which is likely another work of Paracelsus. Bartoletti, 1619b, 136. There are many other references to book titles without authors, some of which were very likely works of Paracelsus or Paracelsians.

28. Zanier, 1985, 640–42, also points out that there were many references to the works of Paracelsus and at least one reference to a work of Daniel Sennert. A professor of medicine at the University of Wittenberg, Sennert sought to integrate a modified Paracelsian chemical medicine into traditional Galenic medicine. Debus, 1977, 1:191–200.

29. "[Q]uod Tyrones eorum argumenta futilia cognoscant, ut Hermeticas fraudes evitare possint." Bartoletti, 1619b, 27. This is also quoted in Zanier, 1985, 640.

tise about the production of substances from metals and vegetative matter through fermentation, the application of heat and water, and distillation, very much a Paracelsian approach.[30] Bartoletti allowed that both true *philosophi* (traditional Galenists) and Hermetic *physici* (natural philosophers) could agree that the *virtus germinativa* (germinative spirit) was a form of the *facultas vegetativa* (vegetative faculty).[31] He gave credit to the Hermetics for having found a method to "germinate" (i.e., produce substances from) metals as nature does it.[32]

Bartoletti allowed that the dogmatics and the Hermetics had some common interests and similar methods. Both sought to discover the formal constitution and the efficient causes of disease and manifested some methodological similarities. Both the Galenist and the "irrationalis Hermeticus" (irrational Hermetic) looked for symptoms of disease in urine.[33] Bartoletti discussed balsam (an oily, gummy substance from trees, and by extension, any soothing ointment composed of animal, vegetative, or metallic matter), an important part of medical Paracelsianism. But he denied that it had more than a limited, soothing therapeutic quality; he did not see balsam as causing burning or producing perspiration.[34]

Bartoletti criticized Hermetics for their wrong ideas about humors, the heart of Galenism, and affirmed Galen throughout. He discussed sulfur, mercury, and salt, key Paracelsian principles, but unlike Paracelsus, did not see them as fundamentally different from other elements. Moreover, he saw them as mixed, not pure. And Bartoletti did not believe in alchemy. But he welcomed the search for chemical remedies for diseases and expressed confidence in chemical processes.[35] In summary, while remaining a Galenist, Bar-

30. Bartoletti, 1619b, 128–35. However, it should be noted that information about distillation techniques might come from sources other than Paracelsus. Multhauf, 1956, argues that Renaissance medical chemists learned more from traditional medieval and Renaissance distillers than from Paracelsus.

31. "Germinatio est crescentia vegetabilis à propria facultate, mediante calido & humido." Bartoletti, 1619b, 128; also quoted by Zanier, 1985, 641.

32. "Hermetici modum adinvenerunt quo, ad modum naturae germinare, faciunt metalla; ex quorum germinibus medicamenta summae admirationis parant: quae artificiosa germinatio naturali similis est, sed non univoca, quia non fit ab eodem agente univoco, à facultate scilicet germinatrice; est enim potius metalli quaedam elongatio à calore facta per modum fermentationis, sicut fermentum ex digestione crescere solet: analogia autem talis est, nam germinatio naturalis nil aliud est, quam terrae imbibitio. Solis autem calor nil aliud, quam Solis destillatio, tales humiditates sursum attrahentis; unde Hermeticus similibus imbibitionibus, et destillationibus metallorum germinationem moliri poterit." Bartoletti, 1619b, 129; also quoted by Zanier, 1985, 641 note 26. Note that Bartoletti saw "facultate" and "germinatrice" as synonymous.

33. Zanier, 1985, 642.

34. Bartoletti, 1619b, 136–39. The title of the section is "De spiritu innato, seu Balsamo radicali, impostur Hermetica." See also Thorndike, 1923–58, 7:179.

35. Thorndike, 1923–58, 7:178–80, makes these points.

toletti was open to some of the new ideas that came under the broad label of Paracelsianism, even though he found fault with much of the Paracelsian system. Like some of the northern European Paracelsians, Bartoletti wished to integrate medical chemistry into traditional medicine. But he had no time for the cosmological philosophizing of Paracelsus.

Bartoletti did more than present some aspects of Paracelsian chemical medicine as congruent with Galenism. He experimented in chemical medicine, the process of extracting chemical components from animal substances by means of heat, evaporation, or distillation, and made an original contribution. In the section on hygiene, Bartoletti discussed milk, which he divided into *butyrum* (butter or butter fat), *serum* (whey), and *caseus* (cheese).[36] Serum was the watery part of milk, which could be cooled or warmed. Bartoletti wrote that by evaporating the serum, one could extract lactose, the white crystalline sugar in milk. Lactose could then be mixed with other substances for use as medicines and lubricants in the treatment of various conditions and diseases. Indeed, later in the century lactose was used to treat gout. In a later work, Bartoletti described the process that he followed in extracting lactose: it involved repeated boiling plus coagulation (the change from a liquid to a soft, semisolid state).[37] Bartoletti was the first to extract and identify lactose.

Bartoletti's discussion of Paracelsianism and discovery of lactose demonstrated that he had a strong interest in exploring the chemical composition of animal products for therapeutic uses. Although a Galenist, he was also an innovator. Bartoletti may have been the most important Italian practitioner of chemical medicine in the first third of the seventeenth century. This combination would be very important for the University of Mantua, which would include a professorship of chemistry and Paracelsian medical scholars, as well as teachers of traditional medicine.

Bartoletti's interest in Paracelsian chemical medicine must have intrigued Ferdinando Gonzaga, who had petitioned the Holy Office in Rome for permission to read the works of Paracelsus while a student at the University of Pisa. And after he became a cardinal, he had a laboratory in Rome with instruments, glass vessels, and other equipment enabling him to perform chemical medicine and alchemical experiments. In June 1611 Giovanni Antonio Magini, who guided his efforts, recommended to Ferdinando a Paracelsian treatise, Philip Müller's *Miracula chymica et mysteria medica* (Chemical miracles and medical mysteries), published in Wittenberg, 1611. Müller (1581–1659) listed the instruments and equipment needed to carry on chemical and alchemical experiments, then discussed the transmutation of metals through fire, which was standard alchemical matter, followed by sections on mercury,

---

36. Bartoletti, 1619b, 168–69. See also Busacchi, 1943, 67–68; and De Renzi, 1846, 50, 239.
37. Bartoletti, 1633, book 5, p. 400. Busacchi, 1943, 67, quotes the key passages.

sulfur, balsam, simples, and much else. The largest part of the book described the production of secret remedies, some of them quite ridiculous to modern eyes, which would cure every disease.[38]

As stated above, Bartoletti dedicated his book to Duke Ferdinando. One wonders if he knew of Ferdinando's interest in alchemy and chemical medicine or if the dedication was the consequence of encouragement from Ferdinando. In any case, Duke Ferdinando would remember a professor who shared his interest in Paracelsus.

In 1620 Bartoletti received a promotion at Bologna, as he became one of the seven ordinary professors of practical medicine, a much more prestigious position than surgery and anatomy. In 1622 he received a salary of 300 Bolognese lire, which was still not very high.[39] He also taught anatomy along with five to seven others. This indicated a strong commitment to anatomy, because he was not obliged to teach anatomy once he became an ordinary professor of practical medicine. He held the two positions through the academic year 1624–25.[40] As ordinary professor of practical medicine, he taught a three-year cycle of texts that included "de morbis particularibus" (which might have been book 9 of Rhazes' *Liber Almansoris*, which briefly described more than a hundred complaints and diseases), in the first year, followed by "de febribus" (On fevers, a section of Avicenna's *Canon*, book 4, fen 1) the second year, and he lectured on humors from Avicenna's *Canon*, book 1, fen 4, in the third.[41] Although the texts were traditional, by the early seventeenth century professors taught them freely and added material from their own research and other works.[42]

The students at Bologna were so pleased with Bartoletti's teaching that in 1624 the arts and medicine student organization hung a plaque praising him in the Archiginnasio, the university building. Carrying the names of the prior and consuls of the student organization, it praised Bartoletti for his acumen in logic, perspicacity in philosophy, experience in surgery, dexterity in anatomy, roundness of knowledge in medical theory, and method in practical medicine. It also mentioned his eloquence and the muses, a reference to the fact that he wrote poetry.[43] A century later the University of Bologna honored Bartoletti

---

38. Chambers, 1987, 128–29. For Müller's work, see Thorndike, 1923–58, 7:163–65.

39. Busacchi, 1943, 58. Some senior arts and medicine professors were paid 1,400 and 1,650 lire.

40. *I rotuli dello Studio Bolognese*, 1888–1924, 2:346, 347, 350, 351, 354, 355, 357, 359, 361, 363, 366, 367. He was also listed as teaching at Bologna in the academic year 1625–26, although he had left for Mantua.

41. See the references in *I rotuli dello Studio Bolognese*, 1888–1924, cited in note 40; and Grendler, 2002, 324 note 26, for identifications of the texts.

42. This is the theme of Siraisi, 1987. Although she studied the teaching of theoretical medicine, the same was likely true for practical medicine.

43. Fantuzzi, 1965, 365, quotes the plaque in full. Medici, 1857, 108, quotes part of it; and Forni,

for his anatomical teaching and research. His carved wooden bust was one of the twelve depicting famous anatomists added to the permanent anatomical theater between 1733 and 1737. The eminent dozen began with Hippocrates and Galen, then skipped to modern figures, all of whom taught at Bologna.[44] Vesalius, never a professor at Bologna, was not included.[45]

### 3. THE COURTING OF BARTOLETTI

Whether or not Bartoletti and Duke Ferdinando met or exchanged letters in or before 1619, they did communicate in the next few years. Both looked ahead. Ferdinando thought about his future university, while Bartoletti wished to improve his lot. On August 31, 1622, Alessandro Senesi, the duke's representative in Bologna, forwarded Bartoletti's good wishes to the duke and to "Madama," Duchess Caterina de' Medici.[46] Bartoletti had met her while she was convalescing, perhaps at a spa. And he had met Duke Ferdinando, who had expressed a desire to found a university.[47] On September 10, 1622, Bartoletti wrote to the duke that he had procured medicine to relieve Senesi's asthma. Although the medicine might not cure him, it would at least ease his distress, Bartoletti wrote. In additional letters of September and November 1622 Senesi forwarded some medicines that Bartoletti had procured for the duke and for one Laura Gonzaga.[48]

The friendly correspondence continued in 1623. Senesi in Bologna remained in contact with Bartoletti, while Bartoletti corresponded with Ferdinando. On

---

1948, 107, prints it in full except for the names of the student organization leaders. According to Simeoni, 1940, 25, the plaque is located on the left side of the loggia on the ground floor of the Archiginnasio, which has hundreds of plaques and coats of arms. Because I was unaware of its existence, I did not look for it at my last visit.

44. The existing wooden anatomical theater, inside the Archiginnasio, was erected between 1639 and 1647, with the carved wooden busts added between 1733 and 1737. Simeoni, 1940, 25. I have seen Bartoletti's bust there; there is a poor illustration of it in Forni, 1948, 107.

45. At the invitation of medical students, Vesalius did conduct anatomical demonstrations at Bologna in January 1540.

46. Alessandro Senesi to Ferdinando, August 31, 1622, Bologna, in ASM, AG, Bu. 1173, Lettere di diversi, f. 124r.

47. "Si riccorda V(ostra) S(ignoria) Ill(ustrissi)ma che gl'anni passati a Perto quando l'Altezza Serenissima di Madama era ivi convalescente, si trattò con risolutione di principiare lo studio." Bartoletti to Duke Ferdinando, July 9, 1625, Bologna, in ASM, AG, Bu. 1173, f. 651v. Perto has not been located.

48. Senesi to Ferdinando, September 21, 27, and November 16 (two), 23 (two), 30, 1622, always from Bologna, and Bartoletti to Ferdinando, September 10, 1622, Bologna, in ASM, AG, Bu. 1173, Diversi, ff. 130r (Bartoletti), 134r, 154r, 170r, 172r, 182r, 184r, 188r. Laura Gonzaga has not been identified.

# The Courting of Bartoletti

March 5, 1623, Bartoletti sent his greetings to Duke Ferdinando and enclosed a sonnet that he had written in praise of Ferdinando. On July 16 Bartoletti wrote that, in conformity with the duke's wishes, he had spoken with "D. Navarro" (possibly another agent of the duke) and was willing to talk some more. On August 7, 1623, Bartoletti wrote that he was willing to serve the duke.[49] In other words, he would consider an appointment.

The discussions over the next twenty-two months cannot be followed because no letters have been located. But they obviously went well. On June 5, 1625, Bartoletti wrote acknowledging the offer of the first-position ordinary professorship of practical medicine at the University of Mantua.[50] This was the beginning of a more elaborate dance of negotiations, as Bartoletti pirouetted away from a final commitment with elegant gestures and words. He graciously thanked the duke for the offer but regretfully concluded that it was not enough. When he looked at the stipend (he did not name the figure), he found it inadequate. And for the first time Bartoletti realized with shock and horror how much he would lose by abandoning his birthplace for the unknown Mantua. Bartoletti described with feeling the comfort of his house in Bologna and the more than 2,000 scudi in earnings from his private practice that he would be leaving behind. He sorrowfully concluded that he could not possibly move without at least 1,000 scudi "of our money." Otherwise he would suffer financially, especially because of his family expenses.[51] He would need a house. This was necessary to relieve the suffering caused by leaving his *patria* and home where, thanks be to God, he had enjoyed some comfort.

Then he dropped a bombshell: others sought his services. He swore to the duke that Cardinal Ludovico Ludovisi in Rome had offered the same and more. But he had not accepted because Bartoletti suffered from quartan fever, a form of malaria in which the paroxysms occurred every fourth day. He meant that Rome's climate would have worsened his condition, and he was not about to jeopardize his health for mere money. But a new opportunity had suddenly appeared: a few days ago the "presidents" of the University of Padua had approached him about filling the chair of "Acquapendente" at a high salary. He concluded with expressions of warm affection for Duke Ferdinando.[52]

Thus Bartoletti described the opportunities available to a talented medical

---

49. Bartoletti to Ferdinando, March 5 (with the sonnet), July 16, and August 7, 1623, Bologna, in ASM, AG, Bu. 1173, ff. 277r, 346r, 362r. Senesi to Ferdinando, February 8, 15, and March 22, 1623, Bologna, in ibid., ff. 263r, 269r, and 297r.

50. Bartoletti to Ferdinando, June 5, 1625, Bologna, in ASM, AG, Bu. 1173, f. 647r.

51. The Pisan provveditore who reported in 1619 that Bartoletti had no wife must have been mistaken.

52. Bartoletti to the duke, June 5, 1625, Bologna, in ASM, AG, Bu. 1173, f. 647r.

scholar. He sang the comforts of patria and home, and let the duke know about his lucrative practice at Bologna. And if his private practice earned 2,000 scudi annually—a big if—it was six times his university salary. The Rome offer was probably an invitation to become personal physician to Cardinal Ludovico Ludovisi, a man of chronic ill health. From Bologna, Cardinal Ludovisi (1595, created cardinal in 1621, died 1632) was the nephew of Pope Gregory XV (1621–23). Although Gregory's death had sharply reduced his influence, Ludovisi remained very wealthy, a collector of antiquities, and generous benefactor to the poor.[53] The Paduan post was the professorship of anatomy and surgery that Girolamo Fabrici d'Acquapendente (ca. 1533–1619), a pioneer in comparative embryology and teacher of William Harvey, had held for many years. It had become vacant in April 1625 when his successor died.[54] But it is not likely that Bartoletti really had an offer. These "presidents" may have been the leaders of the student organization of arts and medicine at Padua, even though the latter were called "rector" and "councillors." And while they sometimes lobbied for appointments, Venetian magistrates, the Riformatori dello Studio di Padova, governed the university and recommended appointments to the Venetian Senate. The senate made the final decisions, often against the wishes of the students.[55] Bartoletti was probably bluffing.

Nevertheless, Bartoletti got his salary wishes, as Duke Ferdinando seldom worried about money. On July 9, 1625, Bartoletti wrote to the duke's representative that he accepted Ferdinando's offer to become the first ordinary professor of practical medicine for a salary of 1,000 ducatoni plus expenses for moving his family to Mantua. But he had to accede to the duke's request that he also do the annual public anatomy scheduled for January 1626; see table 6.1. Bartoletti informed the duke that he had declined an offer from Padua and wanted either a three-year or a five-year contract, which would have underscored his star status.[56] He wished to teach at the last hour of the morning without a concurrent because this was the customary practice for "the eminent one of medicine."[57] He did not mean that he feared competition. Rather,

---

53. For Cardinal Ludovisi, see Pastor, 1891–1953, 27:50–65, 69–73, et passim; and 28:291–93 et passim.

54. Facciolati, 1978, part 3, 389–90.

55. Grendler, 2002, 157–58, 335, 345, 451, including note 70.

56. The longest contract to come to my attention was the lifetime contract granted by the Venetian Senate to Galileo Galilei in August 1609, to begin in the fall of 1610. However, Galilei left Padua in 1610 to become the "Primary Philosopher and Mathematician" to the Grand Duke of Tuscany, thus angering the senators whom Galilei had lobbied for the lifetime appointment. Grendler, 2002, 419.

57. "[C]he Vostra Signore Ill.ma sà che l'eminente di Medicina legge sensa concorrente la

# The Courting of Bartoletti

he implied that the lectures of the leading medical professor were of such value that all the medical students, and possibly some professors, would attend, thus leaving the concurrent in the embarrassing situation of lecturing to empty benches.

In subsequent letters Bartoletti reassured the duke that he was not negotiating with the universities of Padua and Pisa, the first mention of the latter. He renewed his request that he teach in the last hour of the morning, as he found it difficult to lecture after lunch because the combination of his malarial condition and eating upset his stomach. He wanted to lecture on fevers the first year, because the material was important and complex. He did not like the house that the duke's agent located for him because it was too close to the students and university classes for the safety of the "young women" in his family.[58] Bartoletti was animadverting on the topos that university students threatened the virtue of the good women of the town. In the end Bartoletti found a satisfactory house and began teaching at the new University of Mantua in early November 1625.

But Bartoletti did not get his way on everything. He had to teach at the first hour of the afternoon rather than in the morning. Although he had no concurrent the first year, he had one in subsequent years. Nor did he lecture on fevers the first year, but on the *Canon* of Avicenna, book 1, fen 4, which dealt with the general principles of therapy and methods of treatment for disease. The duke wanted him to teach the Avicenna material because professors of practical medicine at Bologna and Padua taught it.[59] This told potential students and the learned world that Mantua would provide the same program of study as the best universities of Italy; it demonstrated in a concrete way Ferdinando's ambition for his university. Bartoletti also had to teach surgery on holidays at the third hour of the morning in the academic year 1625–26, because no surgery professor was appointed. He re-

---

mattina all'ultim'hora, come qui sempre si è custumato." Bartoletti to Duke Ferdinando, July 9, 1625, Bologna, in ASM, AG, Bu. 1173, Lettere di diversi, ff. 651r–v, quote at f. 651r.

58. Bartoletti to Ferdinando, July 16, August 2 (two letters), August (no day), September 9, and October 1, 8, 22, 1625, Bologna, in ASM, AG, Bu. 1173, ff. 653r, 655r, 657r, 659r, 661r, 663r, 667r, 669r. Also "Il Bertoletti fù qui, et per non haver trovata casa à suo modo non essendogli piaciuta quella offrirgli da Vostra Altezza che era del Colombo, dicendo esser troppo vicina ai scolari et alle scuole havendo egli donne giovani di sua famiglia." Caterina de' Medici to Duke Ferdinando, then in Florence, of October 22, 1625, Mantua, in ASM, AG, Bu. 2176, Lettere originali dei Gonzaga 1624 e 1625, ff. 567r–68r, at 567r. Bartoletti might have meant daughters, maid servants, or female relatives. Elisabetta, his wife, gave birth to a short-lived son and possibly other children. Mazzuchelli, 1758, 430.

59. Bartoletti to Ferdinando, September 9, 1625, Bologna, in ASM, AG, Bu. 1173, f. 661r. See table 6.1 for the texts that Bartoletti taught.

linquished it when the university added an ordinary professor of surgery in the following year.[60] Finally, as mentioned above, Bartoletti would conduct the annual public anatomy. Thus, while Bartoletti cost a great deal, the duke and the university got multiple services from him. And Bartoletti attracted students.

Why did Bartoletti leave prestigious Bologna for a new university? Money played an important role. Even though comparing remuneration is difficult when every state had its own monetary system, Mantua clearly offered a much higher salary than Bologna. And although he had to leave behind his lucrative private practice at Bologna, he expected to establish a good practice at Mantua. Second, prestige and visibility probably swayed Bartoletti. At Bologna he was one of six ordinary professors of practical medicine, possibly the most junior.[61] It would take many years for him to be recognized as the leading professor of practical medicine, if it happened at all. Even worse, he had no chance of obtaining the most prestigious medical professorship at Bologna. As a counterweight to its policy of hiring mostly its own subjects, Bologna reserved four professorships, including one in medicine, for eminent non-Bolognese, scholars. These so-called foreigners became highly paid stars at Bologna.[62] But Bartoletti, a native of Bologna, was ineligible. In contrast to the discouraging prospects for advancement at Bologna, Bartoletti would be the star medical professor at Mantua. Third, despite his name dropping, he did not have any other attractive offers. Finally, Duke Ferdinando's enthusiasm may have attracted him. As a relatively young scholar (thirty-eight years of age when he began at Mantua), Bartoletti concluded that appointment as the star professor at a new university generously supported by a prince who valued learning offered the best opportunity to pursue his research and to win fame.

## 4. MORE SEARCHES

The recruitment of Bartoletti from Bologna and of Marta, who taught at Pisa, Padua, and Pavia, were coups. Ferdinando had in hand the two most important professors for the new university. He did not have to worry about theology, philosophy, and the arts, because the Jesuits would fill these positions. But he still needed another ten to sixteen legists and ten to twelve medical scholars to staff the substantial university that he envisioned. So Ferdinando and his chief minister, Alessandro Striggi, asked the duke's agents to

---

60. See the roll for the academic year 1626–27 in ASM, AG, Bu. 3366, f. 108.
61. In the rolls of 1623–24 and 1624–25, Bartoletti was listed last of the six ordinary professors of practical medicine. *I rotuli dello Studio Bolognese*, 1888–1924, 2:358–59, 362–63.
62. Costa, 1912, 32–35; Zaccagnini, 1930, 146–47. The Bolognese government sometimes left these prestigious professorships unfilled for years, which saved money.

## More Searches 145

send confidential reports on the positions, ages, abilities, and possible salary demands of potential appointees currently teaching at Padua and Bologna.[63]

In 1624 Ferdinando and Striggi went a step further: they asked a professor at Padua for names. Ottavio Sagliero, professor of law at the University of Padua for twenty-seven years and a native Paduan, sounded out at least five professors at Padua in the summer and autumn of 1625.[64] The first was Claudio Curtivo of Padua, who held the second-position extraordinary professorship of *Institutes*. Marta also recommended him.[65] The second was Bartolomeo Silvatico, who held the third-position morning ordinary professorship of canon law.[66] The third was Aldreghetto Aldreghetti, another native of Padua, the second-position extraordinary professor of medical theory. All seemed receptive; Aldreghetti told Sagliero that he would also like a professorship for his son, Antonio Luigi Aldreghetti, who in January 1625 had been appointed to the third-position *Institutes* professorship at Padua.[67] Sagliero told the duke that he saw no problem with hiring both.[68] Sagliero also spoke to Benedetto Silvatico, a Paduan, who was the second-position ordinary professor of practical medicine.[69] He added that Bologna wished to hire him at 1,600 scudi but that the Venetian government had denied him permission to move to Bologna. Finally, he mentioned Alessandro Synclitico, a nobleman from Cyprus who held the second-place afternoon ordinary professorship of civil law.[70] In addition to

---

63. For example, see "Mancovestro" (not further identified) to Ferdinando, January 25, 1623, Bologna, and Alessandro Nevola to Striggi, February 21, 1624, Bologna, in ASM, AG, Bu. 1173, Diversi, ff. 255r–56r, 428r.

64. See Sagliero to Duke Ferdinando, June 1, 14, 21, and 28, July 6 and 20, and October 19, 1625, always from Padua. ASM, AG, Bu. 1556, ff. 803r–04r, 806r–v, 823r, 831r–v, 842r, 847r, 925r. Sagliero's letters to the duke began in March 1624, if not earlier, but did not initially deal with the recruitment of professors. See ibid., ff. 195r, 197r, and 285r. Sagliero was first appointed to a minor law professorship at Padua in 1597, then moved up. In the academic year 1624–25 he was the second-position ordinary morning professor of civil law, earning 350 Paduan florins, a middling salary for law professors there. Facciolati, 1978, part 3, 124, 142, 150, 182, 184; and Tomasini, 1986, 253, 258, 262, 265, 271 (misnumbered as 269), 437, 448, 452. There are small discrepancies between the two sources. Sagliero disappeared from the rolls in or about 1632.

65. See Facciolati, 1978, part 3, 146, 158; and Tomasini, 1986, 259, 267, 434, for Curtivo's career at Padua. For Marta's recommendation, see Giovanni Domenico Verasio to the duke, June 1, 1625, Pavia. ASM, AG, Bu. 1756, f. 722r.

66. Facciolati, 1978, part 3, 91; Tomasini, 1986, 244.

67. For Aldreghetto Aldreghetti, see Facciolati, 1978, part 3, 368, 381, and Tomasini, 1986, 312, 451. For Antonio Luigi Aldreghetti, see Facciolati, 1978, part 3, 124, 143, 151, 158, 161; and Tomasini, 1986, 253, 265, 267, 268.

68. Sagliero to Duke Ferdinando, June 14, 1625, Padua, in ASM, AG, f. 806r.

69. Facciolati, 1978, part 3, 333, 339, 353, 358, 372; Tomasini, 1986, 49, 140, 195, 222, 299, 301, 314, 316, 325, 455, 462, 465.

70. For his career at Padua see Facciolati, 1978, part 3, 94, 118, 142; and Tomasini, 1986, 224, 246, 251, 253, 258, 448.

praising these men in measured fashion, Sagliero offered a few personal comments. For example, he found the senior Aldreghetti to be difficult and unstable and concluded that he could not be persuaded to move to Mantua.

Except for the younger Aldreghetti, who was probably a newly graduated doctor of law, these men fitted a pattern. They were mature men, probably in their fifties or older, who had been teaching at the University of Padua for twenty to twenty-five years (Curtivo for thirty-five). All held middle-rank positions and received middling to low salaries; not one was a first-place ordinary professor. And all except Synclitico were Paduans.

This was not happenstance. The Venetian government appointed many Paduans to the faculty of the University of Padua but seldom to first-position professorships. To limit provincialism, and to keep Paduans in their places, the Venetian government preferred to fill most first-place ordinary professorial chairs with the weighty foreign bottoms of distinguished nonsubjects. The Venetian government also forbade Paduan concurrents; that is, two Paduans might not simultaneously fill the first and second places of an ordinary professorship teaching the same text at the same hour.[71] Consequently, able Paduan scholars often found their paths to the highest positions in the university blocked and looked elsewhere.

Sagliero made overtures but did not negotiate for the duke. In September 1625 Giovanni Domenico Verasio, who had represented the duke in face-to-face meetings with Marta in Pavia, came to Padua. He talked to Curtivo and another professor, Giuseppe Angelo of Padua, who was the third-place professor of *Institutes*. Verasio judged both to be able men and Curtivo to possess virtue, eloquence, and presence. Both responded positively to the idea of serving the duke. But first they wished to write to Venice to see if the government would permit them to leave.[72] Although the answers are not known, both remained at the University of Padua.[73] In the end, no Paduan professors moved to Mantua.

Neither did Sagliero. At one point he wrote to Ferdinando that he was coming to the end of his contract at a time when great disturbances were

---

71. Grendler, 2002, 28, 253. In its effort to avoid provincialism, the Venetian government also prohibited its own nobles and original citizens from holding professorships at the University of Padua.

72. Giovanni Domenico Verasio to Duke Ferdinando, September 6, 1625, Padua, in ASM, AG, Bu. 1556, ff. 886r–v. For Angelo's career at Padua, see Facciolati, 1978, part 3, 127, 141, 161, 182, and Tomasini, 1986, 139, 254, 258, 271 (misnumbered as 269).

73. Professors fairly often mentioned that they had to have permission to leave in order to take a position in another university, and they cited the reluctance of governments to give that permission as a reason for declining offers. On the other hand, many professors did move, with or without permission. The role of government permissions in faculty mobility has not been studied.

## More Searches

roiling Italy. He opined that the duke's new university would be a place where alienated youths barred from learning elsewhere might come to study in peace. He predicted that the new university would have a glorious beginning.[74] Even though this looked like a broad hint that he was open to an offer, he stayed at Padua.[75]

Besides Bartoletti, Ferdinando succeeded in persuading only one other professor to leave Italy's two premier universities for Mantua. Andrea Mariani of Bologna taught logic, then natural philosophy, at the University of Bologna from 1618 through 1626. He then taught surgery at the University of Mantua beginning in the academic year 1626–27.[76] The energetic Verasio also tried to persuade two more legists to come from the highly respected University of Pavia, but both declined.[77] The extent to which Duke Ferdinando attempted to recruit professors from Italy's other universities is not known. In any case, no professors are known to have moved from them to Mantua.[78]

Perhaps for this reason, Ferdinando and his agents looked beyond universities. A memorandum from another talent scout assessed the professional experience and qualifications of three legists who were not professors. He recommended Giovanni Petrazzini of Cremona, age fifty-six, who was cur-

---

74. "Mentre nello strepito d'armi, et ne i moti si grandi d'Italia io vivo incaminandomi al fine della mia condotta con una ferma opinione, che cotesta Ser(enità) Alt(ezza) non habbia ad aprir un nuovo studio in tempo, nel quale i giovani, ò alienati dalle lettere, ò portati dall'occasione altrove, ò trattenuti dalle necessità non potrano renderlo cosi numeroso, la dove nella pace per molte conditioni potria haver glorioso principio." Sagliero to Duke Ferdinando, June 1, 1625, Padua, in ASM, AG, Bu. 1556, ff. 803r.

75. Sagliero did receive some reward for his services. In a letter to Duke Ferdinando, he thanked the duke for doing something for a gentlewoman on his request; December 13, 1625, Padua, in ASM, AG, Bu. 1556, f. 999r. It is also possible that Sagliero received some financial reward for his services.

76. See table 6.2 and the Mantuan roll of 1626–27 in ASM, AG, Bu. 3366, f. 108. For his previous career at Bologna, see *I rotuli dello Studio Bolognese*, 1888–1924, 2:338, 342, 346, 350, 354, 358, 362, 367, 371. Although the roll listed him as teaching at Bologna in 1626–27 (p. 371), this was a mistake caused by the fact that university rolls were prepared some time before the beginning of the academic year and, hence, did not reflect late changes.

77. They were Lodovico Vismara, the second-place afternoon civil law professor and Marta's concurrent, and Giovanni Battista Marinoni, extraordinary professor of civil law. See *Memorie di Pavia*, 1970, 88, for their positions. On Vismara see Giovanni Domenico Verasio to the duke, June 1, 1625, Pavia, in ASM, AG, Bu. 1756, ff. 721r–22v. Vismara told Verasio that he needed the permission of the Senate of Milan to leave but this was "almost promised" ("però poscia havere buona licenza dal Senato di Milano dalla quale quasi si promette," Ibid., f. 721v). But he did not come. Marinoni wrote to the duke on October 19, 1625, Pavia, declining his offer, adding that he was quite happy at Pavia. ASM, AG, Bu. 1756, f. 765r.

78. I have checked through all the lists of professors and other material in the printed primary and secondary literature known to me without result. Of course, the available scholarship varies greatly from university to university, and there is less information on the seventeenth century than on the sixteenth.

rently teaching law privately to important clients in Cremona. He had lived in Rome for many years and had served as a judge for the papal nuncio to the Holy Roman Emperor in Prague. More recently he had been the visitor general for Cardinal Pietro Campori (d. 1643), the bishop of Cremona. And in the previous year he had dealt with Chancellor Alessandro Striggi. Petrazzini was willing to deliver two or three lectures in the presence of Duke Ferdinando to prove his ability. The talent scout concluded that he was capable of filling an ordinary professorship in either civil or canon law. Petrazzini was appointed first-position morning ordinary professor of canon law in 1625 and later became second-place afternoon ordinary professor of civil law.[79]

The talent scout next recommended the thirty-seven-year-old Cesare Chiozzi of Casalmaggiore, a town in the southern part of the Mantovano. Although he had made his reputation as a legal consultant, probably meaning that he had written useful consulte and consilia for clients, he had great talent as a teacher, not least because he was also an excellent philosopher, in the opinion of the talent scout. He could fill one of the ordinary law professorships. Chiozzi was appointed to the extraordinary professorship of legal procedures (*De actionibus*). Finally, the talent scout recommended a younger man, Claudio Zocchi, age twenty-seven, for the *Institutes* professorship, the introductory law course. Possessed of an excellent intellect, Zocchi had an active legal practice in Milan and was acquainted with a Milanese senator, who would, presumably, endorse him. However, Zocchi was not hired.[80]

Finally, Ferdinando could draw talent from Mantua and the Gonzaga court. A number of native Mantuans and other subjects with law degrees, many with connections to the Gonzaga court, were available. And years of Gonzaga patronage had created a medical establishment. Duke Ferdinando and his advisers called on these men, some of them accomplished scholars, to fill out the roll of law and medicine professors, as will be seen in chapter 7.

---

79. Undated (possibly 1625) and unsigned memorandum in ASM, AG, Bu. 3366, f. 347r. See tables 6.1 and 6.2 for Petrazzini's appointments.

80. Undated and unsigned memorandum in ASM, AG, Bu. 3366, f. 347r–v. For Chiozzi's professorship, see table 6.1.

CHAPTER 6

# The Peaceful University of Mantua

uke Ferdinando issued a proclamation, as he had done for the Jesuit Public Academy the year before. On September 16, 1625, he told the youth of the state that he had established a complete university that, beginning in November, would teach every discipline. It would boast distinguished professors of law and medicine and every other subject. He invited all to learn virtue and knowledge and promised that students would enjoy their customary privileges. Ferdinando commanded his subjects to study at the University of Mantua. He further ordered those currently studying at other universities to return within two months under pain of "our disfavor." But he promised that everyone who came would be received with paternal love.[1] The proclamation expressed Ferdinando's high hopes for the university.

## 1. FINAL PREPARATIONS AND CRISES

There was much to do as the opening of the new university approached. Duke Ferdinando was out of town, mostly in Venice. As he often did, he named Duchess Caterina de' Medici temporary regent, meaning that she had the authority to act in his name.[2] She presided over a small group that included Ferdinando's chief minister, Count Alessandro Striggi, Giacomo Antonio Marta, and Rocco Piazzoni, the syndic of the new university, which undertook the final preparations. Striggi (1573–1630), the son of a court musician of the same name, has a small place in music history as the author of the libretto of Claudio Monteverdi's first opera, *La favola di Orfeo*, performed in

---

1. ASM, AG, Bu. 3366, f. 78.
2. Quazza, 1922, 106.

## FERDINANDO PER LA GRATIA DI DIO
### Duca di Mantoua, & di Monferrato, &c.

OVENDO porsi in esecutione questo Nouembre prossimo il pensiero, c'habbiamo hauuto da vn tempo in quà d'aprire in questa nostra Città di Mantoua vno Studio vniuersale di tutte le scienze, con hauer Noi già proueduto per tal effetto d'huomini insigni, & eminenti, così nella professione legale, come in quella di medicina, & d'ogni altr'arte, che negli altri Studij d'Italia si professa, i nomi de i quali saranno descritti nel Catalogo de i Lettori, che questo Ottobre si darà fuori. Inuitiamo con la presente tutti i giouani studiosi, amatori della virtù, à venir à godere degli effetti di questa nostra buona volontà, promettendo loro ogni commodo, & fauore particolare in tutte le loro occorrenze, come da i priuilegij degli Scolari, che si manderanno alla Stampa, distintamente potran vedere. E' quanto à i nostri Sudditi, così di questo Stato, come di quello di Monferrato, espressamente comandiamo, che volendo essi studiare fuori di casa loro, debbano farlo in questa Città, prohibendo l'andarsene in altri Studij, & ordinando à quelli, che già vi fossero, il ritornare dentro il termine di due mesi, se saranno in Italia, & di quattro se si trouassero in altra Prouincia: che si come coloro, che non vbbidiranno, insieme con i loro Padri incorreranno nella disgratia nostra, & in altra pena ancora à Noi arbitraria; così quei, che verranno, saranno da Noi con paterno amore riceuuti, e trattati, & benignamente protetti.
Di Mantoua li 16. Settembre 1625.

**FERDINANDO.**

Luogo del Suggello.

V.' Striggius.

*Franciscus Cominus Cancell. man. Seveniss. Domine vel. D. Iacobi Pecorelli eius Cels. à Secretis. subscr.*

Pecorellus.

FIG. 10. Proclamation of the opening of the Peaceful University of Mantua. ASM, AG, Bu. 3366, f. 78. *With permission of the Ministero per i Beni e le Attività Culturali, Archivio di Stato di Mantova.*

# Final Preparations and Crises 151

Mantua in 1607. He also wrote the texts of other musical works and corresponded with Monteverdi after the latter left Mantua in 1612. A capable man who held many positions under the Gonzaga and had been given the title of count, Striggi was as committed to the new university as was Ferdinando.[3] After the meetings, Caterina wrote to the duke outlining the options, sometimes making a recommendation, and asking the duke for a decision. She then implemented his wishes; occasionally Ferdinando left it to her to make final dispositions. Caterina was clear headed and sensible.

A last-minute crisis arose over the metaphysics lectureship. Count Striggi noticed that the roll of Jesuit professors sent by the Jesuit provincial lacked a metaphysics lecturer.[4] Since the father provincial happened to be in Mantua, Striggi spoke to him. The provincial said that Father Vincenzo Serugo of Forlì would deliver the metaphysics lecture in the morning in addition to his morning and afternoon lectures in logic. Serugo had lectured twice a day on a combination of natural philosophy and metaphysics at the Jesuit Public Academy of Mantua (see table 3.1) in the academic year 1624–25; now he would deliver three lectures a day on two different subjects.

Striggi objected that this would be bad for the reputation of the university, inconvenient for the students, and difficult for the lecturer.[5] All three of Striggi's objections had merit, especially the first. What the father provincial proposed did not conform to Italian university practice in which ordinary professors taught a single subject, delivering one lecture a day, five days a week. The fame of Italian universities came from the fact that professors concentrated on a single subject, delivering original and weighty lectures that students came from afar to hear. A university with a Jesuit delivering three lectures daily on two subjects would not meet student expectations.

Striggi proposed that another Jesuit, the eminent scholar Francesco Manfredini of Modena, currently at Parma, should come to Mantua to teach logic, while Father Serugo would teach metaphysics. But the father provincial objected that Manfredini had a problem with his eyes. Striggi countered by suggesting that a Father Cabeo should teach metaphysics, and Serugo logic, to which the provincial also objected.[6] The exasperated Striggi charged that

---

3. Striggi appears repeatedly in Quazza, 1922, 1926.
4. For what follows see Caterina to Ferdinando, October 15, 1625, Mantua, in ASM, AG, Bu. 2176, ff. 553r–54v.
5. Caterina de' Medici to Ferdinando, October 15, 1625, Mantua, in ASM, Bu. 2176, ff. 553r–54v.
6. Manfredini did teach logic, natural philosophy, and metaphysics at the University of Mantua from 1626 to 1629. See ASM, AG, Bu. 3366, ff. 108, 109; table 6.2; and the appendix. Caterina's letter, written by a secretary, referred to "Padre Gabeo." This was probably a mistake for Niccolò Cabeo of Ferrara, S.J. (1586–1650), who taught logic, natural philosophy, and metaphysics at the University of Parma, 1618 through 1621, and was an able mathematician. He had some contacts with Duke Ferdinando and taught mathematics at the Jesuit school in Mantua in

the father provincial favored the University of Parma and had little enthusiasm for the new university in Mantua. Upon being apprised of all this, the duchess resolved to send a personal representative to the provincial to convince him to allow Father Manfredini to come to Mantua. But Striggi persuaded the duchess to consult with the duke to see if he wished to contact the father provincial personally or handle the matter differently.[7]

In the end the Jesuits did not provide a metaphysics professor for the first year of the new university. Instead, Father Ludovico Busti of Venice, not a Jesuit, filled the position (see table 6.1), while Father Serugo delivered two daily lectures on logic. Busti was an interim solution. In the academic year 1626–27, Antonio Morando, a Jesuit, taught metaphysics, and Busti disappeared from the roll. Exactly what lay behind the father provincial's reluctance to provide another Jesuit is not clear. Perhaps the Society was short of university-level teachers, and the father provincial decided that Parma, with its established part-Jesuit university and its school for noble boys, was a higher priority. In any case, the incident pointed to the complicated structure of the University of Mantua, in which the Jesuits, not the duke, named one-third of the lecturers.

Duchess Caterina, Count Striggi, and others dealt with the preparation and printing of the roll, that is, the list of professors, their places in the roll, the texts that they would teach, and the lecture hours. Marta organized the teaching of the legists.[8] And someone else had to get from professors the titles of the texts that they would teach. His job was made more difficult because some professors were out of town, including the Jesuit professor of cases of conscience, who had gone to Rome "for his devotion."[9] On October 22, Caterina wrote to the duke that they had decided to proceed, even though she had not yet received his approval of the roll of the medical professors, on the presumption that he had no objections.[10] So, the roll went to the printer. Caterina added that the students were beginning to arrive and that they needed a matriculation procedure. Marta and Piazzoni proposed that they prepare a form modeled on the printed forms used at the University of Padua, and that the student nations and their officers should be involved. And she

---

1624 according to ARSI, Veneta 71, f. 111v–12r, although he did not appear in the roll of the Jesuit Public Academy of Mantua of 1624–25. For more on Cabeo, see Sommervogel, 1890–1932, 2:483–84; Ingegno, 1972; Baldini, 2002, 296; and *Giambattista Riccioli*, 2002, ab indice.

7. Caterina de' Medici to Ferdinando, October 15, 1625, Mantua, in ASM, AG, Bu. 2176, ff. 553r–54v.

8. Duchess Caterina to Ferdinando, October 17, 1625, Mantua, in ASM, AG, Bu. 2176, f. 558v.

9. "Non hò potuto saper di certo la materia del casisca, essendo egli andato per sua devotione à Roma." Alessandro Nevola to the duke, October 10, 1625, Mantua, in ASM, AG, Bu. 2768, f. 303r.

10. Caterina de' Medici to the duke, October 22, 1625, Mantua, in ASM, AG, Bu. 2176, f. 567r.

# Final Preparations and Crises 153

was happy to tell the duke that the renovations to the building that would be used for the law and medicine lectures were proceeding well.[11]

Some professors requested special treatment or complained about their positions in the roll. The Sicilian Pietro Antonio Cavalli, appointed to the extraordinary professorship of medical theory, asked for a higher salary so that he could bring his family to Mantua. He must have gotten his wish, because he received 350 scudi, while the second-place ordinary professor of medicine, a person normally paid more than an extraordinary professor, received 300 scudi.[12]

Another professor believed that he had been denied his rightful place in the roll. Giacomo Francesco Palperia, ordinary professor of medical botany, complained that Cavalli, an extraordinary professor, was listed ahead of himself, an ordinary professor, in the roll. He charged that Cavalli had convinced those drafting the rolls to do this because it was the practice of the University of Padua. Palperia conceded that this might be the practice at Padua. But, he added, Mantua had committed itself to follow the practice of Bologna, where the professor of medical botany preceded all the extraordinary professors of medicine. And the universities of Pavia and Pisa, where he had studied, did the same.[13] Palperia had a better case than he knew. Paduan rolls at this time listed the ordinary professor of medical botany, as well as all the other ordinary professors of medicine, ahead of the extraordinary professors of medical practice and theory. Cavalli had pulled a fast one.[14]

Some of the legists needed stroking. Giacomo Filippo Rattazzi was appointed first-position morning *Institutes* professor at 200 scudi but wanted more. Caterina consulted with Marta, who recommended increasing Rattazzi's stipend to 300. The duke agreed.[15] Another law professor apparently suffered from shyness and lack of confidence, a very rare occurrence in a law professor. Giovanni Petrazzini had been appointed first-position professor of

---

11. Duchess Caterina to the duke, October 22, 1625, Mantua, in ASM, AG, Bu. 2176, ff. 567v–68r.

12. Duchess Caterina to the duke, October 17, 1625, Mantua, in ASM, AG, Bu. 2176, f. 558v; and the undated list of salaries of professors of medicine in ASM, AG, Bu. 3366, f. 349r.

13. Giacomo Francesco Palperia to Duke Ferdinando, November 5, 1625, Mantua, in ASM, AG, Bu. 2768, f. 327r–v.

14. See the printed arts rolls of the University of Padua for 1617–18 and 1622–23 in ASM, AG, Bu. 1592, no pag. (That rolls of the University of Padua are in the archive of Mantua indicates how much Ferdinando and his ministers intended to follow the practices of established universities.) By contrast, the Bologna rolls do not completely support Palperia's case, because they are somewhat organized according to lecture hours rather than rank. For example, see the roll of the artists for 1624–25 in *I rotuli dello Studio Bolognese*, 1888–1924, 3:362–63.

15. Duchess Caterina to Ferdinando, October 22, 1625, Mantua, and his reply, October 25, Venice, in ASM, AG, Bu. 2176, ff. 567v, 529v. Incidentally, the undated list of the salaries of the legists in ASM, AG, Bu. 3366, f. 369, lists his stipend as only 150 scudi. Obviously, this was changed.

canon law at 300 scudi. Nevertheless, he wished to prove himself by delivering a lecture in the presence of the duchess, but without any other professors there. This was arranged—except that Marta hid behind a door curtain. After the lecture Marta praised him, as did others who heard about the lecture, or who may have shared Marta's hiding place.[16] The episode raises an intriguing question: was Caterina so well educated in Latin and law, or reputed to be so, that Petrazzini believed that she could evaluate his lecture?

## 2. FINANCES

Although the duke, the duchess, and other members of the Gonzaga government had recruited and stroked professors, prepared the rolls, and renovated a building, they had not taken one essential step. Astonishing as it seems, they did not have a tax to finance the university.

The majority of Italian governments financed their universities by taxing the commerce of the host city, or by taxing the food and services consumed by the population of the host city and its surrounding area. A tax on goods coming into the city supported the University of Bologna, and a tax on wine entering the city paid for the University of Rome. At Catania a tax on goods leaving the port supported the university. Turin levied a tax on wine and meat, and Ferrara on meat only, for their universities. At Macerata a tax for the service of grinding grain and other products supported the university. Supplementary funds might come from other sources; for example, a tax on prostitutes helped fund the University of Padua for a short time. But taxes on commerce, food, and services provided the bulk of the funds.[17] Mantua looked in the same direction.

Ferdinando initially imposed a tax on chickens entering the gates of the city but ordered it stopped in September 1625.[18] The duke being out of town, his advisers and the duchess met in council to discuss alternatives on September 25. They considered increasing the tax on meat by one soldo. Another proposal was to increase the duty on wine. Still another proposal was to impose a small tax on the famous wool knitwear that Mantua produced. Such a tax had several advantages: these goods were not currently taxed, only foreigners who bought the knitwear would be obliged to pay the tax, and no

---

16. "Il Rev. Petrazani Cremoneze nominato nel sudetto cattalogo per lettione del canonica la mattina con trecento scudi di stipendio volse far prova di se con una lettione alla presenza mia, et essendo stato sentito dal Marta dietro ad una portiera (perch'egli non volse che ci fusse presente alcuno dei lettori) e stato grandemente da lui et dagl'altri comendato." Caterina de' Medici to the duke, October 22, 1625, Mantua, in ASM, AG, Bu. 2176, f. 567v.

17. Grendler, 2002, 14, 23, 59, 98, 100, 106, 113.

18. This paragraph is based on Alessandro Striggi to the duke, September 25, 1625, Mantua, in ASM, AG, Bu. 2771, f. 265r–v.

burden would be imposed on the peasants (*contadini*), as the poultry tax presumably did. A consensus favored the tax on knitwear. So, Caterina instructed Striggi to write to the duke for his approval. Striggi also politely urged Ferdinando to make a quick decision, because money would soon be needed to pay for the remodeling of the university building and salaries of the professors.

Ferdinando must have agreed, because the government informed the wool merchants that it would tax knitwear at the rate of 1.5 soldi per pound of the finished product. However, the merchants presented a memorandum raising a series of objections, the most important of which was that the tax would be very damaging to an industry that was just now flourishing. If the tax were imposed, this industry would decline, just as the silk industry had. Believing that the objections had merit, the duchess sought alternatives from her advisers. She reported the results to the duke in a long letter of October 15, 1625.[19]

Rocco Piazzoni, the syndic of the new university and a native of Padua, recommended that they follow the practice of the Venetian government for funding the University of Padua.[20] A tax of three *sesini* (small copper coins worth six denari each) per month was levied on every "mouth" (*boccadego*), with mouth defined as every person aged three or older, in the *contado* (surrounding territory) of Padua with the proceeds used to fund the university. The Mantuan council rejected a head tax, because it felt that the contadini of the Mantuan state were so poor that they could not bear any more taxes and would ask for relief from their current imposts. Another proposal was to levy a tax of 20 soldi on every pair of silk hose produced in Mantua. Such a tax would copy the practice of Rome and other cities. Some of Caterina's advisers objected on two grounds: it would damage an industry already in decline because of other taxes, and it was not likely to raise enough money.[21] A third idea was to levy a tax of 1 soldo on every quire of paper sold. However, it was believed that this would produce only 2,000 scudi annually, not enough for the university. Moreover, it would take more than a month to

---

19. Duchess Caterina to the duke, October 15, 1625, Mantua, in ASM, AG, Bu. 2176, f. 555r. Although Caterina wrote that she enclosed the memorandum from the wool merchants, it is not there. However, on October 13, 1625, the knitwear guild did submit a petition protesting a proposed new tax of 37 1/7 soldi on every "weight" (*peso*) of knitwear. A peso amounted to four dozen (48) stockings or caps. Coniglio, 1962, 358 note 12. Coniglio was unaware that the purpose of the proposed tax was to support the university.

20. One wonders if Rocco Piazzoni was related to Francesco Piazzoni of Padua, who taught surgery and anatomy at the University of Padua from 1619 until his death in 1623. Facciolati, 1978, part 3, 390; Tomasini, 1986, 80, 138, 303, 444, 447, 494.

21. It is true that the silk cloth industry was not doing well. See chapter 1, section 2, and the bibliography cited therein.

register all the shops selling paper. The majority of her advisers favored adding one sesino per pound to the tax on meat sold throughout the state (presumably both the Mantovano and Monferrato), thus making the rate the same as for the city of Mantua.[22]

However, some of the Jesuits argued that it was not permissible to burden people of the contado when only the inhabitants of the city would derive benefit or use from the university.[23] Here "benefit" probably meant both the opportunity to study and the increased income that city dwellers would derive from the students who spent money on food and lodging. But other theologians held a contrary opinion and "not without foundation" (*non senza fondamento*), in the view of the duchess. It could not be denied that some inhabitants of the state paid taxes for purposes that did not benefit all, she pointed out. And the duchess recalled that the duke had earlier stated that the tax on meat would not burden the contadini, because they did not buy meat but ate only the animals and chickens that they raised. The duchess suggested that after the first of November the government should add one sesino per pound on pork slaughtered in the city. The date was appropriate for two reasons: the university would begin in November, and so would slaughtering to produce cured meat for the winter. The duchess endorsed an increase of the tax on meat, although she added that it be might be necessary to tax paper as well to get the necessary funds for this year and for the future, when the professors would merit higher stipends based on their accomplishments, as was the practice in other universities. Duchess Caterina finished by requesting that the duke let them know his preference as quickly as possible.[24]

It is remarkable that Ferdinando and his government had not imposed a tax to pay for the university three weeks before the beginning of classes. He had already laid out substantial sums to support the Jesuits and had hired twenty professors for law and medicine. The need for money was very acute if the duke intended to pay professorial salaries in three equal installments (*terzerie*), typically November 1, March 1, and August 1, as was the practice in some universities.[25] However, one suspects that Ferdinando did not intend to

---

22. Duchess Caterina to the duke, October 15, 1625, Mantua, in ASM, AG, Bu. 2176, f. 555r–v. A sesino was a coin worth 6 denari, or pennies, thus, a "sixpence"; it was widely used in Lombardy. The soldo was worth 12 denari.

23. Caterina may have consulted the Jesuits because Ferdinando did not have a personal theologian at this time. Father Paolo Bombino, S.J. (1576–1648?), who had been Ferdinando's theologian, left for Rome in 1622 and was not replaced. Baldini, 2000, 199. The unidentified "other theologians" with a different opinion mentioned below may have been other local clergymen.

24. Duchess Caterina to the duke, October 15, 1625, Mantua, in ASM, AG, Bu. 2176, f. 556r–v.

25. For example, the University of Pisa paid professors three times a year. See the payment records in Verde, 1994. On the other hand, the University of Parma paid its professors in four

pay the first installment on November 1, before the university began. Thus, he had a grace period in which to raise the necessary funds.

Although the duke was slow in putting a tax in place, there were good reasons for proceeding cautiously. Caterina, the duke's advisers, and presumably Ferdinando himself worried about the impact of any tax on the city's manufacturing base as well as the ability of the population to bear more taxes. Caterina listened to the objections from the wool merchants, and the royal couple decided not to tax knitwear, the city's most important product and export. They were also concerned about the plight of the peasantry. And they were troubled enough about the fairness of imposing a tax on many for a university that would benefit a few that they consulted theologians. All this spoke well of the moral sensibilities of the royal couple. But they postponed action to the last minute, which revealed even more about the way that Ferdinando ran his state.

The discussion was not quite over. Sometime after October Piazzoni renewed his argument.[26] He again proposed that Mantua adopt a Paduan-style head tax of 3 sesini per month to be imposed on all inhabitants over the age of three. He stated that this tax produced 17,000 ducats annually for the University of Padua.[27] He noted that the head tax had not been accepted earlier because it was seen as weighing too heavily on the poor, and that it would last too long. Piazzoni proposed that the head tax be limited to three years, time enough to bring the new university to perfection. To the earlier objection that the tax should not be levied on everyone, he argued that having a university in Mantua was such a universal good that all would be happy and honored to help pay for it. Everyone in Mantua would be particularly pleased to support the university, because it benefited the gentleman, the merchant selling his goods, the shopkeeper providing the necessities of life, and even the Jew, although the benefit to Jews was not explained and is hard to understand. Thus, a head tax was appropriate for all. With the money generated, the

---

installments, and Macerata paid every two months. Grendler, 2002, 161. Information on the payment schedule for the University of Mantua has not been located.

26. Piazzoni's memorandum addressed to the duke in ASM, AG, Bu. 3366, f. 397r–v. Although undated, it refers to the discussion of October, but not "ottobre passato." Hence, it is likely that it was written not too far into the academic year 1625–26.

27. Piazzoni slightly exaggerated the amount of money that taxes raised to support the University of Padua. The figure was 13,706 ducats in 1617. Relazione of Giovanni Dandolo, one of the two governors of Padua, of November 28, 1617, in *Relazioni in Terraferma*, 1975, 171. Moreover, Piazzoni did not mention (and may not have known) that a tax on vehicles and several smaller taxes also raised money for the university. Nor did he mention that tax revenues did not produce enough money to meet the expenses of the University of Padua, with the result that professors were not always paid on time. Of course, Padua was a larger university than Mantua, with many highly paid professors. De Bernardin, 1975, 479; Grendler, 2002, 34, 497.

university could be brought to perfection through the creation of a residence college for poor students, an anatomical theater, a botanical garden, and bookstores, all without touching the ducal treasury. And the tax would be only 12 *parpagiole* (small coins used in Lombardy, worth 18 denari) per year per person.[28] When the tax ended after three years, the duke's subjects would be consoled and pleased that they had contributed to such an excellent work. However, Piazzoni's renewed argument failed to convince the royal couple, who opted for the expanded tax on butchered meat at the rate of 6 soldi per pound to pay for the university.[29]

### 3. THE PACIFICO GYMNASIO MANTUANO BEGINS

The great day approached. On Tuesday, November 4, 1625, Duke Ferdinando issued a solemn proclamation for the new Pacifico Gymnasio Mantuano (the Peaceful University of Mantua), the name that he chose.[30] The Public Academy of Mantua, the Jesuit upper school of the academic year 1624–25, disappeared, because the Jesuit lectures became part of the larger university. The proclamation named all the subjects that the new university would teach and affirmed on the basis of previous imperial decrees of emperors Sigismund I and Frederick III that the new university was empowered to grant degrees. And the proclamation added something new: the student rector of the university would have count palatine authority to confer degrees, again thanks to imperial authorization.[31] Obtaining this power for the student rector of the University of Mantua further signified that Ferdinando would do everything possible to make his university a success.

The formal inauguration of the Peaceful University of Mantua occurred on Wednesday, November 5, 1625. It began with a pontifical high Mass in the cathedral, San Pietro, just across the piazza from the ducal palace, sung by Vincenzo Agnelli Soardi, the bishop of Mantua, with professors and the no-

---

28. The coins mentioned permit calculations of the proposed cost per person of the tax. As mentioned earlier, the sesino was worth 6 denari. Since each person would pay 3 sesini monthly, the annual amount would be 216 denari (18 × 12). Piazzoni stated that the total tax would be 12 parpagiole (*parpagliole* in modern spelling). Hence, 1 parpagliola was worth 18 denari, and the annual tax per person would be 216 denari (18 soldi), per person per year. This might not have been burdensome to a master mason earning 40 soldi per day (see Values of Some Coins and Monies of Account ca. 1625 in the front matter), but it was probably a significant sum to a peasant family of five or more.

29. "[B]asta dire che si accrebbero soldi sei per libra sopra la carne del publico macello, che all'anno montava ad una considerabilissima somma." Gorzoni, 1997, 146. The tax seems a little high. I have been unable to determine how much money was raised.

30. "Gymnasium" originally meant a Greek public school for higher studies and was a synonym for *studium* or university in the Renaissance.

31. ASM, AG, Decreti 55, ff. 1r–3v.

## The Pacifico Gymnasio Mantuano Begins 159

bility of the city in attendance.[32] Giacomo Antonio Marta then delivered the inaugural oration, also in the cathedral. It was published as *De Accademiae Mantuanae institutione et praestantia oratio habita Mantuae in Cathedrali Ecclesia die v. Novembris 1625. A Doctore Marta Neapolitano eiusdem Accademia primario Iurisconsulto. Nunc primùm in lucem data a Iosepho a Bubalo Mirandulano eiusdem Accademia Scholastico. Ad Illustrissimum & Excellentiss. Dominum Don Hiacynthum Gonzagam, Serenissimi Ferdinandi filium, eiusdem Accademiae Protectorem* (Oration on the education and excellence of the University of Mantua. Delivered in the cathedral church of Mantua, 5 November 1625, by Doctor Marta of Naples, first jurisconsult in the same university, now first published by Joseph Bubalo of Mirandola, student of the same university. To the most illustrious and most excellent Lord Don Hyacinth, son of the most serene Ferdinand, protector of the same university), in Mantua.[33]

Although the publication lacked a date, it carried a dedicatory letter of February 8, 1626, written by the editor. Bubalo addressed the protector of the university, Giacinto Gonzaga, Ferdinando's son from his annulled marriage to Camilla Faà. He alluded to Don Giacinto's youth—he was eight years and eleven months old at the moment of Marta's lecture—but was sure that he would grow in learning and would watch over the teachers. Bubalo, a matriculated student at the university, praised Marta as his professor.[34]

Marta began by extolling the institution, saying that a wise legal scholar had given the name "university" to the place that accommodated all disciplines, and that a prince established one for the common good, to eradicate error, and to propagate the veneration of God. He noted that universities have most excellent men for philosophy, medicine, public and private customs, sacred laws and institutions, liberal arts, and law, and mentioned the growth of the best disciplines in Mantua. He praised Duke Ferdinando as a most learned man and founder of the university.[35]

Then he celebrated rulers in history who established universities or otherwise arranged for their subjects and people to learn. He began with Moses, who gave laws to the people of Israel to be taught in synagogues, which Marta likened to universities. He next mentioned Jehoshaphat, king of Judah, who in the third year of his reign sent his officers and priests to teach the law of the

---

32. Gorzoni, 1997, 146. A pontifical Mass is a solemn Mass celebrated by a bishop in his capacity as bishop; he wears his episcopal robes and, at certain points, his miter.

33. Marta, 1626. The work is a small quarto volume of eighteen numbered pages including the title page and the blank verso of the title page, or signatures A4, B5. The Bibliotheque Nationale de France–Paris has the only known copy, which is used here.

34. Dedicatory letter of Bubalo, February 8, 1626, in Marta, 1626, 3–4. Bubalo appears in the undated list of matriculated students in ASM, AG, Bu. 3366, f. 384r. Don Giacinto Gonzaga was born on December 4, 1616. Quazza, 1922, 22 note 5; Benzoni, 1996, 247.

35. Marta, 1626, 7–9.

# DE ACCADEMIÆ MANTVANÆ INSTITVTIONE, ET PRÆSTANTIA.

## ORATIO

HABITA MANTVAE IN CATHEDRALI Ecclesia die v. Nouembris 1625.

A DOCTORE MARTA NEAPOLITANO *eiusdem Accademiæ primario Iurisconsulto.*

Nunc primùm in lucem data

A IOSEPHO A BVBALO MIRANDVLANO *eiusdem Accademiæ Scholastico.*

Ad Illustrissimum, & Excellentiss. Dominum Don HIACYNTHVM GONZAGAM, Serenissimi FERDINANDI filium, eiusdem Accademiæ Protectorem.

MANTVÆ, Ex Typis Aurelij, & Ludouici Osannæ fratrum, Ducalium Impressorum. Superiorum permissu.

FIG. 11. Title page of Giacomo Antonio Marta, *De Accademiae Mantuanae institutione et praestantia oratio*. Mantua: Aurelio & Ludovico Osanna, no date, but 1626. *Courtesy of the Bibliothèque nationale de France.*

Lord to his people.³⁶ He praised the Egyptian Ptolemaic kings for establishing the academy of Alexandria. He lauded Caesar for bringing mathematicians from Egypt, Augustus for supporting learning, Hadrian for bringing scholars to Germany, Constantine the Great, and Sarro, a king of the Gauls, who responded to ferocious barbarians with books and learning. Marta argued that learning prevented tyranny, and noted that Julian the Apostate, who deserted true religion, was an opponent of the Christian university. Skipping over the Middle Ages, he praised popes Nicholas V (1447–55), Pius II (1458–64), and Leo X (1513–21) for establishing colleges and universities. He lavished praise on Cosimo de' Medici (1389–1464) for bringing learned Greeks to Italy to teach.³⁷ Marta did not refer to any university foundation by name but emphasized rulers. He linked Ferdinando to past emperors and popes who supported learning. Returning to the present, Marta praised the Jesuits and the current bishop of Mantua, who would preside over the conferral of degrees.³⁸

Although he mentioned that the university would teach medicine, philosophy, and the liberal arts, Marta did not dwell on these fields. The only scholar he named was Bartolo da Sassoferrato. Always the legist, Marta animadverted on how the university would teach divine and human law, as well as the decrees of peoples, the deliberations of senates, edicts, constitutions, and everything else that law created and promulgated. The new university will benefit the common good, it will be a house of virtue, and it will entice young people to the sweetness of learning, he orated. The university will be useful to Mantua and to the "universal republic" by promoting virtue, integrity, peace, and tranquility. Marta finished as he began, by hailing Duke Ferdinando for founding the University of Mantua.³⁹

After Marta's oration, the other professors, laymen and Jesuits, delivered their own inaugural orations in classrooms. And so the wheel of the great machine of the university began to turn, wrote the Jesuit chronicler in an uncharacteristic rhetorical flourish.⁴⁰ The Jesuits taught their classes in a building located at the end of their island; it had previously belonged to a certain "marchesa di Grana" and had been renovated by the duke. The professors of law and medicine taught in another building, described as a palace with large rooms appropriate for lectures, that had once belonged to a

---

36. Jehoshaphat, who ruled about 870–848 B.C., was one of the good kings of Judah. Although Marta gave no references anywhere in the oration, he probably referred to 2 Chronicles 17:7–9.

37. Marta, 1626, 10–13. Sarro has not been further identified.

38. Marta, 1626, 14, 18.

39. Marta, 1626, 9, 14, 18.

40. "Fece la prima oratione de' studii il famoso et eccellente signor dottore Marta, qual poi, seguitato susseguentemente nelle scuole private dagl'altri et anche da' nostri padri, diè come prima ruota il moto et il corso a tutta la gran machina dello studio." Gorzoni, 1997, 146.

Marchese Prospero Gonzaga. Although outside the Jesuit island, it was contiguous with the building in which the Jesuits taught.[41] No permanent anatomical theater was built, which meant that a temporary wooden structure would be erected in January for the annual anatomy, the practice in universities lacking permanent theaters. The demonstration of medicinal plants would take place in the ducal botanical garden located in the courtyard of a wing of the vast ducal palace, and the chemical demonstrations in a local distillery (see chapter 7, section 2).

Ordinary lectures began on Friday, November 7, 1625, and ended on June 30, 1626. The calendar for the academic year 1625–26 listed ninety-six days of ordinary lectures and forty-two days of extraordinary lectures. A number of Sundays were designated extraordinary lecture days.[42] On the other hand, no lectures were held on many religious holidays, including June 21, the Feast of Blessed Luigi Gonzaga. Although the number of lectures was not high, Mantua's calendar conformed to the practice of other Italian universities in the early seventeenth century.[43] The calendar decreed a carnival vacation of thirty-eight days (including Sundays) and an Easter vacation of twenty-one days. Carnival was not a complete vacation from classes, because the annual public anatomy took place at that time and could last for two weeks. It attracted many, including nonmedical students and outsiders.

In the academic year 1625–26 the University of Mantua had twenty-nine professors who filled thirty-six positions as ordinary professors, extraordinary professors, and special positions such as plant demonstrator. The faculty divided into three nearly equal parts. Eleven men (ten ordinary professors, another one teaching on holidays) taught law, with four positions vacant. Eight men filled eleven medical positions, with two places vacant. Bartoletti held three positions: he was the first-position afternoon ordinary professor of medical practice, he lectured on surgery on holidays, and he conducted the public anatomy during carnival. Pietro Antonio Cavalli held two positions: he was extraordinary professor of medical theory, and he taught chemistry on holidays. The arts, philosophy, and theology part of the university consisted

---

41. See map 3. ASM, Ms. Carlo d'Arco 80, Mambrino, "Dall'historia di Mantova," pp. 971, 973; Amadei, 1956, 383; Gorzoni, 1997, 146: "Lo studio delle arti e scienze non nostre s'aperse nel palazzo contiguo al nostro collegio, che termina l'isola verso la chiesa di Santo Stefano, dove in grandi saloni, resi usuali per questo, si leggeva il *ius* civile e canonico e le arti della medicina."

42. The printed calendar for the 1625–26 academic year is found in ASM, AG, Bu. 3366, f. 74.

43. For example, the calendar of the University of Padua for the academic year 1641–42 listed 111 ordinary lecture days and 50 extraordinary lecture days between November 5 and June 30, with the usual very long carnival and Easter vacations and various religious holidays. Printed calendar of the University of Padua for 1641–42, found in ASB, Assunteria di Studio, Bu. 76, no pag. However, at Padua and elsewhere, unauthorized holidays reduced the number of lectures to about what the Mantua calendar listed. Grendler, 2002, 495–96.

TABLE 6.1
University of Mantua Roll, 1625–1626

| Lecture, a.m./p.m. hour: texts | Lecturer |
|---|---|
| Canon law, 2nd a.m: de constitutionibus | Giovanni Petrazzini of Cremona |
| | Second position vacant |
| Canon law, 2nd p.m.: de accusationibus | Andrea Malaguzzi of Reggio Emilia |
| | Second position vacant |
| Civil law, 1st a.m: ff. si certum petatur | First position vacant |
| | Paolo Sghibini of Mantua |
| | Giovanni Domenico Verasio of Nizza Monferrato* |
| Civil law, 1st p.m: ff. de verborum obligationibus | Giacomo Antonio Marta of Naples |
| | Angelo Angelelli of Perugia |
| | Third position vacant |
| *Institutes*, 3rd a.m: de tutelis | Giacomo Filippo Rattazzi of Monferrato a Castronovo |
| *Institutes*, 3rd a.m: de obligationibus | Bartolomeo Galvani of Mantua |
| *Institutes*, 3rd p.m: books 3 and 4 | Andrea Lavezzari of Valtellina |
| | Francesco Paraleoni of Mantua |
| De actionibus, extraordinary holiday, 2nd p.m. | Cesare Chiozzi of Casalmaggiore |
| Sacred Theology, 2nd a.m: de sacramentis in genere, de Eucharistae sacramento et missae sacrificio | Francesco Rossano of Forlì, S.J. |
| Sacred Theology, 2nd p.m: Aquinas, 1st and 2nd questions de vitijs, peccatis, de legibus, and de gratia | Giacomo Filippo Trezzi of Innsbruck, S.J. |
| Sacred Scripture, 3rd p.m: *Psalms* | Giovanni Battista Noceto of Genoa, S.J. |
| Cases of Conscience, 2nd p.m: de restitutione et de contractibus | Emilio Zucchi of Parma, S.J. |
| Metaphysics, 2nd a.m: *De anima* | Ludovico Busti of Venice† |
| Medical Theory, ordinary 1st a.m: Avicenna *Canon*, bk. 1, fen 1 | Pietro Francesco Oclerio of Trino |
| | Giacomo Ferrari of Mantua |
| Medical Practice, ordinary 1st p.m: Avicenna *Canon*, bk. 1, fen 4‡ | Fabrizio Bartoletti of Bologna |
| | Second position vacant |
| Anatomy, anatomical dissection during Carnival; other hour to be announced** | Fabrizio Bartoletti of Bologna |
| Medical Botany, 3rd a.m: Dioscorides, *De materia medica* | Giacomo Francesco Palperia of San Salvatore Monferrato |
| Medical Botany Demonstration; to begin in the botanical garden on May 2, 1626, hours to be determined | Zanobio Bocchi of Florence |
| Natural Philosophy, 2nd a.m: 8 books of the *Physics*, *De caelo*, bk. 4, and *De generatione*, bk. 1 | Antonio Morando of Piacenza, S.J. |
| Natural Philosophy, 2nd p.m: same texts†† | Antonio Morando of Piacenza, S.J. |

*(continued)*

TABLE 6.1
*(continued)*

| Lecture, a.m. / p.m. hour: texts | Lecturer |
|---|---|
| Medical Theory extraordinary, 2nd a.m: classes of diseases in their circumstances, causes, and symptoms | Pietro Antonio Cavalli of Sicily |
| Medical Practice extraordinary | Vacant |
| Chemistry, vacation days, 2nd a.m: distillation and the preparation of chemical medicines; every application will be demonstrated in the hall of the distillery of Fausto Vialardi, ducal distiller | Pietro Antonio Cavalli of Sicily |
| Moral Philosophy of Aristotle, 3rd a.m: 10 books of the *Nicomachean Ethics* | Matteo Torto of Verona, S.J. |
| Surgery 3rd a.m: on wounds | Vacant. In the interim Fabrizio Bartoletti will lecture on holidays |
| Logic, 2nd a.m: Porphyry, *Isagoge*; Aristotle, *Categories, On interpretation,* and *Analytics,* bk. 4 | Vincenzo Serugo of Forlì, S.J. |
| Logic, 2nd p.m: same texts†† | Vincenzo Serugo of Forlì, S.J. |
| Mathematics, 1st a.m: Euclid, *Elements*; Clavius, *Sphaera*; and astrolabe | Cesare Moscatelli of Bologna, S.J. |
| Latin Humanities, 2nd a.m: Cicero, *Orator* and *Verrines*; Q. Curtius Rufus, *History of Alexander the Great* | Alessandro Simonetta of Milan, S.J. |
| Latin Humanities, 2nd p.m: Horace; Virgil, *Aeneid*, bk. 8 | Alessandro Simonetta of Milan, S.J. |
| Greek Humanities, 3rd p.m: Basil the Great, *Letter to Gregory the Theologian* | Alessandro Simonetta of Milan, S.J. |

*Source: Rotulus Excellentissimorum Dominorum Doctorum legentium in Almo* Pacifico Gymnasio Mantuano *infrascriptas lecturas, quas aggredientur die v. mensis Novembris anni instantis MDCXXV. Mantuae, Apud Aurelium & Ludovicum Osannam fratres, Ducales Impressores,* 1625. ASM, AG, Bu. 3366, f. 64. It is a large printed sheet, 36 x 50 cm. The table conveys the information in the roll, but it is not a translation, and it has been reorganized slightly for clarity. Further explanation of some of the lectureships and teaching is found in chapter 7. Latin place names have been rendered into Italian, and some names have been standardized according to the best available information. The roll does not indicate which professors were Jesuits; hence, "S.J." has been added to those who were. When two professors taught the same subject at the same hour, the first listed held the first position, and the second held the second position, usually at a lower salary.

*His place of origin is listed as "Nitiensis." Given his service to Duke Ferdinando in the recruitment of professors, he was likely a subject of the duke and came from Nizza Monferrato rather than Nice.

†Busti was a priest but not a Jesuit.

‡Avicenna (Ibn Sina, 980–1037) was the most important Arab medical writer; his *Canon of Medicine* was a major curriculum text in medieval and Renaissance medical teaching.

**Carnival began on Saturday, January 17, 1626, and lasted until Ash Wednesday, February 25. The roll reads "Administrabit Anatomen tempore carnispriuij. Hora aliàs declaranda." The meaning of the last phrase is not completely clear.

††The description does not indicate if the same or different texts of Aristotle were to be taught in the morning lecture and afternoon lecture.

# The Pacifico Gymnasio Mantuano Begins 165

of nine Jesuits and Father Ludovico Busti, the last-minute substitute metaphysics professor; together they delivered fourteen daily lectures. This was a medium-sized university, about the size of the universities of Rome and Turin in the early seventeenth century, and slightly larger than Parma, the other part-Jesuit university.[44]

The University of Mantua had two beadles, one for arts, one for law. Their duties included announcing feast days and vacations, counting the number of students who attended lectures, and checking to see if the professor showed up on time, at the middle of the hour, or not at all. Beadles were also present at general disputations, and they began and ended circular disputations.[45]

The Peaceful University of Mantua had one officer not found in other Italian universities, syndic of the university, filled by Rocco Piazzoni. Duke Ferdinando may have viewed the syndic as the person to oversee the university on his behalf. Almost all princes and communes governed universities in their states through an intermediate body of elected or appointed officials with some independence, usually called Riformatori dello Studio or Ufficiali dello Studio, thus keeping the university at arm's length from the sovereign. By contrast, the Medici grand dukes of Tuscany ruled the University of Pisa through the Provveditore dello Studio di Pisa. He was an appointed official who resided in Pisa and reported to an official just below the grand duke. The provveditore prepared the roll, recommended appointments and stipend increases for the professors, generated ideas for attracting more students, and had the authority to incarcerate students.[46] Given his studies at the University of Pisa and extensive contacts with Grand Duke Ferdinando I de' Medici, Ferdinando Gonzaga surely was familiar with the office. Piazzoni's participation in the discussions over the finances of the University of Padua suggests that his role was intended to be like that of a provveditore. If so, his tenure was short. The rolls of 1626–27 and 1627–28 did not list Piazzoni or any other syndic.[47]

The salary expenses for the law and medicine parts of the new university were high. The legists received 4,070 Mantuan scudi.[48] The medical professors

---

44. Grendler, 2002, 61, 97–98, 132, 515.

45. The calendar of the academic year 1625–26 listed two beadles, Salomon Porta and Antonius Andreasius. ASM, AG, Bu. 3366, f. 74. The duties of the arts beadle are given in ibid., f. 365r.

46. Cascio Pratilli, 1975, 54–55, 128–31, 171, 195–96; De Rosa, 1983; Marrara, 1993, 89–101.

47. ASM, AG, Bu. 3366, ff. 108, 109.

48. To be precise, Marta received 1,500 scudi; Angelelli and Malaguzzi 450 scudi each; Sghibini, Verasio, Lavezzari, and Petrazzini 300 each; Rattazzi 150 (later raised to 300); Galvani 70; and Chiozzi 50. No figure was given for Paraleoni, while 200 scudi was set aside for the second-position morning canon law professor, which was not filled in 1625–26. See an undated and untitled list of the salaries of the legists in ASM, AG, Bu. 3366, f. 369r. It was a provisional listing of the professors and their salaries. Although it lacks a date, it must be September or October 1625, because the names and positions almost exactly match the 1625–26 roll. The exchange rate used

received about 2,850 scudi, making a total of 6,920 scudi.[49] Two beadles, two booksellers (one for law, one for arts), and a notary cost about another 150 scudi, bringing the salary costs, excluding the Jesuits, to about 7,070 scudi annually.[50] And Ferdinando had awarded the Jesuits land and an annuity designed to give them about 1,500 scudi annually for their university teaching. Hence, the total cost of the University of Mantua was about 8,500 scudi. The salary expenses of the University of Mantua were higher than those of the University of Rome and the University of Pisa, but about half the cost of the University of Padua salaries.[51]

Marta received the highest stipend of 1,500 scudi, while Bartoletti received 1,200 scudi. The remuneration levels for the professors of various disciplines, and distribution among higher and lower ranking positions, were typical for Italian universities. Marta received about 21 percent of the total allocated to law and medicine salaries, while Bartoletti received about 17 percent. Giving the star legist and leading medical professor disproportionate fractions of the total salary money available was common practice.

As the university continued, the vacant positions were filled and new positions added. In 1625–26 the first-position ordinary morning professor of civil law, traditionally the second most important law position in a university, was left vacant. In 1626–27 Fausto Soncini of Brescia was appointed to the position at a salary of 500 scudi at 5 lire to the scudo. But he complained to the duke that he thought he was going to be paid in scudi worth 7 lire, hence, 700

---

at this time was 5 lire = 1 Mantuan scudo. See Fausto Soncini to the duke, November 23, 1626, Mantua, in which he asked for more money from the duke. ASM, AG, Bu. 2775, f. 548r.

49. Bartoletti received 1,000 scudi plus a rented house and another 200 scudi to teach surgery as a temporary arrangement. Oclerio received 500 scudi, and Cavalli received 350 for the position of extraordinary professor of medical theory. His chemistry position is not mentioned. Ferrari received 300 scudi, and Palperia 200. There is no mention of Bocchi (plant demonstrator) or Busti, who taught metaphysics. Three hundred scudi were intended for a "medico Mattias" from Casale as Bartoletti's concurrent. But the 1625–26 roll does not list him. Hence, the total of 2,850 scudi is approximate. See the provisional list of medical professors and salaries in ASM, AG, Bu. 3366, f. 349r. Although it lacks a title and date, it must be September or October 1625, because of its congruence with the roll of 1625–26.

50. The document giving the salaries of the legists (ASM, AG, Bu. 3366, f. 369 r) listed two beadles costing 50 scudi (whether for each or together is not clear); two "librari," one each for arts and law, at 50 ducats combined; and a notary with no salary indicated. Perhaps the total was about 150 scudi. On November 11, 1625, one Domenico Torre wrote to the duke asking for the job of notary for the university. He argued that he knew Latin and the vernacular well, and had experience in drafting legal documents. It is not known if he got the position. ASM, AG, Bu. 2768, f. 334r–34bis r.

51. Grendler, 2002, 61, 74, 497 note 77. The Pisan comparison assumes that a Florentine florin was worth about the same as a Mantuan scudo, while the Paduan florin was worth 5 lire, the same as the Mantuan scudo. Of course, all comparisons are only estimates, because money systems were different, the value of monies fluctuated, and the cost of living varied from place to place.

Mantuan scudi. Although he avowed that he was the duke's "creature," he believed that for the sake of his honor and that of the university, a first-position professor (*primario lettore*), should be paid 700 scudi.[52] Whether he got the higher stipend is not known.

The 1626–27 roll listed thirty-four professors (fourteen legists, ten medical scholars, and ten Jesuits) who filled forty-two ordinary and extraordinary lectureships: seventeen in law, eleven in medicine, and fourteen in arts, philosophy, and theology. The most notable additions were the civil law professorship filled by Soncini, a *Pandects* (humanistic jurisprudence) professorship, and a professorship of feudal law. Andrea Mariani of Bologna, who had previously taught at the University of Bologna, became professor of surgery, relieving Bartoletti of that responsibility. The university now had both a lecturer on medical botany and a plant demonstrator. A Jesuit taught metaphysics, replacing Father Ludovico Busti.[53]

The university expanded a little more in the academic year 1627–28 by adding three professors, making it thirty-seven men who delivered forty-two lectures. Compared with the academic year 1625–26, the university had about a quarter more faculty members (thirty-seven to twenty-nine) and one-sixth more lectures (forty-two compared with thirty-six). The faculty was about the size of the University of Perugia, and it approached Pisa.[54] In 1627–28 fourteen legists delivered sixteen lectures, with two legists holding both ordinary and extraordinary (holiday) lectureships, plus two vacancies. There were twelve medical scholars filling thirteen lectureships with no vacancies. Bartoletti still held the first-position ordinary afternoon professorship of practical medicine and did the annual anatomy. Ten Jesuits and one layman delivered thirteen lectures daily in theology, philosophy, logic, and the humanities.[55] Two hard-working Jesuits gave two lectures daily. Thus, the university was approaching the goal of each professor teaching a single course and delivering one lecture a day. It is likely that salary costs amounted to at least 1,000 more scudi than in 1625–26, making the total a minimum of about 9,500 scudi or a little more.[56] The roll of 1627–28 probably marked what Duke Ferdinando and

---

52. Fausto Soncini to the duke, November 23 and December 7, 1626, Mantua, in ASM, AG, Bu. 2775, ff. 548r–v, 570r. Soncini's name first appeared in the letter of Giovanni Battista Tiberio to the duke, May 13, 1627, Bologna. ASM, AG, Bu. 1174, f. 133r.

53. The 1626–27 roll (a large printed page, 36 x 50 cm.) is found in ASM, AG, Bu. 3366, f. 108.

54. Grendler, 2002, 68, 74, 515.

55. That the number of arts, philosophy, and theology lectures declined by one is a tentative statement. It is not clear from the roll of 1627–28 whether Giovanni Francesco Natta, the Jesuit humanities professor, delivered more than one daily lecture or alternated days and hours for the Greek and Latin texts that he taught.

56. It is assumed that Soncini had to be content with 500 scudi, and that the other new positions, traditionally not well paid, amounted to another 500 scudi or a little more.

TABLE 6.2
University of Mantua Roll, 1627–1628

| Lecture, a.m. / p.m. hour: texts | Lecturer |
|---|---|
| Canon law, 2nd a.m: de constitutionibus | Paolo Sghibini of Mantua |
| | Second place vacant |
| Canon law, 2nd p.m: *Decretum,* bk. 5; de purgatione canonica; de poenitentijs et remissionibus; and seqq. titulos | Andrea Malaguzzi of Reggio Emilia |
| | Second place vacant |
| Civil law, 1st a.m: *Digest,* ff. de officio eius, cui mandata | Fausto Soncini of Brescia |
| | Francesco Vecchi of Siena |
| Civil law, 1st p.m: *Digest,* ff. de novis operis nuntiatione | Giacomo Antonio Marta of Naples |
| | Giovanni Petrazzini of Cremona |
| *Pandects* (Humanistic Jurisprudence), 2nd a.m: *Old Digest* | Andrea Lavezzari of Valtellina |
| *Institutes,* 3rd a.m: tit.de usucap., de longi temp. praescript. and de donat.; tit.de tutelis, cum seg. Ad materiam spectantibus | Francesco Paraleoni of Mantua |
| | Francesco Andreasi of Mantua |
| *Institutes,* 3rd p.m: tit. de fideiuss. cum seq. ad materiam spectan.; tit. de obligationibus et sequentes | Giacomo Filippo Rattazzi of Monferrato a Castronovo Incise |
| | Bartolomeo Galvani of Mantua |
| *De regulis iuris,* 2nd a.m. | Giulio Camillo Marta of Naples |
| *De feudis,* extraordinary, holidays 1st a.m. | Giacomo Filippo Rattazzi of Monferrato a Castronovo Incise |
| Criminal law, extraordinary, holidays 2nd a.m. | Andrea Lavezzari of Valtellina |
| *Institutes, de actionibus,* extraordinary, holidays 1st p.m. | Giacomo Antonio Grandi of Mantua |
| *Institutes, de obligationibus,* extraordinary, holidays, 2nd p.m. | Giacomo Torrolo of Mantua |
| Sacred Scripture, 3rd p.m: *Genesis,* ch. 1 | François Remond of Dijon, S.J. |
| Sacred Theology, 2nd a.m: questions on God three and one | Francesco Rossano of Forlì, S.J. |
| Sacred Theology, 2nd p.m: questions on justice and law | Giacomo Filippo Trezzi of Innsbruck, S.J. |
| Cases of Conscience, 2nd p.m: ecclesiastical censures | Lorenzo Megli of Sarzana, S.J. |
| *De anima & Metaphysics* (Metaphysics), 2nd p.m: *De generatione,* bk. 2; *Metaphysics,* bk. 12 | Vincenzo Serugo of Forlì, S.J. |
| Medical Theory, 1st a.m: Hippocrates, *Aphorisms* | Pietro Francesco Oclerio of Trent |
| | Giacomo Ferrari of Mantua, concurrent |
| Medical Practice, 1st p.m: particular diseases of the thoracic cavity | Fabrizio Bartoletti of Bologna |
| | Giovanni del Monte of Mantua, concurrent |
| Anatomy: manage the anatomy to begin on January 17, 1628, hour to be announced* | Fabrizio Bartoletti of Bologna |
| Medical botany, 3rd a.m: "Leget de Aquis Thermalibus"† | Giuseppe Guerrero of Guastalla |

*(continued)*

TABLE 6.2
*(continued)*

| Lecture, a.m. / p.m. hour: texts | Lecturer |
|---|---|
| Medical botany demonstration: to begin on May 2, 1628, in the botanical garden at the determined hour | Galeazzo Coccapani of Carpi |
| Natural philosophy, 2nd a.m: 8 books of the *Physics*, 4 books of *De caelo,* and *De generatione,* bk 1 | Francesco Manfredini of Modena. S.J. |
| Natural philosophy, 2nd p.m: same texts | Francesco Manfredini of Modena. S.J. |
| Medical theory, extraordinary, 2nd a.m: art of medicine‡ | Giacomo Francesco Palperia of San Salvatore Monferrato |
| | Luigi Mazzuchi of Mantua |
| Medical practice, extraordinary, 2nd hour p.m: syphilis** | Andrea Zatta of Mantua |
| | Carlo Tonolo of Mantua |
| Chemistry, 3rd p.m: teaching about minerals and metals in the chemical way; begin chemical operations eight days before the anatomy†† | Jean Clave of France |
| Moral philosophy of Aristotle, 3rd a.m: classes of moral virtues | Matteo Torto of Verona, S.J. |
| Surgery, 3rd a.m: on tumors‡‡ | Andrea Mariani of Bologna |
| Logic, 2nd a.m: Porphyry, *Isagoge*; Aristotle, *Categories, On interpretation, Prior* and *Posterior Analytics* | Orazio Fontana of Bologna, S.J. |
| Logic, 1st p.m: same texts | Orazio Fontana of Bologna, S.J. |
| Mathematics, 1st p.m: Euclid, *Elements*; Clavius, *Sphaera*; pseudo-Aristotle, *Mechanics* | Cesare Moscatelli of Bologna, S.J. |
| Tacitus, 3rd p.m. | Antonio Possevino of Mantua |
| Greek and Latin Humanities, alternate days and different hours: Cicero, *Orator* and *Pro Milone*; Aristole, *Rhetoric*; Virgil, *Aeneid,* bk. 6; Isocrates, *To Demonicus* | Giovanni Francesco Natta of Monferrato, S.J. |

Source: *Rotulus Excellentissimorum Dominorum Doctorum legentium in Almo* PACIFICO GYMNASIO *Mantuano infrascriptas lecturas, quas aggredientur die v. Novembris MDCXXVII*. Mantuae, Ex Officina Typographica Fratrum de Osannis, Ducalium Impressorum, 1627. ASM, AG, Bu. 3366, f. 109. It is a large printed sheet, 36 x 50 cm. The table conveys the information in the roll, but it is not a translation and has been reorganized slightly for clarity. Latin place names have been rendered into Italian, and some names have been standardized according to the best available information. The roll does not indicate which professors were Jesuits; hence, "S.J." has been added to those that were. Further explanation of some of the lectureships and teaching is found in chapter 7. When two professors taught the same subject at the same hour, the first listed held the first position, and the second held the second position, usually at a lower salary. Concurrent may mean a slightly higher second position.

\*The roll states that the anatomy was to begin on the feast of St. Anthony (of Padua), which was January 17, 1628.
†The meaning of "de Aquis Thermalibus" is not clear.
‡The Latin is "Legent artem medicinalem," which might refer to Galen's *Ars medica*, his introductory treatise.
\*\*The Latin is "de morbo Gallico."
††For more discussion of this lectureship, including the Latin roll description and Clave, see chapter 7.
‡‡Whether "de Tumoribus" was a generic description of the teaching or referred to a precise medical work, such as one of Galen's short treatises, or a section in a longer medical work, is unclear.

Chancellor Striggi saw as the full size of the university, even though Duke Vincenzo II now ruled Mantua.

### 4. STUDENTS

The Peaceful University of Mantua instituted a matriculation process that yielded the names of 238 students for the academic year 1625–26.[57] About 51 percent of the matriculated students came from the Gonzaga state: eighty-seven came from the Mantovano excluding Mantua, and thirty-four from the duchy of Monferrato. About 47 percent came from northern Italy outside the Gonzaga state, two came from Florence, one from Naples, and one from Palermo. The university had four matriculated German students but no other non-Italians.[58]

The northern Italian students' places of residence suggest the universities with which the University of Mantua successfully competed. Thirty-nine students came from the Venetian Republic. Numerous laws obliged subjects of the Republic of Venice to attend the University of Padua, and most probably did. Nevertheless, thirty-nine Venetian subjects attended the University of Mantua.

About a dozen students came from Lombardy, whose university was Pavia. Another twenty came from Ferrara and its territory, which had a university in Ferrara. Fourteen students came from Trent, which had no university. Most of the eighty-seven students from the Mantovano, plus the unmatriculated students from Mantua itself, would have attended the nearby universities of Parma, Bologna, Ferrara, Padua, and Pavia if Mantua did not exist. And it is likely that some of the thirty-four students from Monferrato would have attended the University of Turin, which was much closer than Mantua. Thus,

---

57. The names come from "Not. scholares studentes in Almo Pacifico Gymnasio Mantuano, super matricula descripti" in ASM, AG, Bu. 3366, ff. 381r–86v. As the title indicates, this is a summary list of matriculated students, not the original matriculation records. Although undated, it is clearly 1625–26. For example, it lists Giulio Camillo Marta as a student on f. 383v. He received a doctorate in law in both laws on April 23, 1626, and became a professor in 1626–27. In addition, "Joseph Bubalo of Mirandola" (D. Josephus d. Bubalo Mirandolensis), who published Marta's inaugural oration in February 1626 and called himself Marta's student, is also listed as a student at f. 384r.

58. The list gives each matriculated student's name and provenance, and indicates if he was a councillor of a student nation. The list of students and places not from the Gonzaga state is as follows: Verona 15, Trent 14, Reggio Emilia 12, Brescia 11, Cremona 9, Mirandola 8, Padua 6, Carpi 4, Ferrara 4, Vicenza 4, Milan 3, Bergamo 2, Correggio 2, Faenza 2, Florence 2, Piacenza 2, Como 1, Concordia 1, Lavena 1, Modena 1, Naples 1, Palermo 1, and Venice 1. The four German students were Johann Vesling from Minden, one from Westphalia, and two brothers simply called "Theutonici." The places of origins of five students are unclear or unreadable. ASM, AG, Bu. 3366, ff. 381r–86r.

despite the existence of six universities in northern Italy, including the famous Bologna and Padua, Mantua competed successfully for students.

The above figures included matriculated students. But not all students at Italian universities matriculated, and this was the case at Mantua.[59] Members of the clergy, especially the regular clergy, traditionally were not required to matriculate. This must have been true at Mantua, because the list did not include any clergymen, not even any Jesuits. But some Jesuits did study at the university: the college in Mantua had sixteen scholastics in residence in 1625, sixteen in 1627, and eight in 1628.[60] As the name indicates, scholastics were Jesuit students, usually intended for the priesthood. Hence, the scholastics attended the university courses in theology, biblical studies, metaphysics, and so on. In addition, the university enrolled an unknown number of clergymen from other religious orders plus secular clergymen. They attended universities in increasing numbers because the Council of Trent strongly encouraged clergymen to obtain university degrees and made possession of a theology doctorate a prerequisite to hold some benefices.

Students from the host city traditionally were not required to matriculate. This was true of Mantua: the list of 238 students included only one Mantuan.[61] But men from the host city normally constituted one of the largest, sometimes the largest, student cohorts. If the total number of unmatriculated students (sixteen Jesuit scholastics, an unknown number of other clergymen, and an unknown number of Mantuans) came to fifty to sixty, then the University of Mantua had 288 to 298 students in 1625–26. This was comparable to some of Italy's smaller universities and an encouraging figure for the first year of a new university.[62]

Like established universities, the Peaceful University of Mantua had student organizations called nations, which were formal associations of students from a particular region, each with at least one officer, a councillor.[63] In 1625–26 it had sixteen student nations. Most of the nations represented students from north Italian towns outside the Gonzaga state: Correggio, Cremona,

59. On the lacunae in matriculation records, a phenomenon needing further investigation, see Del Gratta, 1983, xi–xvi (University of Pisa); and Brizzi, 1988, 251–53, 256–58 (University of Bologna).

60. ARSI, Veneta 39 I, ff. 132r (catalog of Jesuits at Mantua in 1625), 197r–v (catalog of Jesuits at Mantua in 1628); Veneta 71, ff. 142v–43r (catalog of Jesuits at Mantua in 1627).

61. "Horatius Garba Mantuanus." ASM, AG, Bu. 3366, f. 385v.

62. A figure of 288 to 298 made Mantua about the same size as small universities, such as Catania, Macerata, or Perugia around 1600. By contrast, Bologna and Padua probably had about 1,500 students at that time. Grendler, 2002, 19, 34, 36, 69, 107, 115, 515. A caution: all enrollment figures for Italian universities at this time are only educated guesses based on limited documentation.

63. For the nations at the University of Pisa in the late sixteenth and the seventeenth centuries, see Marrara, 1993, 110–16.

Milan, Modena, Padua, Reggio Emilia, Venice, and Verona, plus Rome in central Italy. There were four nations of students from the two parts of the Gonzaga state: Bozzolo, Guastalla, and Viadana from the Mantovano, as well as the Monferrato nation. And Mantua had three ultramontane nations: England, Germany, and Poland. By contrast, the University of Bologna had over forty law nations and about twenty arts nations in the early seventeenth century.[64]

Because the University of Mantua had no students from England, Poland, or Rome, Italians served as councillors for these nations; for example, Silvestro Ripa of Brescia became the councillor of the Polish nation.[65] Since there were no Polish students to vote for him, it is likely that Piazzoni, Striggi, or the duke appointed him. Ferdinando insisted that his new university should have all the features of established universities from the beginning, possibly in order to attract students from distant lands.

Like other Italian universities, Mantua particularly wished to attract German students. Princes and republics wanted them because they believed that a large number of German students enhanced the prestige of the university. Many German students were nobles or otherwise privileged; after obtaining degrees, usually in law, they assumed leadership roles in their home states. In addition, civic authorities, merchants, and landlords saw German students as free spenders who aided the local economy. Consequently, Italian universities welcomed German students, including Protestants. At Padua, for example, the Venetian government quietly blocked the Inquisition of Padua from pursuing German Protestant students at the university even when they committed insulting anti-Catholic acts.[66]

However, the 1625–26 list of matriculated students included only four Germans.[67] So Duke Ferdinando and his chief minister tried harder. In August 1626, a delegation of German students from Padua, representing a larger group of Germans who were considering coming to Mantua, visited the city. They spoke first to Fabrizio Bartoletti, which suggests that some of them were medical students, and that his reputation attracted them, just as it had brought Johann Vesling from Padua to Mantua (see chapter 7, section 3). The

64. Simeoni, 1940, 66–67.
65. ASM, AG, Bu. 3366, f. 386r.
66. See the report of the former nuncio to Venice, Alberto Bolognetti, ca. 1581, about how the Venetian government would not allow the Paduan Inquisition to pursue and prosecute German Protestants students even in the face of provocations. Stella, 1964, 277–79. See also Grendler, 2002, 190–94.
67. ASM, AG, Bu. 3366, "Not.scholares studentes in Almo Pacifico Gymnasio Mantuano, super Matricula descripti," ff. 382r, 384v. In addition, there were fifteen students from Trent, who may have been German speaking.

delegation next asked Count Striggi if Mantua would offer the same privileges as the German nation of students enjoyed at Padua.[68] Striggi answered yes and showed them the list of privileges that the duke was prepared to give them. He also showed them lists of the privileges that the universities of Siena and Bologna granted their German nations in order to prove that Mantua's privileges would be the same. And Striggi brought forth a letter from a certain Baron of Bemelbergs (sic), who had promised to send "a quantity of students" from the Tyrol (in western Austria) to Mantua.[69] The baron was certain that once students discovered the quiet University of Mantua, and how well students were treated there, many would come and the university would flourish.

Duke Ferdinando kept his word. On September 8, 1626, he issued a proclamation detailing the privileges conferred on the German nation of the University of Mantua.[70] As promised, they matched the privileges of other Italian universities. The goods of German students and their servants entering the Gonzaga state would not be assessed customs duties or taxes. The German nation had the right to elect its officers, and the latter had jurisdiction over students accused of some crimes, although not capital offenses. The student leaders had the right to be present when German students were questioned in order to prevent language misunderstandings and to make sure that immunities were honored. Officers of the German nation were permitted to participate in the examination of degree candidates. The duke's action indicated how much he wanted German students because, while the university had other student nations with rights and privileges, Ferdinando did not issue separate proclamations for them.

Issues of precedence in official events sometimes produced disputes and fighting among the representatives of student nations. So, in an effort to keep the peace, Don Giacinto Gonzaga in his capacity as protector of the university issued rules that gave precedence to the councillors of ultramontane nations over councillors of Italian nations. This included preference in placing their coats of arms in the university building.[71] In other words, Duke Ferdinando

---

68. Striggi to the duke, August 13, 1626, Mantua, in ASM, AG, Bu. 2774, f. 126r–v.

69. The "Barone di Bemelbergs" has not been identified. However, the Tyrol, a Catholic region, was ruled from 1619 to 1632 by Leopold V Habsburg from a cadet branch of the family, and Duke Ferdinando had Habsburg relatives. Perhaps the baron was part of the Habsburg connection.

70. A copy of the proclamation of September 8, 1626, is found in ASM, AG, Decreti Liber 55, ff. 4v–5v.

71. Undated statement of the rules of precedence beginning "Per conservar la pace tra ss.ri scholari dello Studio di Mantova circa la precedentia de' ss.ri Consiglieri." ASM, AG, Bu. 3366, f. 401r–v. Obviously, Don Giacinto, aged nine or ten, did not write the rules.

and his advisers hoped and expected that the coats of arms of noble ultramontane student officers would soon grace the building of the University of Mantua as they did the Archiginnasio, the university building in Bologna.

The University of Mantua began to award degrees. On April 23, 1626, it conferred a doctorate in both laws on Giulio Camillo Marta of Naples, the nephew of Giacomo Antonio Marta. The procedure copied the forms of other Italian universities. Young Marta was given *puncta* (passages) to defend, and he underwent private and public examinations. As ordered by the papal bull *In sacrosancta beati Petri* of November 13, 1564, he publicly professed his Catholic faith, a condition for receiving degrees from universities in Catholic lands.[72] After obtaining the doctorate, Giulio Camillo Marta became an ordinary professor of civil law teaching *De regulis iuris* in the academic years 1626–27 and 1627–28.[73] The university also began awarding medical degrees.[74]

Duke Ferdinando took advantage of his new university in the most appropriate way: he attended Bartoletti's public anatomy and the accompanying lectures and formal arguments. A remark that he made about applying anatomical dissection techniques to plants inspired a Mantuan scholar to write a treatise on that subject.[75] He philosophized and published a work on disputed and controversial philosophical propositions.[76] Ferdinando became a student again.

72. ASM, AG, Bu. 3366, ff. 88r–91r, for the doctoral degree of Giulio Camillo Marta. He is listed as a student and identified as Marta's *nepos* (nephew) in the matriculation list of 1625–26. ASM, AG, Bu. 3366, f. 383v.

73. For the roll of 1626–27, see ASM, AG, Bu. 3366, f. 108. For the roll of 1627–28, see table 6.2.

74. There are two pieces of indirect evidence. In November 1626 the rector of the Jesuit college complained that the "Signori medici" had passed a decree stating that they could award a doctorate without the participation of the Jesuit professors of philosophy. The "Signori medici" may have been professors and other members of the college of doctors of medicine. Father Girolamo Furlani to Duke Vincenzo II, November 19, 1626, in ASM, AG, Bu. 2775, f. 539r. And in September 1627 the vice prior of the college of physicians of Mantua warned that "i giovani medici nuovamente addottorati in questa Università" (the young physicians newly doctored in this university) who wished to practice medicine still had to complete two years of "prattica" (probably practice under the supervision of licensed physicians) before treating patients on their own. Chancellor Alessandro Striggi to Duke Vincenzo II, September 23, 1627, Mantua, in ASM, AG, Bu. 2777, f. 80r. "Signore medico Bagni," the vice prior, was probably "Doctor Balneus a Balneo," who was admitted into the Mantuan college of physicians in 1608. Carra, Fornari, and Zanca, 2004, 138. I have not looked for doctoral diplomas in the notarial records of Mantua.

75. Franchini et al., 1979, 130.

76. *Diverse propositioni filosofiche controverse e disputate*. Mantova: Aurelio e Ludovico Osanna, 1625, as listed in Pescasio, 1971, 266.

CHAPTER 7

# Medicine, Law, and Tacitus

edical and legal teaching and research at the University of Mantua combined innovation and tradition. Gonzaga support for medical, botanical, pharmaceutical, and alchemical scholarship in Mantua over the previous half century moved the university toward Paracelsian chemical medicine. The university created a chemistry professorship, found in only one other Italian university at this time. Bartoletti did pioneering anatomical and clinical research, while Doctor Marta continued to publish. The university also taught Tacitus, which rarely happened in Italian universities.

### 1. BOTANICAL MEDICINE

Having secured Bartoletti and Mariani from Bologna, Duke Ferdinando found the rest of the professors of medicine mostly among his own subjects and the court. Of the fourteen medical scholars who taught at the university between 1625 and 1629, seven came from Mantua and other towns in the Gonzaga state, and two others, while born elsewhere, had served the Gonzaga for years.[1] At least four came from the botanists, physicians, and alche-

---

1. The Gonzaga subjects were Giacomo Ferrari of Mantua, Giovanni del Monte of Mantua, Luigi Mazzuchi of Mantua, Carlo Tonolo of Mantua, Andrea Zatta of Mantua, Giuseppe Guerrero of Guastalla, and Giacomo Francesco Palperia of San Salvatore Monferrato. In addition, as explained below, Zanobio Bocchi of Florence definitely and Jean Clave of France possibly were in the employ of the Gonzaga long before 1625. The five who did not come from the Gonzaga state were Fabrizio Bartoletti, Pietro Antonio Cavalli of Sicily, Galeazzo Coccapani of Carpi, Andrea Mariani of Bologna, and Pietro Francesco Oclerio of Trent. However, one cannot exclude the possibility that Cavalli, Coccapani, and Oclerio may have been in Gonzaga service as well. See

mists attached to the court, as the university harvested the fruits of Gonzaga medical and scientific patronage. Through these men the scholarly interests of the dukes, and Ferdinando in particular, influenced the university's teaching and research.

Like other princes of the time, the Gonzaga dukes supported studies in natural history, medicine, botany, pharmacology, and alchemy, areas of study not viewed as totally distinct from each other.[2] Duke Guglielmo, an intellectually curious man, began to build up the court's medical resources in the 1570s.[3] Duke Vincenzo I to some extent, and Duke Ferdinando enthusiastically, pursued new medical and scientific knowledge. And the Gonzaga were second to none in their willingness to spend money in the quest. Of course, intellectual curiosity was not the only motivation: the dukes wanted able physicians and a supply of the best medicines to ensure good health and long life for themselves and their spouses and offspring. Their hopes went unrealized, but it was not for lack of support for medical research or failure to ingest medicines. In addition, medical scholarly patronage, like artistic and musical patronage, proclaimed Gonzaga munificence and culture.[4]

Natural history came first. Sixteenth-century scholars and patrons eagerly acquired and studied plants, animals, and objects, both for reasons of curiosity and to create new medical compounds. They searched for new and exotic plants, strange objects, freaks of nature, and evidence of fanciful creatures, then displayed the results in museums. Ulisse Aldrovandi (1522–1605), professor at the University of Bologna and a pioneering natural historian, created the best-known natural history museum of the day for his large collection of unusual and bizarre specimens and objects. Princes and others followed suit. Inspired by two local physicians with their own collections, Duke Guglielmo Gonzaga established a natural history museum at the court in the early 1580s.[5] Aldrovandi came to Mantua to assist in its creation and to promote the study of natural history.[6]

A botanical garden came next. The *De materia medica* of Dioscorides (fl.

---

the rolls for 1625–26 and 1627–28 in tables 6.1 and 6.2. For the roll of 1626–27 see ASM, AG, Bu. 3366, f. 108.

2. Emperor Rudolf II (1548, ruled 1576–1612) was the most celebrated ruler to support these areas of learning, while the Medici grand dukes Francesco I and Ferdinando I, were Italian examples. For Rudolf, see Evans, 1984.

3. This is the theme of Franchini et al., 1979; see also various chapters in *Mantova e i Gonzaga*, 1978.

4. Findlen, 1994, 346–92.

5. Franchini et al., 1979, 44–55.

6. Aldrovandi spent considerable time in Mantua and wrote many letters. His name appears in over 80 percent of the pages describing the creation and expansion of the Gonzaga natural history collection in Franchini et al., 1979.

# Botanical Medicine

A.D. 50–70), which cataloged some six hundred plants, thirty-five animal products, and ninety minerals with medicinal properties, stimulated the development of medical botany in the sixteenth century. Scholars searched for new plants and minerals, while Italian universities founded botanical gardens and established professorships of medical botany. Duke Vincenzo I joined them. In 1600 he brought the Franciscan Friar Minor Zanobio Bocchi of Florence (1570?–after 1626) to Mantua to construct a botanical garden. Bocchi, who had served as an assistant to the curator of the botanical garden at the University of Pisa from 1595 to 1600, created a garden similar to that of Pisa.[7] Located in a courtyard of the new wing (built ca. 1480) of the ducal palace, it grew simples, that is, medicinal plants.

On August 23, 1603, Bocchi wrote an open letter to the physicians, surgeons, and pharmacists of Mantua, informing them that the Gonzaga family had created a botanical garden for the benefit of all. He boasted about its commodious site and promised that physicians would find in it plants gathered from afar, all clearly identified and well organized. Physicians might come and find the medicinal plants needed to cure the people of Mantua. Two days later Bocchi arranged for publication of a map of the Gonzaga botanical garden. In 1611 Duke Vincenzo I appointed Bocchi general superintendent of all the ducal gardens: the botanical garden, another garden at the ducal palace, the pleasure gardens of several Gonzaga villas, and the fish pond at the Villa Porto in the countryside.[8]

In 1625 Bocchi became the botanical demonstrator at the University of Mantua. According to the roll, Bocchi began teaching in the botanical garden on May 2, 1626. He continued to improve the garden for the benefit of professors and students, always with the support of Duke Ferdinando. On June 26, 1626, he wrote to the duke informing him that he had organized the garden in a way never done before so that it could serve all the professors of medicine. He added a printed list of the plants there and a bill for the expenses of procuring them.[9]

The list of plants, as well as a description of the contents of the Gonzaga museum of natural history, appeared in a medical work published in 1625 by another professor of medicine at the university, Giacomo Francesco Palperia.[10] From San Salvatore Monferrato in the other half of the Gonzaga state,

---

7. Garbari, Tomasi, and Tosi, 1991, 106 note 99, 124, 163. Bocchi's life dates are unknown. Since he began at the Pisan botanical garden in 1595, it is likely that he was born about 1570. He lived at least through the fall of 1626. Someone else was listed as the plant demonstrator at the University of Mantua in the roll of 1627–28.

8. Franchini et al., 1979, 130–33.

9. Franchini et al., 1979, 131 and document 59 on pp. 236–37.

10. Franchini et al., 1979, 133. The book was *Iacobi Francisci Palperiae Monferratensis a S. Salvatore, Philosophiae, & Medicinae Doctoris; Medicamentorum facultates in Mantovano Gymnasio publicè*

Palperia became the ordinary professor of medical botany of the University of Mantua. He lectured on *De materia medica* of Dioscorides, the standard text for medical botany, in the third hour of the morning.

## 2. CHEMICAL MEDICINE

The Gonzaga enthusiasm for alchemy bubbled over into the new university. As mentioned earlier, Duke Vincenzo I had a passion for alchemy and supported alchemists at his court. Although Duke Francesco III dismissed them in 1612, Ferdinando brought them back.[11] In 1614 Bocchi wrote to Duke Ferdinando that, in response to the duke's command, he was searching for a formula to create gold. He reported that "the Frenchman" (*il franzese*) was helping him.[12]

Medical chemistry with its Paracelsian base was alchemy's close sibling and a new field for teaching and research; indeed, for many there was no dividing line between the two. The roll for the academic year 1625–26 of the Peaceful University of Mantua included a professorship of chemistry (*Ad lecturam Chymiae*). The professor lectured on distillation procedures and the preparation of chemical medicines and demonstrated every application in the lecture hall of the shop of Fausto Vialardi, distiller to the duke.[13] The class met on vacation days at the second hour of the morning. The professor was Doctor Pietro Antonio Cavalli of Sicily, who also held the morning extraordinary professorship of theoretical medicine, which class also met in the second hour of the morning on extraordinary teaching days. In other words, Cavalli lectured on medical theory, a traditional subject, most of the time and chemistry on vacation days, which could have been saints' days sprinkled throughout the year or days in the long carnival and Easter vacations in which ordinary lectures did not meet.[14]

---

*docentis Lectio prima*. Mantuae, 1625. Apud Aurelium, & Ludovicum Osannam fratres, Ducales Impressores. See Zanca and Galassi, 1978, 414. There is an illustration of the title page in Franchini et al., 1979, 129, which also reproduces the list of plants at 123–36.

11. See the relazione of Pietro Gritti of 1612 in *Relazioni*, 1912, 118; and Franchini et al., 1979, 122.

12. Bocchi to Ferdinando, October 24, 1614, Mantua, in Franchini et al., 1979, 136, and document 56 on pp. 235–36. There are three references to "il franzese" in the letter.

13. "Leget de Distillatione, ac praeparatione medicamentorum Chymicorum omnium verò praxim (Fausto Vialardi Ducali distillatore operante) monstrabitur in Aulica officina Distill. diebus vacantibus. Hora secunda matutina." ASM, AG, Bu. 3366, f. 64, roll of 1625–1626. The original capitalization and punctuation have been retained.

14. The meaning of lectures on vacation days is not entirely clear. According to the calendar for the academic year 1625–26 (ASM, AG, Bu. 3366, no foliation), there were many religious holidays in which neither ordinary nor extraordinary lectures met. In addition, there were the long carnival and Easter vacations, plus the shorter Christmas vacation. Chemistry lectures may have been held on some of the religious holidays. It is more likely that they were held during the

# Chemical Medicine

In the academic year 1626–27 chemistry rose to become an ordinary professorship meeting at the third hour of the afternoon on ordinary teaching days. The professor was now "Doctor Ioannes Clavius Gallus," that is, "Doctor Jean Clave [or Clavé] Frenchman," whom the roll charged with explaining the theory of chemistry and demonstrating practical applications.[15] One suspects that this was the Frenchman who helped Bocchi in his search for a formula to create gold in 1614. Clave continued to hold the chemistry professorship, now described as lectures on minerals and metals in the chemical way, in 1627–28. The class met at the third hour of the afternoon, and Clave was required to begin discussing chemical applications eight days before the public anatomy.[16] Since the public anatomy began on the Feast of St. Anthony (January 17, 1628), instruction on chemical applications began on or about January 9, 1628.[17] Clave probably lectured on minerals and metals in November and December and switched to practical applications in January.

Chemistry instruction meant teaching students which substances to heat, burn, distill, or evaporate, how to mix them together, and then demonstrating the processes. Because of the variety of substances and the number and complexity of the actions, teaching chemistry must have resembled the slow unveiling of the mysteries of a semisecret art. The Mantuan professors of chemistry probably lectured on what they learned from northern European Paracelsians plus their own experiments. Then they demonstrated practical techniques in the distillery of Vialardi.

Paracelsian chemical medicine enthusiasts sought to produce medicines that were typically compounds of mercury, antimony, gold, other metals and minerals, and plant and animal products. The process began with a compound from which the distiller expected to get a purer substance. Distillation consisted of heating a mixture to separate the more volatile from the less volatile parts, then cooling and condensing the result to produce a more pure or refined substance. Sometimes the process was repeated several times with

---

long carnival and Easter holidays, which encompassed twenty-nine days (excluding Sundays) for the carnival vacation, and eighteen days (excluding Sundays) for the Easter vacation.

15. "Ad lecturam Chymiae. Excellentiss. Artium, & medicinae Doctor D. Ioannes Clavius Gallus. Chymiae Theoricam explicabit, eiusque; operationes practicas demonstrabit. Hora tertia pomeridiana." ASM, AG, Bu. 3366, f. 108, roll for 1626–27. Cavalli now held only the extraordinary professorship of practical medicine.

16. "Ad lecturam Chimiae. Excellentiss. Art. & med. Doct. D. Ioannes Clavius Gallus. Leget de mineralibus, & metallicis in via chimica, & incipiet operationes chimicas octo dierum spatio ante anathomen. Hora tertia matutina." ASM, AG, Bu. 3366, f. 109, roll for 1627–28.

17. See the roll for 1627–28, which gives the date of the beginning of the public anatomy, which was also the beginning of the carnival vacation, plus the academic calendar for 1625–26, in ASM, AG, Bu. 3366, f. 109 and no foliation respectively; and Capelli, 1983, 100. While cold weather was required for some chemical operations, it is more likely that academic reasons dictated the schedule.

different mixtures and heat levels. Distillation was not new; medieval and Renaissance physicians practiced it.[18] But Paracelsianism chemical medicine brought new attention and popularity to it.

A typical Paracelsian procedure produced laudanum from opium. The distiller took a quantity of opium, cut it into pieces, then placed the pieces into bowls and put the bowls into an oven. Heat was applied until the opium gave off a smell of sulphur, which gradually vaporized. Then the opium was ground, mixed with distilled vinegar, and heated over a slow fire. The resultant distillate was strained through paper and allowed to coagulate. Elaborately prepared powdered coral and pearl were blended in. Finally, a sticky plant substance was added, so that the mixture could be made into pills.[19]

Another favorite Paracelsian preparation was *aurum potabile* (drinkable gold), which began as a pearl or coral powder mixed into alcohol. Then oil or tartar was poured on the solution, perhaps sulphuric acid, and finally, purified gold, already prepared through various processes. After heating and distillation, the result was used as a diaphoretic, a medicine producing heavy sweating that was thought to expel the evil matter making the body sick.[20] Although such chemical medicines probably did not do the patient any good, neither did bleeding, the Galenic therapy for many ills. And the result might be something more quotidian and useful, such as an ointment to apply to a wound or suppurating ulcer. In any case, medical chemistry involved experimentation, observation, and learning to manipulate compounds, and this led to greater knowledge of the properties and uses of many substances.

The Peaceful University of Mantua had a professorship of chemistry more than one hundred years earlier than all other Italian universities and before most universities in Europe. The University of Marburg established the first known professorship of chemistry (which it called *chymiatria*) in 1609, appointing Johann Hartmann (1568–1631), a Paracelsian and philosophical eclectic, to the position, which he held until 1621.[21] The University of Jena had a professorship of chemistry in 1612, and other German universities followed in the second half of the seventeenth century. The University of Leiden established a professorship of chemistry in 1669, Montpellier in 1675, Oxford in 1683, Louvain in 1685, Paris in 1698, and Cambridge in 1702.[22]

Italian universities were much slower to create professorships of chemistry or to accept chemical medicine. Besides Mantua, only one other Italian uni-

---

18. Multhauf, 1956; plus Moran, 2005, for a good survey.

19. The description is based on the laboratory journal of Johann Hartmann, professor of chemistry at the University of Marburg. Moran, 1991, 45–58.

20. Moran, 1991, 62–65.

21. Moran, 1991, 13–17, 51. Hartmann was succeeded by one of his students, which suggests that the position continued.

22. Debus, 1991, 141–46; Porter, 1996, 546.

versity had a known Paracelsian in the early seventeenth century. The University of Pisa appointed Giacomo Macolo, a Scot, to teach chemical medicine in 1614, and he continued to teach through the 1617–18 academic year. The name Macolo, and sometimes Macolone, was an Italian version of a Scottish name, which might have been McCole, McCaul, or MacCallough. Macolo published works in Florence, 1616, and London, 1622, defending Paracelsiansim and showing the influence of Peter Severinus (Peder Sørensen of Denmark, 1542–1602), author of a major Paracelsian synthesis and an opponent of Galenism.[23] The chemical medicine position disappeared at Pisa in 1618. Nevertheless, a Portuguese professor of medical theory who taught at Pisa from 1618 to 1637 also supported Paracelsian ideas.[24] The two non-Italian Paracelsian professors underscored the reluctance of Italian universities to accept Paracelsian medicine. Other Italian universities did not have professorships of chemistry until much later. The University of Bologna discussed establishing a professorship of chemistry in 1617 and again in 1633, but did not do so until 1737. The University of Ferrara founded a professorship of chemistry only in 1743, Rome in 1748, Padua in the middle of the century, Pavia about 1773, and Siena in 1780.[25]

The Paracelsian influence at the University of Mantua extended beyond the professorship of chemistry. Giacomo Ferrari of Mantua, part of the Gonzaga medical circle, obtained a doctorate and was accepted into the Mantuan college of physicians in 1599.[26] He was appointed to the second-place ordinary professorship of medical theory, which required him to teach the traditional fare of Galen, Hippocrates, and Avicenna.[27] But he strongly endorsed and

---

23. Barsanti, 1993, 522–23, 559. For Macolo's ideas and works, see Zanier, 1985, 645–46. For Severinus, see Debus, 1977, 1:128–31 et passim; and Debus, 1981.

24. This was Stefano Rodrigo De Castro (1559–1637) from Portugal, also called Estevam Rodrigues de Castro and Stephanus Rodericus Castrensis. His works were published posthumously. See Barsanti, 1993, 516, 555; and Zanier, 1985, 646–47.

25. For Bologna, see Costa, 1912, 25; and Simeoni, 1940, 110, 117. For Ferrara, see *I maestri di Ferrara*, 1991, 103, 152, 261; and Pulidori, 2004. For Rome, see *I maestri di Roma*, 1991, 2:984. For Padua, for which three possible dates (1738, 1748, and 1760 are given), see Facciolati, 1978, part 3, 248, 351; and Ongaro, 2001, 187. For Pavia, see Vaccari, 1957, 156, 186; and Belloni, 1970, 108. For Siena, see Vannozzi, 1991, 162. Although the dates are based on the best available information, sometimes the exact year in which a position was established or teaching began is not always clear.

26. Carra, Fornari, and Zanca, 2004, 137.

27. In 1625–26 he and his concurrent taught book 1, fen 4, which dealt with fevers, of Avicenna's *Canon*. In 1626–27 they taught the *Ars parva*, or *Prognostics*, of Galen, an introductory treatise. In 1627–28 they taught the *Aphorisms* of Hippocrates. See tables 6.1 and 6.2 and ASM, AG, Bu. 3366, ff. 64, 108, 109. All were traditional texts taught in Italian universities from at least the late fourteenth century. See Grendler, 2002, 314–24. I have been unable to discover Ferrari's life dates, and there is no biography in DBI.

diffused French Paracelsian chemical medicine ideas and believed that Galen and Paracelsus could be reconciled.

In 1601 Ferrari published a work on theriac and mithridate based on the work of an earlier Mantuan pharmacist.[28] Theriac, which sought to replicate the complexity of human physiology, had many ingredients, each believed to correspond to a body part or function. For Galen, theriac consisted of sixty-four simples, minerals, and animal products, such as unicorn horns ground into dust. The flesh of a serpent became a key ingredient in the sixteenth century. Theriac was expected to cure any ailment, especially the effects of poison. Mithridate, a version of theriac, was named for Mithridates VI (120–63 B.C.), king of Pontus in northern Asia Minor, who, according to legend, ingested poisons in gradually increased dosages until he became immune to them. Although mithridate lacked the flesh of a serpent, medical scholars saw it as an antidote to all poisons. Pharmacists and physicians of the sixteenth and seventeenth centuries created many theriacs and mithridate potions with exotic ingredients.[29]

Ferrari's short book praised medicine in general, lauded theriac and mithridate, discussed vipers and other ingredients, commented on Galen's views on the viper, and included a short chapter devoted to Avicenna. The work was dedicated to the young prince Francesco Gonzaga and included Latin poems paying homage to the late Duke Guglielmo Gonzaga as a supporter of learning, as well as praise for Duke Vincenzo I, the Mantuan college of medicine, and the city of Mantua.[30]

Ferrari's next book strongly endorsed Paracelsian chemical medicine. In 1619 he published an Italian translation of the *Pharmacopoea dogmaticorum restituta* (1607 with many reprints), by Joseph Du Chesne, called Quercentanus (ca. 1544–1609). Du Chesne was a Huguenot physician to King Henry IV and a major Paracelsian with a European-wide reputation; his work discussed the preparation of chemical medicines.[31] Ferrari's translation, later revised by

---

28. *Idea theriacae et mithridatii, ex optima atque omnium excellentissima Antonii Berthioli pragmatia: ipsorumque interim ingredientium simplicium exactissima discussio, & praesertim de viperis scitu dignissima non hucusque ab alio quopiam Physiologo e nucleata, nunc demum a Jacobo Ferrario philosopho, & Medico Mantuano, partime ex doctissimi olim Flamminii Evoli scriptis, partim ex prorijs excerpta, & ad commune commodum edita.* Venetiis, Apud Jo. Antonium & Jacobum de Franciscis, 1601. The NLM copy has been used. It was reprinted in Mantua, 1602, and Venice, 1606. Antonio Bertioli, or Berthioli (ca. 1550–after 1608), was pharmacist to the Gonzaga. Zanca and Galassi, 1978, 409, 419; Franchini et al., 1979, 55, 127.

29. On theriac and mithridate in the sixteenth and seventeenth centuries, see Findlen, 1994, 241–43, 267–86 passim.

30. Ferrari, 1601.

31. *Le ricchezze della riformata farmacopoea del Sig. Giuseppe Quercetano medico e consiglier regio. Nuovamente di favella latina traportata* (sic) *in italiana dal Sig. Giacomo Ferrari medico, e filosofo mantovano. Sono li seguenti, cioè discorsi varij. . . . Oltre nuove osservationi, pensieri gratiosi, utilissime*

# Chemical Medicine

another Italian, was reprinted at least five times in Italy through 1684. Ferrari dedicated his translation to Duke Ferdinando with extravagant praise.

In his introduction Ferrari pleaded the cause of chemical medicine to the pharmacists of Italy.[32] He began by noting that because Du Chesne was French, France was ahead of Italy in this area. Ferrari's Italian translation would help Italy to catch up. He then praised the efficacy and usefulness of Du Chesne's book and chemical medicine generally. Ferrari noted that some Italians opposed Du Chesne and chemical medicines on the grounds that they did not produce the desired results, that they involved excessive and useless expense, and that distillation techniques worked better in France, a cooler country. Ferrari responded to the criticisms in reverse order. Extracts from simples produced their "natural force" wherever they were prepared. The cost of chemical medicines was no higher than the cost of other medicines, because very small doses of chemical medicines were as efficacious as large doses of conventional medicines. And chemical medicines were effective if the physician observed the necessary conditions and distilled correctly. Bad results came from ignorance of the properties of simples and from poor distillation.

Ferrari then named another Mantuan Paracelsian with ties to the Gonzaga. He praised Count Francesco Bruschi of Mantua, physician (*archiatro*) to Duke Ferdinando, for achieving good results from medicines prepared and distilled for him by Girolamo Gilberti, pharmacist to Duke Ferdinando.[33] Ferrari told readers that Bruschi had spent time in Paris when he was in the service of Vincenzo I. This was true; Bruschi was in Paris sometime after 1593, at which time he studied with Du Chesne. Bruschi then obtained a medical doctorate and became a member of the Mantuan college of physicians in 1597. In 1623 Bruschi published, in Mantua, a book defending chemical medicine and attacking traditional medicine. Like several northern European Paracelsians, he wished to introduce iatrochemistry into Galenic medicine. Although not a professor in the university, he became prior of the Mantuan college of physicians in 1633 and published another medical work in 1634.[34]

---

inventioni, *Avvertimenti necessarij per la compositione di molti medicamenti Heremetici: fatiche veramente degne d'esser lette, & rilette da ogni gran Personaggio, & da qualunque persona, che desidera medicarsi citò, tuto, & iocunde*. In Venetia, 1619. Appresso Giovanni Guerigli. The NLM copy has been examined. It was reprinted in 1638, 1646, 1655, 1665, and 1684. DuChesne's work is a text on the preparation of chemical medicines. See Debus, 1977, 1:160–68 et passim; and Debus, 1991, 51–59 et passim.

32. "Alli spetiali di tutta l'Italia apologia di Giacomo Ferrari." In Ferrari and Du Chesne, 1619, no pag. or signatures.

33. For what follows, see Ferrari, "Alli spetiali di tutta Italia," in Ferrari and Du Chesne, 1619, no pag.

34. Zanier, 1985, 642–43; Zanca and Galassi, 1978, 414, 420; Carra, Fornari, and Zanca, 2004, 137, 138. Ferrari also mentioned a third Italian physician, Giovanni Antonio Magno of Como, a

In 1627 Ferrari published another book, again in Mantua, in which he called himself *protomedico* as well as ordinary professor of medicine.[35] That is, he was either the chief medical officer of Mantua, or a member of the committee that, in conjunction with the college of physicians, oversaw the medical profession. As protomedico he licensed apothecaries and ensured that their medicines, theriacs, and mithridates conformed to specifications and were fresh, an appropriate duty for Ferrari.[36] The book consisted of a series of Italian dialogues in which he discussed sulfur, mercury, and salt according to the "chemists." And he argued that Galenism and Paracelsianism were not completely opposed.

The net result of the professorial appointments of Cavalli, Clave, and Ferrari, the latter two from the Gonzaga medical circle, was to make the Peaceful University of Mantua a center for Paracelsian chemical medicine.

### 3. BARTOLETTI'S RESEARCH ON ANGINA PECTORIS

As important as the professorship of chemistry and other appointments were, Fabrizio Bartoletti remained the major medical scholar at the University of Mantua. He justified his high status and salary by isolating and identifying the symptoms of a heart disease that normally led to death, plus additional research into diseases of the thoracic cavity, containing the heart, lungs, and esophagus.

The 1627–28 roll of the University of Mantua announced that Bartoletti would lecture on particular diseases of the thoracic cavity that resulted in his most important work.[37] In 1633 a Bolognese publisher issued Bartoletti's *Methodus in dyspnoeam seu de respirationibus libri iv. Cum synopsibus quibus quintus pro colophone accessit de curationibus ex dogmaticorum et hermeticorum poenu depromptis. Opus rarum, practicantibus admodu. necess.um anno MDCXXVIII publicis lectionibus explicatum a' Fabritio Bartoletto Bonon. philosopho, et medico, practicae medicae, et anatomes in Mantuana Academia primario professore* (Four books of a systematic treatise on dyspnea, or on respiration. With synopses, to which a fifth has been added as a colophon on bringing forth treatment of the suffering according to the dogmatics and Hermetics. A rare work explained in public lectures in 1628 by Fabrizio Bartoletti of Bologna, philosopher and physician,

---

physician to the Holy Roman Emperor, who had given him chemical medicines when Ferrari visited the imperial court at Prague. Magno has not been identified further.

35. *Democrito et Eraclito. Dialoghi . . . del Sig. Giacomo Ferrari Protomedico e Teorico ordinario nello Studio di Mantova*. In Mantova, appresso Aurelio & Lodovico Osanna fratelli, stampatori ducali, 1627. The book is listed in Michel and Michel, 1967–84, 3:34. Zanier, 1985, 643–44, discusses it.

36. Palmer, 1981, 57–59, 61; Findlen, 1994, 261–72, 278–82.

37. "Legent de morbis particularibus à Thorace infra." Roll of 1627–28 in ASM, AG, Bu. 3366, f. 109.

first professor of practical medicine and anatomy at the University of Mantua). It is a quarto-sized volume of about 560 pages. As the title indicated, it presented material from Bartoletti's lectures in 1628, which meant either the 1627–28 academic year, the 1628–29 year, or both. It also included anatomical research and patient diagnoses done at Bologna and Mantua.[38]

The book was a comprehensive treatise on dyspnea (difficulty in breathing) and the pathological conditions of throat, lungs, and other parts of the thoracic cavity in patients suffering from it.[39] The format and content reflected the new ways in which medical scholars presented their research. Although scholars continued to use Galen and Hippocrates as reference points, they increasingly wrote independent treatises on a single topic based on their own research.[40] While Bartoletti paid homage to Galen with many references to his *De difficultate respirationis* (On difficulty breathing) and *De locis affectis* (On the affected parts), he presented his own clinical observations, anatomical research, reasoning, and conclusions.

Bartoletti began with general comments on how to classify the traits, causes, and signs of dyspnea, using Aristotelian logic and summary tables. The book devoted substantial sections to numerous kinds of breathing difficulties. Typical was the discussion of suffocative catarrh, an inflammation of the mucous membrane of the throat and nose producing so much mucus that

---

38. The publishers dedicated the book to Carlo I Gonzaga-Nevers, Duke of Mantua and Monferrato, in the dedicatory letter dated and signed "Bonon. xxviij Apr. MDCXXXVIII . . . Bernardinus & Petrus Dozza fratres." Bartoletti, 1633, no sig. The NLM copy has been used. The date of 1638 is obviously a typographical error, because Carlo I Gonzaga-Nevers died in 1637. The question is, should the correct date be 1633 (MDCXXXIII) or 1628 (MDCXXVIII)? It must be 1633, because in the dedicatory letter the publishers stated that Bartoletti fell while in the middle of the race of life but nevertheless won glory with this book, an allusive reference to his death on March 30, 1630, at the age of forty-two. The letter continued to say that the book languished half dead until, thanks to the favor of the duke, it moved. This suggests that Carlo I Gonzaga-Nevers provided publication funding. The title page displayed the Gonzaga coat of arms.

As with the *Encyclopaedia hermetico-dogmatica* of 1619, some older sources list other editions. For example, Fantuzzi, 1965, 365, listed an edition of Bologna, 1632, published by "Theobaldum." Since Tebaldini was the printer (not the publisher) of the 1633 edition, Fantuzzi probably expanded the printer and publisher of the 1633 volume into two editions. Crespi, 1964, 553, lists editions of 1630 and 1632, which are probably ghosts. Busacchi, 1943, 70, found only the 1633 edition in his search through Italian libraries and the Bibliothèque National in Paris, and I have found only the 1633 edition. Unless other editions are located, it is assumed that the 1633 edition was the only one.

39. See Bartoletti, 1633, plus the very useful translation of substantial sections with introduction and commentary in Jarcho, 1980, 122–40, 382–83, for this and the following two paragraphs. See also Busacchi, 1943, 62–66.

40. Jarcho undervalues Bartoletti's format and originality when he writes that Bartoletti's book "amounts to a commentary on the Galenic treatise, with important additions." Jarcho, 1980, 123A.

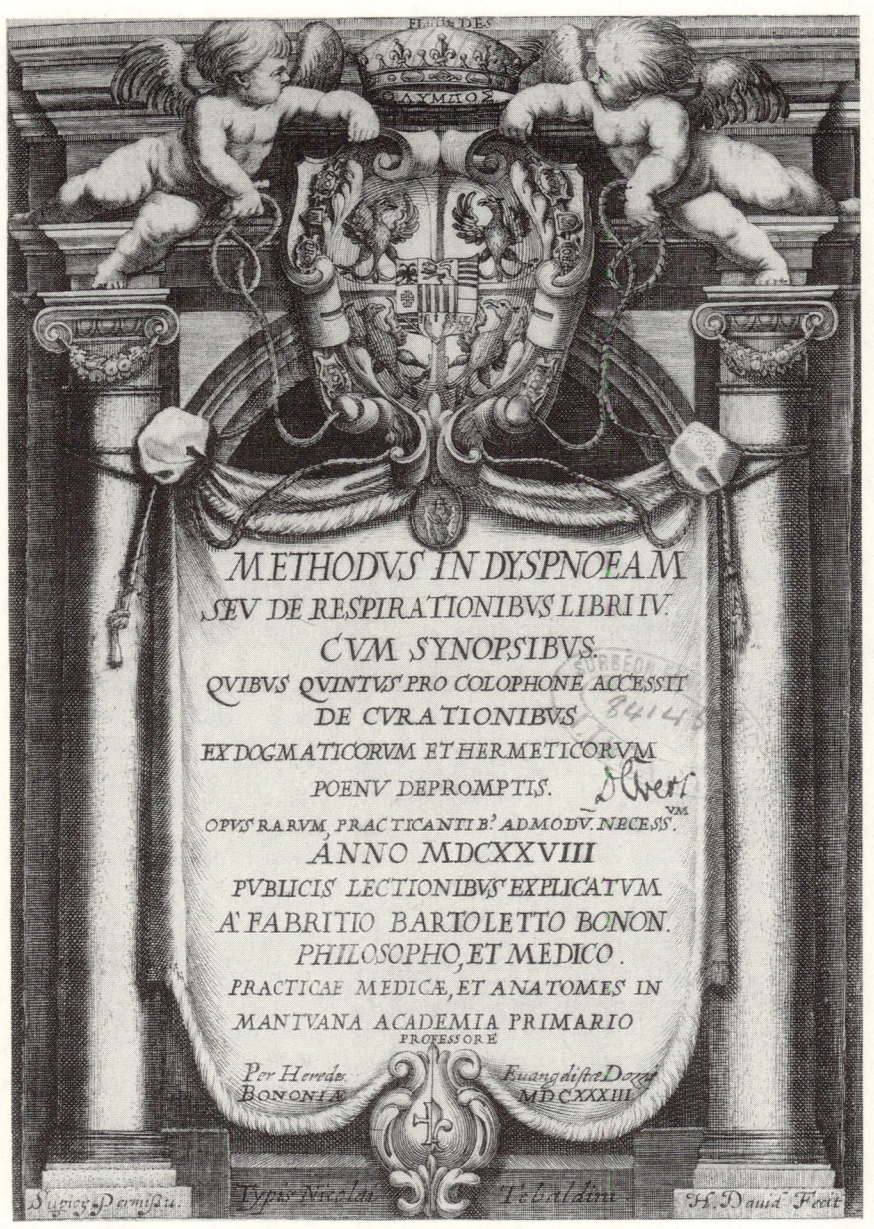

FIG. 12. Title page of Fabrizio Bartoletti, *Methodus in dyspnoeam seu de respirationibus libri iv.* Bononiae: Heredes Evangelistae Dozze, 1633. Typis Nicolai Tebaldini. *Courtesy of the National Library of Medicine.*

the patient has difficulty breathing and feels as if he is suffocating. For each condition, Bartoletti isolated and differentiated symptoms, such as difficulty in breathing, throat pain, secretions, and so on, through close observation. For example, he devoted considerable space to a discussion of hydrothoraxy, abnormal amounts and unusual kinds of fluid in the thoracic cavity. After listing symptoms and giving some patient histories, including whether they recovered or (more often) died, Bartoletti presented the results of autopsies. And he recommended therapies. Dyspnea was the entry point for a wide-ranging examination of pathologies of the chest.

In his investigations, Bartoletti combined two techniques. The first was close observation of the patient and a careful recording of his symptoms over time. This was a natural expansion of the procedures of clinical medicine that rose in importance in the sixteenth century. The other was morbid anatomy, that is, autopsies that concentrated on cataloging the exact conditions of the interior of humans who died after experiencing a precise set of symptoms. The goal was to connect a set of symptoms with the interior pathology of the body, especially a part of it, the thoracic cavity for Bartoletti. For centuries physicians and medical scholars had been performing autopsies to discover why patients died. What was new, or at least more organized and goal oriented than before, was the convergence of anatomy and pathology.

Bartoletti several times mentioned Mantuan patients, sometimes by name, and their symptoms, plus autopsies done there.[41] At one point he differentiated between suffocative catarrh and other kinds of throat pain and used his university colleague Antonio Possevino as an example. He wrote that "a few weeks ago the eminent Antonio Possevino, the fluent professor of Tacitean eloquence in our university at Mantua, was attacked by this kind of angina [i.e., a feeling of strangulation] caused by inflammation of the throat. By phlebotomy [blood-letting] alone I rescued him from the imminent danger of suffocation, beyond the expectation of everyone."[42]

---

41. Bartoletti, 1633, 318B; "was seen recently in Master Mario Carbonelli at Mantua"; English translation from Jarcho, 1980, 130A; and Bartoletti, 1633, 319B; "In Mantua in 1627 I saw two men who had suffered for a long time from dropsy of the chest and who died of supervening acute disease. One was autopsied in St. Dominic, the other in the church of St. Ambrose." English translation from Jarcho, 1980, 130B-31A. It is likely that St. Dominic was a hospital, while St. Ambrose was a parish church on the northwest side of Mantua. Bartoletti referred to other autopsies, at least one of which was done in the presence of many professors, e.g., "In Ecclesia Patrum Carmelitanorum meo suasu fuit exenteratus coram multis Professoribus." Bartoletti, 1633, 290A. In addition to Bolognese patients, Bartoletti several times referred to patients examined in Mantua. For examples, see Bartoletti, 1633, 291A and 319B (which is translated in Jarcho, 1980, 131A.)

42. Bartoletti as translated by Jarcho, 1980, 128A. I have added the phrases in brackets. For the Latin, see Bartoletti, 1633, 234A. I have changed Jarcho's "college" to "university," because the Latin is "Gymnasio," which meant "university." There is another reference to Possevino and his breathing problem in Jarcho, 1980, 131B: "As I observed recently in the eminent Dr. Possevino,

The book included an original contribution to medicine. In book 4, part 4, chapter 3, Bartoletti wrote about a form of unexpected death that was presaged only by difficult breathing.[43] In his view, this was a syndrome that neither Galen in his *De difficultate respirationis* nor any modern scholar had discussed. Bartoletti saw this as a particular set of symptoms and circumstances. The person suddenly has great difficulty breathing. If walking, he must stop walking and other physical activities. If reclining when experiencing sudden difficulty breathing, the patient must rise upright to breathe. The ill person has a feeling of suffocation and feels acute pain at the sternum. But the pulse normally remains steady, and there is no frothing at the mouth, a common sign of pulmonary edema (an abnormal accumulation of fluid in the lungs). The ill person does not suffer fainting spells or palpitations of the heart, and has little or no swelling of the feet or legs. At least twice in his treatise Bartoletti mentioned that he had done morbid anatomies on ten or more persons who had died after suffering breathing problems.[44] Autopsies revealed no empyema (accumulation of pus in the thoracic cavity, such as from the lungs). Bartoletti also eliminated abdominal dropsy, that is, liquid filling the abdominal cavity, as a possibility.

For those who suffered this form of suffocating dyspnea, Bartoletti counseled that the only solution was quiet and relaxation. Those afflicted might experience intervals in which they had only minor problems and conclude that they were no longer ill. But they would be wrong. In time patients would suffer additional and more severe attacks of dyspnea. The sick person might live for a year in great difficulty until without warning he would suddenly die. Bartoletti many times referred to "sudden death" and "unexpected death." Although he listed some traditional therapies, Bartoletti concluded that the physician could do nothing for the body of the ill person. Nevertheless, the physician who recognized the symptoms could inform the patient so that he might prepare his soul for death, and he could protect his own reputation by avoiding inaccurate prognoses.

---

distinguished professor of Tacitean oratory in our college (=university) at Mantua." Latin in Bartoletti, 1633, 320B. Here the Latin is "Academia," which also meant "university" rather than "college" in context.

43. For this and the following paragraph, see Bartoletti, 1633, 381–87. Curiously, Jarcho, 1980, did not translate this section. However, Cova, 1955, 59–60, provides a partial Italian translation. See also De Renzi, 1846, 156, 442; Busacchi, 1943, 64–66, who reproduces Bartoletti's synoptic table; and Crespi, 1964, 552–53.

44. "[P]lusquam enim decem cadavera thoracis hydrope suffocata meismet manibus apervi." Bartoletti, 1633, 317AB. Jarcho's translation is "for I myself with my own hands have opened more than ten cadavers suffocated by dropsy of the thorax." Jarcho, 1980, 129B. Also "ex decem enim cadaveribus, quae apervi, vix duo eperi, quibus aqua utroque in ventre stagnaret." Bartoletti, 1633, 318B; English translation in Jarcho, 1980, 130A.

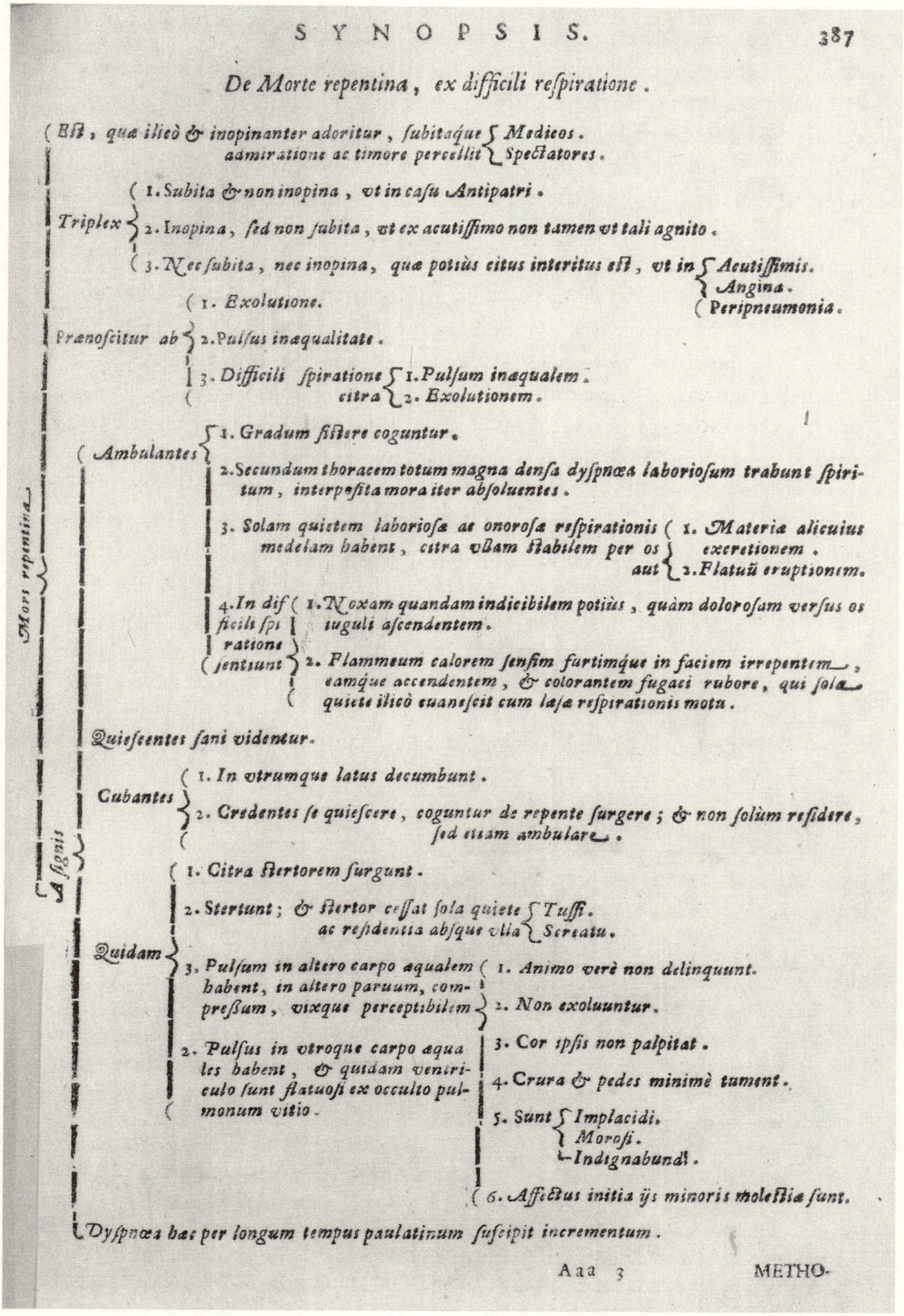

# SYNOPSIS. 387

### De Morte repentina, ex difficili respiratione.

Est, quæ ilico & inopinanter adoritur, subitaque { Medicos.
admiratione ac timore percellit { Spectatores.

Triplex
{ 1. Subita & non inopina, ut in casu Antipatri.
{ 2. Inopina, sed non subita, ut ex acutissimo non tamen ut tali agnito.
{ 3. Nec subita, nec inopina, quæ potiùs citus interitus est, ut in { Acutissimis.
{ Angina.
{ Peripneumonia.

Prænoscitur ab
{ 1. Exolutione.
{ 2. Pulsus inæqualitate.
{ 3. Difficili spiratione { 1. Pulsum inæqualem.
{ citra { 2. Exolutionem.

Mors repentina

Ambulantes
{ 1. Gradum sistere coguntur.
{ 2. Secundum thoracem totum magna densa dyspnœa laboriosum trahunt spiritum, interposita mora iter absoluentes.
{ 3. Solam quietem laboriosæ ac onorosæ respirationis { 1. Materia alicuius medelam habent, citra ullam stabilem per os { excretionem.
aut { 2. Flatuũ eruptionem.
{ 4. In difficili spiratione sentiunt
{ 1. Noxam quandam indicibilem potiùs, quàm dolorosam versus os iuguli ascendentem.
{ 2. Flammeum calorem sensim furtimque in faciem irrepentem, eamque accendentem, & colorantem fugaci rubore, qui sola quiete ilico euanescit cum lassa respirationis motu.

Quiescentes sani videntur.

Signis

Cubantes
{ 1. In utrumque latus decumbunt.
{ 2. Credentes se quiescere, coguntur de repente surgere; & non solùm residere, sed etiam ambulare.

Quidam
{ 1. Citra stertorem surgunt.
{ 2. Stertunt; & stertor cessat sola quiete { Tussi.
ac residentia absque ulla { Screatu.
{ 3. Pulsum in altero carpo æqualem habent, in altero paruum, compressum, vixque perceptibilem
{ 1. Animo verè non delinquunt.
{ 2. Non exoluuntur.
{ 2. Pulsus in utroque carpo æquales habent, & quidam ventriculo sunt flatuosi ex occulto pulmonum vitio.
{ 3. Cor ipsis non palpitat.
{ 4. Crura & pedes minimè tument.
{ 5. Sunt { Implacidi.
{ Morosi.
{ Indignabundi.
{ 6. Affectus initia ijs minoris molestiæ sunt.

Dyspnœa hæc per longum tempus paulatinum suscipit incrementum.

FIG. 13. Synopsis of symptoms of sudden death from difficult breathing. Fabrizio Bartoletti, *Methodus in dyspnoeam*, p. 387. *Courtesy of the National Library of Medicine.*

Bartoletti presented a classic description of difficulty in breathing accompanied by chest pain, a disorder that points to heart attack for modern physicians, although he did not identify the heart as the ultimate source of the deadly disorder. Even though Bartoletti could not prescribe a cure, he isolated and listed the symptoms of the disease. This enabled physicians and medical scholars to look for it, diagnose it, study it, and communicate their findings.

One hundred forty years later, an English medical scholar named this combination of symptoms angina pectoris (from *angere,* to choke, and *pectoris,* of the chest). In July 1768 William Heberden (1710–1801), a London physician, delivered a paper entitled "Some Account of a Disorder of the Breast" to the Royal College of Physicians of London and published it in 1772.[45] He described, sometimes in words nearly identical to those of Bartoletti, a set of symptoms he called angina pectoris and sometimes pectoris dolor. He based his analysis on twenty patients initially, and nearly one hundred patients eventually. But unlike Bartoletti, he did very few autopsies. Like Bartoletti, Heberden did not identify heart disease as the cause of the symptoms. But he did give the disorder the name that endured.[46] Heberden apparently never mentioned Bartoletti, even though his scholarship was available to a limited degree. Bartoletti's *Methodus in dyspnoeam* of 1633 was republished as part of the Venetian 1735 and 1772 editions of the *opera omnia* of the famous medical scholar Lazare Rivière (1589–1655). Other Italian scholars were aware of Bartoletti's research.[47]

Bartoletti's *Methodus in dyspnoeam* combined old and new. It was old because he respected Galen and the Hippocratic corpus and followed them most of the time. It was also old because he did not mention William Harvey's book on the circulation of the blood, which appeared in 1628.[48] It was new research because he dissented from Galen. Bartoletti was a polite man

---

45. Heberden's paper, "Some Account of a Disorder of the Breast," was published in the *Medical Transactions of the Royal College of Physicians* 2 (London, 1772), 59–67. Not seen. But see the short paragraph from the 1772 paper in Silverman, 2003, 48. *Cardiac Classics,* 1941, 222–24, prints three pages with a description of *pectoris dolor* from a larger work of Heberden published posthumously in 1802. Again, some words are almost identical to Bartoletti's words, allowing for the differences between Latin and English.

46. Bartoletti did use the term "angina maligna." Bartoletti, 1633, 244B.

47. Busacchi, 1943, 70. There is a copy of *Lazari Riverii . . . Opera medica omnia . . . accedunt Fabritii Bartholeti . . . De dyspnoea, seu de respirationibus, libri quinque,* Venetiis, ex typographia Balleoniana, 1772, in the Bancroft Library of the University of California at Berkeley, which I have not seen. Ippolito Francesco Albertini (1662–1738), who taught at the University of Bologna and wrote about the heart, did mention Bartoletti. Jarcho, 1980, 325, 334, 337, 338.

48. Harvey's book was published in Frankfurt, 1628. Bartoletti would have had to have obtained a copy immediately to incorporate it into his own research. On the other hand, since Bartoletti did not identify the heart as the source of the problem, he may not have judged Harvey's book to be relevant, even if he knew about it.

who stated his disagreements in measured terms. He did not denounce Galen or modern scholars, as Vesalius sometimes did. Bartoletti's medicine was also new because he employed the methods of close clinical observation and extensive anatomical dissection pioneered by sixteenth-century Italian professors. The heart of the book consisted of careful examination and listing of patient symptoms and histories, followed by morbid anatomies, to study the pathological conditions of the thoracic cavity and its organs.

Thanks to his discovery of lactose, an exercise in chemical medicine, and his identification of the symptoms of angina pectoris, Bartoletti has a place in the history of medicine. He lived between the age of Vesalius and other anatomists of the late sixteenth century, and that of Marcello Malphigi (1628–94) and his microscopic anatomical discoveries of the second half of the seventeenth century. These two left very large footprints in medical history. Bartoletti took smaller but still significant steps forward in medical knowledge.

Duke Ferdinando and Chancellor Striggi hoped that Bartoletti would bring German students to Mantua. Bartoletti attracted, taught, and inspired one German student who became better known than his teacher. Johann Vesling (1598–1649) came from the Catholic bishopric of Minden in north-central Germany.[49] He studied medicine in Leiden, Venice, and Bologna, where he probably met Bartoletti, whom he credited with stimulating his love for anatomical studies. He followed Bartoletti to Mantua and matriculated as a student at the Peaceful University in 1625.[50] In the winter of 1627–28 he appeared in Venice, where he performed an anatomical demonstration that greatly impressed local physicians. He then went to Cairo, ruled by the Ottoman Turks, in the company of the Venetian political representative. Vesling studied Egyptian flora, visited Palestine, and continued his anatomical and embryological studies.

In early 1633 he became professor of anatomy and surgery at the University of Padua, in which capacity he received great praise because he made a number of anatomical discoveries. In the academic year 1641–42 he held two positions at Padua. He was the first-position ordinary professor of anatomy who both lectured and performed the annual public anatomy, and he was the ordinary professor of medical botany who lectured on Dioscorides and demonstrated the medicinal properties of plants in the university's botanical garden.[51] In 1641 he published *Syntagma anatomicum,* which went into many Latin

---

49. Hintzsche, 1981.

50. "Not. D. Joannes Weslingius Mindensis Ph. et M. D," in the list of matriculated students in ASM, AG, Bu. 3366, f. 384v.

51. Vesling is listed as the holder of these two positions in the 1641–42 printed roll of the University of Padua found in ASB, Assunteria di Studio, Bu. 76, no pagination. The fact that one can find a roll of the University of Padua in the archive of the University of Bologna demonstrates that universities kept a close eye on each other.

editions; was translated into Dutch, English, and German; and became the standard university anatomy text for half a century. He also published a major botanical work on the plants of Egypt. In 1648 he undertook a botanical expedition to Crete, where he became ill and returned to Padua to die in 1649. His studies on embryological and comparative anatomy were published posthumously.[52]

## 4. LAW PROFESSORS AND MARTA'S RESEARCH

The number and different kinds of law professorships at Mantua were very similar to what was found in other Italian universities. In 1625–26 Mantua had two professors of canon law and nine of civil law (see table 6.1). Like other Italian universities, Mantua taught little canon law. All Italian universities sharply reduced the number of canon law professorships over the course of the sixteenth century for two reasons. Civil law and the state grew in influence at the expense of canon law and the church; therefore, canon law needed less attention. And the papacy in 1564 forbade publication of interpretive material on the canons of Trent without papal permission, thus sharply restricting the legal tradition that could be erected on Trent and leaving less to be taught.[53] At Mantua the number of canon law professorships remained at two in the next two years.

By contrast, the number of civilians rose to fifteen, then fourteen, in the two academic years following 1625–26.[54] Mantua offered the same range of law professorships and specializations as established Italian universities.[55] Law instruction began with the *Institutes,* taught by four professors, which introduced the student to civil law and legal principles in general. The most important positions were the morning and afternoon ordinary professorships of civil law, filled by Giacomo Antonio Marta and three or four other men. Like other Italian universities, Mantua offered specialized courses after the first year of its existence. Mantua had a professorship of criminal law, which concentrated on the parts of the *Digest* dealing with the definition and prosecution of crime, and a professorship of feudal law, important in an age of disputed fiefs. Mantua provided a *Pandects* professorship, which was humanistic jurisprudence. It taught *De actionibus* (On legal actions), which explained the kinds of legal actions that could be brought and the relations between them. Mantua offered a course entitled *De regulis juris* (On the rules of law),

---

52. Hintzsche, 1981. The NLM has fifteen editions of Vesling's works.
53. See Grendler, 2002, 443–47, 455 table 13.3.
54. See ASM, AG, Bu. 3366, f. 108 for the roll of 1626–27 and table 6.2 for 1627–28.
55. For further discussion of the law professorships in Italian universities, see Grendler, 2002, 430–73.

taught by Giulio Camillo Marta, which dealt with legal procedure and juridical logic. And it had a professorship called *De obligationibus* (On the obligations [of words], from the *Digest,* bk. 45, ch. 1), which discussed the legal obligations arising from words, as in contracts. The number of professors and the courses offered made Mantua a middle-sized law university, such as Ferrara and Siena were at the end of the sixteenth century.[56]

Localism dominated law appointments in Italian universities in the seventeenth century, and Mantua followed suit. After Marta and his nephew were hired, local men and Gonzaga subjects filled most of the rest of the positions. Nine of the seventeen professors of law who taught at the university between 1625 and 1628 were Gonzaga subjects, six from Mantua and three from Monferrato.[57] At least three of them served the Gonzaga as diplomats, administrators, and lawyers during the War of the Mantuan Succession.[58] So far as is known, only one of the homegrown law professors published a book.[59]

But Marta did. He justified his star status and high salary by publishing another large legal work, *Consilia . . . summi practici* (Turin, 1628) while at Mantua.[60] It was a collection of consilia, that is, advisory legal opinions on cases brought to him by litigants and their attorneys. Consilia were ubiquitous, because people embroiled in legal disputes believed that a consilium written by an uninvolved legist might provide a fresh perspective and more legal ammunition. Perhaps litigants also felt that a mound of supporting consilia would impress a judge or prince. Or a critical consilum from a disinterested lawyer might make it clear that settling or withdrawing was advisable. Governments also sought consilia to guide or justify policy. All distinguished scholars and many ordinary lawyers wrote consilia, for fees, of course. The more famous published collections of their consilia.

Marta's *Consilia* was a folio-sized volume of seven hundred double-

56. Grendler, 2002, 464–65, 469.

57. See tables 6.1 and 6.2 and ASM, AG, Bu. 3366, f. 108.

58. Andrea Lavezzari accompanied one of the Gonzaga on a mission to Vienna in December 1629. Quazza, 1926, 1:524 note 4. Francesco (here called Giovanni Francesco but probably the same person because he was called "dottore") Paraleoni was part of a diplomatic mission to German princes in October 1628. He also served as a messenger in December 1629, and defended Gian Francesco Gonzaga when he was accused of crimes in 1632. Quazza, 1926, 1:268, 514, 516; 2:345. Giacomo Filippo Rattazzi helped restore order in Casalmaggiore for Duke Carlo Gonzaga-Nevers after the town was occupied in February 1629. Quazza, 1926, 1:304–5.

59. Paolo Sghibini of Mantua, second-place morning ordinary professor of civil law from 1625 through 1627, then morning ordinary professor of canon law in 1627–28, was probably the author of a 1619 vernacular work on a water dispute. Pescasio, 1971, 264. Perusal of the catalogs of many libraries, most of them in North America, has not uncovered any other legal works by Mantuan legists.

60. See Marta, 1628, for the full citation. Copies in the Library of Congress and the Robbins Law Library of the University of California at Berkeley have been examined.

columned pages. It began with a long preface addressed to Giulio Camillo Marta consisting of eighty-seven maxims of advice for a practicing legist. Number eighty-six stated that the lawyer who acted for a modest fee was a contemptible person of little value. Number eighty-seven added that he should not expect to receive anything from paupers.[61] Next came fifty-four pages of various indexes, followed by two hundred consilia. Each consilium began with a summary. Then came a title, which was a statement of the legal argument, followed by the consilium itself. The first paragraph gave the names of the people involved and the action brought. Then came many numbered paragraphs in which Marta commented on the legal issues and heaped up citations.

Marta wrote these undated consilia at various times and places in his long career. They dealt with primogeniture claims, wills, inheritances, intestate disputes, fiefs, religious orders and their properties, excommunication, and other church-state issues, in which Marta seemed to favor civil jurisdiction. One consilium offered legal advice to the senate of Milan.[62] Another discussed the order of precedence of members of the college of doctors of Padua in meetings and processions, the kind of petty dispute for which professors were notorious. Marta argued that doctors who were nobles had precedence over doctors who were not (*doctores sempliciter*).[63]

Some consilia dealt with Duke Ferdinando and Mantuan issues and were probably written while at the university. In one of them Marta argued that Ferdinando was the rightful ruler of the principality of Bozzolo, a tiny state ruled by a cadet branch of the Gonzaga some twenty-seven kilometers west of Mantua. Marta cited a 1522 proclamation of Emperor Charles V castigating Federico da Bozzolo, the emperor's feudatory, as a rebel and bestowing Bozzolo on Marquis (later Duke) Federico Gonzaga (ruled 1519–40).[64] Despite Marta's consilium, Bozzolo remained in the possession of the cadet branch. Marta offered advice to the Jesuits about inheritance and property issues.[65] And he wrote a consilium for a case concerning the legal rights of University of Mantua students, who claimed the traditional immunity from prosecution so long as they did not commit treason or sedition. However, some of them

---

61. "Advocatus pro modico salario est persona vilis" and "Nam si eris advocatus pro modico salario, eris vilis, & contemptibilis," followed by "a pauperibus nihil recipiendum est" and "A pauperibus verò nihil recipias." "Summaria Praefationis" and "Praefatio super methodo respondendi, et allegandi de iure ad Iulium Camillum Martam I.U.D.," in Marta, 1628, signatures †3 recto and †5 verso.

62. Marta, 1628, consilium 142, pp. 225v–26v.

63. Marta, 1628, consilium 91, pp. 166r–v.

64. Marta, 1628, consilium 197, pp. 309v–13v. Consilium 110, pp. 189v–91r, also involved a fief that the Gonzaga held.

65. Marta, 1628, consilium 11, pp. 34Bv–37Av.

had allegedly killed a man in Mantua and taken refuge in a church, claiming ecclesiastical sanctuary. They were captured, then they escaped and were apprehended again, this time within forty steps of the wall of the church, which raised a new issue.[66] Marta continued to be an active scholar.

## 5. THE TACITUS PROFESSORSHIP

The roll of 1627–28 listed an ordinary professorship of Tacitus at the third hour of the afternoon filled by a layman. This was a different and more specialized humanities professorship than the Jesuit humanities professorship, and Tacitus was far from a curriculum author. Why did the University of Mantua have a Tacitus lectureship?

Cornelius Tacitus (ca. 55–after 116) was the preeminent historian of the early Roman Empire, which he described in his *Annals* and *Histories,* while his *Germania* and *Agricola* narrated the history of the Germanic tribes. Practically unknown in the Middle Ages, he was rediscovered in the Renaissance; then various humanists worked on the difficult texts of his works until Justus Lipsius established definitive versions in 1574.[67] With minor changes the recension of Lipsius is followed today.

Even with an established text, Tacitus did not become a curriculum author; only two Italian universities taught Tacitus, and then for only a year or two. At the University of Rome the distinguished humanist Marc'Antoine Muret (1526–85) taught an intense, detailed course on the first three books of the *Annals* in the academic years 1580–81 and 1581–82; he then published a commentary on the first five books. In his lectures Muret mentioned Pope Paul III and Grand Duke Cosimo I de' Medici as rulers who made good use of Tacitus, thus emphasizing Tacitus as a book of wisdom for princes.[68] At the University of Pisa, Domenico Mancini (d. 1595), a humanities professor of no known distinction or publications, taught Tacitus in the academic year 1590–91.[69]

Nevertheless, a Tacitus wave swept across Europe and especially Italy.[70] At

---

66. Marta, 1628, consilium 177, pp. 278v–79v. There is another version of this consilium: an undated six-page pamphlet by Marta entitled "Responsum super immunitate ecclesiae Dominiis Scholaribus concedenda, qui capti fuerunt in Ecclesia." ASM, AG, Bu. 3366, ff. 373r–76v.

67. Lipsius made small emendations in subsequent editions. For a brief history of the recovery of the manuscripts and textual criticism on Tacitus before Lipsius, see D'Amico, 1988, 112–26, 257–62.

68. Etter, 1966, 50–58; Schellhase, 1976, 121–22; Renzi, 1985, 33–34.

69. Schmitt, 1972, 254; Schmitt, 1983b, 22 (with the misprint "Bartolomeo" for the correct "Domenico"); and Barsanti, 1993, 524, 566. I have been unable to discover anything more about Mancini.

70. For what follows, see De Mattei, 1963; Toffanin, 1921, 121; Etter, 1966; Burke, 1969, and its

least 45 editions of the *Annals* and *Histories* appeared in the late sixteenth century, and another 103 in the seventeenth. Numerous translations into Italian and other modern languages appeared, and more than a hundred authors wrote commentaries on Tacitus between 1580 and 1700. Historians greatly admired and imitated him, even though he wrote in a difficult aphoristic style very different from the rounded periods of Cicero. Tacitus became an essential text for discussions about reason of state, a powerful and controversial idea. Tacitus had seen little good in the ancient Roman emperors and offered skeptical, sometimes cynical and pessimistic, judgments about the behavior of rulers, especially in books 1 to 6 of the *Annals,* which covered the dissimulation and ruthlessness of Tiberius. Some saw similarities between Tiberius and the rulers and courtiers of seventeenth-century absolutist states. Italian and other commentators linked Tacitus to Machiavelli, whose works were prohibited by the Index of Prohibited Books but widely read. Scholars, historians, theologians, and princes read Tacitus for political wisdom, sometimes to endorse his cynical advice, other times to prove him wrong, while dramatists such as Ben Jonson (1572–1637) wrote tragedies based on Tacitean themes.

Given the nature of the texts, it is not surprising that the holder of the Mantuan Tacitus lectureship was a layman, rather than a Jesuit. The professor was Antonio Possevino (1566–1629), a nephew of Antonio Possevino, S.J. The young Possevino came to the Tacitus professorship via medicine, history, and Gonzaga patronage.

Antonio Possevino was born in Mantua, probably the son of Giovanni Battista, brother of Antonio the Jesuit.[71] The young Possevino studied medicine in Rome, learned several languages, and traveled in northern Europe, where he met scholars. In 1600 he published *Theoricae morborum libri quinque,* in which he described illnesses in Latin hexameter verse in imitation of Girolamo Fracastoro's *Syphilis sive morbus gallicus* (1530; revised edition 1547).[72]

---

shortened form in Burke, 1991; and Schellhase, 1976. This is just an introduction to a large topic. Tacitus was also a key figure in works that argued for or against Machiavelli in the late sixteenth and the seventeenth centuries.

71. Unless otherwise indicated, this and the following paragraph are based on Beghelli, 1978; Zanca and Galassi, 1978, 411; and Pescasio, 1971, 219, 264. Some of the sparse biographical information comes from Possevino's dedication letter to Duke Vincenzo I of Rome, 1600, in Possevino Junior, 1600, 3–5. See the next footnote for the full title. Possevino mentioned his famous uncle in the first sentence of the dedication letter.

72. *Antoniii Possevini Iunioris philosophi, ac medici Mantuani, theoricae morborum libri quinque. Addita Methodus studiorum Medicinae ex Bibliotheca selecta eius Patrui.* Mantuae, Franciscus Osanna Ducalis Impressor excudebat, 1600. The NLM copy has been used. Incidentally, the imprimatur (sig. A3verso) indicates that Antonio Possevino, S.J., read and certified to the inquisitor and bishop of Mantua that the book was useful and free of doctrinal error.

Book 1 described diseases of the head and the thoracic cavity, book 2 diseases of the circulatory and digestive systems, book 3 illnesses of the genital-urinary and gynecological-obstetric tracts, and books 4 and 5 discussed fevers. Returning to Mantua in 1608, Possevino, who had a doctorate of medicine, was accepted into the college of physicians in January 1609.[73] Duke Francesco III named him protomedico in 1612 and charged him with writing a history of the Gonzaga family. When Francesco died after a few months, malicious tongues attributed his death to Possevino's ineptness, which suggested that he was the duke's personal physician as well. Possevino spent the next three years in Rome until Duke Ferdinando called him back, probably in 1616, to finish the history of the Gonzaga.

Published as *Gonzaga, calci operis addita genealogia totius familiae* (Mantua: Francesco Osanna, 1617), it is an attempt to describe the illustrious lineage of the Gonzaga family.[74] It praised illustrious members of the family and tried to document Gonzaga claims to territories. After it appeared, Ferdinando asked the advice of the scholar Gaspare Scioppio, who reported that the book invented claims for which there were no documents, falsified history, and was badly written. Ferdinando commissioned Scioppio to write a better book.[75] Nevertheless, Possevino's history was reprinted in 1628, again in Mantua.

Possevino continued to pursue both medicine and history. In 1617 he published another medical work. And he wrote an account of the 1612–18 war over Monferrato, possibly on commission from Ferdinando, which was eventually published in 1637.[76] Then he appeared as an ordinary humanities professor in 1627, teaching Tacitus, which appointment could not have occurred without the approval of Ferdinando.

The most likely explanation for the Tacitus professorship is that, as a historian, Possevino wanted to teach the texts of an ancient master, and the generous Ferdinando agreed. And perhaps Ferdinando, a ruler with broad intellectual curiosity, was intrigued by the notion that his new university would have a course about statecraft based on study of a master historian. Whatever the reason, the Tacitus professorship once again demonstrated the innovative nature of the Peaceful University of Mantua.

73. Carra, Fornari, and Zanca, 2004, 138.

74. The title is taken from the second edition of 1628; copy in Houghton Library, Harvard University. D'Addio, 1962, 131 note 132, gives a slightly different title for the first edition, which is rare.

75. D'Addio, 1962, 131–33. Scioppio's work, published in 1619 (see ibid., 133 note 135, for the title) was better, but it also engaged in some creative philological interpretations of the documents.

76. The medical work was *De morbis et modis eos curandi*. Mantua: Aurelio e Ludovico Osanna, 1617. The historical work was *Belli Montisferratensis historia ab anno 1612 usque ad annum 1618*. No pl., 1637. Beghelli, 1978, 387–88.

CHAPTER 8

# The Jesuit Professorships

he Jesuit professors offered a comprehensive program based on the *Ratio studiorum* of 1599 but similar to the instruction offered in civic universities. The Jesuits taught humanities, mathematics, moral philosophy, logic, natural philosophy, metaphysics, theology, casuistry, and Scripture. The only other Jesuit school to teach all of them was the Collegio Romano.[1] The Jesuits at Mantua deviated a little from the prescriptions of the *Ratio studiorum* because the Peaceful University of Mantua had to teach the same subjects and the same texts as civic universities to justify Ferdinando's claim that his university was the equal of established universities. On the other hand, the University of Mantua offered a bonus: it taught casuistry, a subject not taught by lay universities.[2]

Although the Jesuits taught the same arts subjects and mostly the same texts as professors in non-Jesuit universities, a subject-by-subject comparison of the research and teaching of Jesuits and lay professors in civic universities reveals many similarities and significant differences. The Jesuits had their own

---

1. See the list of professors and subjects taught at the Collegio Romano in Villoslada, 1954, 322–36. The Collegio Romano also had a professorship of Hebrew at this time, which Mantua lacked. The half-civic, half-Jesuit University of Parma (founded in 1601) had a professorship of Sacred Scripture only in 1621. See Brizzi, 1980, 170–73, for eight lists of Jesuit professors at Parma between 1600 and 1622. See also ARSI, Veneta 71, ff. 11r–12v (list of Jesuit professors at Parma in 1624), 140r–41r (1627 list), 158r (1628), 227r–28r (1633), 237r–38r (1634), 248r–49v (1636). Why Parma lacked a professorship of Scripture is unknown. Incidentally, in Grendler, 2002, page 134, table 4.8, Domenico Zanetti, S.J., is listed as teaching "Moral philosophy." That should be corrected to "Moral theology."

2. "Lay universities" and "civic universities" (used interchangeably) refer to Italian universities lacking Jesuit professors. Of Italy's fifteen universities at this time, only Parma was like Mantua, a half-civic, half-Jesuit university. The Collegio Romano was exclusively Jesuit and did not teach law and medicine. Hence, it was an incomplete university.

approach to Aristotle, which some lay professors found wanting. The Jesuit *Ratio studiorum* conceived of education as an integrated hierarchical process, which was not the case in civic universities. The career patterns of Jesuit professors also diverged from their lay colleagues. Because it was a half-civic and half-Jesuit institution, two academic cultures co-existed in the University of Mantua.

## 1. THE JESUIT CURRICULUM AND TEACHING

Little separated Jesuit professors and lay professors in civic universities in the teaching of the Greek and Latin literary classics. The *Ratio studiorum* instructed Jesuit teachers to give priority to Cicero for Latin prose, and they did. The Jesuit humanities professors at Mantua taught several oratorical works of Cicero, Aristotle's *Rhetoric* and *Poetry*, Virgil's *Aeneid*, Horace, and a tragedy of Seneca. Professors in lay universities taught the same texts and emphasized Cicero.[3] On the other hand, the *Ratio studiorum* instructed Jesuit humanities professors not to teach Terence (195–159? B.C.), the great comic playwright often taught in lay universities, and some Latin poets, for moral reasons, and the Mantuan Jesuits did not teach them.[4] The *Ratio studiorum* recommended the insertion of a Latin historian into the curriculum now and then. Hence, in 1625–26 the Jesuit professor taught the *History of Alexander the Great* of Quintus Curtius Rufus (first century A.D.), a rhetorical history seldom, if ever, taught by lay professors.[5] For Greek the Jesuit professors taught orations of Isocrates and the *Letter to Gregory the Theologian* of St. Basil the Great (ca. 329–379).[6] Professors in non-Jesuit universities frequently taught Isocrates but not the works of Basil the Great. The *Ratio studiorum* also prescribed intensive grammar drill and the assignment and correction of written compositions, exercises obviously intended for younger students.

---

3. For comparison with the texts taught by the humanities professor at the University of Pisa between 1565 and 1600, see Schmitt, 1972, 254; and Schmitt, 1983b, 23 note 13. This is briefly summarized in Grendler, 2002, 240. See ibid., 229–47 passim, for more information on the Latin and Greek classics that became curricular texts in Italian universities. For the Jesuit emphasis on Cicero's oratorical works and other recommended Latin and Greek classics, see *Ratio Studiorum*, 2005, paragraphs 375, 380, 387, 395–96, pp. 155, 159, 163, 166–67. The instructions to the teachers of the lower grammar classes are not relevant here.

4. "[I]n our schools we avoid entirely the books of poets or whatever material can injure moral integrity and good character, unless they have first been expurgated of unseemly language and subject matter; otherwise, if they can not be completely expurgated, as Terence cannot, it is better that they not be read, so that the nature of the material does not damage anyone's innocence." *Ratio Studiorum*, 2005, paragraph 57, p. 25.

5. See Goodyear, 1982, 641–42; Drury, 1982, 891.

6. This was probably one of the letters of St. Basil, bishop of Caesarea, to St. Gregory Nazianzus (ca. 325–ca. 389).

Since university students were older and, presumably, already knew Latin well, the Jesuit humanities professor at the University of Mantua probably simply lectured.

A Jesuit professor taught mathematics at the University of Mantua, as did lay professors in civic universities. Mathematics did not fit neatly into the Jesuit curricular hierarchy but grew in importance over the years.[7] The *Ratio studiorum* directed Jesuit professors of mathematics to teach Euclid's *Elements*, the famous Greek work on geometry composed about 300 B.C., for about two months. When the students were familiar with it, the teacher should add "something about geography or the Sphere or about those things that are usually of interest."[8] The "Sphere" was *De sphaera*, written ca. 1220 by Johannes de Sacrobosco (John of Holywood, d. 1244 or 1256). It summarized Ptolemaic astronomy and was the most used and commented on astronomical work in medieval and Renaissance universities. The distinguished Jesuit mathematician, astronomer, and friend of Galilei, Christoph Clavius (1537 / 8– 1612), who taught at the Collegio Romano, published a commentary on Sacrobosco's *De sphaera* in 1570, which Jesuit teachers often used.[9] It is likely that the Mantuan professors of mathematics taught it.

The Jesuit professors of mathematics added other "things . . . of interest." In the academic year 1624–25 the Jesuit mathematician at the Public Academy of Mantua lectured on sundials, which were still the most reliable instruments for measuring time. In 1625–26 the Jesuit mathematician at the Peaceful University of Mantua added instruction on the use of the astrolabe. In 1626–27 he added material on optics. And in 1627–28 the additional matter consisted of "Questions on the Mechanics of Aristotle," which was the pseudo-Aristotelian *Quaestiones Mechanicae*.[10] The work combined mathematics and physics to solve problems in dynamics, statics, weights, and velocity as Aristotle had not done. Many professors of mathematics at lay universities also taught the *Mechanics*, including Galilei, who wrote a commentary (now lost) on it.

In short, the Jesuits taught exactly what professors of mathematics and astronomy in non-Jesuit Italian universities taught. The sundial, astrolabe, optics, and the material that came under the heading of mechanics reflected some of the research interests of seventeenth-century Italian Jesuit mathematicians, who focused on practical applications and relied on observation

---

7. For the development of the Jesuit interest in mathematics in the sixteenth century, see Romano, 1999, 43–180; for later growth, see Harris, 1995.

8. *Ratio Studiorum*, 2005, paragraphs 239–41, pp. 109–10 (quote on 109).

9. There is a large bibliography on Clavius. Start with Homann, 2001.

10. Written in the third century B. C., the *Mechanics* was ignored in the Middle Ages. Aldo Manuzio first printed it in Greek in 1497, and a Latin translation appeared in 1517. It helped scholars develop mathematical techniques to solve physical problems. See *Mechanics*, 1969, and Rose and Drake, 1971.

and experiment as well as computations.[11] Many non-Jesuit professors of mathematics did the same. Jesuits mathematicians did not teach astrology or cast horoscopes. Most of their counterparts in lay universities had also abandoned astrology by this date, even though many outside the academy, including Duke Ferdinando, remained starstruck.[12] The Jesuits did not accept heliocentrism as physical reality because it contradicted Scripture and Aristotelian natural philosophy. They did accept the work of Copernicus as a useful mathematical fiction that could explain phenomena. Many non-Jesuit professors of mathematics and astronomy did not completely accept Copernicus either at this time.[13] Even though mathematics was a lesser subject in the Jesuit curriculum, seventeenth-century Italian Jesuit mathematicians were very active, and their contributions have been much studied by historians.[14]

The Jesuit Academy of Mantua in 1624–25 and the Peaceful University of Mantua had a professor who taught Aristotle's *Nicomachean Ethics*. Moral philosophy was a minor subject taught by a single professor paid a low stipend in larger Italian universities in the sixteenth and early seventeenth centuries but not taught in smaller ones. The curriculum text was always Aristotle's *Nicomachean Ethics*, but no particular teaching and commentary tradition dominated. Humanistically inclined teachers and commentators saw the *Ethics* as a guide to life for the man in society serving his family and patria. Other professors applied formal philosophical analysis using scholastic and philological analytical tools to explicate the text of the *Ethics* without necessarily offering advice on living. They made the *Ethics* more a philosophical text to be analyzed than a guide to life.[15]

The Jesuits also viewed moral philosophy as a minor subject. The Society introduced a professorship of moral philosophy into the Collegio Romano in

---

11. Harris, 1995, 243, argues that the Jesuits were one of the most important agents legitimizing practical mathematics across Europe.

12. Italian university mathematicians usually taught astrology as well as mathematics and astronomy in the fifteenth century. But astrology almost disappeared from their teaching and writing in the course of the sixteenth century. Grendler, 2002, 408–29 passim.

13. The acceptance and rejection of Copernicus, and the many in-between positions held by Italian Jesuits and non-Jesuits, cannot be discussed here.

14. There is considerable bibliography on the contributions of seventeenth-century Italian Jesuit mathematicians. Some important recent studies include Baldini, 1992, 1999, 2000, 2002; Dear, 1995, 32–123; Feldhay, 1999; Borgato, 2002; Fiocca, 2002; Gavagna, 2002; and *Giambattista Riccioli*, 2002. Giuseppe Biancani (1566–1624), Niccolò Cabeo (1586–1650), and Riccioli (1598–1671) were part of a Parma school of Jesuit mathematicians that probably taught or influenced the mathematicians who taught at Mantua. For Jesuit mathematics in France, see Romano, 1999, 2006.

15. See the comprehensive study of Lines, 2002, and the brief comments in Grendler, 2002, 393–407, for moral philosophy in Italian universities.

1562, but not until 1593 did it become a permanent lectureship. And among Italian Jesuit schools, only the Collegio Romano and the part-Jesuit University of Parma are known to have offered courses in moral philosophy in the early seventeenth century. Again Mantua included it in order to be comparable to civic universities. The teachers at the Collegio Romano viewed moral philosophy as separate from, but with some connections to, theology; hence, their commentaries on the *Ethics* added references to Scripture, Thomas Aquinas, and other philosophical and religious authors.[16] On the other hand, the *Ratio studiorum* instructed professors of moral philosophy to teach the *Nicomachean Ethics* without digressing into theological questions.[17] It is likely that the Jesuit professor at Mantua followed the *Ratio studiorum*.

The next step in the ascending Jesuit curriculum was the philosophical trio of logic, natural philosophy, and metaphysics based on Aristotle. In the forty to fifty years before the promulgation of the final version of the *Ratio studiorum*, the Jesuits debated how to use Aristotle and the rest of the traditional philosophical inheritance, and concluded that his works could provide rational philosophical grounds for Catholic belief. They searched for a unified approach, what they called a common doctrine, that all Jesuit teachers might follow.

In their printed works the Jesuits sought to establish Aristotelian axiomatic foundations, that is, propositions on which all could agree.[18] Then they systematically constructed arguments that would be philosophically sound and would serve, ultimately, as the underpinning of theology. Like other philosophers using scholastic methodology, the Jesuits made *quaestiones,* or disputed questions, the heart of their teaching and books. After a translation or summary of a bit of Aristotelian text, Jesuit authors and teachers stated a question, then carefully studied Aristotle's thought on the basis of his own words. They started with basic Aristotelian principles, then built toward a conclusion by reconstructing Aristotle's meaning as they saw it, which might go beyond Aristotle's cryptic words. This approach differed somewhat from philosophers who started with Aristotle, then constructed arguments based on a combination of Aristotle's words and those of other philosophers, typically commentators on Aristotle. And the Jesuit method also differed from philoso-

---

16. Villoslada, 1954, 334, lists the professors of moral philosophy at the Collegio Romano. For teaching and commentaries there, see Lines, 2002, 348–83.

17. *Ratio Studiorum,* 2005, paragraphs 234–36, pp. 108–9 (quote 108). It also directed that thirty to forty-five minutes of daily instruction in ethics should be given to the metaphysics students in schools lacking a professor of moral philosophy.

18. This and the following paragraph are especially based on Simmons, 1999; plus Lohr, 1976, 1995. Fois, 2000, offers a good survey of the Jesuit upper school between 1550 and 1650. There is much more bibliography on individual Jesuit philosophers.

phers who offered line-by-line commentaries of an Aristotelian work or presented a topically organized *summa,* as Thomas Aquinas did.

At the same time, the Jesuits were products of the Renaissance and did not limit themselves to Aristotle and Aquinas. They read, cited, and answered if necessary ancient Greek commentators (Themistius, Alexander of Aphrodisias, and others) whom Italian university philosophers had inserted into philosophical discourse around 1500. The Jesuits read and used Arab commentators, medieval scholastics from different traditions, humanists such as Marsilio Ficino, and sixteenth-century Italian university philosophers, sometimes with reservations. And Jesuit philosophers differed among themselves, although not on fundamental principles.

The Jesuits viewed logic, natural philosophy, and metaphysics as a three-year unit. The *Ratio studiorum* expected that a Jesuit professor might teach all three in successive years, which some did.[19] According to the *Ratio studiorum,* the curricular texts for logic were Aristotle's *Categories, On Interpretation, Prior Analytics, Topics,* and *On Sophistical Refutations,* five of the six works sometimes called the *Organon.* In addition, at the end of the year the teacher was expected to explain some of the prolegomenous matter of Aristotle's *Physics* and the definitions in Aristotle's *On the soul,* both of which would be primary texts for the course in natural philosophy in the next year.[20] The *Ratio studiorum* also stated that Jesuit professors might use material from logic manuals of two Jesuits, Francisco de Toledo (1532–96) and Pedro de Fonseca (1528–99).[21]

The Jesuit professors of logic at Mantua departed a little from the *Ratio studiorum* in order to bring their logic instruction in harmony with the practice of other universities. Fifteenth- and sixteenth-century professors of logic at non-Jesuit universities normally taught Aristotle's *Organon,* including the *Posterior Analytics.* They also taught the *Isagoge* of Porphyry (ca. 234–301), a logic manual that served as an introduction to the *Categories,* and sometimes a medieval text, such as the *Liber sex principiorum* of Gilbert of Poitiers (ca. 1075–1154). The Jesuit professors at Mantua taught four of the six books of the

---

19. In its "Rules for the Professor of Philosophy," the *Ratio studiorum* discussed the teaching of logic, natural philosophy, and metaphysics in a unified way. *Ratio Studiorum,* 2005, paragraphs 207–34, pp. 99–108. See Baldini, 2002, 295–97, for several examples of Jesuits who taught logic, natural philosophy, and metaphysics in that order in successive years at the University of Parma, and this volume's appendix for Mantuan Jesuits who did the same.

20. *Ratio Studiorum,* 2005, paragraphs 215–20, pp. 101–3.

21. Toledo wrote two well-known logic manuals: *Introductio in dialecticam Aristotelis* (Rome, 1561), with many reprints, and *Commentaria una cum quaestionibus in universam Aristotelis logicam* (Rome, 1572), with reprints. Pedro de Fonseca wrote *Institutionum dialecticarum libri octo* (Lisbon, 1564), with reprints. *Ratio Studiorum,* 2005, 242 note 19. For short biographies, see Donnelly, 2001, and Vaz de Carvalho, 2001b.

*Organon* plus the *Isagoge* of Porphyry, which was not mentioned (and, hence, not recommended) by the *Ratio studiorum*. This was a return to earlier practice, because Italian Jesuits had taught Porphyry throughout the sixteenth century before the *Ratio studiorum* was promulgated.[22] They were not the only Jesuits to depart from the *Ratio studiorum* on this. The Jesuit professor of logic at the University of Graz in Austria initially used Fonseca's manual but in 1602 returned to Porphyry because he preferred it.[23]

The Mantuan Jesuits may also have taught the *Posterior Analytics* (not mentioned in the *Ratio studiorum*) because it was a key text in discussions about demonstrative regress, a matter of intense interest to late sixteenth-century logicians, including some at the Collegio Romano. Demonstrative regress enabled a scholar to reason from phenomena grasped by the senses to universal principles and back again, always within an Aristotelian context. It enabled scholars, including Galilei, to separate necessary causes from effects.[24]

Natural philosophy meant Aristotelian science consisting of a broad discussion of the physical world, of concrete entities, and how they could be understood through their conditions and causes, rather than through measurements. Natural philosophers in Renaissance and seventeenth-century lay universities analyzed the nature of science and the inanimate world by lecturing on the *Physics*, which explained basic principles, and on *De caelo et mundo* and *De generatione et corruptione* for the heavens, elements, compounds, and the atmosphere. They also taught Aristotle's *On the soul*, *Meterology*, and sometimes his so-called animal books and the *Parva naturalia*. Professors of natural philosophy, like the logicians, also tried to develop a logic appropriate for scientific investigation.[25]

The Jesuits concurred with faculty at non-Jesuit universities that natural philosophy should teach Aristotelian science. They agreed on the Aristotelian texts to be taught, except that the *Ratio studiorum* transferred the teaching of *On the soul* to the metaphysics class and to the logic class.[26] The Jesuits viewed

---

22. For example, in response to the first *Ratio studiorum* of 1586, which dismissed Porphyry as an impious man and the *Isagoge* as of little merit to Christians, the Jesuits of the Province of Milan objected, noting that his *Isagage* was a common text in all the universities and was taught by all the doctors. "Nulla ratione videtur dimittendus Porphyrius, cum in omnibus academiis sit usitatus, et ab omnibus doctoribus expositus." *Monumenta Paedagogica*, 1965–92, 6:263. See also ibid., 6:261, 265, and 5:100, for the harsh words of the 1586 *Ratio studiorum*. There are many references to the teaching of Porphyry by the Jesuits earlier in the sixteenth century in *Monumenta Paedagogica*, 1965–92, vols. 1–4.

23. *Monumenta Paedagogica*, 1965–92, 7:504 paragraph 1, 510. Hellyer, 2005, 27, first pointed this out.

24. For logic instruction in Italian Renaissance universities, see Grendler, 2002, 249–66. For demonstrative regress, see Wallace, 1995, 1996, 300–308.

25. For a brief summary and bibliography, see Grendler, 2002, 267–71, 279–81.

26. *Ratio Studiorum*, 2005, paragraphs 221–23, pp. 103–4.

their philosophical teaching as a way of proceeding through cosmological and ontological reality, a passage through different kinds of being. The *Physics*, which discussed corporeal substances in general, came first. Next came simple eternal substances based on *De caelo et mundo*. Then came simple non-eternal substances, discussed with the aid of *De generatione et corruptione*, followed by mixed inanimate substances based on the *Meterology*. Finally came mixed animated substances, for which the text was *On the soul*, taught in the metaphysics class.[27]

The *Ratio studiorum* did not mention Aristotle's animal books or *Parva naturalia*, because the *Ratio studiorum* did not view natural philosophy as preparation for the study of medicine. Indeed, in the directions for teaching book 2 of *On the soul*, the *Ratio studiorum* told the metaphysics teacher that "he should not digress into anatomy and the rest of the things that are the concerns of medical doctors."[28] The rolls demonstrated that the Jesuit professors of natural philosophy at the University of Mantua followed the *Ratio studiorum*, except that they omitted the *Meterology*.

However, the Jesuit approach to *On the soul* uncovered an area in which the Jesuits differed profoundly from the teaching of natural philosophy by some lay professors. The philosophical question at issue was, according to Aristotelian philosophy, is the individual human soul mortal or immortal, material or immaterial? And the corollary, can Aristotelian philosophy without assistance from Revelation demonstrate the immortality of the human soul? The issue had a long and controversial history that went beyond the lecture hall.

Italian universities in the Middle Ages and in the Renaissance viewed natural philosophy as preparation for and a complement to medical studies, the study of the human being and his activities. Hence, professors of natural philosophy discussed the human intellective soul. According to Aristotle, every living being has an organic soul, which is the form or life principle appropriate to it. The organic soul is the source that directs those life functions tied to the bodies of living beings and are dependent on them, such as sensation, memory, reproduction, and digestion. *On the soul*, especially books 2 and 3, provided the approach and direction of these studies.

Aristotle in *On the soul*, book 3, 4–5, raised the questions, how does the human intellect know, and what is the relationship between sense knowledge and abstract thought? Answering these questions provoked an intense debate among Renaissance philosophers over the nature of the intellective soul, that

---

27. Baldini, 1999, 252 and note 15. Indeed, the entire discussion of Jesuit teaching in natural philosophy, metaphysics, and mathematics is indebted to Baldini, 1992, 19–73; 1999; 2002. Hellyer, 2005, 79–84 et passim, also provides a good analysis of the Jesuit approach to natural philosophy.

28. *Ratio Studiorum*, 2005, paragraph 224, p. 104.

is, the human mind. Does it know independently from sense experience and is, therefore, independent of the body and not material in substance? Or does the intellective soul depend entirely on sense experience in order to know and is, therefore, material in substance? The latter view, plus acceptance of two other secular Aristotelian propositions, the eternity of the world and the universal intellect in which the human intellect participates only during his or her lifetime, challenged core Christian belief. The discussion inevitably led to other important issues, such as how to approach the study of the human soul, the claims of knowledge of philosophy and theology, and the relations between the two. It appears that the majority of Renaissance and early seventeenth-century Italian philosophers, almost all of whom were Aristotelians, held that the human soul was immortal and that God created the world.[29]

But there were exceptions, the most famous of whom were Pietro Pomponazzi (1462–1525) and the still living Cesare Cremonini (1550–1631), professor of natural philosophy at the University of Ferrara 1578 to 1590, and the University of Padua from 1591 to 1629, and the most visible natural philosophy professor in Italy. In several books Cremonini held tenaciously to the position that the individual human intellective soul was mortal according to Aristotelian philosophy, and that reason alone could not reach a different conclusion. He argued that a philosopher who followed Aristotle strictly and a theologian honoring Christian Revelation must reach different conclusions about the immortality of the soul and the eternity of the world.[30]

The Jesuits saw this issue as a question about how they should approach Averroes (Ibn Rushd, 1126–98), the Arab commentator on Aristotle who rejected individual immortality and saw the world as eternal. Not all Jesuits initially opposed teaching Averroes, who offered useful comments on many other Aristotelian issues as well. In 1564 Benedetto Perera (or Benito Pereira, 1535–1610), who taught logic, natural philosophy, and theology at the Collegio Romano, argued that Jesuit philosophers should teach the opinions of Averroes and his important medieval and Renaissance followers.[31] Some of his fellow Jesuits criticized him for this position.[32] And in the last third of the

---

29. Di Napoli, 1963, remains a fundamental survey. See also Grendler, 2002, 281–96, and the bibliography cited.

30. The bibliography on Cremonini is extensive. Start with Della Torre, 1968; Schmitt, 1980; Poppi, 1993; and Kuhn, 1996.

31. "Leggere Averroe è molto utile, sì per la sua dottrina, come per la fama che ha in Italia; et per poterlo intendere, leggerà li suoi seguaci, come Janduno, Barleo, Paulo veneto, Zimarra, Nipho." *Monumenta Paedagogica*, 1965–92, 2:665–66. The followers were John of Jandun, ca. 1275–1328; Walter Burleigh 1275–1343; Paul (Nicoletti) of Venice, ca. 1369–72/1429); Marco Antonio Zimara, ca. 1475–1532; and Agostino Nifo, 1473–1546. On Perera, see Solà, 2001.

32. Hellyer, 2005, 24, 30–31.

# The Jesuit Curriculum and Teaching

century, Italian Jesuits turned decisively against Averroes, denouncing him as a "destroyer of truth," "troubler of souls," "impious," and "atheistic." The Jesuits did not attack Pomponazzi, Cremonini, or other modern philosophers by name but called them Averroists (*averroistis*) or the "sect of the Averroists" (*sectam averroistarum*).[33] German Jesuits also strongly condemned Averroist opinions and any Jesuits attracted to Averroist positions.[34]

Even though it is not likely that many professors of philosophy in non-Jesuit universities agreed with Pomponazzi and Cremonini, the very possibility frightened Italian rulers and parents who feared that university philosophers might teach their sons atheism. The Jesuits exploited this concern. In 1570, when the rector of the Jesuit college in Turin was trying to persuade the duke of Piedmont-Savoy to turn over philosophy instruction at the University of Turin to the Society, he promised that the Jesuits would teach "Christian philosophy" in place of "that secular philosophy tending toward atheism."[35] In 1599, when the Jesuits were negotiating their participation in the new University of Parma, Antonio Possevino, S.J., told Duke Ranuccio I Farnese that lay professors of philosophy were likely to teach "pestilential errors about the mortality of the soul."[36] The presence of Jesuits in a university would assure rulers and parents that Christian philosophy was being taught.

Despite many Jesuit denunciations of Averroes, the *Ratio studiorum* of 1599 took a more measured approach. It stated that the goal of logic, natural philosophy, and metaphysics was to prepare students for theology and to know God. And it told philosophy teachers not to follow Aristotle "if he contradicts orthodox belief."[37] It then warned teachers against the Averroists

---

33. For some examples, see *Monumenta Paedagogica*, 1965–92, 2:487, 499, 502 (1564); 4:198 (1574), 248 (1573), 664–65 (1576); 5:100–101 (1586, *sectam averroistarum* on 100); 5:283 (1591); 6:39 (1585, *averroistis*), 267 (a very strong denunciation of Averroes from the Jesuits of the Province of Venice). On the other hand, Perera differed with his colleagues at the Collegio Romano and continued to insist that Averroes and other "Gentiles" should be taught, albeit carefully. *Monumenta Paedagogica*, 1965–92, 6:261.

34. Hellyer, 2005, 17–19.

35. "Dopo ch'io son qui quanto ho potuto ho faticato in questa materia e ne son già a bon termine, gioverà grandissima per introdur philosophia cristiana, poiché l'istesso duca et questi signori sogliono dir spesse volte che hanno toccato con mano che questa philosophia secolare tende all'atheismo, del quale non vi manca qui semenza e il duca lo ha in grande orrore, e dice che in questo si confida che la Compagnia qui abbia dar far frutto grande." Father Achille Gagliardi to Father General Francisco Borja, September 13, 1570, Turin, in ARSI, Epistolae Italiae 139, f. 220r (entire letter ff. 219r–220v). It is also quoted in Scaduto, 1992, 332.

36. "Altri potrebbono pretendere letture di filosofia benché fossero secolari, la quale quando è letta da chi non è prima buon Teologo, serve spessissimo per introdurre pestilenti errori della mortalità dell'anima, o di altro." Memorandum by Antonio Possevino, S.J., summarizing his discussion with Duke Ranuccio I concerning the proposed University of Parma, no date but 1599, printed in Brizzi, 1980, 188 (entire memorandum 183–93).

37. *Ratio Studiorum*, 2005, paragraphs 207–11, pp. 99–100, quote 99.

and Alexandrians, meaning those who held to the view that the human soul was mortal and the earth eternal. It told Jesuit professors to be very selective in their use of interpreters of Aristotle "who do not serve Christianity well," and to be careful that students did not become well disposed toward such interpreters.[38] But the *Ratio studiorum* did not forbid their use entirely. The Jesuits were confident that they understood Aristotle and the rest of the philosophical tradition well enough that they could refute Pomponazzi and Cremonini on their own grounds.[39]

There was also a quantitative difference between the teaching of natural philosophy at the University of Mantua and at civic universities. The University of Mantua had only a single professor of natural philosophy, a Jesuit. By contrast, medium-sized and large civic universities had several professors of natural philosophy. The University of Rome had two, the University of Padua had five, and the University of Bologna had ten to thirteen in the 1620s.[40] Even though university statutes required all professors of natural philosophy to teach the same texts, professors had their own approaches and styles, which produced instructional variety and different viewpoints. This quantitative difference did not appear or was less important in other arts subjects, such as the humanities and mathematics, because, like the University of Mantua, civic universities usually had only one, and occasionally two, professors for these subjects.

Despite the differences, much of Jesuit natural philosophy instruction resembled what lay professors taught. So far as can be determined, Jesuit professors and their students produced scholarship on scientific issues within the Aristotelian context comparable to that produced by lay professors and their students. Jesuit scholars favored research employing observation and experiment and were at least as innovative as other Aristotelians.[41]

The third of the Jesuit philosophical trio was metaphysics. In civic uni-

---

38. *Ratio Studiorum*, 2005, 100 (quote). Note 126 on page 100, states that the "Alexandrians" (Nulli sectae, ut averroistarum, alexandraeorum, et similium vel se vel suos addicat), whose views the *Ratio studiorum* tells Jesuits to avoid, referred to followers of Alexander of Hales (d. 1245). It is much more likely that "Alexandrians" referred to Renaissance professors such as Pietro Pomponazzi, who allegedly followed Alexander of Aphrodisias (fl. ca. 200) to argue that the individual human intellect died with the body.

39. Lohr, 1976, 218–19.

40. For Rome, see *I maestri di Roma*, 1:191–215 passim, and 2:1083. For Padua see Facciolati, 1978, part 3, 275–76, 280–81, 285, 289, 292; and Tomasini, 1986, 307, 309, 319–21. For the University of Bologna, see *I rotuli dello Studio Bolognese*, 1888–1924, 2:366–83 passim.

41. An examination of thirteen Jesuit theses in natural philosophy written between 1612 and 1674 at Jesuit schools in Parma, Rome, Florence, and Milan showed that Jesuit Aristotelian natural philosophy was innovative and open to mathematics and experiment. Baroncini, 1981. See also the comments of Baldini, 1999, 261, 263–67, 278; and Baldini, 2002, 286–88.

versities metaphysics served as preparation for scholastic theology. Major universities usually had two metaphysicians: a friar from a local Franciscan convent or a hermit or canon from an Augustinian convent taught Scotist metaphysics as preparation for Scotist theology, and a Dominican friar taught Thomistic metaphysics as preparation for Thomistic theology. They commonly taught as concurrents. The universal text was Aristotle's *Metaphysics*, especially books 1, 7, and 12. Metaphysics was not highly regarded: professors in other disciplines looked down on metaphysics as an easy subject pursued only by members of religious orders.[42]

The University of Mantua had one professor, a Jesuit, who taught metaphysics in preparation for the Jesuit form of Thomistic theology. He taught students the conceptual and linguistic tools needed to study theology and further explained some principles of natural philosophy.[43] Because metaphysics was of greater importance in the Jesuit curriculum than in civic universities, it received more time and involved more texts. The *Ratio studiorum*-decreed that metaphysics teachers would teach book 2 of *On generation and corruption,* plus the *Metaphysics,* and *On the soul.*[44] This is what happened at Mantua. In 1625–26 the lectureship was called "Ad lecturam de Anima," and the text was *On the soul,* taught by a non-Jesuit priest, because there was no Jesuit available. However, in 1626–27 and in 1627–28 the professorship at the University of Mantua was renamed "Ad lecturam de Anima & Metaphysica" and expanded to two lectures daily delivered by a single Jesuit. He taught books of *De generatione* and the *Metaphysics* in the morning and *On the soul* in the afternoon. In their teaching and research on metaphysics, Jesuit scholars developed a distinctive approach to being and essence that did not echo Thomas Aquinas.[45]

The philosophical trio of logic, natural philosophy, and metaphysics prepared students for theology, the highest subject in the Jesuit curriculum, as well as casuistry and biblical studies. The University of Mantua had two professors of theology, one professor of cases of conscience, and a professor of Scripture, all of them Jesuits. This was a slightly larger commitment to religious studies than that of contemporary universities lacking Jesuits and a considerable increase over the past. Italian universities in the Middle Ages and the Renaissance taught little theology. Some had one or two professors of theology, while several did not teach it at all, or only intermittently, until after

---

42. Grendler, 2002, 353–92 passim, especially 385–89 for the texts taught and negative comments about metaphysics.
43. Baldini, 1999, 260–61.
44. *Ratio Studiorum,* 2005, paragraphs 224–25, p. 104.
45. See especially Di Vona, 1968; plus Lohr, 1976; and Simmons, 1999.

Trent. For example, not until 1566 did the University of Bologna create a continuing professorship of theology. Like metaphysics, theology had a low reputation in lay universities.[46]

Civic universities did not emphasize biblical studies either. In 1546 the Council of Trent instructed princes and city governments to introduce lectureships of Sacred Scripture into universities lacking them—which meant all Italian universities. About two-thirds, mostly large and middle-sized universities, established professorships of Scripture by the end of the sixteenth century; the others did not.[47] And no Italian university taught casuistry until Parma, the other half-Jesuit university founded in 1601, introduced a professorship of casuistry.[48]

The *Ratio studiorum* strongly emphasized that the Jesuits should be scholastic theologians and follow Thomas. Indeed, it devoted many pages to a list of the questions in the *Summa theologica* of Thomas to be discussed, how to address them, what should be emphasized, and what could be omitted.[49] And the Jesuits did follow Thomas. For example, between 1618 and 1623 Cosma Alamanni (1559–1634), an Italian Jesuit who taught philosophy and theology for many years in Milan, published a five-volume work that combined texts of Thomas with his own commentary.[50] Jesuit theologians proceeded in a careful, orderly, and logical progression full of questions and answers couched in scholastic terminology and with many references to Thomas Aquinas.[51] This was particularly true in dogmatic theology, which explicated the theoretical truths of faith concerning God and his works, including man.

But the Jesuits treated Thomas freely, and contemporary influences, above all Renaissance humanism, made Jesuit scholasticism, as it is sometimes called, quite different from medieval scholasticism. The intellectual struggles with the Protestants over the origins of the Christian Church encouraged the development of positive theology, that is, the scriptural, patristic, and other bases for theological doctrines. Hence, the Jesuits emphasized positive theol-

---

46. For a summary of theology in Italian Renaissance universities and more bibliography, see Grendler, 2002, 353–92, esp. 381–83 for Bologna, and 387–88 for negative comments about theology.

47. Grendler, 2002, 371, 374, 376, 377, 380, 382–83.

48. Brizzi, 1980, 170–72.

49. *Ratio Studiorum*, 2005, 69–94.

50. Di Vona, 1968, 133–36, although Alamanni's work did not have great influence among the Jesuits. See also Zanfredini, 2001.

51. The following brief summary of Jesuit theology, which overlaps discussions of what some scholars call second scholasticism, which included the Dominicans and other religious orders, is based on Ryan, 1936; the relevant chapters in Giacon, 1944–50; Villoslada, 1954; Broderick, 1961; González, 1975, 197–203; Mondin, 1996, 284–323; Dietrich, 1999; Knebel, 2000; Brunet et al., 2001; Elorduy, 2001; Cesareo, 2004, 613–21; and Höpfl, 2004. There is much more bibliography on specific individuals and topics.

ogy more than did medieval scholastics, including Thomas. Jesuit scholars studied the ancient sources of Catholicism in their original languages and filled their writings with references to the early Church Fathers, which was not the case with medieval scholastics. Jesuit theologians had a much stronger sense of history than did medieval Scholasics, another consequence of humanism.

Jesuit theologians emphasized man's capabilities, including the individual's life in society and his freedom to make informed moral decisions. Major Jesuit theologians, above all Francisco Suárez (1543–1617), who taught theology at the Collegio Romano from 1580 to 1585, wrote extensively on the law and the state in ways relevant to the times. And when Suárez argued that under certain, very limited circumstances an individual might commit tyrannicide, many denounced him and the Jesuits generally for subverting the authority of the state. The Jesuits engaged in controversial theology, which concerned itself with refuting error, more than their medieval predecessors. The most celebrated theological work penned by an Italian Jesuit of this era was Robert Bellarmine's *Disputationes de controversiis christianae fidei adversus huius temporis haereticos* (three volumes published in 1586, 1588, and 1593, with many printings), based on his lectures at the Collegio Romano between 1576 and 1587.

As expected, Jesuit theology strongly supported the canons of the Council of Trent. It was triumphalist, because Jesuit theologians confidently expected that true religion, Catholicism, would prevail. Jesuit theology was also universalist, as it kept in mind the missionary goal of spreading Catholicism throughout the world. The Society's theologians showed themselves to be sensitive to the problems of converting non-Europeans and more readily accepted the customs of non-European peoples than theologians of other Catholic religious orders. In short, Jesuit theology was as much a product of its age as it was medieval and scholastic.

While Jesuit theology was broad and multifaceted, the rolls suggest that the theologians at the Public Academy were a cautious lot. The first Jesuit professor of theology lectured on topics in dogmatic theology, including the Incarnation of the Divine Word, the sacraments, especially penance and matrimony, the Eucharist, the Mass, and the Trinity. The second professor of theology followed a more eclectic path. In 1624–25 he lectured on angels, the state of blessedness, and human actions. In subsequent years he discussed moral theology topics, including vice and sin, grace, justice and law, as well as faith, hope, and charity, according to St. Thomas.[52] Whether they broached other areas, such as topics in controversial theology, the methodology of positive theology, or the issues that Suárez addressed, is unknown.

The University of Mantua had a professorship of cases of conscience, or casuistry, a branch of moral theology designed to aid confessors. While casu-

---

52. See tables 3.1, 6.1, 6.2, and ASM, AG, Bu. 3366, f. 108.

istry was a part of medieval scholastic theology, it became more important when the Council of Trent in 1551 obligated Catholics to confess their mortal sins to a priest at least once a year.[53] Trent also insisted that parish priests obtain the theological education needed to administer and understand penance and other sacraments. The Jesuits responded. By the 1570s the larger Jesuit colleges across Italy offered two or three casuistry lectures a week primarily intended for local priests.[54] As the *Ratio studiorum* stated, the professor of cases of conscience "should strive to devote all his effort and energetic activity to the training of skilled parish priests or ministers of the sacraments."[55] The Collegio Romano instituted a professorship of casuistry in 1553 and by the early seventeenth century often had two Jesuits teaching it.[56]

At the end of the sixteenth century Jesuit scholars began to publish manuals for confessors. One of the most important came from Francisco de Toledo, who developed his ideas while teaching the subject at the Collegio Romano from 1562 to 1569. Copies of his lectures and student notes circulated for some time until his *Summa casuum conscientiae, sive de instructione sacerdotum, libri septem* was published in 1598, followed by many reprints and epitomes. Toledo used the Ten Commandments for his framework and emphasized human behavior and sin in a social context. Hence, he discussed theft and restitution, which was repairing the social damage of theft. He explained usury, a person's duties in a court of law, whether a clergymen could hold several benefices, and many other human actions that had social consequences, including the question of whether one might kill to defend the faith, country, friend, or neighbor.[57] Toledo's work helped set the direction of Jesuit casuistry.

The Spanish Jesuit Juan Azor (1536–1605), who also taught theology for many years at the Collegio Romano, published a large and influential manual entitled *Institutiones morales* (three volumes, 1600–11).[58] Volume 1 began with a section on human actions, followed by discussions of the habits, passions, and virtues of the soul, sin, divine and human laws, church precepts, and the Ten Commandments. He devoted volumes 2 and 3 to the Ten Commandments and the increasingly complex sins, penalties, and conditions for absolution.

---

53. See session 14, "Canons concerning the most holy sacrament of penance," especially canons 4, 6, and 8, in *Decrees*, 1990, 2:711–13.

54. Grendler, 2004, 488, 492, 495, 496, 498.

55. *Ratio Studiorum*, 2005, paragraph 197, p. 95.

56. Villoslada, 1954, 325, 326.

57. Keenan, 2004. See Turrini, 1991, 483–92, for a list of fifty-five printings of Toledo's work published between 1599 and 1645; more followed.

58. Villoslada, 1954, 75, 97, 98, 121, 323, 324, although Azor never held the casuistry professorship. For a brief description of Azor's *Institutiones morales* and a list of the editions of it through 1622, see Turrini, 1991, 181–83, 364–65.

# The Jesuit Curriculum and Teaching

Many more manuals guiding confessors in dealing with sinners and moral dilemmas followed in the seventeenth century.

Casuistry, and moral theology generally at this time, put heavy emphasis on duties and laws, producing what might be called a morality of obligation.[59] The key factor was the individual human conscience, which supplanted the focus on prudence in medieval casuistry. Conscience became a judge with freedom of choice. It could not formulate or modify moral or civil laws, but because the circumstances of human actions varied so much, the individual human conscience had to interpret the situation and possessed the moral freedom to act. While Jesuit casuistry emphasized laws and sins, it also strongly endorsed the freedom of the conscience. This was another legacy of Renaissance humanism, which focused on the individual and his or her responsibility before God.

The need for principles to assist the conscience and to aid confessors to resolve morally unclear cases led to the formulation of systems of moral theology, in which the Jesuits played a major role. The most influential was probabilism; in its most expansive form, it argued that one might do what was morally probable, even if another action was more probable.[60] In other words, the individual human conscience was permitted to follow a course of action so long as its moral acceptability was probable and supported by good reasons, even if the opposite view was based on better reasons. Bartolemé Medina (1528–80), a Spanish Dominican, first formulated probabilism, but Jesuit casuists developed it and added variations—and were accused of moral laxity. Again, Jesuit theologians were men of their times; Thomas Aquinas did not devote much analysis to cases of conscience, nor did he formulate probabilism.

Even though the content of their lectures is unknown, the Jesuit professors of casuistry at Mantua probably followed the mainlines of Jesuit casuistry. In 1624–25 the casuist at the Public Academy of Mantua lectured on the Ten Commandments. In 1625–26, now at the University of Mantua, he focused on restitution and obligations; in 1626–27 on obligations and censures; and in 1627–28 on ecclesiastical censures.[61]

Jesuit biblical scholarship and teaching manifested similar tendencies as Jesuit theology and again reflected Renaissance developments. In the first thirty-five years of the sixteenth century, Italian biblical humanists learned Greek, Hebrew, and Aramaic in order to read the Bible in its original lan-

---

59. For the following brief description of Jesuit moral theology and casuistry, see Angelozzi, 1981; Turrini, 1991, passim; Pinckaers, 1995, 254–73; and Brunet et al., 2001, 3739–43, 3747.

60. For an exhaustive and exhausting study of probabilism, see Deman, 1936. See also Turrini, 1991, 162–76 et passim; Pinckaers, 1995, 273–77; Brunet et al., 2001, 3745–47. See also Maryks, 2008, which offers a fresh look at Jesuit probabilism.

61. See tables 3.1, 6.1, 6.2, and ASM, AG, Bu. 3366, f. 108.

guages. They often corrected the Vulgate, the accepted Latin translation attributed to St. Jerome (342–420). They emphasized the importance of the early Church Fathers as authentic witnesses, studied medieval Jewish commentaries, and used historical materials in order to understand obscure passages. By contrast, they paid little attention to medieval scholastic biblical commentaries and rejected most allegorical and mystical interpretations. Their emendations of the Vulgate and explanations of passages drew sharp criticism from conservatives, especially those of the Faculty of Theology of the University of Paris.[62]

Jesuit biblical scholarship built on these foundations. The commentaries on the four gospels, first published in 1596 and 1597, of Juan Maldonado (1533–83), probably the ablest Jesuit biblical scholar of the era, demonstrated this.[63] In his commentary on the Gospel of Matthew, Maldonado used his knowledge of Greek, Hebrew, Aramaic, and Syriac (i.e., ancient Syrian Aramaic) to explain obscure points and words. Maldonado made extensive use of the Septuagint, a Greek translation of the Hebrew Old Testament prepared in Egypt in the second century. Although aware of problems with the Latin Vulgate, he did not correct it, possibly because a papal commission of scholars was preparing a revised edition, which was finally promulgated in 1592. Instead, he delved into the linguistic, social, and political history of the ancient world to explain passages.[64] He drew on his extraordinarily comprehensive knowledge of the early Church Fathers for explanations and interpretations. While almost ignoring medieval scholastics, including Thomas Aquinas. Maldonado referred to "the followers of Luther and Calvin" and corrected their interpretations but restricted his disagreements to biblical explanations and did not devote much space to refuting Protestants. He treated Hebrew commentators the same way. On the other hand, Maldonado did not follow the paths of some humanists, such as Erasmus, who drew out the moral lessons of the gospels. Maldonado produced a literal and historical explanation of every phrase and, when necessary, every word of the gospels.

62. See Grendler, 2008, with more bibliography.
63. For a brief survey of Jesuit biblical scholarship for the period 1563–1660, see Gilbert, 2001, 438–40. For Maldonado's life and additional bibliography, see Tellechea, 2001. Maldonado's immense gospel commentaries were reprinted at least thirty-one times in the century after publication. For what follows, see Maldonado, 1888.
64. For example, in Matthew 3:11, John the Baptist preaches that he is preparing the way for one coming after him who is mightier and adds, "I am not fit to carry his sandals." Maldonado, 1888, 1:91–92, explains that the phrase came from the custom of taking off one's shoes when entering holy places, and "that persons of higher rank had slaves to carry their shoes when they had taken them off." Maldonado further described the shoes as sandals consisting of soles with fasteners.

# The Jesuit Curriculum and Teaching

The twenty short paragraphs that the *Ratio studiorum* devoted to guiding the professor of Sacred Scripture reflected a century of biblical study and controversy.[65] It generally endorsed the kind of scholarship that Maldonado practiced but advised caution at several points. The *Ratio studiorum* began by instructing the professor of Sacred Scripture to explain the sacred texts "according to their genuine and literal meaning" (*germanum literalemque sensum*), a humanist approach. The revised Vulgate, which had eliminated errors, should be followed, although some room was allowed for discussion of differences between it and Hebrew or Greek original texts. The *Ratio studiorum* urged great respect for the Septuagint and told the professor to "follow reverently in the footsteps of the holy Fathers." On the other hand, the professor of Scripture "should not treat questions proper to Sacred Scriptures in the Scholastic manner." He was permitted to use "Hebraic rabbinical writings." But he should use them in a way as to keep his listeners from becoming well disposed toward them, especially "those who wrote after the times of Christ the Lord." This was a warning against the great medieval Jewish scriptural scholars, such as Rashi (Rabbi Solomon Ben Isaac, 1040–1105) and David Kimhi (1160–1234), who combined immense erudition with occasional criticism of Christian interpretations and Christians generally. Maldonado used Hebrew commentaries more freely.

The *Ratio studiorum* enjoined the Scripture professor to respect the canons of popes and councils when they offered views about the meaning of passages. He was permitted to mention disagreements with heretics but should not linger over them, because his job was to teach Scripture. The *Ratio studiorum* also told him not to spend time over biblical chronology and other historical details unless the passage demanded it, a command that Maldonado would have found irksome. The *Ratio studiorum* instructed the professor of Scripture to teach a single book of the Bible every year, alternating between the New and Old Testaments, "unless occasionally some other arrangement is judged to be better."[66] In 1624–25 the professor of Scripture at the Public Academy of Mantua taught parables from the gospels, obviously an "other arrangement." In 1625–26 at the University of Mantua, he taught the Psalms; in 1626–27 Paul's Epistle to the Romans; and in 1627–28 the first chapters of Genesis.[67] In short, he followed the prescriptions of the *Ratio studiorum* and probably the scholarship of Maldonado, in so far as he was able, in his teaching at the University of Mantua.

---

65. For what follows, see *Ratio Studiorum*, 2005, paragraphs 149–68, pp. 55–60, quotes on pp. 57, 59, 58 respectively.
66. *Ratio Studiorum*, 2005, paragraphs 149–68, pp. 55–60, quote on p. 60.
67. See tables 3.1, 6.1, 6.2, and ASM, AG, Bu. 3366, f. 108.

## 2. THE CAREER PATHS OF JESUITS AND LAY PROFESSORS

Professors in lay universities and Jesuits followed different career paths. In the former, local men from prominent or professional families obtained doctorates from the local university and began teaching there at about age twenty-five. A few humanities professors lacked doctorates but were still local men. Most lay professors spent their entire professional lives teaching, although professors of medicine often had private practices as well, and legists wrote consilia for clients. Only academic stars enjoyed opportunities to move from one university to another. The rest, whether learned or mediocre, could only hope to ascend to higher positions and salaries in their university through merit and the mortality of senior professors.

Professors in civic universities seldom changed disciplines, except for some medical scholars and natural philosophers who began by teaching logic, considered an introductory course useful to students in all fields. Other than that, legists taught law, medical scholars taught medicine, mathematicians taught mathematics, and humanists taught the Latin and Greek classics. They might teach different sectors of their disciplines. Some legists taught both civil and canon law in the course of their careers or different aspects of civil law. A man with a medical doctorate might teach surgery and anatomy, then theoretical medicine, followed by practical medicine.

Jesuit professors had different career trajectories. They often joined the Society of Jesus in their late teens and then underwent probation as novices, followed by extensive education, religious exercises, various ministries, and ordination, a program that consumed ten years and more. Although a handful, such as Bellarmine, were sent to study in lay universities, the vast majority studied in Jesuit schools. Very little is known about where the Mantuan Jesuit professors studied, but they likely did their philosophical and theological studies in Parma, and a few at the Collegio Romano. So far as can be determined, very few Italian Jesuits possessed doctorates, and those who did acquired them before entering the Society.[68] While Jesuit schools had papal authorization to confer doctorates in philosophy and theology to candidates who passed rigorous examinations, they awarded very few degrees.

On the other hand, Jesuit professors usually had considerable teaching experience. Many taught grammar, humanities, and/or rhetoric in Jesuit lower schools for one or several years during their own education and religious training. By the time they completed the philosophical trio plus theology, and were called on to teach these courses, they were probably ordained

---

68. Of the Jesuits who taught at the University of Mantua, Cesare Moscatelli and Carlo Zamberti obtained doctorates before entering the Society of Jesus, which they did at the ages of about twenty-four and twenty-one respectively. See the appendix.

and had professed the four vows of the Society. Most of the Jesuit teachers at the University of Mantua were men in their thirties and forties (see the appendix).

Unlike professors at civic universities, Jesuit professors taught different subjects in their pedagogical careers. Jesuit professors commonly taught logic, natural philosophy, and metaphysics in successive years, and then either repeated the cycle or taught theology next. At the University of Mantua, fathers Francesco Manfredini, Antonio Morando, and Vincenzo Serugo did exactly that, and Morando taught theology in his fourth year (see appendix). The unique subject matter of mathematics made it an exception; hence, Jesuit mathematicians often taught only that subject for many years.[69] Jesuit teachers frequently moved from college to college within a province. For example, Father Luca Parenti taught logic, natural philosophy, and metaphysics at the University of Parma from 1621 to 1626, then went to Mantua, where he taught casuistry in 1626–27 and theology in 1628–29. Alessandro Simonetta taught six different subjects at Mantua, Parma, and Bologna in the course of his career (see appendix).

Jesuit teachers did not move or teach different subjects in pursuit of more money or prestige, but in response to the needs of the Society as perceived by their superiors. At the same time it is likely that they had some voice in their careers, because they sometimes resisted transfers. And teaching was only one of several possible ministries for a Jesuit priest. He might be a teacher, confessor, preacher, missionary to rural areas, rector of a college, or all of them, in the course of his life.[70] The Jesuit professors of arts, philosophy, and theology at Mantua had professional careers quite different from the professors of law and medicine.

### 3. TWO ACADEMIC CULTURES

Only a few differences in the content of what was taught separated the Jesuits from lay professors in the same disciplines at civic universities. Differences in pedagogy and academic culture were more significant. Some professors and students at non-Jesuit universities held that the Jesuits did not teach directly from Aristotle but taught from summaries and textbooks. According to the critics, the Jesuits taught Aristotle poorly and failed to serve the academic needs of students. Even though enemies of the Jesuits were casting about for stones to throw, real differences existed.

In 1572, non-Jesuit professors at the University of Ingolstadt in Bavaria

---

69. Baldini, 2002, 288, 294–316 passim.

70. Although the Jesuits are best remembered for their schools, only about 10 percent of Italian Jesuits were actually teaching at any one time in the 1570s. Grendler, 2004, 517 et passim.

charged that the Jesuits there so neglected Aristotle that students graduated without ever seeing a text of the Greek master. They further complained that the Jesuits taught logic in a way that was of no help to law and medicine students and only useful to philosophy and theology students. These complaints must be taken with a grain of salt, because Ingolstadt was embroiled in a bitter struggle: non-Jesuit professors believed that their authority in the university and their very jobs were threatened, while the Jesuits sought a larger role and more positions. Indeed, the Jesuits came to dominate the faculties of arts and theology, and they eventually replaced many of the incumbents in arts, philosophy, and theology.[71] Nevertheless, the complaints anticipated what Italian professors would say about Jesuit university teaching.

In early December 1591 the leader of the organization of arts and medicine students of the University of Padua claimed that the Jesuits in their school at Padua, which was not part of the university, taught logic and philosophy by means of modern *Summisti* (summaries) without lecturing from the text of Aristotle. Students could not become good philosophers without studying Aristotle directly, he believed.[72] Two weeks later Cesare Cremonini, second-place ordinary professor of natural philosophy at the university and an implacable foe of the Jesuits, charged that Jesuit teachers read from sheets of paper containing either "anti-knowledge" (*anti dottrina*) or knowledge borrowed from others.[73] Teaching from these notes, the Jesuits in their school at Padua got things wrong or produced secondhand knowledge, he concluded.

There was more. In Turin in 1593 an anonymous memorandum opposing transfer of philosophy and theology teaching from the university to the Jesuits offered a more elaborate version of the same criticism. There were three different ways of teaching Aristotle, it began. One could teach from the text only, like a grammarian, a method that was poor and lacked substance. One could teach Aristotle by ignoring the text completely and just teaching the questions, a method condemned as too sophisticated and barbarous, words implying a medieval scholastic approach. Or one could teach Aristotle through the text with digressions on the questions in their place, which method the Greeks and Averroes followed. This was the correct approach. But the Jesuits followed the second method, according to the memorandum.[74]

---

71. Mobley, 2004, esp. 231 and 233 for the comments about Aristotle and logic.

72. "[L]eggendo come fanno la logica, et filosofia senza però il testo d'Aristotile, ma solamente alcuni moderni Summisti non approvati dalle Università de' studi generali." The governors of Padua to the Venetian Senate, December 5, 1591, printed in Favaro, 1877–78, 487–88.

73. "[D]el loro modo d'insegnare, s'egli è superficiale, o fondato . . . se leggono su quelle carte, che tengono in anti dottrina, ch'essi intendono, o dottrina tolta imprestito da altri." Cremonini's oration to the Venetian Senate on December 20, 1591, asking it to close the Jesuit school in Padua. Favaro, 1877–78, 494.

74. "Et di più tre sono i modi con i quali fino qui sie letto la filosofia, uno tropo digiuno et

The charges touched on aspects of Jesuit pedagogy that the Jesuits themselves debated. In 1583 a Jesuit visitor sent to evaluate Jesuit teaching at the University of Vienna reported that the teacher in the logic class had hardly lectured on a line of Aristotle during the year.[75] Moreover, Italian Jesuits were well acquainted with *Summisti,* which they called (in Latin) *Summula* or *Summulae.*[76] *Summisti,* or *Summulae,* were compendia or textbooks that covered all the material for a year's course of study in a subject. They were not the same as commentaries on a text of Aristotle in which a scholar offered a word-by-word explication of the text. Indeed, they were a little removed from the text but better structured; their goal was to impart the body of knowledge of a course in an organized way.

The Society was of two minds about *Summulae* and textbooks in general in the late sixteenth century. The Jesuits of the Province of Lombardy did not like *Summulae* at all and in 1586 recommended that their professors should be forbidden to dictate from them.[77] By contrast, in 1585 the professors at the Collegio Romano discussed at length whether the Society should produce a textbook for theology that all Jesuits would be obliged to use. Those favoring a universal textbook argued that it would offer uniformity in the opinions to be taught and the pedagogy. Further, it would be a useful book of reference; it would aid less well-prepared teachers and help eliminate heretical opinions.

---

povero, legendo il testo solo di Aristo(ti)le, come farebbe un grammatico; un troppo sofistico et barbaro, lasciando il testo d'Aristotile affatto, ma sempre trattando quistioni; et uno di mezo legendo il testo d'Aristotile e' digredendo nelle questioni a' suo luogho, il qual modo tengono i greci et Averroe; [ma] questi Reverendi Padri si sono apigliati al modo secondo quistionoso." AST, Istruzione Pubblica, Regia Università, Mazzo 1, no. 7.2, labeled in a nineteenth-century hand: "Ragioni, colle quali si dimostra il danno, che risultarebbe al Pubblico qualora le lezioni di tutte le parti della Filosofia, e della Teologia si separassero dalle pubbliche Scuole di Torino, e si leggessero nel Collegio de' Padri Gesuiti," October 8, 1593, no pagination. Although the memorandum to the commune of Torino was anonymous, it clearly emanated from one or more persons in university circles.

75. "[H]oc toto spatio temporis vix lineam de Aristotele legerit." *Monumenta Paedagogica,* 1965–92, 7:445. Hellyer, 2005, 77, first located this passage. To date I have not found comparable descriptions of or discussions about Italian Jesuit schools in the nearly five thousand pages of the *Monumenta Paedagogica.*

76. For example, see *Monumenta Paedagogica,* 1965–92, 6:260, 261, 263, 267, always in 1586. The comments from the provinces of Rome, Naples, Lombardy (also called Milan), and Venice responded to the 1586 version of the *Ratio studiorum,* which was largely an attempt to codify Jesuit educational practices to date. Some of the references to *Summula* referred specifically to the *Institutiones dialeticae* of Pietro de Fonseca, which the 1586 *Ratio studiorum* liked (*Monumenta Paedagogica,* 1965–92, 5:97), but many Jesuits did not. Other references to *Summulae* were generic and referred generally to textbooks in logic, natural philosophy, or casuistry.

77. "Prohibendum est expresse, ne dictetur a magistro Summula vel seorsim detur discipulis." and "Summulae nihil dictetur, nisi brevissimae annotationes." *Monumenta Paedagogica,* 1965–92, 6:263 under points 6 and 18.

All teachers and students would be free to concentrate on more interactive academic exercises, such as disputations and repetitions.[78]

Those opposed believed that if a comprehensive textbook were available, professors would become lazy and stop consulting the sources. Most important, they feared that a textbook would limit the opinions that professors might hold and teach and, thus, block the development of new ideas. Proponents responded by proposing that seven scholars should jointly write the theology textbook, thus ensuring a diversity of viewpoints. And they believed that professors would still be free to express their own views to some extent.[79]

Nothing came of the comprehensive theology textbook. The *Ratio studiorum* of 1599 did mention three Jesuit works that were de facto textbooks: the logic manuals of Fonseca and Toledo and the rhetoric of Cypriano Soares.[80] This suggested endorsement but did not bind. The Society as a whole never commissioned or adopted any textbooks.

Nevertheless, in the early seventeenth century the Jesuit leadership sought more uniformity in teaching, and this probably led to greater acceptance and use of textbooks of one kind or another. The introduction of internal prepublication censorship procedures within the Society in 1601 signaled a preference for greater unanimity and less tolerance for diversity, even though the procedures had loopholes.[81] Then in 1611 General Aquaviva wrote to the leaders of all provinces to express what he believed was the necessity of "solidity and uniformity in knowledge" (*soliditas et uniformitas doctrinae*), by which he primarily meant greater allegiance to Thomas Aquinas. In 1613 Aquaviva followed with a longer and stronger admonition toward uniformity in teaching. He wanted teachers to follow Aquinas in theology, and he wanted a single approach to Aristotle in philosophy.[82]

The Jesuits had several kinds of course summaries and textbooks in the early seventeenth century. The logic works of Fonseca and Toledo, Alamanni's Thomistic summary, Toledo's manual for confessors, and Suárez' works have been mentioned. Philosophical compendia, which were summaries of a year's course in logic, natural philosophy, or metaphysics, or all three, also began to appear. The *Cursus philosophicus*, first published in 1632, of Rodrigo de Arriaga, S.J. (1592–1667) claimed to explain philosophy as it was actually taught in Jesuit schools.[83] Printed compendia made extensive use of questions, assertions, objections, and responses, and were well organized.

78. *Monumenta Paedagogica*, 1965–92, 6:34–35.
79. *Monumenta Paedagogica*, 1965–92, 6:35–36, 42; and well summarized by Hellyer, 2005, 25–27. A textbook with seven authors strikes one as unlikely to satisfy anyone.
80. *Ratio Studiorum*, 2005, paragraphs 215, 263, 353, pp. 101, 119, 147.
81. Baldini, 1992, 75–119.
82. *Monumenta Paedagogica*, 1965–92, 7:657–64; also noted in Hellyer, 2005, 33–35.
83. Hellyer, 2005, 74–75. On Arriaga see Baciero, 2001.

Manuscript compendia or *cursus* prepared by professors also circulated and may have been as important as printed works. Students in the upper-level Jesuit school were advised to bring loose sheets of paper to the lectures to take detailed notes. Later they could fill in the gaps in their notes during repetitions (recapitulation and review exercises) to produce notebooks that would be useful for disputations and compositions.[84] At the end of the course, the Jesuit student had a detailed set of lectures that could be made available to other students or used as the basis for his own lectures when he became a teacher.[85]

All of this provided some of the solidity and uniformity of instruction that General Aquaviva sought. It also meant that the criticism by Cremonini and others was accurate to some degree. Inevitably Jesuit lecture notes and course compendia were not so tightly connected to Aristotle's texts as were traditional commentaries. And the Jesuit professor who used compendia and lecture notes from a course that he attended was not creating original knowledge. Jesuit teachers and students did read and study Aristotle, but their pedagogy differed from the traditional lecture-paraphrase and commentary approach that Italian professors claimed that they used.

Cremonini made two further accusations in 1591. He charged that the Society put young and inexperienced Jesuits in the classroom to teach. And he accused the Jesuits of using more advanced students to teach the less advanced.[86]

The Jesuits responded to the accusations of Cremonini and the broader charges.[87] They pointed out that Jesuit professors read and interpreted the

84. Nelles, 2007.

85. William A. Wallace has located the manuscript lectures of various Jesuit professors of logic and natural philosophy who taught at the Collegio Romano and demonstrated that much of the material concerning logic methodology found in the notebooks of the young Galilei came from the lecture notes of Collegio Romano professors. Since Galilei never attended the Collegio Romano, Jesuit manuscript lectures must have circulated outside Jesuit circles. No doubt they circulated even more widely within the Society. Wallace, 2006, provides a brief summary of his conclusions and points to his more detailed studies. See also Hellyer, 2005, 75; and Nelles, 2007, esp. 102–4.

86. "[S]e gli uomini posti da loro in Cattedra sono giovani da esercitare sè stessi; o provetti da istruir gli altri." Cremonini's oration to the Venetian Senate, December 20, 1591, in Favaro, 1877–78, 494.

87. This and the following three paragraphs are based on the responses to Cremonini of five Jesuits probably writing between late December 1591 and February 1592. They were not printed or presented publicly to Venetian authorities, so far as is known. They were too late and not likely to have changed the mind of the senate, which ordered the Jesuits not to enroll any non-Jesuits in their school in Padua. The Jesuits then closed the school. The Jesuit responses did circulate privately and were intended to furnish arguments for Venetian nobles sympathetic to the Jesuits, who would, in the future, urge the senate to permit the reopening of the Paduan school. The Jesuit authors were Ludovico Gagliardi, Paolo Comitoli, Giovan Domenico Bonac-

same Aristotelian texts, dealt with the same difficulties and questions, and employed the same ancient and modern Latin, Greek, and Arabic commentators as did lay professors. They argued that Jesuit teachers, even the younger ones, were learned and well prepared to teach because they had studied for ten years and more, including three years of philosophy and four of theology.[88] The implied comparison was to non-Jesuit university professors who obtained doctorates after about five years of study and immediately began teaching. The Jesuits did not respond to Cremonini's charge that they used older students to teach younger students, because they did use advanced students to help the teacher with drills and other mundane tasks in the lower school.[89] But they did not do this in the upper school, so far as is known. And, as mentioned earlier, most Jesuit teachers were both experienced and in their thirties and forties.

In response to the major objection, that Jesuit professors lacked originality and relied on the commentaries and summaries of others, one Jesuit turned the accusation back at Cremonini, by asking if he taught only his own ideas and never relied on the works of others. If so, he gave Cremonini mock praise as a miraculous doctor who had all the learning of the ages in his head. The Jesuit concluded that availing oneself of the wisdom of distinguished scholars of the past was a good idea.[90]

Going over to the attack, the Jesuits charged that university professors did not offer a thorough and integrated understanding of an Aristotelian text or Aristotelian philosophy as a whole. They jumped about, teaching passages here and there, skipping over half of it, leaving so many gaps that students could not understand the "method and marrow" of Aristotle. Nevertheless, these same professors conferred doctorates on students who did not understand the whole of philosophy.[91] The Jesuits also pointed out that Jesuit teachers delivered three hundred or more lectures in the academic year, while a University of Padua professor delivered only sixty or seventy lectures in the

---

corsi, Benedetto Palmio, and Antonio Possevino. Their responses are conveniently printed from manuscript texts in ARSI by Sangalli, 2001, 79–175. Donnelly, 1982, 61–71; and Sangalli, 1999, 260–75, summarize and analyze the responses well. The discussions about teaching were only small parts of the Jesuit *apologiae*, and there is some repetition among the responses. In the notes that follow, only the author and the pages from Sangalli, 2001, are given.

88. Sangalli, 2001, 124, 125 (Bonaccorsi), 149, 150 (Palmio), 173, 174 (Possevino).
89. See paragraph 360 on decurions in the lower school. *Ratio Studiorum*, 2005, 150.
90. Sangalli, 2001, 125 (Bonaccorsi).
91. "Anzi a punto sarebbe volo et salto il non farne tante, perciochè il non leggere pezzi di Aristotele, et lasciarne buona parte di mezo, et fare tante parentesi in sì breve periodo de' tempi ne' quali i scolari vi vogliano o possano attendere, et nondimeno il dottorare per filosofi quei che non hanno udita intiera filosofia, né per conseguente hanno potuto comprendere la metodo et midolla." Possevino, in Sangalli, 2001, 174.

university academic year.⁹² Both numbers were correct. One professor at the Collegio Romano who taught the three-year philosophical trio delivered 1,100 lectures in three academic years, November 1589 through early September 1592, an average of 367 per year. He delivered more than 300 lectures annually because for the better part of the metaphysics year, he delivered two lectures daily, one on the *Metaphysics* and the other on *De anima*. Moreover, the Jesuit academic year began in early November and lasted to the end of August or early September of the following year.⁹³

By contrast, although the University of Padua calendar mandated about 135 ordinary lectures in an academic year that began in early November and lasted into early June, unauthorized holidays, professorial absenteeism, and student disturbances had reduced the number to sixty to seventy in the early seventeenth century.⁹⁴ Other universities fared no better. Of course, the Jesuits who taught in the University of Mantua followed that university's calendar and did not deliver three hundred lectures per year, although the Jesuit metaphysician at Mantua delivered two daily lectures in the academic years 1626–27 and 1627–28.

The Jesuits added that their professors combined lecturing with many exercises for the students, including daily review of the material covered, and that professors and students engaged in monthly disputations, which helped them to learn.⁹⁵ This was true, but it did not mean that universities lacked student exercises. As mentioned earlier, the statutes of many Italian universities obliged professors to engage in circular disputations. At the end of every lecture, or once a week, professor and students were required to gather in a circle outside the classroom, often in a courtyard or piazza, to dispute with one another and with the professor over the conclusions reached in the lecture.⁹⁶ Overall, the Jesuits were able to answer most of the accusations leveled against them.

But the Jesuits were more inclined to use textbooks than non-Jesuit Italian professors. In this the Jesuits were part of a European pedagogical shift labeled by a modern scholar as "the rise of the philosophical textbook."⁹⁷ Beginning in the late sixteenth century and continuing throughout the seventeenth, Catholic and Protestant scholars across Europe generated more textbooks to teach Aristotle. They had concluded that a simple exposition of Aristotle had pedagogical disadvantages, and they wanted to insert new material not found in Aristotle. The number of straightforward commentaries on

92. Sangalli, 2001, 124 (Bonaccorsi), 134 (Palmio).
93. Wallace, 2006, 318–19.
94. Grendler, 2002, 495–96.
95. Sangalli, 2001, 124 (Bonaccorsi), 150 (Palmio).
96. Grendler, 2002, 156 with documentation.
97. This is the title of Schmitt, 1988. For what follows, see also Schmitt, 1983a.

Aristotle declined, except in Italy, where many university professors, like Cremonini, still used commentaries as a primary means of presenting their interpretations of Aristotle. Since the Jesuit approach to higher education owed much to the student experiences of Loyola and the first Jesuits in the colleges of the University of Paris, it is not surprising that the Jesuits favored ultramontane practices and endured criticism from Italian professors. The difference over the use of textbooks was part of a larger division in European university education.

Even allowing for the fact that the criticism of the Jesuits came from professors protecting their universities and jobs from competition, the charges, responses, and other evidence suggest that differences in pedagogy and academic culture between civic universities and the Jesuits existed. Jesuit professors probably sacrificed some direct contact with the texts of Aristotle, notoriously difficult to understand without a guide, in favor of an integrated approach learned from their teachers, from notes, and from the published works of more learned Jesuits. A Jesuit professor sought to impart an integrated understanding of Aristotelian philosophy, rather than his own original interpretation. (Of course, Bellarmine, Suárez, and others were brilliant exceptions.)

By contrast, professors in civic universities, who also used previous scholarship a great deal, strove to offer some original commentary on the statutory texts, because this was the path toward publication and recognition, a road that Cremonini traveled, even though he ignored the new Galilean developments in his field. Although it must have been difficult to be original in disciplines dominated by Aristotle, this remained the ideal. In practice, the overwhelming majority of arts professors in seventeenth-century lay universities published nothing and probably did not offer anything original in their lectures. There were more opportunities for original research and teaching in law and medicine, because an endless supply of new legal disputes demanded analysis, while new medical research bubbled out of a cauldron of anatomy, chemical medicine, and experimentation.

Two different views about a university education existed. Through much experimentation and analysis over half a century, the Society of Jesus had worked out a rational, integrated, and comprehensive curricular and pedagogical plan and codified it in the *Ratio studiorum* of 1599. Italian universities had no such document, no curricular plan, and hardly any organization. They were not structured to impart a unified university education or systematic preparation in any discipline, let alone a group of disciplines. They consisted of independent professors, either brilliant or mediocre, who offered their own lectures without concern for whether they fitted into a structured curriculum. So long as the professor adhered to statutory guidelines, which only told him which texts to teach within broad parameters, he was free to present his own ideas or those of other scholars. The absence of structure gave the professor great freedom to teach a subject as he chose and to display his originality, if he had any.

Students enjoyed the same freedom. They were not required to attend particular lectures or to take courses in any order. They might choose to attend a set of lectures because the professor was brilliant, or because he was good at teaching the puncta, the brief passages from the statutory texts on which degree candidates were examined. Or a student might attend the lectures of a professor in a position to advance his career. Note taking, studying, academic exercises, and private tutoring were the student's responsibility. When the student felt ready, he presented himself for the doctoral examinations. By contrast, students in Jesuit institutions were obliged to become part of an integrated curriculum in the humanities, mathematics, logic, natural philosophy, metaphysics, and theology that had a unified approach, a point of view, and mandatory exercises.

The University of Mantua did not last long enough for friction between the two academic cultures to strike fire. Still, there were signs of heat. As noted in chapter 6, in November 1626 the rector of the Jesuit college complained that the medical scholars of the university had passed a decree saying that they could award doctorates without the participation of the Jesuit professors of philosophy. He probably meant that the Jesuits were excluded from the committees composed of professors and other members of the local college of doctors of medicine that examined doctoral candidates. The rector pointed out that it was customary for professors of philosophy to participate in such academic exercises (which was true), and that the Jesuits were equal in status with other professors.[98] Had the Peaceful University of Mantua lasted longer, this issue might have made the university less peaceful.

In the same letter he complained that some "doctors" (presumably meaning professors) were teaching privately in their homes the same philosophy that the Jesuit professors taught in their university lectures. He pointed out that this was contrary to university rules and, if not stopped, would lead to empty lecture halls.[99] Private teaching for additional income was a much condemned but near universal practice. The professor taught privately the same material on which he lectured publicly, or he offered supplemental material.[100] And the student received more attention than he received in the

---

98. Girolamo Furlani, S.J., to Duke Vincenzo II, November 19, 1626. ASM, AG, Bu. 2775, f. 539r. Although the salutation does not make it clear that the letter is addressed to Vincenzo II, it ends by wishing him "every condolence," an appropriate wish, because Duke Ferdinando had died on October 29, 1626.

99. Girolamo Furlani, S.J., to Duke Vincenzo II, November 19, 1626, in ASM, AG, Bu. 2775, f. 539r.

100. Grendler, 2002, 486–90.

lecture hall. But professors who taught privately did not normally teach subject matter from other disciplines. One wonders if some lay professors were teaching privately an Aristotle counter to what the Jesuits taught. For example, the Paracelsians on the faculty viewed Aristotle very differently than did the Jesuits. This issue had the potential for conflict.

The Mantuan Jesuits and their students also endured a little harassment. On December 1625 some law students from Mantua and Casale Monferrato came to the logic and natural philosophy lectures taught by Jesuits and made insolent remarks. Then they forcefully entered the humanities class (the middle class in the lower school), grabbed the book out of the hands of the Jesuit teacher, made filthy and insulting remarks, and left, but threatened to return after dinner. The Jesuit vice rector immediately asked Duke Ferdinando for protection, reminding him that the boys in the class were the sons of the highest nobility of Mantua.[101] In June 1627 some men, not necessarily students, left a pasquinade with a list of alleged sodomites in one of the Jesuit classes.[102] Two incidents in an era of rampant student rowdiness were not that significant. Still, they pointed to some hostility toward the Jesuits.

Two university cultures coexisted in the half-civic, half-Jesuit University of Mantua: the traditional laissez faire culture in law and medicine, and the integrated Jesuit program in arts, philosophy, and theology. One wonders how this worked in practice. Was the law student who took the course in logic taught by a Jesuit prepared to understand the legal logic presented in law lectures? Did the student who attended the natural philosophy course taught by a Jesuit feel adequately prepared for lectures in theoretical and practical medicine? Or was the University of Mantua a university of three separate parts, law, medicine, and arts and philosophy, in which professors and students in one part had little to do with professors and students in the other two? It may be that Mantua's students took the two cultures in stride and went about pursuing knowledge and degrees without worrying about the separation. Perhaps the University of Mantua pointed to the twenty-first-century university in which professors and students of one division seldom have anything to do with professors and students in other parts of the university beyond cheering for the sports teams.

---

101. Giovanni Battista Tiberio, vice rector of the Jesuit college, to Duke Ferdinando, December 10, 1625, in ASM, AG, Bu. 2768, f. 358r. Tiberio wrote on the same day as the incident. He was the de facto rector because the previous rector had left at the end of September and a new rector had not yet been appointed. Gorzoni, 1997, 150.

102. Antonio Porta, captain of justice, to Duke Vincenzo II, June 25, 1627, in ASM, AG, Bu. 2777, f. 107r–v. Porta arrested four men, all of whom denied having written the pasquinade.

CHAPTER 9

# The End of the University of Mantua

hile the university flourished, political events cast an ominous shadow over the Gonzaga and Mantua. Premature deaths and a failure to produce heirs created a disputed succession. Further miscalculations by a Gonzaga ruler led to the disastrous War of the Mantuan Succession, 1627–31, and the terrible sack of Mantua. The University of Mantua became a casualty of the war.

## 1. THE CRISIS OF THE MANTUAN SUCCESSION

Despite the intricate diplomacy, military campaigns, and maneuvering of the protagonists, the basic story was simple. The direct male line of the Gonzaga of Mantua died out, leaving no clear successor to rule the duchies of Mantua and Monferrato. Two claimants emerged, and several other states concluded that securing one candidate over the other was vital to their interests. The aggressive actions of Italian princes and the self-interests of the Holy Roman Empire, France, and Spain collided, producing a war from which the people and city of Mantua suffered grievously.

While the crisis had been building for years, the premature deaths of two Gonzaga dukes and the feckless marriage of the second precipitated it. Duke Ferdinando had not been in good health for some time. As early as 1615 the Venetian ambassador noted that Ferdinando took numerous medications every time he was angry, upset, or depressed. The ambassador opined that he took too many pills and would be better off if he ignored the advice of his doctor.[1] Whatever the effect of the pills, Ferdinando had serious health prob-

---

1. Relazione of the Venetian ambassador Giovanni da Mula, 1615, in *Relazioni*, 1912, 139–40.

lems by 1624.² As his health deteriorated further in the spring and summer of 1626, he probably took many more medicines, with a predictable lack of improvement.³ He came down with a fever in October 1626. After suffering for fifteen days, he died on October 29, 1626, at the age of thirty-nine, a few days before the beginning of the second year of the Peaceful University of Mantua.⁴ He lived only long enough to enjoy his university for one year.

Ferdinando worked hard to preserve the Gonzaga lands in the face of war and diplomatic threats. He inherited a state consisting of two widely separated territories, with Piedmont-Savoy determined to seize one of them. Nevertheless, he used his political, diplomatic, and military resources well enough to fend off the aggression of Carlo Emanuele I in 1613 and to keep his state intact. He successfully promoted the interests of his family through dynastic marriages with the more powerful, including the union of his sister Eleonora to Emperor Rudolf II. He was sincerely religious, manifested through his commitment to the Jesuits and a lively Baroque piety. Ferdinando may have been the most intellectually and artistically gifted prince ever to rule an Italian state. His patronage was exemplary: Ferdinando supported artists, scholars, and musicians generously, and founded a university. But the costs of war, diplomacy, marriages, patronage, the court, and the university were very high. He inherited a huge debt from his father and made no effort to curb expenditures. And he could not resolve the structural problem of a separated state, one part of which was coveted by another power. The only real solution would have been a land swap, that is, giving up Monferrato in exchange for smaller but contiguous territories, which did not happen. Finally, his inability to produce a legitimate male heir left his state vulnerable and caused him to engage in some disreputable actions to continue the Gonzaga line.⁵

---

2. See Ferdinando's letter of July 23, 1624, Florence, to Chancellor Striggi in ASM, AG, Bu. 2176, f. 112r–v. In addition, in an undated letter Ferdinando wrote about passing fourteen kidney stones and other health problems but still managed to quote Hippocrates. Quazza, 1922, 134–35 note 3. Gorzoni, 1997, 150, also referred to his chronic ill health.

3. See Antonio Ruggiero, a pharmacist, to the duke, May 15, 1626, Rome. It presented a bill of about 20 scudi for a list of medicines three pages long. The resident ambassador in Rome had ordered them for Ferdinando who, according to the letter, had been ill for some time. ASM, AG, Bu. 1031, Diversi, no pag.

4. ASM, Ms. Carlo d'Arco 80, "Historia di Giovanni Mambrino," p. 976. Gorzoni, 1997, 150, wrote that Ferdinando, already suffering from fevers and other ailments, spent himself dealing with crises and fighting Mantua's enemies. The autopsy suggests that Ferdinando suffered from chronic intestinal infection and obstruction, which might have been caused by inflammatory bowel disease, gall stones, or both. Malacarne, 2007, 291.

5. See also the less favorable assessments of Luzio, 1974, 52–53 (lack of willpower and gluttonous appetites); Quazza, 1922, 134–35; and Malacarne, 2007, 294. Gorzoni, 1997, 150–51, offered a more positive assessment, partly because Ferdinando was a good friend to the Jesuits. He also

# The Crisis of the Mantuan Succession

Because his marriage to Caterina de' Medici produced no children, and Ferdinando's one child, Giacinto, had not been legitimized, his younger brother Vincenzo II succeeded him.[6] Vincenzo II (1594–1627), the third and last son of Duke Vincenzo I, had a Jesuit teacher and confessor as a youth, with few positive results.[7] He was feckless, morally obtuse, and physically weak. After Ferdinando renounced his cardinal's hat to become duke of Mantua and Monferrato, Vincenzo became the family cardinal on December 2, 1615. But in August 1616 he secretly married Isabella Gonzaga di Novellara (1578–1630), daughter of Alfonso Gonzaga, marquis of Novellara (a principality ruled by a cadet branch of the Gonzaga), and widow of Ferrante Gonzaga, the marquis of Bozzolo (another principality ruled by a cadet branch). As a result he lost his cardinal's hat on September 5, 1616.[8] It may have been a love match, and it may also have had the long-range goal of bringing Bozzolo or Novellara into the hands of the Gonzaga of Mantua. But it was an irresponsible marriage, because Isabella was thirty-eight years of age. Although she had borne eight children, she was unlikely to bear more.[9]

Because both Duke Ferdinando and Prince Vincenzo were in declining

---

noted the genuine grief of the court and the city at Ferdinando's death. One wonders if Ferdinando's chronic ill health played a role in the failure of Ferdinando and Caterina to produce children. Caterina de' Medici, who did not remarry, returned to Florence in June 1627 and became governor of Siena. She died of smallpox in 1629. Quazza, 1922, 163.

6. What follows is a brief history of the War of the Mantuan Succession. While the crisis and the war were episodes in the Thirty Years' War and had Europe-wide consequences, this narrative will concentrate on the actions of the Gonzaga rulers and the consequences for Mantua. It is based on a number of excellent sources. Quazza, 1922 and 1926, follow the politics, diplomacy, and military actions day-by-day, and are fundamental. Good shorter histories are Quazza, 1933, 173–211; and Mazzoldi, 1963, 90–116, 119–38. Pastor, 1891–1953, 28:201–48, discusses the diplomacy and war from the papal perspective and blames Spain and the Holy Roman Empire for much of what happened. For the limited involvement of Venice, see Cozzi, Knapton, and Scarabello, 1992, 112–16. Older accounts and general histories of the period tend to see the two Gonzaga claimants to the duchies of Mantua and Monferrato as clients and stalking horses for France, the Empire, and Spain from the beginning. However, Parrott, 1997a and 1997b; and Oresko and Parrott, 1997, take a fresh look and assign much responsibility to Carlo Gonzaga-Nevers and Carlo Emanuele I for precipitate, even reckless, actions that drew the initially reluctant major powers into a war in Italy. Unless otherwise cited, what follows is based on the above sources without additional footnotes. A few notes offer support for some details and interpretations.

7. "Fu questo padre (Luca Drago) di rara simplicità, capace però d'esser adoprato per maestro del prencipe che fu poi duca Vicenzo II." Father Drago died on June 7, 1630, probably of the plague, at the age of sixty-five. Gorzoni, 1997, 166. Baldini, 2000, 198, states that Domenico Benini, S.J. (1546–1617), was Vincenzo's confessor.

8. Pastor, 1891–1953, 25:336.

9. Although Quazza, 1922, 137, stated that she had borne five children, genealogical table no. 3 of the Gonzaga of Bozzolo in Coniglio, 1967, no pag., gives the names of eight children.

health and had no legitimate children,[10] diplomats in chancelleries across Italy and Europe watched closely. So did male members of cadet branches of the Gonzaga. Just as lions from the next savannah draw near as the patriarch of the pride weakens, other Gonzaga moved to Mantua to ingratiate themselves with the sickly ducal brothers and to pounce when they died.

Since Vincenzo was the last male member of the direct line of the Gonzaga of Mantua, he had to marry again to produce legitimate offspring. Vincenzo now repented of his marriage, and he and Ferdinando frantically tried to undo it. They easily obtained an annulment from the compliant bishop of Mantua, but not from Pope Paul V, because the marriage fulfilled canonical conditions. The Gonzaga brothers then resorted to lying, bullying, and, possibly, attempted murder. Some whispered that the Gonzaga tried to poison Isabella. Then in 1622 Vincenzo charged that Isabella had used a magic potion to overcome his will and obtain his consent to the marriage. A Mantuan ecclesiastical court predictably found Isabella guilty of witchcraft on the basis of the confession of a woman who allegedly administered the potion. But Rome needed to review the case. Isabella went to Rome and willingly accepted confinement in Castel Sant'Angelo in Rome, a prisoner but safe from Gonzaga poisons, while the Congregation of the Holy Office examined the case. The alleged accomplice of Isabella retracted her confession, declaring that Duke Ferdinando and Count Striggi had threatened her with a beating if she did not do what they wished. The Congregation declared Isabella innocent of witchcraft in January 1624.[11]

Vincenzo next may have tried to assassinate his wife. Three men confessed that they had been sent to kill her by one Federico Gonzaga from another cadet branch. Since Federico commanded the ducal militia for Vincenzo, many wondered if the murder order originated with Vincenzo. The trio was hanged, but Federico and Vincenzo suffered no punishment beyond malicious rumors. Fortunately, Isabella was not alone during her troubles, as members of the two cadet branches of the family closest to the Gonzaga of Mantua rallied to her support.[12] They hoped that the ducal crown would come to one of them if Vincenzo failed to remarry and father a son.[13]

---

10. Illegitimate children did not count. Duke Vincenzo II fathered three bastard sons, for whom he tried to obtain ecclesiastical benefices. Two of them died of the plague in Mantua in 1630. Quazza, 1922, 136 note 3 (which also gives the names of their mothers), 188 note 2, 190; and Quazza, 1933, 189.

11. Quazza, 1922, 139 note 2; Mazzoldi, 1963, 92–93, 120–21; Coniglio, 1967, 416–23; and Malarcarne, 2007, 247–51, 356–58, 360–61.

12. For example, when Isabella di Novellara was imprisoned in Castel Sant'Angelo, Carlo Gonzaga-Nevers provided her with money and assistance. Quazza, 1922, 139 note 2.

13. Quazza, 1922, 137–38; Mazzoldi, 1963, 93, 120–21; Coniglio, 1967, 423.

After he became duke, Vincenzo II badly needed money. The most saleable asset was the ducal art collection, begun in the fifteenth century and constantly enlarged. Indeed, Duke Ferdinando had continued to buy art and books while spending on everything else as well.[14] To cite one example, in 1622 he was interested in purchasing a painting of il Parmigianino (Francesco Mazzola, 1503–40), while his agent in Parma also mentioned three paintings of "Gioachem Brughel d'Olanda" (probably Jan Brueghel, 1568–1625, son of Pieter Brueghel the Elder) that might be available.[15] Renaissance masterpieces and lesser works filled rooms and lined corridors of the vast ducal palace. Duke Ferdinando, always short of money, had considered selling some paintings before he died.

Almost immediately after ascending the ducal throne in late October 1626, Duke Vincenzo II let it be known that all or most of the collection was for sale, and King Charles I of England, an avid collector, wanted it.[16] A merchant of unknown provenance acted for the English king, and Striggi for Duke Vincenzo II. By January 1627 the two sides were exchanging lists of paintings and prices. By early September they had come to an agreement on a sale of a great quantity—the exact number is unknown—of paintings, including masterworks of Mantegna, Giorgione, Raphael, Michelangelo, Johann Brueghel the Younger, Titian, Tintoretto, and Caravaggio, for 62,000 ducatoni, a pittance compared to their value even then. When in early September knowledge about the sale circulated abroad, a Gonzaga agent in Venice reported that he had heard much murmuring about the sale.[17] Although Italians had little national feeling, they did not want their masterworks to leave Italian soil. Striggi justified the sale on the grounds that the money was needed; he only regretted that news about the sale had leaked.[18] The paintings were sent clandestinely to Murano in the Venetian lagoon in September 1627 to avoid

---

14. For example, see the letter of a Venetian bookseller concerning 90 ducats in Venetian money owed by the duke to a Venetian publisher. Giacomo Scaglia, July 13, 1624, Venice, in ASM, AG, Bu. 1556, f. 329r. Ferdinando also received letters from writers requesting support, and he probably often responded. For example, Guidobaldo Benamati, who called himself the poet of Duke Ranuccio I Farnese, sent some of his poems to Ferdinando. Letter of Benamati, March 8, 1622, Parma, in ASM, AG, Bu. 1383, no pag. The fact that Duke Ranuccio I had just died (March 5) might have caused him to turn to Ferdinando.

15. Parmenio Calestrani to Duke Ferdinando, February 14, 1622, Parma, in ASM, AG, Bu. 1383, no pag.

16. Luzio, 1974, tells the story with many documents. See also Malacarne, 2007, 294–303.

17. "Tengo lettera del Signor Cristino venutami questa mattina da Venetia per staffetta, con cui mi dice d'haver sentito molta mormoratione colà per la vendita dei quadri." Minute of Striggi, September 8, 1627, in ASM, AG, Bu. 2777, number 71. The relevant parts of the letter are also printed in Luzio, 1974, 143.

18. Striggi to Girolamo Parma, Mantuan resident ambassador in Venice, September 8, 1627, Mantua, in ASM, AG, Bu. 2777, letter 70. Relevant parts are printed in Luzio, 1974, 143.

attracting notice and scorn from other courts. They then went to England, where they became the Renaissance core of the royal collection.

While trying to get an annulment or otherwise dispose of Isabella, Duke Vincenzo II sought to arrange a new marriage with his niece, Maria Gonzaga (1609–60), the daughter of his brother Francesco and Margherita of Piedmont-Savoy.[19] Such a marriage would have prevented Maria from marrying someone else, an important consideration because Maria and her husband would have a strong claim on Monferrato, which could be inherited through the female line. But even in the unlikely chance that a marriage between uncle and niece might receive papal dispensation from various canons, it was not generally favored.

As his health deteriorated, Vincenzo II abandoned the effort to get rid of Isabella of Novellara and made a last-ditch effort to ensure an orderly succession. Both he and Duke Ferdinando had been edging closer to Carlo Gonzaga-Nevers, making it clear that they preferred him, rather than Ferrante II Gonzaga, as successor. Vincenzo II completed the process by arranging for Maria Gonzaga to marry Carlo Gonzaga, duke of Rethel (1609–31, hereafter called Gonzaga-Rethel), the son of Gonzaga-Nevers. Again a papal dispensation was needed. It arrived on December 24, 1627, and Maria Gonzaga and Carlo Gonzaga-Rethel were immediately married at the bedside of Duke Vincenzo II, who died on the night of December 25.[20] Duke Vincenzo hoped that this marriage would ensure that the duchies of Mantua and Monferrato would be passed on intact to the Gonzaga-Nevers branch of the family, and that the Piedmont-Savoy claim on Monferrato would be thwarted.

## 2. THE CONTENDERS

Carlo Gonzaga-Rethel was more than a hastily married eighteen-year-old. He was the stalking horse for his father, Carlo Gonzaga-Nevers, who expected to be the successor to Vincenzo II. And the son's marriage to Maria would help secure Monferrato for his father.

Gonzaga-Nevers was the French Gonzaga. In 1549 the Gonzaga sent ten-year-old Ludovico Gonzaga (1539–85), the younger brother of Guglielmo

---

19. Quazza, 1930; Tamalio, 2008. Maria Gonzaga later became duchess then regent of Mantua for her son Carlo II (1629, ruled 1637–65).Several Gonzaga women, including Eleonora of Austria, Caterina de' Medici, Maria Gonzaga, and Margherita of Piedmont-Savoy (1589–1655), played significant political roles and merit further study.

20. The immediate cause of death was gangrenous infection, but he had other ailments as well. Malacarne, 2007, 324. It is noteworthy that while Father Giuseppe Gorzoni marked the deaths of Vincenzo I, Francesco III, and Ferdinando Gonzaga with restrained but dignified praise, he simply recorded the death of Vincenzo II. Gorzoni, 1997, 154. He did the same when Ferrante II Gonzaga and Duke Carlo I Gonzaga-Nevers died.

# The Contenders

Gonzaga, who would become duke of Mantua and Monferrato in 1550, to Paris to secure a Gonzaga presence at the Valois court (see genealogical chart 1). Although the Gonzaga of Mantua were allies and clients of the Habsburgs, they practiced the traditional politics of small powers in all centuries of making sure they had a family member in the court of their patron's chief rival. Ludovico did well at the Valois court as a soldier for the French crown and as a strong opponent of the Huguenots.[21] In due time he married a Frenchwoman who brought him the duchy of Nevers in north-central France. Their son, Carlo Gonzaga-Nevers (1580–1637), did even better. He also served the French monarchy as a soldier and acquired additional small territories, including the tiny duchy of Rethel in northeastern France. Ambitious, a gambler by nature, and not always reliable, he never forgot his Gonzaga heritage. When he learned of the ill health of Ferdinando and Vincenzo Gonzaga and their lack of legitimate heirs, he sent Gonzaga-Rethel in December 1625 to live in Mantua, to cultivate good relations with the Gonzaga brothers, and to create a network of allies at the court.[22]

Alerted that Vincenzo II was dying, Carlo Gonzaga-Nevers left his capital of Charleville in northern France and dashed to Mantua, traveling through Germany to avoid Piedmont-Savoy. He arrived on January 17, 1628. Gonzaga-Nevers immediately assumed power as duke of Mantua and Monferrato. He had the support of Striggi, now grand chancellor, and cemented his loyalty by making him a marquis with an annual stipend of 500 scudi. And he distributed honors to others to win their support.[23] Although five degrees of consanguinity separated him from the late duke, he was the closest legitimately born male relative. Moreover, his son had just married the daughter of a former duke and niece of Vincenzo II. His prospects looked good.

But there was no constitution determining succession, especially in complicated cases. The principles of exclusive male succession and *feudo feminino* were traditions, not written rules.[24] Hence, the approval or grudging consensus of interested parties, above all the major powers, had to be obtained for arrangements that would determine a crown. Previous generations of Gonzaga knew this and had secured imperial approval for the marriage that brought them Monferrato in the 1530s. Approval was secured by an intricate round of diplomacy, including appeals, favors granted and returned, and negotiated compensations. The last were really bribes, such as money, a lesser title, a marriage, or small territorial adjustments, offered to disappointed

---

21. For a comprehensive study of the French careers of Ludovico Gonzaga and Carlo Gonzaga-Nevers, see Boltanski, 2006; for a short account see Parrott, 1997b, 154–69.
22. Quazza, 1922, 159; Parrott, 1997b, 172.
23. Quazza, 1922, 207–8; Parrott, 1997a, 45.
24. Parrott, 1997a, 25–26.

rivals in exchange for grudging approval. Time would then ratify the succession. All of this required elaborate, time-consuming diplomacy.

Neither the assumption of power by Gonzaga-Nevers nor the marriage of Gonzaga-Rethel and Maria Gonzaga pleased the great powers, because these actions were unilateral, done without securing the acquiescence of other parties whose interests were affected. Duke Vincenzo II died before he could complete negotiations, and Gonzaga-Nevers, the beneficiary of the marriage, did not negotiate.[25] He had not secured the approval of Piedmont-Savoy, which saw its quest to acquire Monferrato by fair means or foul again thwarted. Outsiders saw Gonzaga-Nevers as a French agent and his ascension to power in Mantua as bolstering French influence in northern Italy. But he had not consulted Paris, which was surprised rather than pleased. Above all, he did not have the support of the Holy Roman Empire or Spain. Support from the former was essential, because Mantua and Monferrato were imperial fiefs.

And there was a rival claimant, Ferrante II Gonzaga (1563–1630), duke of Guastalla. As noted in chapter 1, section 1, Emperor Charles V had created the marquisate of Guastalla from a small area of Lombardy contiguous to the Mantovano (see map 1). He awarded it to Don Ferrante Gonzaga (1507–57) who had served Charles for many years and in many lands as soldier and viceroy. Don Ferrante was a younger brother of Duke Federico II Gonzaga, who ruled Mantua from 1519 to 1540. In other words, the tie to the Gonzaga of Mantua went one generation further back than that of Gonzaga-Nevers, making the link between Ferrante II and Duke Vincenzo II one of six degrees of consanguinity (see genealogical chart 1).

When his father, Cesare, died in 1575, Ferrante II became marquis of Guastalla at the age of twelve under a regency. In 1621 he became duke of Guastalla when the emperor raised Guastalla to a duchy. Like his father and grandfather, Ferrante II was a soldier who commanded troops for the emperor, but the paucity of Habsburg wars meant that he had fewer opportunities to win military fame. Nevertheless, he acquired a high decoration and received the plum assignments of escorting a Habsburg empress and a Spanish queen-to-be on state trips, which indicated that he was in good odor at the two Habsburg courts. He had served the Gonzaga as governor of Monferrato in the early 1590s, and he lived nearby, unlike Gonzaga-Nevers. Ferrante II moved to Mantua during Duke Vincenzo's last months in order to win over the court. And he sent his son, Cesare II (1592–1632), to Vienna to seek support for his candidacy. He proposed to Vincenzo II that Cesare, rather than Gonzaga-Rethel, should marry Maria Gonzaga, but was rebuffed.[26]

25. Parrott, 1997a, 49–50, emphasizes this point.
26. For a brief history of the Gonzaga of Guastalla, see Coniglio, 1967, 486–93, at 489–90 for Ferrante II.

Gonzaga-Nevers made it clear from the beginning that he did not intend to divide the inheritance or to give Piedmont-Savoy any land in Monferrato,[27] and he had not secured the approval of the emperor for the marriage of his son to Maria Gonzaga. Yet he applied for imperial investiture as duke of Mantua and Monferrato. However, he did not wait for it to arrive but called himself duke and demanded that the nobility of both duchies swear allegiance. He minted coins with his image and titles.[28] He clearly expected that France would support him in any conflict.

The precipitant actions of Gonzaga-Nevers made it easier for the emperor to accede to the entreaties of Ferrante II and his son. On March 20, 1628, Emperor Ferdinand II promulgated an edict of sequestration stating that Gonzaga-Nevers had acted unlawfully. He placed the Gonzaga lands under the authority of an imperial commissary pending investigation of the disputed succession claims.

Piedmont-Savoy did not like this decision, because it sidelined its attempt to obtain part or all of Monferrato. While Vincenzo II was still living, Carlo Emanuele I had pressed his demands in a variety of ways. For example, he demanded payment of a dowry debt. In 1485 the marriage contract between the daughter of the Paleologo marquis of Monferrato and the then ruler of Piedmont-Savoy included the promise of a dowry of 80,000 ducats to be paid to the Savoia. It was never paid. So in 1627, some 142 years later, Carlo Emanuele I demanded that Vincenzo II, as successor to the Paleologo and duke of Monferrato, pay the dowry along with compound interest, a total of 700,000 scudi, or hand over a substantial part of Monferrato.[29] It was clear that Carlo Emanuele I would use any means, including a military invasion as in 1613, to seize Monferrato.

### 3. WAR, PLAGUE, AND THE SACK OF MANTUA

Both Gonzaga-Nevers and Carlo Emanuele I expected that France would support their positions. But Cardinal Richelieu, the de facto ruler of France, had laid siege to the Huguenot stronghold of La Rochelle and was unwilling or unable to offer concrete support to either side. So Carlo Emanuele I went to Spain. In return for Spanish aid, he offered to divide Monferrato into two, the fortress of Casale Monferrato and its surrounding land for Spain, most of the rest of Monferrato for Piedmont-Savoy. Spain was not eager to enter into a war over Monferrato. But it did feel that it had to protect its interests on the western flank of the duchy of Milan, especially since it saw

---

27. Parrott, 1997a, 49.
28. Parrott, 1997a, 50–51.
29. Parrott, 1997a, 32–33.

Piedmont-Savoy as an ally of France. So the army of Don Gonzalo Fernández de Córdoba, the governor of Milan, laid siege to Casale Monferrato on April 2, 1628.[30]

Gonzaga-Nevers fought back. He raised a small army from his French possessions and sent them to attack the northern, French-speaking part of Piedmont-Savoy. Thus, he took the war to Piedmont-Savoy, even though his troops were routed in August 1628. His military action did not help him with the imperial court, but it did finally persuade France to send an army into Piedmont-Savoy in early March 1629. Carlo Emanuele I quickly abandoned his alliance with Spain and allowed the French army to move through Piedmont to relieve Casale Monferrato, under siege by Spanish troops from Spanish-controlled Lombardy. The French took Casale Monferrato, and Carlo Emanuele I was rewarded with parts of Monferrato.

At this point the war over the succession became part of the larger Thirty Years' War. Richelieu's action raised the stakes for Spain, which was worried about French control of Casale Monferrato and concluded that Piedmont-Savoy was a French client. In the fall of 1629 Spanish troops moved from Lombardy westward to lay siege again to Casale Monferrato and its fortress, at that time occupied by French troops. France now viewed the struggle in Italy as a battle against the combined forces of the empire and Spain and acted accordingly. Richelieu launched a new invasion of Monferrato to relieve his troops at Casale Monferrato.

The outbreak of war with foreign powers fighting on Italian soil shocked Italy. Except for a few military actions of limited scope and short duration, such as Piedmont-Savoy's invasion of Monferrato in 1613, Italy had been at peace since 1559 and had witnessed no large-scale military operations since the 1530s. The war galvanized the diplomats into action. Eager mediators from France, the papacy, and the empire shuttled between the warring parties. If Gonzaga-Nevers had been more inclined to negotiate and less quick to take military action, and above all, had he been willing to accept significant losses of territory in Monferrato, a larger war might have been avoided. But the two duchies had been an essential part of the Gonzaga heritage and geopolitical position, and Monferrato a lucrative source of revenue, since the 1560s.

Until early 1629 all the military action took place in Monferrato and Piedmont-Savoy, leaving the Mantovano untouched. Then Gonzaga-Nevers took a chance. In late February 1629 he gathered about 2,500 troops, traveled along the Po River, crossed the border into the Cremonese, part of Spanish-ruled Lombardy, and seized the town of Casalmaggiore barely inside the

---

30. Gonzalo Fernández de Córdoba played a key role in the war, but his story cannot be followed here. See Fernandez Alvarez, 1955.

border. Although the duke had ordered his troops not to molest the inhabitants or enter religious convents, they did so anyway.[31]

This action was a serious political mistake. It helped the Spanish to make the case with the emperor that Gonzaga-Nevers really was a threat to imperial fiefs and authority.[32] It may have caused the imperial court to make up its mind. Emperor Ferdinand II now rejected the claim of Gonzaga-Nevers to Mantua and Monferrato and decided to support Spain against Mantua. By early May 1629 the first imperial troops had moved through Alpine passes, and by late August 1629 some thirty thousand infantry and six thousand cavalry, all Germans, had mobilized in the duchy of Milan. They invaded the Mantovano on October 17 and marched inexorably toward Mantua, burning houses and crops and killing peasants on the way. Sometimes the desperate peasants replied in kind. Because the distances were short and the Gonzaga troops did not offer much resistance, the imperial troops moved quickly.

Gonzaga-Nevers was in a terrible situation. His small army had to defend both Monferrato and Mantua against much superior forces. And once Spain entered the fray, he could not move troops back and forth between the two duchies. While Gonzaga-Nevers enjoyed diplomatic support from Pope Urban VIII, only the Republic of Venice provided military assistance. Traditionally anti-Spanish and fearful of a Habsburg encirclement of northern Italy, Venice sent 70,000 ducats and an army of three thousand men to Mantua in the fall of 1629.[33] But the Venetian Senate was not unified in support of military action, and the tepid leadership of the Venetian general reflected this indecision. The Venetian army did little fighting.

As the imperial army approached Mantua in the autumn of 1629, Gonzaga-Nevers prepared for a siege. He leveled buildings near the city to deny them to the enemy army. And he taxed the inhabitants, including the clergy, of Mantua for funds in order to acquire the supplies with which to hold out against the coming siege. The Jesuit college had to contribute hundreds of scudi.[34] In November the imperial army laid siege to Mantua and attacked the city between December 22 and 24, 1629. But Mantuan defenses held. Because of bad winter weather and logistical problems, the imperial troops withdrew.

In the meantime a more deadly enemy arrived. The first verified case of malignant fever and buboes in Mantua was discovered on November 2, 1629. The plague had appeared in Lombardy a little earlier, and German soldiers may have brought it into the Mantovano.[35] It swept across northern Italy

---

31. Quazza, 1926, 2:304–6; Parrott, 1997a, 63.
32. Giuseppe Gorzoni, the Jesuit chronicler, made this point. Gorzoni, 1997, 160.
33. Quazza, 1933, 181, for the number of Venetian troops.
34. Gorzoni, 1997, 160.
35. Quazza, 1933, 183; Segala, 1993–94, 75.

from 1629 to 1631, with many towns and cities losing one-third to one-half of their populations. No historian has described the plague's human cost so well as Alessandro Manzoni in *I promessi sposi*.

Refugees or Gonzaga soldiers probably brought the plague into the city of Mantua, which was crowded with people, many of them already malnourished and weak. Heavy rains, floods, and storms had reduced the harvest of 1627, leading to scarcity and famine in areas of the Mantovano in 1627, 1628, and 1629.[36] Then the war and its attendant destruction drove refugees from the countryside into Mantua. In 1625 the city had 29,710; this swelled to nearly 39,000 in 1629 and possibly 60,000 in the months before July 1630.[37]

The plague roared through the city. There were 1,176 deaths in Mantua in January 1630, followed by 1,088 deaths in February, 1,100 deaths in March, 2,243 deaths in April, then 3,978 deaths in May, and 1,152 deaths in the first seven days of June. This made a total of 10,737 in five months and one week, after which the records spoke no longer. This contrasted with a normal monthly death total of 100 to 180 and about 1,500 deaths annually. Other reports, difficult to verify, state that by mid-summer 250 to 300 died daily and a total of 25,000 civilians and soldiers died in a four-month period.[38] Deaths from the plague continued for the rest of the year and into the next, although numbers are not available. When the city ran out of wood to burn the bodies, it dropped the weighted corpses into the lakes. Nobles fled the city, while some 400 servants and workers at the ducal court who could not leave, died, leaving the huge palace nearly empty.[39]

The imperial army again laid siege to Mantua in May 1630. By the middle of June the city had only seven hundred infantry and fifty cavalry soldiers left to defend it. The troops were no longer able to man their posts by the causeways, which were the entry points. The imperial troops broke through the weak defenses of the city on July 18, 1630. The commander, Count Johann von Aldringen, gave his troops permission to sack the city for three days, July 18 through 20. Sacking was the customary military punishment for cities that resisted sieges, in this case two sieges in a period of about eight months. Looting, killing, extortion, and wanton destruction were the order of the day.[40] As always, the violence was unfocused, sparing some individuals and

---

36. See the comments of Gorzoni, 1997, 157, 168.

37. The figure of 29,710 in 1625 comes from a census and is found in several sources, including Coniglio, 1962, 392. The figures of 39,000 and 60,000 come from a chronicle and an archival source; Segala, 1993–94, 146, 143. Gorzoni, 1997, 164, also presented the figure of 60,000.

38. Quazza, 1933, 187.

39. Quazza, 1933, 187–90. Segala, 1993–94, 138–46, summarizes well the number of deaths and other data about the plague in Mantua.

40. See the account in Quazza, 1926, 2:119–81. See *Mantova: La storia*, 1963, 712–19, for some contemporary descriptions of the sack.

buildings, while devastating others. The printing establishment of Aurelio and Ludovico Osanna, the city's most important publisher, was sacked and burned with much destruction of books and equipment.[41] By contrast, the Jesuits boarded the doors and windows of their college for the three days of the sack and suffered only limited forced entrances and minor damage.[42] Much of the city was not so fortunate. The soldiers thoroughly looted the ducal palace. Mantua's Jews particularly suffered; they had to pay large sums of money, and their quarters were ransacked anyway. Then they were forced to leave the city and not permitted to return until the end of the year.[43]

Key figures of the succession struggle did not survive the deadly summer of 1630. Count Alessandro Striggi died of the plague on June 16, 1630, in Venice, where he had gone to ask the republic for more help. Don Giacinto Gonzaga, who commanded some of the defenders of Mantua, died of the plague in the middle of June 1630. So did Ferrante II Gonzaga on August 6, 1630, also in Mantua, and Isabella di Novellara on August 17, at Bozzolo. On the other side, Duke Carlo Emanuele I of Piedmont-Savoy died on July 27, 1630, apparently not of the plague.

Gonzaga-Nevers surrendered and did not have to suffer through the sack. He was permitted to leave with his entourage of fifty nobles and servants to take refuge in the duchy of Ferrara, part of the Papal States, because Pope Urban VIII had consistently supported his candidacy. He arrived at the Ferrara border on July 19.[44] When military order was restored after the three-day sack, Aldringen and three thousand soldiers remained in the city as its rulers. After having robbed and killed during the sack, they now levied taxes on each parish church, which had to get the money from the parishoners. Even the Jesuits had to pay, even though they had no parish. They borrowed money, putting up some of the artwork of the chapel of Blessed Luigi Gonzaga in their church as collateral.

Peace treaties dictated by the major powers, who mostly preferred a return to the status quo before the war, were signed at Ratisbon and Cherasco on April 6, 1631. The emperor invested Carlo Gonzaga-Nevers as ruler of the duchies of Mantua and Monferrato. But a substantial portion of the Monferrato, although not Casale Monferrato, was given to Vittorio Amedeo I, the new duke of Piedmont-Savoy. On the other hand, parts of his duchy had also been devastated by war. In addition, Reggiolo and Luzzara, two small parts of

---

41. Pescasio, 1971, 276.

42. Gorzoni, 1997, 184–85.

43. Simonsohn, 1977, 46–60, who includes some interesting details about events in Mantua as a whole based on the accounts of Jewish chroniclers.

44. See letter 1049 of Giulio Sacchetti, papal legate of Ferrara, July 20, 1630, Ferrara, along with additional material in *La legazione di Ferrara*, 2006, 2:791–95. There are many letters about the war in the two volumes.

the Mantovano, were given to the new duke of Guastalla, Cesare Gonzaga. Count Aldringen left Mantua in late May 1631, and the German troops began to leave the Mantovano as a whole in June. The remaining troops left Mantua between September 4 and 20, 1631. Gonzaga-Nevers and his family returned on September 21, 1631.[45]

Economic recovery in the Mantovano was slow because the occupying soldiers stayed so long. What happened in the Jesuit properties at Fabrico and Correggio was typical. The soldiers destroyed houses, farm buildings, and livestock when they first arrived. Then the Jesuits, like people across the Mantovano, were forced to use the limited food and income from their devastated farms and villages to feed these same soldiers for weeks and months. The Jesuits were fortunate to be able to call on outsiders for help; for example, the Province of Venice loaned money to the Mantuan college.[46] Matters were far worse for the peasants and townspeople across the Mantovano who lacked assistance. In these circumstances those who could flee to other parts of Italy did so. But the departure of farmers and workers further weakened the economy. The knitwear industry never recovered because it needed many hands, and Mantua and the Mantovano no longer had them. Mantua had only 8,000 souls in 1632, while the population of the Mantovano declined from 170,000 before the war to 43,000 at the end of the war. Mantua did not regain its earlier glory, and the Mantovano never again reached its former population and prosperity heights in the seventeenth and eighteenth centuries.[47] Even in 1676, Mantua had only about 19,000 people, and the Mantovano about 78,000.[48]

## 4. THE IMPRISONMENT AND DEATH OF DOCTOR MARTA

The succession crisis had a direct effect on the university's most prominent scholar, Doctor Marta. Both Carlo Gonzaga-Nevers and Ferrante II Gonzaga asked legal scholars to write works supporting their claims for use in presentations to rulers and circulation in European capitals. After Gonzaga-Nevers seized power in January 1628 three local men wrote legal treatises. Senator Francesco Negri Ciriaco, the most important, wrote at least three works arguing that Gonzaga-Nevers was the legitimate successor to Vincenzo II.

45. Mazzoldi, 1963, 143–44; Gorzoni, 1997, 187.
46. Gorzoni, 1997, 169–71, 179, 182, 184.
47. Belfanti, 1982, 116. Gorzoni, 1997, 164, states that the population of the city was reduced from 60,000 to between 5,000 and 6,000. This does not mean that 53,000 to 54,000 people died in Mantua in the siege, sack, and occupation. Rather, it means that the surviving refugees returned to their villages. The figures of 170,000 and 43,000 come from Quazza, 1933, 210–11.
48. Belfanti, 1982, 116; Mozzarelli, 1987, 116.

# The Imprisonment and Death of Doctor Marta 241

The longest was *Allegationes in iure octo articulis distincte per Franciscum Nigrum Cyriacum I. C. Mantuanum, et in patria senatorem,* published between March and June 1628 in Mantua, followed by publication elsewhere under different titles.[49] It included material written by two more men from the inner circle of the Gonzaga government, Ercole Ripa, president of the Mantuan Senate, and Federico Bosio, cameral auditor and a member of the ducal council.

All three were close to the dead Duke Vincenzo II and Gonzaga-Nevers. For example, Negri Ciriaco and Bosio were two of the five men who witnessed Vincenzo's last will and testament of December 15, 1627.[50] The Mantuan Senate, to which Negri Ciriaco and Ripa belonged, was not a legislative body but the highest court in Mantua, with jurisdiction over a wide range of issues. It might be seen as one of those "grand tribunals" whose decisions Marta collected and edited in his effort to found *ius commune* on the opinions of legal bodies. It had about six members, all appointed by the duke for long periods, and the president of the senate was a member of the ducal council.[51] Gonzaga-Nevers used material from the *Allegationes* in his arguments against the imperial commissary. And the work apparently circulated among imperial electors and in Rome, where Pope Urban VIII liked it. Several political figures wrote against it or, at least, had counter arguments prepared.[52]

Negri Ciriaco also published a short work on the order of Gonzaga-Nevers: *De jure legitimae successionis Ser. Ducis Caroli Gonzagae Ludovici ducis Nivernii filii in ducatibus Mantuae et Montisferrati. . . . Auctore Francisco Nigro Cyriaco J. C. Mantuano,* published in Mantua in 1628.[53] And in 1629 he published in Frankfurt an Italian *relazione* which offered a short history plus documents summarizing

---

49. The book had three titles, depending on where and when it was printed. Quazza, 1922, 205–6 note 3, gives the title of *Allegationes* given in the text plus the titles of the eight articles or sections. He used a copy found in ASM but does not indicate if it was a manuscript or printed work. Since one of the article titles mentioned the imperial edict of sequestration issued on March 20, 1628, and the ducal representative in Rome referred to a printed version on June 11, 1628, it was written, or at least finished and printed, between those dates. Quazza, 1926, 1:169 note 2. It was published under two other titles as well, first as *Controversarum forensium* in 1628 in Mantua by Aurelio and Ludovico Osanna, printers to the duke. Pescasio, 1971, 266; and Ascheri, 1989, 248. According to ibid., this edition had two books. It then appeared as *Ducatus Mantuae, sive disquisitio juridica articulis octo comprehensa . . . Edita pro Carlo, Duce Mantuae . . . Accessit disquisitio alia articulis aliquot distincta in eadem causa conscripta a F. Bosio. . . .* Frankfurt, 1629; copy in the British Library. Ascheri, 1989, 248, also refers to an edition of three books published in Frankfurt, 1629, under the title of *Controversiae forenses.* And he lists an edition of Cremona, 1639, which contained book 3; plus a complete edition of Geneva, 1652–1664; and an edition of Venice, 1664, with four books.

50. Quazza, 1922, 188 note 2.
51. For the story of the Mantuan Senate, see Mozzarelli, 1978.
52. Quazza, 1926, 1:144, 169, 359, 369, 385, 403.
53. Pescasio, 1971, 266, 276.

the dispute up to March 1629. It again defended the legitimacy of the claim of Gonzaga-Nevers.[54] Naturally other rulers with different views sought and obtained consilia as well. An Italian legist published two books supporting the claim to Monferrato of Carlo Emanuele I.[55] Phillip IV, king of Spain, obtained from legists at the University of Salamanca a book arguing that the emperor had the right to sequester the duchies of Mantua and Monferrato, and that the king of Spain might defend imperial authority through the use of arms.[56] A Milanese senator wrote a defense of the claim of Ferrante II Gonzaga.[57]

Giacomo Antonio Marta also had an opinion. Ferrante II asked him for a consilium on the question of the Mantuan and Monferrato succession, which Marta probably wrote in early 1628, certainly before April. Although the consilium has not been located, contemporaries judged that it favored the duke of Guastalla over Gonzaga-Nevers.[58] Marta received 200 ducats or ducatoni for his consilium.[59]

Negri Ciriaco immediately replied. In his *De jure legitimae successionis* he twice referred to the fact that Marta had written in favor of Ferrante Gonzaga, once using the words "Martha qui pro Guastalla scripsit" (Marta here wrote for Guastalla). He then presented arguments and legal references countering Marta's argument. He and Bosio did the same in the larger *Allegationes*.[60]

Gonzaga-Nevers responded in a harsher way: he had Marta arrested and thrown into the castle prison (part of the ducal palace) in April 1628.[61] He

---

54. *Relatione di quanto è successo degno di consideratione negli affari di Mantova dal dì della morte del Sig. Duca Vincenzo II, che seguì al 25 di Decembre 1627 sino al marzo dell'anno presente (1629)*. Frankfurt, 1629. Quazza, 1926, 1:46 note 2. There is a copy in the British Library. Quazza, 1926, cited documents printed in this work several times in his two volumes.

55. Paglia, 1886, 5.

56. Quazza, 1926, 1:359.

57. This was Papirio Cattaneo, not further identified. Paglia, 1886, 6; Quazza, 1922, 163 note 3, 206.

58. It is not in Marta's *Consilia* of 1628, his last publication. Nor was it listed in the death inventory of Marta's goods, and Paglia, 1886, could not find a copy. There is no evidence that it was printed, and it is possible that Gonzaga-Nevers ordered it destroyed. Or the consilium may have disappeared when the ducal palace was sacked in July 1630.

59. In the inventory of Marta's possessions and papers of 1629, there is a reference to a letter of credit from "Ill. S. D. Ferrante di Guastalla" of 200 ducats in favor of Marta to be paid in Naples to a certain "Sig. Cesare Greco," plus an acknowledgment that this was done. Paglia, 1886, 24, 25. The Jesuits also discovered this credit when they examined his papers: "Altri crediti havea con la medesima camera e con gl'agenti del signor duca di Guastalla, che egli havea nel regno di Napoli, e questi eran di 200 ducatoni." Gorzoni, 1997, 161. It seems likely that the 200 ducats or ducatoni were payment for the consilium on the Mantuan succession.

60. Paglia, 1886, 29–30, provides short excerpts against Marta from Negri Ciriaco's works.

61. "Ibi, illust. Jur. Cons. Napolitanus d. Jacobus Antonius . . . in carceribus castri predicti." Introduction to his testament printed in Paglia, 1886, 8. For the beginning of his imprisonment

remained in prison until he died on September 22, 1629, seventeen to eighteen months later.[62] Marta was never tried for any crime, and no evidence has come to light suggesting that he was involved in the struggle in any other way. A simple consilium had terrible consequences for Marta.

Despite the reaction of Gonzaga-Nevers, Marta's past legal writings suggest that he wrote a balanced and dry legal document rather than a polemical treatise. He probably assessed the cases for the two candidates carefully. He undoubtedly ranged widely through history for examples and precedents and offered many legal references and qualifications. This was Marta's style in his *Tractatus de iurisdictione* of 1609. Since Marta's previous legal and political works manifested strong respect for the authority of the emperor, it is likely that this work did the same, not least because Mantua, Monferrato, and Guastalla were all imperial fiefs. At the same time, it is unlikely that Marta's consilium offered unilateral support for Ferrante II or totally rejected the claim of Gonzaga-Nevers. Marta probably treated the case of the Mantuan succession as an intricate legal problem to be resolved by his considerable erudition. But Gonzaga-Nevers saw it as a partisan document and threw Marta into prison.

Imprisonment was a heavy penalty for writing an advisory consilium. Gonzaga-Nevers may have been infuriated to learn that the leading law professor at the University of Mantua, located a few blocks from the ducal palace, opposed him. A man whose salary he paid argued that he was not the rightful ruler of Mantua and Monferrato, assuming that was Marta's message. It must have been embarrassing to have this coming from Marta, while his diplomats were distributing copies of the treatises of Negri Ciriaco, Bosio, and Ripa across Europe. To make matters worse, Marta had a far greater legal reputation than the Mantuan trio.

Marta ignored a simple reality: princes and governments of all centuries expect judges and lawyers under their rule to support their positions, whether reasonable or unlawful, and will do what is necessary to secure that result. Legal scholars knew this and acted accordingly. For example, no professor from the University of Padua wrote anything favoring papal jurisdiction dur-

---

sometime in April, see the statement of Gorzoni, 1997, 161: "Hebbe (Marta) qualche credito con la camera, cioè il salario del mese di marzo 1628, perché l'aprile vegnente fu carcerato e stette carcerato finché morì; nel qual tempo dissero che non correva il salario della lettura." Gorzoni, 1997, 161. That is, Marta was owed his professorial salary for March 1628, which the Jesuits, as his heirs, could try to collect. But his salary ceased when he was imprisoned. See also Paglia, 1886, 6, 22–23.

62. Paglia, 1886, 6, gives his death date from a necrological document found in ASM. Gorzoni, 1997, 161, gives the same date of death possibly from Jesuit college records. See also Quazza, 1926, 1:415 note 2.

ing or after the Venetian Interdict. Marta failed to support the local prince and was imprisoned, which also stopped him from writing more consilia. He was courageous and foolhardy.

While in prison Marta wrote his last will and testament on May 27, 1628. He began by noting that he had never had a wife and had no living forebears or descendants. He wrote that he had begun to live under the protection of Father Alfonso Salmerón in his tenth year and had been raised by the Jesuit fathers. In gratitude he willed everything to the Jesuits of Mantua. He asked them to take custody of his library and to see that none of his manuscripts would be printed after his death. He asked only to be buried under the first step of the altar of St. Ignatius Loyola (canonized in 1622), one of the side altars in SS. Trinità, with a marble plaque reading "Hic iacet Doctor Martha" (Here lies Doctor Marta).[63]

His goods included his library, some jewelry, and a diamond cross. His library had over a thousand printed and manuscript volumes, the largest part on law, plus works of devotion, sacred and profane erudition, theology, Latin literature, and vernacular literature. Marta also listed credits of thousands of scudi in an account with the Monte di San Giorgio in Genoa and in Naples, as well as a letter of exchange for 200 ducatoni from Ferrante II Gonzaga.[64]

But the Mantua Jesuits discovered that it was an imaginary inheritance, which brought them years and years of troubles and then more trouble.[65] There was no account with the Monte di San Giorgio, while creditors and their descendants came out of the woodwork. When they learned that the Mantuan college was Marta's heir, they wrote to the father general of the Society and to Roman cardinals demanding payment. The father general told the Mantuan Jesuits to get rid of the mess. So the honest Jesuits sent the diamond cross and the letter of exchange from Ferrante II Gonzaga to one of the creditors—only to discover that it was a fictitious claim. They sent the library to Bologna to be sold to satisfy the true creditors. By 1652 they were able to satisfy all the claims. Nevertheless, in 1671 another person wrote to

---

63. "Et perchè io non ho havuto mai moglie, nè ho ascendenti nè discendenti ... et perchè io son allevato dal decimo anno della mia vita dalli Padri Gesuiti, da qual tempo cominciai a vivere sotto la protezione del padre Salmerone ... ho risoluto ... di lasciare herede di tutti i miei beni presenti e futuri di qualsiasi genere il colleggio di detti Padri Gesuiti." "Prego dicti M. R. Padri che dopo la mia morte facino sepelire il mio corpo sotto terra, sotto il primo scalino dell'altare di S. Ignazio ed un sol marmo dove siano scritte queste sole parole: Hic iacet Doctor Martha." Will of May 27, 1628, printed in full in Paglia, 1886, 8, 10 for the quotes. He left nothing to his nephew, Giulio Camillo Marta, because the latter had received an inheritance from his father. Paglia, 1886, 27.

64. Paglia, 1886, 9, 24–25.

65. "Ma in poco tempo si scoperse per una eredità imaginaria, per cui non solo hebbimo per anni et anni disturbi e poi disturbi." Gorzoni, 1997, 162.

# The End of the University of Mantua

them claiming to be a descendant of a previous creditor. The now-wiser Jesuits concluded that this was another fictitious claim and did not respond.[66]

Despite all the difficulties, the Jesuits were grateful to Marta for legal advice, documents, and consilia that he had written on behalf of the college, and for his kind words.[67] They gave him a "most noble" funeral, then buried him under the first step of the altar of St. Ignatius, and placed a stone with an inscription there.[68]

## 5. THE END OF THE UNIVERSITY OF MANTUA

The university continued to function through the deaths of Ferdinando and Vincenzo II, and the accession of Gonzaga-Nevers, despite the imprisonment of its star law professor. Duke Vincenzo II's name appeared as the patron of the university on the faculty rolls for the academic years 1626–27 and 1627–28, and the university added professors in both years. What role Vincenzo II and Carlo Gonzaga-Nevers played in the life of the university is unknown; perhaps the capable Alessandro Striggi oversaw the university. So far as can be determined, the Peaceful University of Mantua functioned normally through the academic year of 1628–29.[69]

The end came in October 1629. As the duke and the city prepared for the coming siege, "the university dissolved like salt in water," according to Giuseppe Gorzoni, the Jesuit chronicler.[70] Professors and students left, leaving the lecterns empty and the classrooms silent at the beginning of November, when classes should have begun. Even the Jesuit professors and students fled; this strained the college's finances, because it had to provide them with funds

---

66. Gorzoni, 1997, 161–63.

67. For example, Marta wrote a consilium concerning a case involving a young Jesuit who renounced his inheritance in favor of the college at Mantua, which claimed it when his father died some fifteen years later. But the father's will was contested; this led to a legal case and Marta's consilium. Marta, 1628, pp. 34Bv–37Av, consilium 11, no date.

68. "Morto, gli fecero i padri nobilissime essequie e fu sepolto in chiesa nostra avanti per appunto alla predella dell'altare di sant'Ignatio, ove hoggidì pure si vede una piccola lapida coll'iscrittione e nome d'un tant'huomo." Gorzoni, 1997, 161. Gorzoni wrote his chronicle between 1701 and 1711.

69. Although no roll for 1628–29 has been located, Gorzoni's description of the university in the fall of 1629 (see the next note) implied that it functioned normally in the academic year 1628–29.

70. "Con quest'occasione lo studio si disfece come sale nell'acqua, absentandosi maestri e scuolari, sì che al principio del novembre le catedre e le scuole amutolirono. Anche li nostri lettori, anche li nostri giovani scuolari partirono di qua, il che fu di non piccol pregiudicio in queste contingenze a questo collegio, dovendosi private di tanto contante per provedere ciascuno di viatici. E questo in città, dove s'ingegnarono di mantenere e trattenere li maestri delle scuole basse." Gorzoni, 1997, 160.

and provisions for their journeys. Most probably went to other Jesuit colleges, such as Bologna and Parma, in the Province of Venice. The Jesuits initially tried to keep their lower school open, but then had to close it. Forced to billet "I do not know how many soldiers" (Gorzoni's words), the Jesuits turned over classrooms to the soldiers defending the city and provided them with heating fires and other support.[71]

Fabrizio Bartoletti, the star professor of medicine, fled Mantua, probably in the autumn of 1629, for his native city of Bologna. But he became ill on the way and died in the little town of Lendinara (near Rovigo in the Veneto) on March 30, 1630, and was buried in a church there.[72] Andrea Mariani was more fortunate. After teaching surgery at the University of Mantua from 1626 to 1628 and probably in 1628–29, he left. A man who respected the social graces, Mariani thanked Duke Ferdinando in 1626 and Vincenzo II in 1627 for his appointments.[73] But in March 1630 he reluctantly wrote to Duke Carlo I Gonzaga-Nevers informing him that he was now teaching at the University of Bologna. He enclosed some sonnets as a goodwill gesture. Mariani continued to teach there until 1642.[74] The fates of the rest of the non-Jesuit professors are unknown. Italian universities always began with much fanfare but shut down quietly. So it was for the Peaceful University of Mantua.

## 6. AFTER THE SACK

Despite the closure of the university and, for a time, the lower school, the Jesuits continued their other ministries through war and disease. They suffered grievous losses. The college had housed fifty or more Jesuits from 1625 through 1628.[75] But three Mantuan Jesuits died in 1629, ten Jesuits died in May

---

71. "Anzi, dovette il collegio ricevere in alloggio non so quanti soldati di quelli che defendevano la città, per il quale alloggio il padre rettore stimò bene assegnargli tutte le scuole, accommodate perciò con camini et altro ad uso di quartiero." Gorzoni, 1997, 160.

72. He had suffered from recurring malarial fever for years. Fantuzzi, 1965, 366; and Crespi, 1964, 552.

73. Mariani to the two dukes, October 14, 1626, Bologna, and August 4, 1627, Mantua, in ASM, AG, Bu. 1174, ff. 66r, 155r.

74. Mariani to Duke Carlo I Gonzaga-Nevers, March 13, 1630, from Bologna, in ASM, AG, Bu. 1174, f. 250r. The sonnets are not found here. *I rotuli dello Studio Bolognese*, 1888–1924, 2:383, 387, 390, 394, 398, 401, 405, 409, 413, 417, 421, 426, 430. There is one inconsistency. "Andrea Mariani of Bologna" was listed as an ordinary professor of medical theory at the University of Pisa in the academic year 1634–35, even though he was also listed as teaching at Bologna. Barsanti, 1993, 524, 555.

75. There were fifty Jesuits in Mantua in 1625, fifty-two Jesuits in 1627, forty or forty-one Jesuits on August 1, 1628, but forty-four Jesuits in Mantua in December 1628. ARSI, Veneta 106 I, f. 2r; Veneta 71, ff. 142v–43r; Veneta 39 I, ff. 197r–v, 166r–68v; and Veneta 71, f. 169r. No figures for 1629 have been located. See also Rurale, 1997, 19, 42 note 31, who suggests that there were sixty-

and June 1630, including the rector of the community, Father Girolamo Furlani, and two more died in 1631.[76] Instead of leaving Mantua as did the other Jesuit professors, François Remond of Dijon, the professor of Scripture, remained, hearing the confessions of those stricken by the plague, especially French soldiers, all through the siege and its aftermath. He died on November 14, 1631.[77] Most of the Jesuits who died were confessors, preachers, and temporal coadjutors, including one who worked as a nurse. They had more contact with the people of Mantua and, hence, a greater chance of contracting the plague or another disease. Because of the deaths, and the flight of professors and scholastics, the Mantuan Jesuit community was reduced to fourteen or seventeen Jesuits in 1630.[78]

Although the university was gone, the dogged Jesuits rebuilt their community and ministries. Numerous deaths in the population at large had one positive outcome: they brought many new bequests to the college. And legacies that supported the benefactor while he or she lived came to the Jesuits more quickly and with more capital when benefactors died sooner than expected. Such legacies helped the Jesuits to rebuild their finances.[79]

Nevertheless, progress was slow. In 1632 there were seventeen Jesuits in Mantua, three of them teachers. One taught cases of conscience and the other two taught grammar and humanity, two classes of the lower school.[80] On August 15, 1633, there were nineteen or twenty-one Jesuits, five of them teachers: cases of conscience, a combination of natural philosophy and mathematics, and three classes in the lower school.[81] On January 1, 1636, there were nineteen Jesuits in Mantua but only the lower school of three classes.[82] The number of Jesuits finally rose to twenty-eight in 1639.[83]

---

one Jesuits in Mantua in 1625. As Rurale points out, the numbers are not always consistent in the documents. Some list many but not all the names of the Jesuits, others are vague about the number of temporal coadjutors (Jesuit brothers), who might constitute one-fourth of the community, while scholastics came and went. Nevertheless, it is almost certain that the Jesuit community annually had fifty or more members from 1625 through at least the end of 1628 and probably until the fall of 1629.

76. Gorzoni, 1997, 159, 165–68, 190.

77. Gorzoni, 1997, 190.

78. There are two lists for 1630, one of which states that there were fourteen Jesuits and the other seventeen. It is likely that the lists came from different times of the year. Two lower-school teachers are listed in both, which suggests that the Jesuits revived the lower school when they no longer had to lodge soldiers in the college. ARSI, Veneta 71, ff. 181v, 191r–v.

79. Gorzoni, 1997, 171–79, 189–90.

80. ARSI, Veneta 71, f. 216r.

81. ARSI, Veneta 39 I, ff. 219r–20r, 278r. As noted earlier, the number of Jesuits fluctuated during the course of the year.

82. ARSI, Veneta 71, f. 251r–v.

83. ARSI, Veneta 39 II, ff. 324r–25v.

By the mid 1640s the number of Jesuits in Mantua stabilized at around forty. The Jesuits again taught four upper-school classes: metaphysics, natural philosophy, logic, and mathematics, as well as the three lower-school classes of rhetoric, humanity, and grammar. In 1646 the metaphysics class had 14 students, the natural philosophy class had 14, logic had 30, and mathematics had 8, making a total of 66. The numbers suggest that a significant number of non-Jesuit students were in attendance. The lower school was much larger; there were 25 students in the rhetoric class, 60 in the humanity class, and 80 in the grammar class, for a total of 165. On religious holidays Jesuit scholastics visited Mantuan churches to teach catechism classes for men and women.[84] In 1681 the Jesuits again had a class in casuistry, and in 1684 they added two lectureships in theology.[85] Thus the Jesuits revived much of their part of the University of Mantua and, thanks to the privileges obtained from emperors and popes long ago, they could award degrees. Still, Mantua never regained its former size and stature; Parma and Bologna remained the most important Jesuit colleges for higher instruction in the Province of Venice.

After the return of Carlo I Gonzaga-Nevers as duke of Mantua and Monferrato in the treaties of 1631, the Gonzaga dynasty clattered and rattled through the rest of the seventeenth century, still fending off attempts by other states to seize Monferrato. It scored a marriage coup when Eleonora Gonzaga (1628–86), sister of Duke Carlo II Gonzaga (1629, ruled 1637–65), became the third wife of Emperor Ferdinand III Habsburg (1608, ruled 1637–57) in 1651. But the Gonzaga and Mantua were never again so important in Italian and European politics, or in art, music, and learning, as in the years between 1584 and 1630. And they did not grow wiser. Ferdinando Carlo (1652, ruled 1665–1708) made the mistake of helping the French in the War of the Spanish Succession (1701–14). The victorious Habsburgs punished him with exile, making him the last Gonzaga duke of Mantua and Monferrato. The Habsburgs incorporated the duchy of Mantua directly into the Austrian Empire in 1708 and assigned Monferrato to Piedmont-Savoy. The French had already demolished the fortress of Casale Monferrato in the 1680s. After nearly four hundred years of both glorious and foolish rule and extraordinary patronage of the arts and learning, the Gonzaga of Mantua came to an end.

The Jesuits and their church suffered a similar fate. In 1773 the Society of Jesus was suppressed, and SS. Trinità was given to the Augustinians. Then in

---

84. ARSI, Veneta 125, a small booklet entitled "Stato spirituale e letterario delli Collegi della Provincia di Venetia," no date, but clearly 1646. It is a summary of the activities of the Jesuits in the Province of Venice in 1646. Although there is no pagination, the enrollment numbers for the college of Mantua and the teaching of Christian doctrine are on pp. 8r–v. The Jesuits taught the same seven classes in 1645, at which time there were thirty-six Jesuits in residence. ARSI, Veneta 71, ff. 388v–89r.

85. Rurale, 1997, 19 and 43 note 33; Rurale, 2002, 63.

# After the Sack

the summer of 1796 a French army under the command of Napoleon Bonaparte laid siege to Mantua. The strategic position of the city still made it difficult to conquer, so the French did not enter until February 2, 1797. The Austrians took Mantua back in July 1799. But the French recaptured Mantua in February 1801, and incorporated it into the Cisalpine Republic and Napoleon's Kingdom of Italy in 1805.[86]

Many Mantuan churches and monasteries were suppressed, and the contents of their buildings sold, during the Napoleonic period. Sometime in the 1790s SS. Trinità was deconsecrated and turned into a storehouse for hay and horse fodder. The remains of Eleonora of Austria, who was buried under the floor in front of the high altar, were transferred to the Capella dell'Incoronata in the cathedral (San Pietro). And the stone over her tomb with the Gonzaga and Habsburg coats of arms was moved to the ducal palace.[87] Unfortunately, no information has come to light concerning the body of Doctor Marta buried under the floor of the chapel of St. Ignatius Loyola. Whether his remains were removed or still rest in the deconsecrated church is unknown.

The triptych of Rubens was still in the ex-church. Because the hay was damaging the paintings, the French general in 1801 gave permission for the paintings to be removed. *The Gonzaga Family in Adoration of the Trinity* was cut into pieces, then the central part of it was sewn back together and remounted in the ducal palace.[88] Unfortunately, the extensive borders with the portraits of the Gonzaga children were not reattached, and these, plus the other two paintings, were dispersed.[89]

The French left in 1814, after which the Austrians ruled Mantua. But the ex-church continued to serve as a storehouse for hay and grain. In 1852 a devastating fire broke out, after which the Austrians extensively altered the building and used it as a military warehouse until Mantua became part of the Kingdom of Italy in 1866. Part of the former church now houses documents for the State Archive of Mantua, which occupies the adjoining former Jesuit college. Although plans to restore the sacristy of SS. Trinità have been prepared, the church remains closed.[90]

A PRINCE AND A RELIGIOUS ORDER, AN UNUSUAL COMBINATION FOR ITALY, jointly created the University of Mantua. Building a university ab uovo was an

---

86. See Giusti, 1963, 291, for the events in Mantua during the Napoleonic era.
87. Gorzoni, 1997, 89.
88. Bazzotti, 1977, 39, 42; see also Navarrini, 1977, 56–58.
89. Today the *Baptism of Christ* is located in the Musée Royal des Beaux-Arts in Antwerp and the *Transfiguration* in the Musée des Beaux-Arts in Nancy, France. Pieces of *The Gonzaga Family in Adoration of the Trinity* are scattered across museums and private collections in Europe and North America.
90. *Il palazzo degli studi*, 1998, 32–35.

audacious undertaking. It took vision, a strong commitment to learning, ample financial resources, and professors, which a religious order could help to supply. For such a venture to succeed, ruling family and religious order had to bond. The Gonzaga had a closer and stronger tie to the Society of Jesus than any other Italian ruling family, thanks to the short, holy life of Blessed Luigi Gonzaga. Duke Ferdinando, who studied at a Jesuit institution and spent evenings conversing with the Jesuit fathers, expanded the union between family and religious order by creating the Peaceful University of Mantua. But it did not survive the fateful politics of his successors.

It is easy to find fault with the Gonzaga. Their statecraft was sometimes reckless, their marital politics irresponsible, and they spent far beyond their means. They were the kind of old regime rulers that Italians of the Risorgimento era despised. But the Gonzaga should also be given credit for their aspirations and accomplishments. By supporting the Jesuits, they provided free Latin education for the boys of Mantua, while Eleonora of Austria funded limited female education. They made it possible for some of the most important writers and musicians of their era to create works of genius. They were intellectually curious and warmly supported scholars. Their piety was genuine. And Ferdinando created a university.

Although the university lasted only four years, and the Jesuit part for five, it accomplished a good deal. It was an innovative institution. While other Italian universities barely noticed chemical medicine, the refined version of Paracelsianism, Mantua embraced it. Had the University of Mantua survived, chemical medicine might have developed more extensively and more quickly in Italy than it did. Mantua also hosted the pioneering research of Fabrizio Bartoletti. Its star legist, Giacomo Antonio Marta, sought to broaden and internationalize mos italicus by establishing ius commune on the jurisprudential practices of courts and justices from across Europe. And he favored civil jurisdiction over ecclesiastical jurisdiction, which was the legal wave of the century. By participating in the University of Mantua, the Jesuits expanded their higher education mission in northern Italy. The Jesuit professors gave their students a thorough education in the humanities, mathematics, logic, philosophy, theology, casuistry, and biblical studies, training comparable to what was found in lay universities. The University of Mantua did well in its few years.

# Appendix
## Jesuit Professors at Mantua, 1624–1630

This is a list with short biographies of the nineteen Jesuits who taught at the Public Academy of Mantua and the Peaceful University of Mantua, 1624–30, plus a rector of the college who did not teach. The place of birth is added because the rolls listed them that way. If no other archival sources are given, the information comes from the rolls of the Public Academy of Mantua (1624–25) and the Peaceful University of Mantua (1625–28) found in ASM, AG, Bu. 3366, ff. 64, 103, 108, 109, which are summarized in tables 3.1, 6.1, and 6.2. This information is supplemented by ARSI, Veneta 71, ff. 108r–v, 111v–12r (1624 list of Jesuit teachers in Mantua), 142v–43r (1627 list), 169r (December 1628 list), 181v, 191r–v (1630 list), plus printed sources as noted. For the one or two inconsistencies between the Mantuan rolls and ARSI documents, the Mantuan rolls are followed.

Accarisi(o), Giacomo, of Bologna. Taught rhetoric and poetry (two daily lectures), 1624–25.
B. 1599 at Bologna; d. May 11, 1653, at Vico Garganico. Accarisi delivered an oration on the death of Archduke Karl of Austria at the church of Santa Barbara in Mantua, which was published with a dedication to Duke Ferdinando in Mantua, 1625. But he left the Jesuits and Mantua by December 1625, at which time he failed to secure a position with Duke Ferdinando. Accarisi obtained a doctorate in philosophy in 1626, probably at the University of Bologna. He taught logic at Bologna in the academic year 1627–28 and was ordained a priest at an unknown date. He then went to Rome, where he became a secretary to Cardinal Guido Bentivoglio, a diplomat. He served as morning ordinary professor of natural philosophy at the University of Rome from 1635 to 1643, then became bishop of Vieste on the Adriatic coast in southern Italy. Accarisi published several funeral and

academic orations, including one in praise of the University of Mantua and Duke Ferdinando. At Rome he published works against Copernicus, against the Paracelsians, and rejecting atomism. Letters to Duke Ferdinando and Chancellor Striggi of December 10, 1625, Milan, in ASM, AG, Bu. 1756, ff. 788r, 790r–v. In the letter to Duke Ferdinando he signed himself as a Jesuit; to Striggi he did not. Petrucci, 1960 (with some errors); *I rotuli dello Studio Bolognese*, 1888–1924, 2:374; *I maestri di Roma*, 1991, 2:1083–84; Sommervogel, 1890–1932, 1:27; Carella, 2007, 134–36.

CURZIO, OMNIBENE, OF VERONA. Taught Scripture 1626–27.

Apparently somewhat older than the others, he died on May 2, 1627. A preacher for many years, he was preparing a treatise on the *Song of Songs* at the time of his death. Gorzoni, 1997, 151.

FERRARI, ORAZIO, OF MODENA. Rector of the college 1622–25 but not a teacher in the university.

B. Modena 1575 or 1576; entered S.J. October 1593; professed four vows May 16, 1613; d. Modena, September 5, 1630. Taught natural philosophy at Parma in 1621–22; named rector of the college in Mantua in September 1622 and negotiated with Duke Ferdinando on the university. He served as rector until October 1625 and may have been transferred at that time. Ferrari published two vernacular books in 1628: on marriage and an account of three Jesuit martyrs in Japan. Baldini, 2002, 296 and note 56; Gorzoni, 1997, 140, 150, 382. Sommervogel, 1890–1932, 3:676, and 12:1062.

FONTANA, ORAZIO, OF BOLOGNA. Taught logic 1627–28, and natural philosophy 1628–29.

B. Bologna July 7, 1595; entered S.J. November 8, 1612; professed four vows March 14, 1632; d. May 7, 1676, at Bologna. Fontana was vice rector then rector of the Mantuan college from 1630 to the middle of 1634 and rector again from 1648 to 1652. He also taught theology. Baldini, 2002, 297 note 66; Gorzoni, 1997, 177, 191, 306.

MANFREDINI, FRANCESCO, OF MODENA. Taught logic 1626–27, natural philosophy 1627–28, and metaphysics 1628–29.

He also taught in the lower school at Parma in 1616–17. ARSI, Veneta 71, f. 169r; Brizzi, 1980, 171.

MEGLI (MELIO), LORENZO, OF SARZANA. Taught cases of conscience, 1627–29. ARSI, Veneta 71, f. 169r.

MORANDO, ANTONIO, OF PIACENZA. Taught logic 1624–25, natural philosophy 1625–26, metaphysics 1626–27, natural philosophy 1627–28, and theology 1628–29.

ARSI, Veneta 71, 169r.

MOSCATELLI, CESARE, OF BOLOGNA. Taught mathematics 1624–29.

B. Bologna ca. 1585; entered S.J. in 1609 after obtaining a doctorate of philosophy; d. Modena, 1644. He studied mathematics at the Jesuit school in Parma, probably with Giuseppe Biancani, and was esteemed as a mathematician. Moscatelli taught in the Jesuit lower school at Parma in 1614–15, logic at Ferrara 1629–30, mathematics there in 1630–31, and then he served in a nonteaching capacity in the Jesuit college in Modena from 1632 to 1644. He constructed mechanical models while at Modena, but no papers have been found. ARSI, Veneta 71, f. 169r; Brizzi, 1980, 171; Baldini, 1992, 422–23, 431, 448 note 129; Baldini, 2000, 184 note 32, 186–87, 198.

NATTA, GIOVANNI FRANCESCO, OF MONFERRATO. Taught humanities 1627–28.

NOCETO, GIOVANNI BATTISTA, OF GENOA. Taught Scripture 1624–26.

B. April 1, 1586, at Genoa; entered S.J. September 1, 1602; d. April 8, 1682, at Genoa. Noceto taught Scripture, Hebrew, and moral theology in his career. In the 1650s and 1660s he published works against astrology, a devotional work, and one on the shroud of Turin. Sommervogel, 1890–1932, 5:1787–89; Casali, 1993.

PARENTI, LUCA, OF VERONA. Taught cases of conscience 1626–27 and theology 1628–29.

B. 1586 at Verona; entered S.J. November 3, 1605; d. October 30, 1648, at Imola. Parenti also taught logic, natural philosophy, and metaphysics at Parma, 1621–26. Baldini, 2002, 296 and note 58, 297.

REMOND, FRANÇOIS, OF DIJON. Taught Scripture 1627–29, 1630–31.

B. October 18, 1561, at Dijon; entered S.J. March 12, 1580, ordained 1588, professed four vows February 2, 1601; d. November 14, 1631, in Mantua. His father, a councillor of the Parlement of Dijon, sent him to study in Rome where he entered the Society of Jesus. He may have obtained a doctorate from the University of Padua. Remond taught logic, natural philosophy, and metaphysics at the Collegio Romano 1592–95, then philosophy at Padua. Remond began teaching theology at the Jesuit school in Parma in 1599 and was invited by Duke Ranuccio I to deliver the inaugural arts oration opening the new university there in November 1600. He stayed to teach theology. The Jesuits then sent him to teach theology at Bordeaux in 1604, and he went back and forth between Parma and Bordeaux in the next twenty-plus years, always teaching theology, until transferred to Mantua. Remond was a famous orator who delivered the inaugural oration for the opening of the academic year of the Collegio Romano in 1586 and funeral orations for several cardinals. His Latin orations, epigrams, and poetry had over thirty-five printings between 1586 and 1626. While ministering to plague victims, he contracted the dread disease and died in Mantua. Bottereau, 2001; Sommervogel, 1890–1932, 6:1652–56 (which gives his birth date as 1558 or 1562); Villoslada, 1954, 327, 329, 332; D'Alessandro, 1980, 32, 40, 60; Baldini, 1992, 570; Gorzoni, 1997, 190; Grendler, 2002, 130.

ROSSANO, FRANCESCO, OF FORLÌ. Taught theology 1624–28.

B. October 18, 1583, at Forlì; entered S.J. November 12, 1602; professed four vows August 15, 1620; d. March 11, 1647, at Piacenza. He taught logic, natural philosophy, and metaphysics at Parma, 1616–22, and later served as rector. Brizzi, 1980, 171–73; Baldini, 2002, 296 and note 50; Grendler, 2002, 134–35.

SERUGO, VICENZO, OF FORLÌ. Taught natural philosophy and metaphysics, 1624–25, logic 1625–26, natural philosophy 1626–27, and metaphysics 1627–28.

ARSI, Veneta 71, ff. 111v–12r.

SIMONETTA, ALESSANDRO, OF MILAN. Taught humanities 1625–26.

B. May 18, 1600; entered S.J. August 3, 1616; professed four vows July 31, 1635; d. October 6, 1671, at Bologna. He taught logic, moral philosophy, and metaphysics at Parma, 1633–36, and taught Scripture for eleven years and theology for three years at Bologna. Simonetta published two vernacular religious works and left manuscripts in philosophy, theology, Scripture, and rhetoric. Sommervogel, 1890–1932, 7:1220–21; Baldini, 2002, 298 and note 70.

TORTO, MATTEO, OF VERONA. Taught moral philosophy 1624–29, 1630–31.

D. March 6, 1652, at Mantua. He was also the prefect of studies for the lower school in Mantua for many years and was briefly vice rector at the college at Castiglione Stiviere in 1630. ARSI, Veneta 71, 169r, 191r–v; Gorzoni, 1997, 227.

TREZZI, GIACOMO FILIPPO, OF INNSBRUCK. Taught theology 1624–28.

B. ca. 1580 in Innsbruck; entered S.J. November 3, 1598; professed four vows November 25, 1618; d. September 30, 1633, at Piacenza. He taught natural philosophy and metaphysics at Parma, 1616–18, and later was a rector. Brizzi, 1980, 171; Baldini, 2002, 296 and note 51; Grendler, 2002, 134.

VULPIO, FRANCESCO, OF MANTUA. Taught humanities 1626–27.

ZAMBERTI, CARLO, OF PIACENZA. Taught logic 1628–29.

B. October 8, 1594, at Piacenza; entered S.J. October 23, 1615, already a doctor *in utroque iure*; professed four vows April 2, 1634; d. April 27, 1650, at Faenza. He taught humanities, later metaphysics at Busseto, then casuistry at Bologna 1634–39 and perhaps longer. He published a work on casuistry ca. 1639. ARSI, Veneta 71, f. 169r; Sommervogel, 1890–1932, 8:1455; Baldini, 2002, 297 and note 66.

ZUCCHI, EMILIO, OF PARMA. Taught cases of conscience 1624–26.

B. ca. 1585 at Parma; entered S.J. 1605; d. 1630 at Parma. He taught Latin grammar to the son of Duke Ranuccio I Farnese at Parma from 1619 to 1621. Emilio was probably the brother of the better-known Niccolò Zucchi, S.J. (1586–1670), a philosopher and mathematician. Brizzi, 1980, 155–56; Baldini, 2000, 195 and note 81.

# Bibliography

### ARCHIVAL

Bologna, Archivio di Stato
    Assunteria di Studio
Macerata, Archivio di Stato
    Archivio Priorale
Mantova, Archivio di Stato
    Archivio Gonzaga
Rome, Archivum Romanum Societatis Iesu
    Epistolae Italiae
    Mediolanensis
    Roma
    Veneta
Torino, Archivio di Stato
    Istruzione pubblica
Torino, Archivio Storico della Città di Torino
    Carte sciolte

### MANUSCRIPT

Mantova, Archivio di Stato
Ms. Carlo d'Arco no. 80, "Dell'historia di Mantova et Analli (sic) ocorsi dall'Edification di essa Città sino al giorno di oggi di et anno 1654 . . . di Capitano Giovanni Mambrino Mantoano."

PRINTED WORKS

Primary Sources, Collections of Documents, and Summaries of Documents

Alidosi Pasquali, 1980. *I dottori bolognesi di teologia, filosofia, medicina e d'arti liberali dall'anno 1000 per tutto Marzo del 1623.* In Bologna per Nicolo Tebaldini, 1623; reprint Sala Bolognese.
Amadei, Federigo, 1956. *Cronaca universale della Città di Mantova. Edizione integrale,* edited by Giuseppe Amadei, Ercolano Marani, and Giovanni Praticò. Vol. 3. Mantua.
Bartoletti, Fabrizio, 1619a. *Anatomia humani microcosmi descripto per theses disposita ex clarissimo Anphiteatro Pisano proposita a Fabritio Bartoleto, medico, et philosopho in Accademia Bononiensi publice chirugiam, et anatomiam profitente.* Bononiae, Typis Sebastiani Bonomii.
Bartoletti, Fabrizio, 1619b. *Encyclopaedia hermetico-dogmatica sive orbis doctrinarum medicarum physiologiae, hygiinae, pathologiae, simioticae, et therepeuticae ad sereniss. Principem D. Ferdinandum Gonzagam Mantuae et Montisferrati ducem.* Bononiae, Apud Sebastianum Bonomium.
Bartoletti, Fabrizio, 1633. *Methodus in dyspnoeam seu de respirationibus libri iv. Cum synopsibus quibus quintus pro colophone accessit de curationibus ex dogmaticorum et hermeticorum poenu depromptis. Opus rarum, practicantibus admodu. necess.um anno MDCXXVIII publicis lectionibus explicatum a' Fabritio Bartoletto Bonon. philosopho, et medico, practicae medicae, et anatomes in Mantuana Academia primario professore.* Bononiae, Per Heredes Evangelistae Dozze. Typis Nicolai Tebaldini.
Carbone, Ludovico, 1596. *Dello ammaestramento de' figliuoli nella dottrina Christiana.* Venetia, Appresso Giovanni Guerigli.
*Cardiac Classics,* 1941. *Cardiac Classics: A Collection of Classic Works on the Heart and Circulation with Comprehensive Biographies and Accounts of the Authors, Fifty Contributions by Fifty-One Authors,* edited by Frederick A. Willius and Thomas E. Keys. St. Louis.
Carra, Gilberto, Luciano Fornari, and Attilio Zanca, 2004. *Gli statuti del Collegio dei medici di Mantova 1313–1559.* Mantua.
*Constitutions,* 1996. *The Constitutions of the Society of Jesus and Their Complementary Norms. A Complete English Translation of the Official Latin Texts.* Saint Louis.
*Decrees,* 1990. *Decrees of the Ecumenical Councils,* edited by Norman P. Tanner, S.J. 2 vols. London and Washington, D.C.
De Paola, Francesco, 1984. *Il carteggio del napoletano Jacopo Antonio Marta con la corte d'Inghilterra (1611–1615). Scorci di storia politica e diplomatica italo-inglese nel sec. XVII attraverso l'epistolario di un giureconsulto napoletano professore in Padova.* Lecce.
Ferrari, Giacomo, 1601. *Idea theriacae et mithridatii, ex optima atque omnium excellentissima Antonii Berthioli pragmatia: ipsorumque interim ingredientium simplicium exactissima discussio, & praesertim de viperis scitu dignissima non hucusque ab alio quopiam Physiologò e nucleata, nunc demum a Jacobo Ferrario philosopho, & Medico Mantuano, partime ex doctissimi olim Flamminii Evoli scriptis, partim ex prorijs excerpta, & ad commune commodum edita.* Venetiis, Apud Jo. Antonio & Jacobum de Franciscis.

# Bibliography

Ferrari, Giacomo, and Joseph DuChesne, 1619. *Le ricchezze della riformata farmacopea del Sig. Giuseppe Quercetano medico e consiglier regio. Nuovamente di favella latina traportata (sic) in italiana dal Sig. Giacomo Ferrari medico, e filosofo mantovano. Sono li seguenti, cioè discorsi varij. . . . Oltre nuove osservationi, pensieri gratiosi, utilissime inventioni, Avvertimenti necessarij per la compositione di molti medicamenti Heremetici: fatiche veramente degne d'esser lette, & rilette da ogni gran Personaggio, & da qualunque persona, che desidera medicarsi citò, tuto, & iocunde.* In Venetia, Appresso Giovanni Guerigli.

Folcario, Antonio, 1598. *Vita della Ser.ma Eleonora Arciduchessa d'Austria, Duchessa di Mantova, et di Monferrato.* Mantova, per Francesco Osanna, Stampador Ducale.

*Fontes narrativi*, 1943. *Fontes narrativi de S. Ignatio de Loyola et de Societatis Iesu initiis*, edited by D. Fernández Zapico and C. De Dalmases. Vol. 1. Rome.

Galilei, Galileo, 1964–66. *Opere.* Nuova ristampa della edizione nazionale. 20 vols. Florence.

Garzoni, Tommaso, 1601. *La piazza universale di tutte le professioni del mondo, Nuovamente ristampata & posta in luce, da Thomaso Garzoni da Bagnacavallo. Aggiontovi in questa nuova Impressione alcune bellissime Annotationi a discorso per discorso.* Venetia, Appresso Roberto Meietti.

Gorzoni, Giuseppe, 1997. *Istoria del Collegio di Mantova della Compagnia di Giesù scritta dal padre Giuseppe Gorzoni. Parte prima*, edited by Antonello Bilotto and Flavio Rurale. Mantua.

*Hermetica*, 1992. *Hermetica: The Greek Corpus Hermeticum and the Latin Asclepius in a new English translation, with notes and introduction.* Introduction, translation, and notes by Brian P. Copenhaver. Cambridge.

*Index*, 1758. *Index librorum prohibitorum Ssmi. D. N. Benedicti XIV Pontificis Maximi iussu recognitus, atque editus.* Romae. Ex Typographia Rev. Camerae Apostolicae.

*Index*, 2002. *Index librorum prohibitorum 1600–1966*, edited by J. M. DeBujanda with the assistance of Marcella Richter. Index des libres interdits, 11. Sherbrooke, Montréal, and Genève.

*Index de Rome*, 1994. *Index de Rome 1590, 1593, 1596. Avec étude des index di Parme 1580 et Munich 1582*, edited by J.M. De Bujanda, Ugo Rozzo, Peter G. Bietenholz, and Paul F. Grendler. Translation by Claude Sutto. With the assistance of René Davignon, Ela Stanek, and Marcella Richter. Sherbrooke and Genève.

*Le istruzioni generali di Paolo V*, 2003. *Le istruzioni generali di Paolo V ai diplomatici pontifici 1605–1621*, edited by Silvano Giardano, OCD. 3 vols. Tübingen.

James I, 1965. *The Political Works of James I. Reprinted from the Edition of 1616.* With an Introduction by Charles Howard McIlwain. New York.

James VI and I, 1994. *Political Writings*, edited by Johann P. Sommerville. Cambridge.

*La legazione di Ferrara*, 2006. *La legazione di Ferrara del Cardinale Giulio Sacchetti (1627–1631)*, edited by Irene Fosi with the collaboration of Andrea Gardi. 2 vols. Vatican City.

*I maestri di Ferrara*, 1991. *I maestri di medicina ed arti dell'Università di Ferrara 1391–1950*, edited by Francesco Raspadori. Florence.

*I maestri di Roma*, 1991. *I maestri della Sapienza di Roma dal 1514 al 1787: I rotuli e altre fonti*, edited by Emanuele Conte. Fonti per la storia d'Italia, 116. 2 vols. Rome.

Maldonado, Juan, 1888. *A commentary on the Holy Gospels by John Maldonatus. S. Matthew's Gospel,* translated and edited by George J. Davie. Second edition. 2 vols. London.

Marta, Giacomo Antonio, 1608. *Decisionum novissimarum almi Collegii Pisani causarum delegatarum, vel ad Consilium Sapientis transmissarum vota Doctoris Martae iurisconsulti Neapolitani in Romana Curia Advocati.* Venetiis. Apud Ioan. Antonium & Jacobum de Franciscis.

Marta, Giacomo Antonio, 1609. *Tractatus de iurisdictione per et inter iudicem ecclesiasticum et secularem exercenda, in omni foro et principum consistoriis versantibus maxime necessarius Doctoris Martae, iurisconsulti Neapolitani, in alma urbe Advocato.* Moguntiae. Typis Ioannis Albini, sumptibus vero Hulderici Rewall.

Marta, Giacomo Antonio, 1613. *Supplicatio ad imperatorem, reges, principes, super causis generalis concilij convocandi. Contra Paulum Quintum.* London: Excudebat Bonham Norton, Serenissimae Regiae Maiestatis in Latinis, Graecis, & Hebraicis Typographus.

Marta, Giacomo Antonio, 1615. *Tractatus de clausulis: de quibus in omnibus tribunalibus hucusque disputatum est . . . cum plurimis additionibus primum impressus, nunc secundo editus cum novis atque omnibus clausulis ad feuda & ultimas testantium voluntates pertienentibus . . . a Doctore Marta.* Venice: Apud Iacobum de Franciscus.

Marta, Giacomo Antonio, 1621. *Totius iuris controversi scientiae, ex omnibus decisionibus universi orbis, quae hucusque impressae fueret: a Doct. MARTA NEAPOLITANO iureconsulto veridico summo pratico, ad instar Digestorum Imperialium nova methoda compilata, sex tomis distincta. Quorum Primus Iudiciorum Civilium, Secundus Criminalium, Tertius Contractuum, Quartus Feudorum, Quintus Ultimarum Voluntatum, Sextus Beneficialium, & Spiritualium materias continent, atque totam legalem scientiam complectuntur. . . . Supera additis omnibus, quae in impressione Veneta praetermissa fuerunt, ac puritati sui nominis, & compilationis authoris correctius restitutum.* Francofurti, Typis Erasmi Kempfferi, Sumptibus Rulandiorum.

Marta, Giacomo Antonio, 1622. *The New Man, or a supplication from an unknown Person, a Roman Catholicke unto James, the Monarch of Great Brittaine, and from him to the Emperour, Kings, and Princes of the Christian World. Touching the causes and reasons that will argue a necessity of a Generall Councell to be forthwith assembled against him that now usurps the papall Chaire under the name of Paul the fifth. Wherein are discovered more of the secret Iniquities of the Chaire and Court, then hitherto their friends feared, or their very adversaries did suspect. Translated into English by William Crashaw, Batchelour in Divinity, according to the Latin Copy, sent from Rome into England.* London, Printed by Bernard Alsop, for George Norton, and are to bee sold in Distaffe-lane, at the signe of the Dolphin.

Marta, Giacomo Antonio, 1626. *De Accademiae Mantuanae institutione et praestantia oratio habita Mantuae in Cathedrali Ecclesia die v. Novembris 1626. A Doctore Marta Neapolitano eiusdem Accademia primario Iurisconsulto. Nunc primum in lucem data a Iosepho a Bubalo Mirandulano eiusdem Accademia Scolastico. Ad Illustrissimum & Excellentiss. Dominum Don Hiacynthum Gonzagam, Serenenissimi Ferdinandi filium eiusdem Accademiae Protectorem.* Mantuae: Ex Typis Aurelij & Ludovici Osanna fratrum, Ducalium Impressorum. No date, but dedicatory letter of February 8, 1626.

Marta, Giacomo Antonio, 1628. *Consilia Doctoris Martae Neapolitani iurisconsulti veridici summi practici. In quibus omnes causae, quae suis temporibus in controversiam vocatae fuerunt iudicio gravissimo definiuntur, Et nova respondendi, & allegandi de iure Methodus exhibetur.* . . . Augustae Taurinorum: Apud HH. Io. Dominici Taurini.

Marta, Giacomo Antonio, 1666. *Doctoris Martae Neapolitani, iurisconsulti veridici, Summi Practici, ac in celeberrimo Papiensi Gymnasio Iuris Civilis Interpretis Primarij, summa totius successionis legalis quatuor partibus complexa. In quibus universa materia ultimarum voluntatum, Testamentorum, Legatorum, Fideicommissorum aliarumque successionum, ad formam iuris communis, item feudalis, ac omnium statutorum, nova methodo copiosissime pertractatur. Editio secunda, et prima veneta.* . . . 2 vols. Venetiis, Apud Bertanos.

Marta, Giacomo Antonio, 1669. *Tractatus de iurisdictione per, et inter iudicem ecclesiasticum & secularem exercenda, in omni foro, et principum consistoriis versantibus, maxime necessarius. Doctoris Martae iurisconsulti neapolitani, in alma urbe Advocati.* Avenone, Apud Ioan. Batistam Bellagambam.

*Mechanics*, 1969. *Mechanics in Sixteenth-Century Italy: Selections from Tartaglia, Benedetti, Guido Ubaldo, and Galileo*, translated and annotated by Stillman Drake and I. E. Drabkin. Madison, Milwaukee, and London.

*Memorie di Pavia*, 1970. *Memorie e documenti per la storia dell'Università di Pavia e degli uomini più illustri che v'insegnarono.* 2 parts. Pavia, 1877–78; reprint Bologna.

*Monumenta Paedagogica*, 1965–92. *Monumenta paedagogica Societatis Iesu*, edited by Ladislaus Lukács. 7 vols. Rome.

Pirri, Pietro, S.J., 1959. *L'interdetto di Venezia del 1606 e i Gesuiti: Silloge di documenti con introduzione.* Rome.

Polanco, Juan Alfonso de, S.J., 1969. *Polanci complementa. Epistolae et commentaria P. Joannis Alphonsi de Polanco e Societate Jesu, Addenda caeteris ejusdem scriptis dispersis in his monumentis.* Vol. 2. Madrid, 1917; reprint Rome.

Possevino, Antonio, S.J., 1594. *Vita, et morte della Serenissima Eleonora Arciduchessa di Austria et Duchessa di Mantova da Antonio Possevino.* Mantova, per Francesco Osanna Stampadore Ducale. No date but the letter of the publisher is October 6, 1594.

Possevino Junior, Antonio, 1600. *Antonii Possevini Iunioris philosophi, ac medici Mantuani, theoricae morborum libri quinque. Addita Methodus studiorum medicinae ex Bibliotheca selecta eius Patrui.* Mantuae, Franciscus Osanna Ducalis Impressor excudebat.

*Ratio Studiorum*, 2005. *The Ratio Studiorum: The Official Plan for Jesuit Education*, translated and annotated by Claude Pavur, S.J. St. Louis.

*Relazioni*, 1912. *Relazioni degli ambasciatori veneti al Senato.* Vol. 1: *Ferrara, Mantova, Monferrato*, edited by Arnaldo Segarizzi. Bari.

*Relazioni in Terraferma*, 1975. *Relazioni dei rettori veneti in Terraferma*, edited by Amelio Tagliaferri. Vol. 4: *Podestaria e capitanato di Padova.* Milan.

*I rotuli dello Studio Bolognese*, 1888–1924. *I rotuli dei lettori legisti e artisti dello Studio Bolognese dal 1384 al 1799*, edited by Umberto Dallari. 4 vols. Bologna.

Salmerón, Alfonso, 1972. *Epistolae P. Alphonsi Salmeronis.* Vol. 2: *1565–1585.* Madrid, 1907; reprint Rome.

Sarpi, Paolo, 1969. *Opere*, edited by Gaetano and Luisa Cozzi. Milan and Naples.

Stella, Aldo, 1964. *Chiesa e stato nelle relazioni dei nunzi pontifici a Venezia: Ricerche sul giurisdizionalismo veneziano dal XVI al XVIII secolo.* Vatican City.

Verde, Armando, 1994. *Lo studio fiorentino 1473–1503: Ricerche e Documenti.* Vol. 5: *Gli stanziamenti.* Presentazione di Eugenio Garin. Florence.

SECONDARY SOURCES

Angelozzi, Giancarlo, 1981. "L'insegnamento dei casi di coscienza nella pratica educativa della Compagnia di Gesù," in *La 'Ratio Studiorum.' Modelli culturali e pratiche educative dei Gesuiti in Italia tra Cinque e Seicento,* edited by Gian Paolo Brizzi. Rome, pp. 121–62.

Antonazzi, Giovanni, 1985. *Lorenzo Valla e la polemica sulla Donazione di Costantino. Con testi inediti dei secoli XV–XVII.* Rome.

Ardenghi, Mario, 1969–70. "Saggio sulla storia dell'Università di Mantova." Tesi di Laurea. Facoltà di Magistero, Università degli Studi di Padova, 1969–70. Copy in ASM.

Ardenghi, Mario, 1972. "Per la storia dell'Università di Mantova." *Civiltà mantovana* 6:209–16.

Ardenghi, Mario, 2000. "L'Università di Mantova. Storia dell'istruzione tra Seicento e Settecento." Mantova. Thesis submitted for the Concorso Fondazione BPA-Poggio-Russo 1999. Copy in ASM.

Ascarelli, Fernanda, 1972. *Le cinquecentine romane: "Censimento delle edizione romane del XVI secolo possedute dalle biblioteche di Roma."* Milan.

Ascheri, Mario, 1989. *Tribunali giuristi e istituzioni dal medioevo all'età moderna.* Bologna.

Baciero, Carlos, 2001. "Arriaga, Rodrigo de." DHCJ 1:243–44.

Bailey, Gauvin Alexander, 1999. " 'Le style jésuite n'existe pas': Jesuit Corporate Culture and the Visual Arts," in *The Jesuits,* pp. 38–89.

Baldini, Ugo, 1992. *Legem impone subactis. Studi su filosofia e scienza dei Gesuiti in Italia 1540–1632.* Rome.

Baldini, Ugo, 1999. "The Development of Jesuit 'Physics' in Italy, 1500–1700: A Structural Approach," in *Philosophy in the Sixteenth and Seventeenth Centuries. Conversations with Aristotle,* edited by Constance Blackwell and Sachiko Kusukawa. Aldershot and Brookfield, Vt., pp. 248–79.

Baldini, Ugo, 2000. *Saggi sulla cultura della Compagnia di Gesù (secoli xvi–xviii).* Padua.

Baldini, Ugo, 2001. "Il pubblico della scienza nei permessi di lettura di libri proibiti delle Congregazioni del Sant'Ufficio e dell'Indice (secolo XVI): verso una tipologia professionale e disciplinare," in *Censura ecclesiastica e cultura politica in Italia tra Cinquecento e Seicento.* VI giornata Luigi Firpo. Atti del Convegno 5 marzo 1999, edited by Cristina Stango. Florence, pp. 171–201.

Baldini, Ugo, 2002. "S. Rocco e la scuola scientifica della provincia veneta: il quadro storico (1600–1773)," in *Gesuiti e università,* pp. 283–323.

Baldini, Ugo, 2006. "Magini, Giovanni Antonio." DBI 67:413–18.

Baroncini, Gabriele, 1981. "L'insegnamento della filosofia naturale nei collegi italiani dei Gesuiti (1610–1670): Un esempio di nuovo aristotelismo," in *La "Ratio Studiorum": Modelli culturali e pratiche educative dei Gesuiti in Italia tra Cinque e Seicento,* edited by Gian Paolo Brizzi. Rome, pp. 163–215.

Barsanti, Danilo, 1993. "I docenti e le cattedre dal 1543 al 1737," in *L'Università di Pisa,* part 2, pp. 505–66.

Baruchson-Arbib, Shifra, 2001. *La culture livresque des Juifs d'Italie à la fin de la Renais-*

*sance*. Presentation Jean-Pierre Rothschild, translated by Gabriel Roth and Patrick Guez. Paris.

Bazzotti, Ugo, 1977. "La pala della Trinità," in *Rubens a Mantova*. Mantova, Palazzo Ducale, 25 settembre / 20 novembre 1977. Milan, pp. 28–54.

Beccari, Camillus, 1913a. "Beatification and Canonization." CE 2:364–69.

Beccari, Camillus, 1913b. "The Blessed." CE 2:597–98.

Beghelli, Silvia, 1978. "Sulle orme del Fracastoro: Il carme medico di Antonio Possevino al tramonto del XVI secolo," in *Mantova e i Gonzaga*, pp. 387–92.

Belfanti, Carlo Marco, 1982. "Una città e la carestia: Mantova, 1590–1592." *Annali della Fondazione Luigi Einaudi* 16:99–141.

Belfanti, Carlo Marco, 1988. "Dalla città alla campagna: industrie tessili a Mantova tra carestie ed epidemie (1550–1630)." *Critica storica* 25:429–56.

Belfanti, Carlo Marco, 2005. *Calze e Maglie. Moda e innovazione nell'industria italiana della magliera dal Rinascimento a oggi*. Mantua.

Belfanti, Carlo Marco, 2006. "Hosiery Manufacturing in the Venetian Republic (16th–18th Centuries)," in *At the Centre of the Old World. Trade and Manufacturing in Venice and the Venetian Mainland, 1400–1800*, edited by Paola Lanaro. Toronto, pp. 245–70.

Belfanti, Carlo Marco, and Marzio Achille Romani, 1987. "Il Monferrato: una frontiera scomoda fra Mantova e Torino (1536–1707)," in *La frontiera da stato a nazione: Il caso Piemonte*, edited by Carlo Ossola, Claude Raffestin, and Mario Ricciardi. Rome, pp. 113–45.

Bellomo, Manlio, 1995. *The Common Legal Past of Europe 1000–1800*, translated by Lydia G. Cochrane. Washington.

Bellonci, Maria, 1956. *A Prince of Mantua. The Life and Times of Vincenzo Gonzaga*, translated by Stuart Hood. New York.

Bellonci, Maria, 1963. *Segreti dei Gonzaga: Il duca nel labirinto, Isabella fra i Gonzaga, Ritratto di famiglia*. Third edition. Milan.

Belloni, Luigi, 1970. "Italian Medical Education After 1600," in *The History of Medical Education*. An International Symposium held February 5–9, 1968. Edited by C. D. O'Malley. Berkeley, Los Angeles, and London, pp. 105–19.

Benzoni, Gino, 1995. "Federico II Gonzaga." DBI 45:710–22.

Benzoni, Gino, 1996. "Ferdinando Gonzaga." DBI 46:243–52

Benzoni, Gino, 1997. "Francesco IV Gonzaga." DBI 49:785–89.

Berti, Giuseppe, 1967. *Lo studio universitario parmense alla fine del Seicento*. Parma.

Biagi, Maria Grazia, 1980. "Gli statuti del Collegio Ferdinando di Pisa in età medicea." *Bollettino storico pisano* 49:87–118.

Biagioli, Mario, 1993. *Galileo, Courtier: The Practice of Science in the Culture of Absolutism*. Chicago and London.

Bianca, Concetta, 1982. "Claudini, Giulio Cesare." DBI 26:157–58.

Birocchi, Italo, 2002. *Alla ricerca dell'ordine. Fonti e cultura giuridica nell'eta moderna*. Turin.

Blackwell, Richard J., 1991. *Galileo, Bellarmine, and the Bible. Including a Translation of Foscarini's Letter on the Motion of the Earth*. Notre Dame, Ind., and London.

Boltanski, Ariane, 2006. *Les ducs de Nevers et l'etat royal: genèse d'un compromise (ca 1550–ca 1600)*. Geneva.

Bonansea, Bernardino M., 1969. *Tommaso Campanella: Renaissance Pioneer of Modern Thought*. Washington.

Borgato, Maria Teresa, 2002. "Niccolò Cabeo tra teoria ed esperimenti: le leggi del moto," in *Gesuiti e università*, pp. 361–85.

Bottereau, Georges, 2001. "Remond, François." DHCJ 4:3331.

Bouwsma, William J., 1968. *Venice and the Defense of Republican Liberty. Renaissance Values in the Age of the Counter Reformation*. Berkeley and Los Angeles.

Brizzi, Gian Paolo, 1980. "Educare il Principe, formare le *élites:* i Gesuiti e Ranuccio I Farnese," in *Università, Principe, Gesuiti: La politica farnesiana dell'istruzione a Parma e Piacenza (1545–1622)*. Rome, pp. 133–211.

Brizzi, Gian Paolo, 1988. "Matricole ed effettivi. Aspetti della presenza studentesca a Bologna fra Cinque e Seicento," in *Studi e memorie per la storia dell'Università di Bologna*, Nuova Serie, vol. 7: *Studenti e università dal XII al XIX secolo*, edited by Gian Paolo Brizzi and Antonio Ivan Pini. Bologna, pp. 225–59.

Brockliss, Laurence, 1996. "Curricula," in *A History of the University in Europe*. Vol. 2: *Universities in Early Modern Europe (1500–1800)*, edited by Hilde de Ridder-Symoens. Cambridge, pp. 563–620.

Broderick, James, 1961. *Robert Bellarmine: Saint and Scholar*. Westminster, Md.

Brunelli, Giampietro, 2001a. "Gonzaga, Ercole." DBI 57:711–22.

Brunelli, Giampietro, 2001b. "Gonzaga, Ferrante." DBI 57:734–44.

Brunet, Robert, et al., 2001. "Teología." DHCJ 4:3720–77.

Burke, Peter, 1969. "Tacitism," in *Tacitus*, edited by T. A. Dorey. New York, pp. 149–71.

Burke, Peter, 1991. "Tacitism, scepticism, and reason of state," in *The Cambridge History of Political Thought 1450–1700*, edited by J. H. Burns with the assistance of Mark Goldie. Cambridge, pp. 479–98.

Busacchi, Vincenzo, 1943. "Precisazioni sulla vita, sulle opere e sulle scoperte di Fabrizio Bartoletti (1587–1630)," in *Atti della riunione sociale in Firenze il 4 ottobre 1942*. Società italiana di storia delle scienze mediche e naturali. Sansepolcro, pp. 57–74.

Camerini, Paolo, 1962–63. *Annali dei Giunti*. Vol. 1 in 2 parts: *Venezia*. Florence.

Camerota, Michele, 1997. "Flaminio Papazzoni: un aristotelico bolognese maestro di Federico Borromeo e corrispondente di Galileo," in *Method and Order in Renaissance Philosophy of Nature: The Aristotle Commentary Tradition*, edited by Daniel A. Di Liscia, Eckhard Kessler, and Charlotte Methuen. Aldershot, pp. 271–300.

Cappelli, Adriano, 1983. *Cronologia, Cronografia e Calendario Perpetuo: Dal principio dell'era cristiana ai nostri giorni*. Fifth edition revised. Milan.

Carafa, Giuseppe, 1971. *De Gymnasio Romano et de eius professoribus*. 2 vols. Rome: Typis Antonii Fulgonii apud S. Eustachium, 1751; reprint Bologna.

Carella, Candida, 2007. *L'insegnamento della filosofia alla 'Sapienza' di Roma nel Seicento. Le cattedre e i maestri*. Florence.

Carpeggiani, Paolo, 1997. " . . . una fortezza quasi inespugnabile e che sarà la chiave di questo stato. . . . ," in *Stefano Guazzo e Casale tra Cinque e Seicento*. Atti del convegno di studi nel quarto centenario della morte, Casale Monferrato, 22–23 ottobre 1993, edited by Daniela Ferrari. Rome, pp. 241–71.

Casali, Elide, 1993. " 'Noceto nocente' e Il Ligure risvegliato. La polemica tra G. B. Noceto e T. Odorico." *Studi secenteschi* 34:287–329.

Cascio Pratilli, Giovanni, 1975. *L'università e il principe: Gli Studi di Siena e di Pisa tra rinascimento e controriforma.* Florence.

Castronovo, Valerio, 1977. "Carlo Emanuele I." DBI 20:326–40.

Catalano, Michele, 1917. *La fondazione e le prime vicende del Collegio dei Gesuiti in Catania (1556–1579).* Catania, 1917. Reprint from *Archivio Storico per la Sicilia Orientale* 13 (1916), 34–80; 14 (1917), 145–86.

Catalano, Michele, 1934. "L'Università di Catania nel Rinascimento," in *Storia della Università di Catania dalle origini ai giorni nostri.* Catania, pp. 3–98.

*CCC anniversario,* 1900. *CCC anniversario della Università di Messina (contributo storico).* Messina.

Cesareo, Francesco C., 2004. "The Jesuit Colleges in Rome under Everard Mercurian," in *The Mercurian Project,* pp. 607–44.

Cessi, Roberto, 1921–22. "L'Università giurista di Padova ed i Gesuiti alla fine del Cinquecento," in *Atti del Reale Istituto veneto di scienze, lettere ed arti.* Vol. 81, part 2, pp. 585–601.

Chambers, David S., 1987. "The 'bellissimo ingegno' of Ferdinando Gonzaga (1587–1626), Cardinal and Duke of Mantua." *Journal of the Warburg and Courtauld Institutes* 50 (1987):113–47.

Chiaudano, Mario, 1972. "I lettori dell'Università di Torino (1566–1580)," in *L'Università di Torino nei sec. XVI e XVII.* Turin, pp. 69–137.

Coniglio, Giuseppe, 1962. "Agricoltura ed artigianato mantovano nel secolo XVI," in *Studi in onore di Amintore Fanfani.* Vol. 4: *Evo moderno.* Milan, pp. 321–92.

Coniglio, Giuseppe, 1967. *I Gonzaga.* Varese.

Costa, Emilio, 1912. "Contributi alla storia dello Studio bolognese durante il secolo XVII." *Studi e memorie per la storia dell'Università di Bologna.* 3:1–88.

Cova, N., 1955. "Fabrizio Bartoletti (1576–1630)," in *Il cuore nella storia della medicina,* edited by Nicola Latronico. Milan, pp. 57–60.

Cozzi, Gaetano, 1958. *Il doge Nicolò Contarini: Ricerche sul patriziato veneziano agli inizi del Seicento.* Venice and Rome.

Cozzi, Gaetano, Michael Knapton, and Giovanni Scarabello, 1992. *La Repubblica di Venezia nell'età moderna. Dal 1517 alla fine della Repubblica.* Turin.

Crespi, Mario, 1964. "Bartoletti, Fabrizio." DBI 6:552–54.

Curzon, Gerald, 2003. *Wotton and His Worlds: Spying, Science, and Venetian Intrigues.* n. pl.

D'Addio, Mario, 1962. *Il pensiero politico di Gaspare Scioppio e il machiavellismo del Seicento.* Milan.

D'Alessandro, Alessandro, 1980. "Materiali per la storia dello *Studium* di Parma (1545–1622)," in *Università, Principe, Gesuiti: La politica farnesiana dell'istruzione a Parma e Piacenza (1545–1622).* Rome, pp. 15–95.

D'Amico, John F., 1983. *Renaissance Humanism in Papal Rome: Humanists and Churchmen on the Eve of the Reformation.* Baltimore and London.

D'Amico, John F., 1988. *Theory and Practice in Renaissance Textual Criticism: Beatus Rhenanus Between Conjecture and History.* Berkeley, Los Angeles, and London.

Davari, Stefano, 1876. *Notizie Storiche intorno allo Studio Pubblico ed ai maestri del secolo XV e XVI che tennero scuola in Mantova. Tratte dall'Archivio Storico Gonzaga di Mantova.* Mantua.

Dear, Peter, 1995. *Discipline & Experience: The Mathematical Way in the Scientific Revolution.* Chicago and London.

De Bernardin, Sandro, 1975. "La politica culturale della Repubblica di Venezia e l'Università di Padova nel XVII secolo." *Studi veneziani* 16:443–502.

Debus, Allen G., 1977. *The Chemical Philosophy: Paracelsian Science and Medicine in the Sixteenth and Seventeenth Centuries.* 2 vols. New York.

Debus, Allen G., 1981. "Severinus, Petrus." DSB 12:334–36.

Debus, Allen G., 1991. *The French Paracelsians: The Chemical Challenge to Medical and Scientific Tradition in Early Modern France.* Cambridge.

Del Gratta, Rodolfo, 1983. *Libri matricularum Studii Pisani 1543–1609.* Pisa.

Del Gratta, Rodolfo, 1993. "L'età della dominazione fiorentina (1406–1543)," in *L'Università di Pisa,* part 1, pp. 33–78.

Della Torre, Maria Assunta, 1968. *Studi su Cesare Cremonini: Cosmologia e logica nel tardo aristotelismo padovano.* Padua.

De Maddalena, Aldo, 1961. *Le finanze del ducato di Mantova all'epoca di Guglielmo Gonzaga.* Milan and Varese.

De Maddalena, Aldo, 1962. "L'industria tessile a Mantova nel '500 e all'inizio del '600. Prime indagini," in *Studi in onore di Amintore Fanfani.* Vol. 4: *Evo moderno.* Milan, pp. 607–53.

Deman, Th., 1936. "Probabilisme," in *Dictionnaire de Théologie Catholique.* Vol. 13, part 1. Paris, columns 417–619.

De Mattei, Rodolfo, 1963. *Il pensiero politico di Scipione Ammirato.* Milan.

De Renzi, Salvatore, 1846. *Storia della medicina in Italia.* Vol. 4. Naples.

De Rosa, Stefano, 1983. "Studi sull'Università di Pisa, II: La riforma e il paradosso: Girolamo da Sommaja Provveditore dello Studio Pisano (1614–1636)." *History of Universities* 3:101–25.

Dietrich, Thomas, 1999. *Die Theologie der Kirche bei Robert Bellarmin (1542–1621). Systematische Voraussetzungen des Kontroverstheologen.* Paderborn.

Di Napoli, Giovanni, 1963. *L'immortalità dell'anima nel Rinascimento.* Turin.

Di Rosa, Pietro, 2001. "De Rosis, Giovanni." DHCJ 2:1061.

Di Vona, Piero, 1968. *Studi sulla scolastica della Controriforma. L'esistenza e la sua distinzione metafisica dall'essenza.* Florence.

Donnelly, John Patrick, 1982. "The Jesuit College at Padua. Growth, Suppression, Attempts at Restoration: 1552–1606." AHSI 51:45–79.

Donnelly, John Patrick, 2001. "Toledo, Francisco de." DHCJ 4:3807–8.

Drake, Stillman, 1981. *Cause, Experiment, and Science. A Galilean Dialogue Incorporating a New English Translation of Galileo's 'Bodies That Stay atop Water, or Move in It.'* Chicago and London.

Drury, Martin, 1982. "Appendix of Authors and Works," in *The Cambridge History of Classical Literature.* Vol. 2: *Latin Literature,* edited by E. J. Kenney and W. V. Clausen. Cambridge, pp. 799–935.

Elorduy, Eleuterio, 2001. "Suárez, Francisco." DHCJ 4:3654–66.

Escalera, José Martínez de la, 2001. "Soares, Cipriano." DHCJ 4:3593.

Etter, Else-Lilly, 1966. *Tacitus in der Geistesgeschichte des 16. und 17. Jahrhunderts.* Basel and Stuttgart.

Evans, R. J. W., 1984. *Rudolf II and His World: A Study in Intellectual History 1576–1612.* Oxford.

Fabroni, Angelo, 1971. *Historiae Academiae Pisanae.* 3 vols. Pisa, 1791–95; reprint Bologna.

Facciolati, Jacopo, 1978. *Fasti Gymnasii Patavini.* 3 vols. Padua, 1757; reprint in one volume, Bologna.

Fanning, William H. W., 1913. "Pension, Ecclesiastical." CE 11:45–46.

Fantuzzi, Giovanni, 1965. *Notizie degli scrittori bolognesi.* Vol. 1. Bologna, 1781; reprint Bologna.

Fasolt, Constantin, 2007. "Hermann Conring and the European History of Law," in *Politics and Reformations: Histories and Reformations.* Essays in Honor of Thomas A. Brady, Jr., edited by Christopher Ocker, Michael Printy, Peter Starenko, and Peter Wallace. Leiden and Boston, pp. 113–34.

Favaro, Antonio, 1877–78. "Lo Studio di Padova e la Compagnia di Gesù sul finire del secolo decimosesto." *Atti del Reale Istituto Veneto di scienze lettere ed arti,* serie 5, vol. 2: 401–535.

Favaro, Antonio, 1911. "Nuovi documenti sulla vertenza tra lo Studio di Padova e la Compagnia di Gesù sul finire del secolo decimosesto." *Nuovo archivio veneto,* serie 3, 21:89–100.

Favaro, Antonio, 1966. *Galileo Galilei e lo Studio di Padova.* 2 vols. Florence, 1882; reprint Padua.

Feldhay, Rivka, 1999. "The Cultural Field of Jesuit Science," in *The Jesuits,* pp. 107–30.

Fenlor, Iain, 1980–82. *Music and Patronage in Sixteenth-Century Mantua.* 2 vols. Cambridge.

Fernandez Alvarez, Manuel, 1955. *Don Gonzalo Fernández de Córdoba y la Guerra de Sucesión de Mantua y del Monferrato (1627–1629).* Madrid.

Ferrari, Marco, 1982. "Alcuni vie di diffusione in Italia di idee e di testi di Paracelso," in *Scienze, credenze occulte, livelli di cultura.* Convegno Internazionale di Studi. Firenze, 26–30 giugno 1980. Florence, pp. 21–29.

Ferri, Andrea, and Mario Giberti, 1997. *I gesuiti a Imola e le scuole cittadine nel complesso di Sant'Agata.* 2 vols. Bologna.

Ferri, Edgarda, 1991. *Luigi Gonzaga 1568–1591.* Milan.

Findlen, Paula, 1994. *Possessing Nature: Museums, Collecting, and Scientific Culture in Early Modern Italy.* Berkeley, Los Angeles, and London.

Fiocca, Alessandra, 2002. "Ferrara e i gesuiti periti in materia d'acque," in *Gesuiti e università,* pp. 339–59.

Fois, Mario, 2000. "I Gesuiti e gli studi superiori (1550–1650)," in *Alle origini dell'Università dell'Aquila. Cultura, università, collegi gesuitici all'inizio dell'età moderna in Italia meridionale.* Atti del convegno internazionale di studi promosso dalla Compagnia di Gesù e dall'Università dell'Aquila nel IV centenario dell'istituzione dell'*Aquilanum Collegium* (1596). L'Aquila, 8–11 novembre 1995. Edited by Filippo Iappelli S. I. and Ulderico Parente. Rome, pp. 57–89.

Forni, G. G., 1948. *La insegnamento della chirurgia nello Studio di Bologna dalle origini a tutto il secolo XIX.* Bologna.

Franchini et al., 1979. Dario A. Franchini, Renzo Margonari, Giuseppe Olmi, Rodolfo Signorini, Attilio Zanca, and Chiara Tellini Perina. *La scienza a corte. Collezionismo eclettico natura e immagine a Mantova fra Rinascimento e Manierismo.* Rome.

Frijhoff, Willem, 1996. "Patterns," in *A History of the University in Europe*. Vol. 2: *Universities in Early Modern Europe (1500–1800)*, edited by Hilde De Ridder-Symoens. Cambridge, pp. 43–110.

Galluzzi, Paolo, 1982. "Motivi paracelsiani nella Toscana di Cosimo II e di Don Antonio dei Medici: alchimia, medicina 'chimica' e riforma del sapere," in *Scienze, credenze occulte, livelli di cultura*. Convegno Internazionale di Studi. Firenze, 26–30 giugno 1980. Florence, pp. 31–62.

Garbari, Tomasi, and Tosi, 1991. Fabio Garbari, Lucia Tongiorgi Tomasi, and Alessandro Tosi. *Giardino dei Semplici. L'Orto botanico di Pisa dal XVI al XX secolo*. Pisa.

Garin, Eugenio, 1966. *Storia della filosofia italiana*. 3 vols. Turin.

Gash, John, 1996. "Caravaggio, Michelangelo Merisi da," in *Dictionary of Art*, edited by Jane Turner. Vol. 5. London and New York, pp. 702–22.

Gavagna, Veronica, 2002. "I gesuiti e la polemica sul vuoto: il contributo di Paolo Casati," in *Gesuiti e università*, pp. 325–38.

Giachi, Gualberto, 2001. "Gonzaga, Luis." DHCJ 2:1779–80.

Giacon, Carlo, 1944–50. *La seconda scolastica*. 3 vols. Milan.

*Giambattista Riccioli*, 2002. *Giambattista Riccioli e il merito scientifico dei Gesuii nell'età barocca*, edited by Maria Teresa Borgato. Florence.

Gilbert, Maurice, 2001. "Biblia sagrada." DHCJ 1:437–43.

Giordano, Silvano, 2006. "Luigi (Alvigi) Gonzaga, santo." DBI 66:499–502.

Giusti, Renato, 1963. "Dalla presa di Mantova (1797) alla prima guerra di indipendenza (1848–49)," in *Mantova: La Storia*. Vol. 3: *Da Guglielmo III duca alla fine della seconda guerra mondiale*. Mantua, pp. 261–526.

Giustiniani, Lorenzo, 1787–88. *Memorie istoriche degli scrittori legali del Regno di Napoli*. 3 vols. Naples.

*I Gonzaga e l'Impero*, 2005. *I Gonzaga e l'Impero. Itinerari dello spettacolo*. Con una selezione di materiali dall'Archivio informatico Herla (1560–1630), edited by Umberto Artioli and Cristina Grazioli. Florence.

González, Justo L., 1975. *A History of Christian Thought*. Vol. 3: *From the Protestant Reformation to the Twentieth Century*. Nashville and New York.

Goodyear, F. R. D., 1982. "History and Biography," in *The Cambridge History of Classical Literature*. Vol. 2: *Latin Literature*, edited by E. J. Kenney and W. V. Clausen. Cambridge, pp. 639–66.

Grendler, Paul F., 1979. "The *Tre Savii sopra Eresia*, 1547–1605: A Prosopographical Study." *Studi veneziani*, N. S., 3:283–340. Also in Grendler, 1981, Study X.

Grendler, Paul F., 1981. *Culture and Censorship in Late Renaissance Italy and France*. London.

Grendler, Paul F., 1989. *Schooling in Renaissance Italy: Literacy and Learning, 1300–1600*. Baltimore and London.

Grendler, Paul F., 1990. "The Leaders of the Venetian State, 1540–1609: A Prosopographical Analysis." *Studi veneziani*, N.S., 19:35–85. Also in Grendler, 2006b, Study XI.

Grendler, Paul F., 2002. *The Universities of the Italian Renaissance*. Baltimore and London.

Grendler, Paul F., 2004. "Italian Schools and University Dreams during Mercurian's Generalate," in *The Mercurian Project*, pp. 483–522.

Grendler, Paul F., 2006a. "The Attempts of the Jesuits to Enter Italian Universities in the Sixteenth and Seventeenth Centuries," in Grendler, 2006b, Study VI, pp. 1–21. For the Italian version see Grendler, "I tentativi dei gesuiti d'entrare nelle università italiani tra '500 e '600," in *Gesuiti e università*, pp. 37–51.

Grendler, Paul F., 2006b. *Renaissance Education Between Religion and Politics*. Aldershot, and Burlington, VT.

Grendler, Paul F., 2008. "Italian Biblical Humanism and the Papacy, 1515–1535," in *Biblical Humanism and Scholasticism in the Age of Erasmus*, edited by Erika Rummel. Leiden, pp. 227–76.

Grendler, Paul F., "Fencing, Playing Ball." "Fencing, Playing Ball, and Dancing in Italian Renaissance Universities," in *Athletes and Athletics, 1000–1650*, edited by John M. McClelland and Konrad Eisenbichler. Toronto, in press.

Grillo, Enzo, 1968. "Biancani, Giuseppe." DBI 10:33–35.

Grmek, M. D., 1981. "Santorio, Santorio." DSB 12:101–4.

Grosso, Michele, and Maria Franca Mellano, 1957. *La controriforma nella arcidiocesi di Torino (1558–1610)*. Vol. 2: *La visita apostolica di Mons. Angelo Peruzzi (1584–1585)*. Vatican City.

Hallman, Barbara McClung, 1985. *Italian Cardinals, Reform, and the Church as Property*. Berkeley, Los Angeles, and London.

Harris, Steven J., 1995. "Les chaires de mathématiques," in *Les jésuites*, pp. 239–61.

Hellyer, Marcus, 2005. *Catholic Physics: Jesuit Natural Philosophy in Early Modern Germany*. Notre Dame, Ind.

Hengst, Karl, 1981. *Jesuiten an Universitäten und Jesuitenuniversitäten: Zur Geschichte der Universitäten in der Oberdeutschen und Rheinischen Provinz der Gesellschaft Jesu im Zeitalter der konfessionellen Auseinandersetzung*. Paderborn.

Hintzsche, Erich, 1981. "Vesling, Johann." DSB 14:12–13.

Homann, Frederick A., 2001. "Clavius, Christophorus." DHCJ 1:825–26.

Höpfl, Harro, 2004. *Jesuit Political Thought. The Society of Jesus and the State, c. 1540–1630*. Cambridge.

Ingegno, Alfonso, 1972. "Cabeo, Niccolò." DBI 15:686–88.

Jarcho, Saul, 1980. *The Concept of Heart Failure from Avicenna to Albertini*. Translations, commentaries, and an essay by Saul Jarcho. Cambridge, Mass., and London.

Jensen, De Lamar, 1999. "Espionage," in *Encyclopedia of the Renaissance*, edited by Paul F. Grendler et al. 6 vols. New York, 2:291–93.

*Les jésuites*, 1995. *Les jésuites a la Renaissance. Système éducatif et production du savoir*, edited by Luce Giard. Paris.

Keenan, James F., S.J., 2004. "The Birth of Jesuit Casuistry: *Summum casuum conscientiae, sive de instructione sacerdotum, libri septem* by Francisco de Toledo (1532–1596)," in *The Mercurian Project*, pp. 461–82.

Knebel, Sven K., 2000. *Wille, Würfel und Wahrscheinlichkeit. Das System der moralischen Notwendigkeit in der Jesuitenscholastik 1550–1700*. Hamburg.

Kuhn, Heinrich C., 1996. *Venetischer Aristotelismus im Ende der aristotelischen Welt: Aspekte der Welt und des Denkens des Cesare Cremonini (1550–1631)*. Frankfurt am Main.

*Libri ebraici a Mantova*, 1996–2003. *Libri ebraici a Mantova*, edited by Giulio Busi. 4 vols. Fiesole.

Lines, David A., 2002. *Aristotle's Ethics in the Italian Renaissance (ca. 1300–1650). The Universities & the Problem of Moral Education.* Leiden, Boston, and Köln.

Lohr, Charles H., 1976. "Jesuit Aristotelianism and Sixteenth-Century Metaphysics," in *Paradosis: Studies in Memory of Edwin A. Quain.* New York, pp. 203–20.

Lohr, Charles H., 1980. "Renaissance Latin Aristotle Commentaries: Authors Pi-Sm." *Renaissance Quarterly* 33:623–734.

Lohr, Charles H., 1995. "Les jésuites et l'aristotélisme du XVI$^e$ siècle," in *Les jésuites,* pp. 79–91.

Loomie, A. J., 2004. "Wotton, Henry," in *Oxford Dictionary of National Biography.* 60 vols. Oxford, vol. 60, pp. 377–82.

Lukács, Ladislaus, S.J., and Giuseppe Cosentino, 1999. *Church, Culture & Curriculum. Theology and Mathematics in the Jesuit Ratio Studiorum,* translated and edited with an introduction by Frederick A. Homann, S.J. Philadelphia.

Luzio, Alessandro, 1974. *La Galleria dei Gonzaga venduta all'Inghilterra nel 1627–28. Documenti degli archivi di Mantova e Londra.* Milan, 1913; reprint Rome.

Mainardi, Antonio, 1871. *Dello studio pubblico di Mantova e de' professori che vi hanno insegnato a tutto l'anno MDCCCXLVIII. Cenni storico-biografici.* Mantua.

Majkowski, Josef, and Fergus O'Donoghue, 2001. "Kostka, Estanislao." DHCJ 3:2219–20.

Malacarne, Giancarlo, 2007. *I Gonzaga di Mantova: una stirpe per una capitale europea.* Vol. 4: *Il duca re: Splendore e declino da Vincenzo I a Vincenzo II (1587–1627).* Modena.

Mancia, Anita, 2000. "La *Ratio studiorum*: genesi e sviluppo in relazione con alcuni ordinamenti coevi fino al 1599," in *L'Università dell'Aquila,* pp. 29–47.

Mango Tomei, Elsa, 1976. *Gli studenti dell'Università di Pisa sotto il regime granducale.* Pisa.

*Mantova e i Gonzaga,* 1978. *Mantova e i Gonzaga nella civiltà del Rinascimento.* Atti del convegno organizzato dall'Accademia Nazionale dei Lincei e dall'Accademia Virgiliana con la collaborazione della città di Mantova sotto l'altro patronato del Presidente della Repubblica Italiana Giovanni Leone. Segrate.

*Mantova: Le lettere,* 1962. *Mantova: Le lettere.* Vol. 2: *L'esperienza umanistica, L'età isabelliana, Autunno del Rinascimento mantovano,* edited by Emilio Faccioli, with a preface by Lanfranco Caretti. Mantua.

*Mantova: La storia,* 1963. *Mantova: La storia.* Vol. 3: *Da Guglielmo III duca alla fine della seconda guerra mondiale,* edited by Leonardo Mazzoldi, Renato Giusti, and Rinaldo Salvadori, with a preface by Ugo Nicolini. Mantua.

Marongiu, Antonio, 1948. "L'Università di Macerata nel periodo delle origini." *Annali della Università di Macerata* 17:3–73.

Marrara, Danilo, 1993. "L'età medicea (1543–1737)," in *L'Università di Pisa,* part 1, pp. 79–190.

Martellozzo Forin, Elda, 1999. "Conti palatini e lauree conferite per privilegio: L'esempio padovano del sec. XV." *Annali di storia delle università italiane* 3:79–119.

Maryks, Robert A., 2008. *Saint Cicero and the Jesuits. The Influence of the Liberal Arts on the Adoption of Moral Probabilism.* Aldershot, U.K., Burlington, Vt., and Rome.

Mazzoldi, Leonardo, 1963. "Da Guglielmo III duca alla fine della prima dominazione austriaca," in *Mantova: La storia,* pp. 3–257.

Mazzuchelli, Giovanni Maria, 1758. *Gli scrittori d'Italia cioè notizie storiche e critiche intorno alle vite e agli scritti dei letterati italiani.* Vol. 2, part 1. Brescia.

Medici, Michele, 1857. *Compendio storico della scuola anatomica di Bologna: dal rinascimento delle scienze e delle lettere a tutto il secolo xviii con un paragone fra la sua antichità e quella delle scuole di Salerno e di Padova.* Bologna.

Michel, Suzanne, and Paul-Henri Michel, 1967–84. *Répertoire des ouvrages imprimés en langue italienne au XVII$^e$ siècle conservés dans les bibliothèques de France.* 8 vols. Paris.

Mobley, Susan Spruell, 2004. "The Jesuits at the University of Ingolstadt," in *The Mercurian Project,* pp. 213–48.

Mondin, Battista, 1996. *Storia della Teologia.* Vol. 3: *Epoca Moderna.* Bologna.

Moran, Bruce T., 1991. *Chemical Pharmacy Enters the University: Johannes Hartmann and the Didactic Care of Chymiatria in the Early Seventeenth Century.* Madison.

Moran, Bruce T., 2005. *Distilling Knowledge: Alchemy, Chemistry, and the Scientific Revolution.* Cambridge, Mass., and London.

Moschea, Rosario, 1991. "Istruzione superiore e autonomie locali nella Sicilia moderna: Apertura e sviluppi dello *Studium Urbis Messanae* (1590–1641)." *Archivio storico messinese* 59:75–221.

Mozzarelli, Cesare, 1978. "Il senato di Mantova: origine e funzioni," in *Mantova e i Gonzaga,* pp. 65–98.

Mozzarelli, Cesare, 1987. *Mantova e i Gonzaga dal 1382 al 1707.* Turin.

Müller, Rainer A., 2002. "The 'Jesuitensystem' in the university structure of early modern Germany," in *Gesuiti e università,* pp. 95–108.

Multhauf, Robert, 1956. "The Significance of Distillation in Renaissance Medical Chemistry." *Bulletin of the History of Medicine* 30:329–45.

Munitiz, Joseph A., S.J., 2007. "St. Aloysius Gonzaga: Autograph Letter in Manresa House Novitiate." AHSI 76:139–49.

Murphy, Paul V., 2007. *Ruling Peacefully: Cardinal Ercole Gonzaga and Patrician Reform in Sixteenth-Century Italy.* Washington.

Navarrini, Roberto, 1977. "I documenti rubensiani conservati nell'Archivio di Stato di Mantova," in *Rubens a Mantova.* Mantova, Palazzo Ducale, 25 settembre / 20 novembre 1977. Milan, pp. 54–64.

Nelles, Paul, 2007. "*Libros de papel, libri bianchi, libri papyracei.* Note-taking Techniques and the Role of Student Notebooks in the Early Jesuit Colleges." AHSI 76:75–112.

Novarese, Daniela, 1994. *Istituzioni politiche e studi di diritto fra Cinque e Seicento: Il Messanense Studium Generale tra politica gesuitica e istanze egemoniche cittadine.* Milan.

Oakley, Francis, 2003. *The Conciliarist Tradition: Constitutionalism in the Catholic Church 1300–1870.* Oxford.

Ojetti, Benedetto, 1913. "Roman Curia." CE 13:147–54.

Oliger, Livarius, 1913. "Scala Sancta." CE 13:505–6.

O'Malley, John W., 1993. *The First Jesuits.* Cambridge, Mass., and London.

O'Malley, John W., 2004. "Concluding remarks," in *I Gesuiti e la Ratio Studiorum,* edited by Manfred Hinz, Roberto Richi, and Danilo Zardin. Rome, pp. 509–21.

Ongaro, Giuseppe, 2001. "Medicina," in *L'Università di Padova. Otto secoli di storia,* edited by Piero Del Negro. Padua, pp. 153–93.

Oresko, Robert, and David Parrott, 1997. "The Sovereignty of Monferrato and the Citadel of Casale as European Problems in the Early Modern Period," in *Stefano Guazzo e Casale tra Cinque e Seicento.* Atti del convegno di studi nel quarto centenario della morte, Casale Monferrato, 22–23 ottobre 1993. Edited by Daniela Ferrari. Rome, pp. 11–86.

Padberg, John W., S.J., 2000. "Development of the *Ratio Studiorum,*" in *The Jesuit Ratio Studiorum: 400th Anniversary Perspectives,* edited by Vincent J. Duminuco, S.J. New York, pp. 80–100.

Pagel, Walter, 1981. "Paracelsus, Theophrastus Philippus Aureolus Bombastus von Hohenheim." DSB 10:304–13.

Pagel, Walter, 1982. *Paracelsus: An Introduction to Philosophical Medicine in the Era of the Renaissance.* Second revised edition. Basel.

Pagel, Walter, 1986. *From Paracelsus to Van Helmont: Studies in Renaissance Medicine and Science,* edited by Marianne Winder. London.

Pagel, Walter, and Pyarali Rattansi, 1964. "Vesalius and Paracelsus." *Medical History* 8:309–28. Also in Pagel, 1986, Study VII.

Paglia, Enrico, 1886. *Il Dottor Jacopo Antonio Marta giureconsulto napoletano giusta i documenti inediti degli archivi mantovani.* Mantua. Reprinted from *Atti della R. Accademia Virgiliana di Mantova,* 1885–86, no pag.

Paitoni, Giovanni Battista, 1740. "De vita ac Scriptis Fabricii Bartholetti medici bononiensis commentarius," in *Raccolta d'opuscoli scientifici e filologici,* edited by Angelo Calogerà. Venice, pp. 387–410.

*Il palazzo degli studi,* 1998. *Il palazzo degli studi. Appunti per una storia dell'istruzione superiore a Mantova. Luoghi e vicende dal Collegio dei Gesuiti al Liceo Ginnasio "Virgilio,"* edited by Ugo Bazzotti and Daniela Ferrari. Second edition. Mantua.

Palmer, Richard, 1981. "Physicians and the state in post-mediaeval Italy," in *The Town and State Physician in Europe from the Middle Ages to the Enlightenment,* edited by Andrew W. Russell. Wolfenbütteler Forschungen, 17. Wolfenbüttel, pp. 47–61.

Palmer, Richard, 1985. "Pharmacy in the Republic of Venice in the Sixteenth Century," in *The Medical Renaissance of the Sixteenth Century,* edited by A. Wear, R. K. French, and I.M. Lonie. Cambridge, pp. 100–17, 303–12.

Pannella, Liliana, 1965. "Basile, Andreana." DBI 7:70–72.

*Paracelsus,* 1998. *Paracelsus: The Man and His Reputation, His Ideas and Their Transformation,* edited by Ole Peter Grell. Leiden.

Parisi, Susan Helen, 1989. "Ducal Patronage of Music in Mantua, 1587–1627: An Archival Study." Ph. D. dissertation, University of Illinois at Urbana-Champaign.

Parrott, David, 1997a. "The Mantuan Succession, 1627–31: A Sovereignty Dispute in Early Modern Europe." *The English Historical Review* 112:20–65.

Parrott, David, 1997b. "A *prince souverain* and the French crown: Charles de Nevers, 1580–1637," in *Royal and Republican Sovereignty in Early Modern Europe. Essays in memory of Ragnhild Hatton,* edited by Robert Oresko, G. C. Gibbs, and H. M. Scott. Cambridge, pp. 149–87.

Pastor, Ludwig von, 1891–1953. *The History of the Popes from the Close of the Middle Ages,* translated by F. I. Antrobus et al. 40 vols. London and St. Louis.

Patterson, W. B., 1997. *King James VI and I and the Reunion of Christendom.* Cambridge.

Pazzini, Adalberto, 1978. "La medicina alla corte dei Gonzaga a Mantova." In *Mantova e i Gonzaga,* pp. 291–351.

Pellizzer, Sonia, 1992. "Eleonora d'Asburgo." DBI 42:419–22.

Pescasio, Luigi, 1971. *L'arte della stampa a Mantova nei secoli XV–XVI–XVII.* Mantua.

Pescasio, Luigi, 1997. *Federico II Gonzaga: V marchese–I duca.* Suzzara (Mantua).

Pescasio, Luigi, 2000. *Don Ferrante Gonzaga: Principe di Molfetta, Signore di Guastalla, Vicerè di Sicilia, Governatore di Milano, Stratega dell'Imperatore Carlo V°*. Mantua.
Petrucci, Armando, 1960. "Accarisi, Giacomo." DBI 1:69–70.
Pignatelli, Antonio M., 2001. "Cepari, Virgilio." DHCJ 1:733–34.
Pinckaers, Servais, 1995. *The Sources of Christian Ethics*, translated from the third edition by Sr. Mary Thomas Noble. Washington, D.C.
Pirri, Pietro, 1955. *Giovanni Tristano e i primordi della architettura gesuitica*. Rome.
Pirri, Pietro, and Pietro Di Rosa, 1975. "Il P. Giovanni De Rosis (1538–1610) e lo sviluppo dell'edilizia gesuitica." AHSI 44:3–104.
Polverini Fosi, Irene, 1984. "Crescenzi, Marcello." DBI 30:641–45.
Poppi, Antonino, 1993. "Cremonini, Galilei e gli inquisitori del Santo a Padova." *Il Santo: Rivista Antoniana di storia dottrina arte*, serie 2, 33, fascicles 1–2: 5–112.
Porter, Roy, 1996. "The Scientific Revolution and Universities," in *A History of the University in Europe*. Vol. 2: *Universities in Early Modern Europe (1500–1800)*, edited by Hilda De Ridder-Symoens. Cambridge, pp. 531–62.
*Profiles in Cardiology*, 2003. *Profiles in Cardiology*, edited by J. Willis Hurst, C. Richard Conti, and W. Bruce Fye. Mahwah, N.J.
Pulidori, Fernando, 2004. "Chimica. Sua istituzione e primi sviluppi nell'Università Pontificia di Ferrara (1742–1860)." *Annali di storia delle università italiane* 8:165–84.
Putelli, Raffaello, 1911. *Il Duca Vincenzo I Gonzaga e l'interdetto di Paolo V a Venezia*. Venice.
Quazza, Romolo, 1922. *Mantova e Monferrato nella politica europea alla vigilia della guerra per la successione (1624–1627) da documenti inediti tratti dall'Archivio Gonzaga*. Mantua.
Quazza, Romolo, 1926. *La guerra per la successione di Mantova e del Monferrato (1628–1631). (Da documenti inediti)*. 2 vols. Mantua.
Quazza, Romolo, 1930. *Margherita di Savoia, duchessa di Mantova e vice-regina del Portogallo*. Turin.
Quazza, Romolo, 1933. *Mantova attraveso i secoli*. Mantua.
Quazza, Romolo, 1950. *Preponderanza spagnuola (1559–1700)*. Second edition. Milan.
Queller, Donald E., 1986. *The Venetian Patriciate: Reality versus Myth*. Urbana and Chicago.
Raviola, Blythe Alice, 2003. *Il Monferrato gonzaghesco: Istituzioni ed élites di un microstato (1536–1708)*. Florence.
Reeve, L. J., 2004. "Carleton, Dudley," in *Dictionary of National Biography*. 60 vols. Oxford, vol. 10, pp. 105–8.
Reinhard, Wolfgang, 1969. "Papst Paul V. und seine Nuntien im Kampf gegen die *Supplicatio ad Imperatorem* und ihren Verfasser Giacomo Antonio Marta 1613–1620." *Archiv für Reformationsgeschichte* 60:190–238.
Reinhard, Wolfgang, 1974. *Papstfinanz und Nepotismus unter Paul V. (1605–1621): Studien und Quellen zur Struktur und zu quantitativen Aspekten des päpstlichen Herrschaftssystems*. 2 vols. Stuttgart.
Renazzi, Filippo Maria, 1971. *Storia dell'Università degli Studj di Roma*. 4 vols. Rome, 1803–6; reprint Bologna.
Renzi, Paolo, 1985. "*Taciti Annales, Mureti schola*: Note sulla didattica della storia allo Studium Romano nel secondo Cinquecento." *Annali del dipartimento di scienze storiche e sociali* 4:27–59.

Robertson, Clare, 1999. "Two Farnese Cardinals and the Question of Jesuit Taste," in *The Jesuits*, pp. 134–47.
Rock, P. M. J., 1913. "Age, Canonical." CE 1:206–9.
Romano, Andrea, 1992. " 'Primum ac prototypum collegium Societatis Iesu' e 'Messanense Studium Generale:' L'insegnamento universitario a Messina nel Cinquecento," in *La pedagogia della Compagnia di Gesù*. Atti del Convegno Internazionale, Messina 14–16 novembre 1991. Edited by F. Guerello and P. Schiavone. Messina, pp. 33–72.
Romano, Andrea, 2002. "Il *Messanense Collegium Prototypum Societatis Iesu*," in *Gesuiti e università*, pp. 79–94.
Romano, Antonella, 1999. *La contre-réforme mathématique. Constitution et diffusion d'une culture mathématique Jésuite à la Renaissance (1540–1640)*. Rome.
Romano, Antonella, 2006. "Teaching Mathematics in Jesuit Schools: Programs, Course Content, and Classroom Practices" in *The Jesuits II: Cultures, Sciences, and the Arts 1540–1773*, edited by John W. O'Malley, S.J., Gauvin Alexander Bailey, Steven J. Harris, and T. Frank Kennedy, S.J. Toronto, Buffalo, and London, pp. 355–70.
Rose, Paul Lawrence, and Stillman Drake, 1971. "The Pseudo-Aristotelian *Questions of Mechanics* in Renaissance Culture." *Studies in the Renaissance* 18:65–104.
Rurale, Flavio, 1992. *I gesuiti a Milano: Religione e politica nel secondo Cinquecento*. Rome.
Rurale, Flavio, 1997. "I Gesuiti a Mantova (secoli XVI–XVIII)," in Gorzoni, 1997, pp. 13–50.
Rurale, Flavio, 2002. "Milano e Mantova: conflitti politici e culturali nei collegi-università della Compagnia di Gesù," in *Gesuiti e università*, pp. 53–68.
Ryan, Edward A., 1936. *The Historical Scholarship of Saint Bellarmine*. New York.
Sadoul, Jacques, 1972. *Alchemists and Gold*, translated by Olga Sieveking. New York.
Saitta, Giuseppe, 1961. *Il pensiero italiano nell'umanesimo e nel Rinascimento*. Vol. 2: *Il Rinascimento*. Florence.
Sangalli, Maurizio, 1999. *Cultura, politica e religione nella Repubblica di Venezia tra Cinque e Seicento. Gesuiti e somaschi a Venezia*. Venice.
Sangalli, Maurizio, 2001. *Università accademie gesuiti. Cultura e religione a Padova tra Cinque e Seicento*. Padua.
Savio, Pietro, 1955. "Il nunzio a Venezia dopo l'interdetto." *Archivio veneto*, serie 5, vol. 56–57: 55–110.
Scaduto, Mario, 1948. "Le origini dell'Università di Messina." AHSI 17:102–59.
Scaduto, Mario, 1968. *Catalogo dei Gesuiti d'Italia 1540–1565*. Rome.
Scaduto, Mario, 1974. *Epoca di Giacomo Lainez, 1556–1565. L'azione*. Rome.
Scaduto, Mario, 1992. *L'opera di Francesco Borgia, 1565–1572*. Rome.
Scaduto, Mario, 2001. "Possevino, Antonio." DHCJ 4:3201–3.
Schellhase, Kenneth C., 1976. *Tacitus in Renaissance Political Thought*. Chicago and London.
Schizzerotto, Giancarlo, 1979. *Rubens a Mantova: Fra Gesuiti, principi e pittori. Con spigolature sul suo soggiorno italiano (1600–1608)*. Mantua.
Schmitt, Charles B., 1972. "The Faculty of Arts at Pisa at the Time of Galileo." *Physis* 14:243–72. Also in Schmitt, 1981, Study IX.
Schmitt, Charles, B., 1980. *Cesare Cremonini: Un aristotelico al tempo di Galilei*. Centro Tedesco di Studi Veneziani. Quaderni, 16. Venice. Also in Schmitt, 1984, Study XI.

Schmitt, Charles B., 1981. *Studies in Renaissance Philosophy and Science.* London.
Schmitt, Charles B., 1983a. "Galilei and the Seventeenth-Century Textbook Tradition," in *Novità celesti e crisi del sapere.* Atti del convegno internazionale di studi Galileiani, edited by Paolo Galluzzi. Florence, pp. 217–28. Also in Schmitt, 1989, Study XI.
Schmitt, Charles B., 1983b. "The *Studio pisano* in the European Cultural Context of the Sixteenth Century," in *Firenze e la Toscana dei Medici nell'Europa del '500.* Vol. 1. Florence, pp. 19–36. Also in Schmitt 1989, Study X.
Schmitt, Charles B., 1984. *The Aristotelian Tradition and Renaissance Universities.* London.
Schmitt, Charles B., 1988. "The Rise of the Philosophical Textbook," in *The Cambridge History of Renaissance Philosophy,* edited by Charles B. Schmitt, Quentin Skinner, Eckhard Kessler, and Jill Kraye. Cambridge, pp. 792–804.
Schmitt, Charles B., 1989. *Reappraisals in Renaissance Thought,* edited by Charles Webster. London.
Schurhammer, Georg, 1973. *Francis Xavier: His Life, His Times,* translated by M. Joseph Costelloe. Vol. 1: *Europe (1506–1541).* Rome.
Segala, Vanna, 1993–94. "La Peste del 1630 a Mantova." Tesi di laurea in storia moderna, Università degli Studi di Bologna, Facoltà di scienze politiche. Indirizzo Storico-Politico. Anno Accademico 1993–94. Copy in ASM.
Sella, Domenico, 1968. *Salari e lavoro nell'edilizia lombarda durante il secolo XVII.* Pavia.
Silverman, Mark E., 2003. "William Heberden and Some Account of a Disorder of the Breast," in *Profiles in Cardiology,* pp. 48–50.
Simeoni, Luigi, 1940. *Storia della Università di Bologna.* Vol. 2: *L'età moderna (1500–1888).* Bologna.
Simmons, Alison, 1999. "Jesuit Aristotelian Education: The *De anima* Commentaries," in *The Jesuits,* pp. 522–37.
Simonsohn, Shlomo, 1977. *History of the Jews in the Duchy of Mantua.* Jerusalem.
Siraisi, Nancy G., 1987. *Avicenna in Renaissance Italy. The Canon and Medical Teaching in Italian Universities after 1500.* Princeton, N.J.
Smith, Logan Pearsall, 1907. *The Life and Letters of Sir Henry Wotton.* 2 vols. Oxford.
Solà, Francisco de Paula, 2001. "Perera, Benito." DHCJ 3:3088–89.
Sommervogel, Carlos, 1890–1932. *Bibliothèque de la Compagnie de Jésus: nouvelle édition.* 11 vols. Bruxelles and Paris.
Spagnesi, Enrico, 1993. "Il diritto," in *L'Università di Pisa,* part 1, pp. 191–258.
Strobel, Ferdinand, 2001. "Soldati, Giorgio." DHCJ 4:3602–03.
Tacchi Venturi, Pietro, 1950. *Storia della Compagnia di Gesù in Italia.* Vol. 2, part 1: *Dalla nascita del fondatore alla solenne approvazione dell'Ordine (1491–1540).* Rome.
Tamalio, Raffaele, 2001a. "Gonzaga, Ferrante." DBI 57:744–46.
Tamalio, Raffaele, 2001b. "Gonzaga, Rodolfo." DBI 57:840–42.
Tamalio, Raffaele, 2008. "Maria Gonzaga." DBI 70:201–3.
Tamalio, Raffaele, and Paola Besutti, 2003. "Guglielmo Gonzaga, duca di Mantova e del Monferrato." DBI 61:1–10.
Tellechea, José Ignacio, 2001. "Maldonado, Juan." DHCJ 3:2484–85.
Terpstra, Nicholas, 1995. *Lay Confraternities and Civic Religion in Renaissance Bologna.* Cambridge.
Thorndike, Lynn, 1923–58. *A History of Magic and Experimental Science.* 8 vols. New York and London.

Toffanin, Giuseppe, 1921. *Machiavelli e il 'Tacitismo.' La 'Politica storica' al tempo della controriforma*. Padua.

Tomasini, Iacopo Philippo, 1986. *Gymnasium Patavinum . . . libri V.* Udine: Nicolai Schiratti, 1654; reprint Sala Bolognese.

Tronti, Mario, 1963. "Baldi, Camillo." DBI 5:465–67.

Turrini, Miriam, 1991. *La coscienza e le leggi. Morale e diritto nei testi per la confessione della prima Età moderna*. Bologna.

Turtas, Raimondo, 1988. *La nascita dell'università in Sardegna. La politica culturale dei sovrani spagnoli nella formazione degli Atenei di Sassari e di Cagliari (1543–1632)*. Sassari.

Turtas, Raimondo, 1995. *Scuola e Università in Sardegna tra '500 e '600. L'organizzazione dell'istruzione durante i decenni formativi dell'Università di Sassari (1562–1635)*. Sassari.

*L'Università dell'Aquila*, 2000. *Alle origini dell'Università dell'Aquila. Cultura, università, collegi gesuitici all'inizio dell'età moderna in Italia meridionale*. Atti del convegno internazionale di studi promosso dalla Compagnia di Gesù e dall'Università dell'Aquila nel IV centenario dell'istituzione dell'*Aquilanum Collegium* (1596). L'Aquila, 8–11 novembre 1995. Edited by Filippo Iappelli S. I. and Ulderico Parente. Rome.

Vaccari, Pietro, 1957. *Storia della Università di Pavia*. Second revised edition. Pavia.

Vallauri, Tommaso, 1875. *Storia delle Università degli Studi del Piemonte*. Second revised edition. Turin.

Vallauri, Tommaso, 1970. *Storia delle Università degli Studi del Piemonte*. 2 vols. Turin, 1845–46; reprint Bologna.

Vannozzi, Francesca, 1991. "L'insegnamento della medicina in Siena dal XVII secolo ai giorni nostri," in *L'Università di Siena. 750 anni di storia*. Siena, pp. 159–73.

Vaz de Carvalho, José, 2001a. "Álvares, Manuel." DHCJ 1:90.

Vaz de Carvalho, José, 2001b. "Fonseca, Pedro da." DHCJ 2:1478.

*Una vergine*, 1965. *Una vergine per il principe: Medici e Gonzaga*. Rome.

Vigna, Guido, 1991. *Il santo dei Gonzaga: San Luigi e il suo tempo*. Milan.

Villoslada, Riccardo G., 1954. *Storia del Collegio Romano dal suo inizio (1551) alla soppressione della Compagnia di Gesù (1773)*. Rome.

Volpi Rosselli, Giuliana, 1993. "Il corpo studentesco, i collegi e le accademie," in *L'Università di Pisa*, part 1, pp. 377–468.

Wallace, William A., O.P., 1995. "Circularity and the Paduan *Regressus:* From Pietro d'Abano to Gaileo Galilei." *Vivarium* 33 (1): 76–97.

Wallace, William A., O.P., 1996. *The Modelling of Nature: Philosophy of Science and Philosophy of Nature in Synthesis*. Washington.

Wallace, William A., O.P., 2006. "Jesuit Influences on Galileo's Science," in *The Jesuits II: Cultures, Sciences, and the Arts 1540–1773*, edited by John W. O'Malley, S.J., Gauvin Alexander Bailey, Steven J. Harris, and T. Frank Kennedy, S.J. Toronto, Buffalo, and London, pp. 314–35.

Wear, Andrew, 1995. "Medicine in Early Modern Europe, 1500–1700," in Lawrence I. Conrad et al., *The Western Medical Tradition 800 BC to AD 1800*. Cambridge, pp. 207–361.

Webster, Charles, 2008. *Paracelsus: Medicine, Magic and Mission at the End of Time*. New Haven and London.

Willson, D. Harris, 1956. *King James VI and I*. New York.

Zaccagnini, Guido, 1930. *Storia dello Studio di Bologna durante il Rinascimento*. Genève.

Zanca, Attilio, and Andriano Galassi, 1978. "Saggio di bibliografia medica mantovana rinascimentale," in *Mantova e i Gonzaga*, 399–421.
Zanetti, Ginevra, 1982. *Profilo storico dell'Università di Sassari*. Milan.
Zanfredini, Mario, 2001. "Alamanni, Cosimo." DHCJ 1:29.
Zanier, Giancarlo, 1983. *Medicina e filosofia tra '500 e '600*. Milan.
Zanier, Giancarlo, 1985. "La medicina paracelsiana in Italia: aspetti di un'accoglienza particolare." *Rivista di Storia della filosofia* 40:627–53.

# Index

*"Gonzaga" means the Gonzaga of Mantua. Other branches are identified by name.*

Accademia degli Invaghiti, 55
Accarisi, Giacomo, S.J., biography, 251–52
Adriatic Sea, dominion over, 99–100
Alamanni, Cosma, S.J., 210
Albert II (emperor), 54
Alciato, Andrea, 120–21
Aldreghetti, Aldreghetto, 145–46
Aldreghetti, Antonio Luigi, 145–46
Aldringen, Johann von: leaves Mantua, 240; permits sack, 238; rules Mantua, 239
Aldrobrandini, Pietro (cardinal), 102
Aldrovandi, Ulisse, in Mantua, 176
Alexander III (pope), 96, 99
Alexander of Aphrodisias, 203
Alexandrians, 208
Álvares, Manual, *De institutione grammaticae*, 50, 51
Angeli, Giacomo, di Barga, 62
Angelo, Giuseppe, 146
Aquaviva, Claudio, S.J.: and Mantua church, 36–37; wants teaching uniformity, 220, 221; mentioned, 44, 45
Archiginnasio (building), 139, 174
Aristotle: comparison of teaching by Jesuits and lay professors, 217–19, 222;
*De caelo et mundo*, 205; *De generatione et corruptione*, 204, 205, 209; logic texts, 51, 203, 204; *Metaphysics*, 209; *Meterology*, 204, 205; *Nicomachean Ethics*, 201, 202; *On the soul*, 203, 204, 205–06, 209; *Parva naturalia*, 204; *Physics*, 204, 205; *Poetry*, 199; *Rhetoric*, 199; textbooks, 223–24
Arriaga, Rodrigo de, S.J., *Cursus philosophicus*, 220
Augustus (emperor), 161
Averroes, Jesuit debate about, 206–08
Avicenna: *Canon*, 139, 143; mentioned, 182
Azor, Juan, S.J., *Institutiones morales*, 212–13

Baldi, Camillo, 135n
Baldo degli Ubaldi, 100, 119, 120
Bartoletti, Fabrizio: *Anatomia humani*, 129; and angina pectoris, 190; death, 246; *Encyclopaedia hermetico-dogmatica*, 130–32, 136–38; extracts lactose, 138, 191; and Galenism, 136–38; and Ferdinando Gonzaga, 130–31, 138, 139, 140, 141, 144; honored by University of Bologna, 139–40; income, 141; *Meth-*

Bartoletti, Fabrizio (*cont.*)
  *odus in dyspnoeam*, 184–90; negotiations with Mantua, 141–44; and Paracelsian medicine, 136–38; studies, 128; at the University of Bologna, 128–29, 139; at the University of Mantua, 142–44, 166; mentioned, 172, 175
Bartolo da Sassoferrato, 100, 119, 120, 161
Basile, Andreana, 66
Basil the Great, St., *Letter to Gregory*, 199
Berretta (woolen cap), 4–5
Bertioli, Antonio, 182n
Biancani, Giuseppe, S.J., mathematical presentation, 66–67
Bocchi, Zanobio, teaches botany, 177
Bonaparte, Napoleon, 249
Borghese, Scipione (cardinal): criticized, 109, 113; mentioned, 102
Borja, Francisco, S.J., 18
Bosio, Federico: witnesses testament of Vincenzo II, 241; mentioned, 242
Botanical garden, at Mantua, 176–78
Bozzolo, principality of, 3, 194
Brahe, Tycho, 59
Branca, Gian Paolo, 56
Brera College, 18, 44
Brueghel, Jan, 231
Brueghel, Johann, the Younger, 231
Brueghel, Peter, the Elder, 231
Bruschi, Francesco, 183
Bubalo, Joseph, 159
Buschetti, Isabella, 9
Busti, Ludovico (professor), 152, 165, 167

Cabeo, Niccolò, S.J., 151
Caesar: *De bello gallico*, 50; mentioned, 161
Cajetan, Tommaso de Vio (cardinal), 97
Cambridge University, 180
Campanella, Tommaso, 86
Campori, Pietro (cardinal), 148
Capello, Bianca, 28
Caravaggio, 66, 231
Carleton, Dudley, Sir: cools toward Marta, 106–07; corresponds with Marta, 101–03; helps Marta, 115–16; mentioned, 99, 108, 114, 121

Carlo Emanuele I. *See* Savoia, Carlo Emanuele I
Casale Monferrato: nobility, 12; mentioned, 11, 41, 76, 235, 239
Casalmaggiore, 236
Castel Goffredo, 43, 46
Castiglione delle Stiviere: principality of, 3; town, 42, 43, 45
Castro, Rodrigo De, 181n
Catarina de' Medici. *See* Gonzaga, Caterina de' Medici
Cavalli, Pietro Antonio: holds two positions, 162; teaches chemistry, 178; wants more money, 153; mentioned, 184
Cepari, Virgilio, S.J., 46
Charles V (emperor), 3, 9, 10, 54, 55, 76
Charville, 233
Chemical medicine, at Mantua, 178–84
Chemistry: in European universities, 180; in Italian universities, 181; at University of Mantua, 178–79
Chiabrera, Gabriello, 72
Chieppio, Annibale, 123
Chiozzi, Cesare, 148
Cicero: texts taught in Mantua Jesuit school, 50–51; mentioned, 199
Circular disputations, 223
Claudini, Giulio Cesare, 128, 135n
Clave, Jean, teaches chemistry, 179, 184
Clavius, Christoph, 200
Clement V (pope), 96
Clement VII (pope), 9, 10, 46
Clement VIII: criticized, 109, 112; mentioned, 102
College of doctors of law of Padua, 105, 114–16
College of doctors of law of Pisa, 89, 91–92, 116
Collegio Romano: and casuistry, 212; debates proposed textbook, 219–20; mentioned, 198, 200, 201–02, 211, 216
Colonna, Marc'Antonio (viceroy), 20
Conciliarism, 111–12
Congregation of the Index, 98–99, 113
Constantine the Great (emperor), 111, 161

# Index

Contarini, Nicolò di Zan Gabriel, 117–18
Copernicus, 59, 60, 201
Córduba, Don Gonzalo Fernández de, 236
*Corpus juris civilis*, 121
Correggio: Jesuit properties devastated, 240; mentioned, 78
Council of Florence, 107
Council of Nicea, 111
Council of Trent: wants more theological education, 212; wants Scripture taught, 210; mentioned, 107, 171
Count palatine doctorates, 55, 116, 158
Cremonese, proposed exchange for Monferrato, 71
Cremonini, Cesare: against the Jesuits, 21; criticizes Jesuit teaching, 218, 221; on the immortality of the soul, 206, 207, 208; mentioned, 118, 222, 224
Curia Romana, 87–88
Curtivo, Claudio, 145, 146
Curzio, Omnibene, S.J., biography, 252

Decio, Filippo, 120
De Rosis, Giovanni, S.J., 36–37
*Digest* of Justinian, 121
Dioscorides, *De materia medica*, 176–77, 178
Distillation, 179–80
Donation of Constantine, 96
Donato, Marcello, 56
Ducal palace of Mantua, 14
Du Chesne, Joseph: *Pharmacopoea dogmaticorum*, 182; mentioned, 183

Eleonora de' Medici. *See* Gonzaga, Eleonora de' Medici
Eleonora of Austria. *See* Gonzaga, Eleonora of Austria
Erasmus, Desiderius, 214
Este, Alfonso II (duke), 27
Este, Isabella, 9
Este, Luigi (cardinal): supports Marta, 86; mentioned, 109
Euclid, *Elements*, 200

Faà, Camilla, 69, 159
Fabrici d'Acquapendente, Girolamo, 28n, 142
Fabrico, Jesuit property devastated, 240
Fachinei, Andrea, 91, 92
Faculty of Theology of the University of Paris, 214
Farnese, Alessandro (cardinal), 76
Farnese, Margherita: marriage, 28; mentioned, 57
Farnese, Ranuccio I (duke): founds university, 22–23; mentioned, 207
Favre, Pierre, S.J., 15
Ferdinand I (emperor), 14
Ferdinand II (emperor): edict of sequestration, 235; invades Mantovano, 237–38; mentioned, 3
Ferdinand III (emperor), 248
Ferrari, Giacomo: promotes Paracelsian chemical medicine, 181–84; *protomedico*, 184; translates Du Chesne, 182–83
Ferrari, Orazio, S.J.: biography, 252; mentioned, 78
*Feudo feminino*, 9, 233
Folcario, Antonio, 26n, 27n
Fontana, Orazio, S.J., biography, 252
Fracastoro, Girolamo, 196
Francisco de Toledo, S.J.: *Introductio in dialecticam*, 203, 210; *Summa casuum conscientiae*, 212
Frederick III (emperor), 54, 158

Gabriello, Girolamo, teaches Marta, 84
Gagliardi, Achille, S.J.: and Christian philosophy, 207; mentioned, 17–18
Galen: *De difficultate respirationis*, 185, 188; *De locis affectis*, 185; texts, 128; mentioned, 140, 190, 191
Galenic medicine, 133, 182, 184
Galilei, Galileo: debates Ferdinando Gonzaga, 67; rebuts Biancani, 67n; and Vincenzo I, 57–58; mentioned, 59, 60
Galli, Taddeo (cardinal), 102
Gallo, Jacopo: death, 117; mentioned, 115

Garzoni, Tommaso, 4
Gazoldo, 3
Ghetto of Mantua, 7
Gilberti, Girolamo (pharmacist), 183
Gilbert of Poitiers, *Liber sex principiorum*, 203
Giorgione, 231
Giraldi Cinzio, Giovanni Battista, 16–17
Gonzaga, Carlo II (duke), 248
Gonzaga, Caterina de' Medici (duchess): and final preparations for university, 149, 151, 152–54; marriage, 69; meets Bartoletti, 140; proposed marriage to Henry Stuart, 103; and university finances, 154–57; mentioned, 77, 78, 229
Gonzaga, Eleonora, marries Rudolf II, 228
Gonzaga, Eleonora, marries Ferdinand III, 248
Gonzaga, Eleonora de' Medici (duchess): marriage, 28–29; opposes alchemists, 57; plays with St. Luigi, 42; supports Jesuits, 39
Gonzaga, Eleonora of Austria (duchess): charities, 26; death, 39; favors Jesuits, 26–27, 29–30; and Jesuit church, 37; marriage, 26; remains moved, 249; wants peace, 45; mentioned, 14
Gonzaga, Ercole (cardinal): attends University of Bologna, 61; and Jesuits, 24–25; legacy, 32; supports press, 58; mentioned, 25, 41, 76
Gonzaga, Federico, would-be assassin, 230
Gonzaga, Federico II (duke), 9, 10, 194, 234
Gonzaga, Ferdinando (cardinal and duke): alchemical experiments, 65; arranges pardon for Caravaggio, 66; and astrology, 72, 201; and Bartoletti, 138, 139, 140; and botanical garden, 177; boyhood friendship with Jesuits, 59; builds Scala Sancta, 73; as cardinal, 63–67; debates Galilei, 67; as duke, 68, 71–73; enjoys company of Jesuits, 73–74; evaluation, 228; first mention of university, 74; grants privileges to German students, 173; honored by Mantuan Jesuits, 65; illness and death, 227–28; imposes tax for university, 154; lacks money, 104; learning, 71–72; looks for professors, 144–45; makes *Spiritual Exercises*, 59, 74; marries Camilla Faà, 69; marries Caterina de' Medici, 69; and Marta, 122–23; moves closer to Gonzaga-Nevers, 232; and music, 63, 66, 71–72; negotiates with Jesuits, 77–78; perennial student, 174; proclaims University of Mantua, 149; regent of Mantua, 68–69; renounces cardinalate, 69; schooling, 60; seeks support of pope, 75–77; supports alchemists, 178; supports medical scholarship, 176; threatens Isabella of Novellara, 230; at University of Ingolstadt, 61; at University of Pisa, 61–63; at Vatican Library, 65; vows to become a Jesuit, 65; wants to read Paracelsus, 63; mentioned, 15, 165, 183, 191, 194, 197, 198
Gonzaga, Ferdinando Carlo (duke), 248
Gonzaga, Francesco (bishop), 47
Gonzaga, Francesco (duke), 9, 14
Gonzaga, Francesco III (duke): death, 68; dismisses alchemists, 178; mentioned, 60, 182, 197
Gonzaga, Giacinto: birth, 69; death, 239; issues rules, 173; not legitimized, 229; protector of university, 159
Gonzaga, Gian Francesco (marquis): hires Vittorino da Feltre, 56; mentioned, 54
Gonzaga, Guglielmo (duke): agreement with Jesuits, 31–32; death, 37; deeds street to Jesuits, 35; hires teachers, 56; invites Jesuits to Mantua, 29–31; marriage, 14, 26; and Monferrato, 11, 13; names Jesuit church, 37; and Pius V, 27; procures right to award degrees, 55; supports medical learning, 176; and will of Ercole Gonzaga, 25; mentioned, 44, 182

# Index

Gonzaga, Laura, 140
Gonzaga, Ludovico (duke of Nevers), 25, 32, 78, 232–33
Gonzaga, Luigi, founder of dynasty, 1
Gonzaga, Margherita, marries Henry of Lorraine, 63
Gonzaga, Margherita Paleologo (duchess), 10, 25
Gonzaga, Maria: marries, 232; mentioned, 68, 105, 235
Gonzaga, Prospero, 162
Gonzaga, Vincenzo I (duke): and alchemy, 178; and botanical garden, 177; fights in Hungary, 58; and Galilei, 57; and Jews, 7; marriages, 27–29; and Monferrato, 13; supports Jesuits, 37, 39, 52; supports medical learning, 176; wants university, 53; mentioned, 33, 47, 60, 66, 182, 183, 229
Gonzaga Vincenzo II (duke): death, 232; marriage and attempted annulment, 229–30; patron of university, 245; sells paintings, 231; wants to marry Maria Gonzaga, 232; mentioned, 234, 235
Gonzaga-Nevers, Carlo (duke): in France, 232–33; imprisons Marta, 242–43; invested as duke, 239; returns to Mantua, 240; seizes power, 233, 235; at war, 236–37
Gonzaga-Rethel, Carlo, marries Maria Gonzaga, 232
Gonzaga family: cadet branches, 3; partible male inheritance, 2; and succession crisis, 227–33
*The Gonzaga Family in Adoration of the Trinity* (painting): dismembered, 249; mentioned, 39, 41
Gonzaga of Bozzolo, Ferrante, 229
Gonzaga of Castel Goffredo, Alfonso, 46
Gonzaga of Castiglione delle Stiviere, Diego, 46
Gonzaga of Castiglione delle Stiviere, Ferrante, 41–44
Gonzaga of Castiglione delle Stiviere, Francesco (marquis), 46, 47
Gonzaga of Castiglione delle Stiviere, Marta Tana: wants peace, 45; mentioned, 41, 43
Gonzaga of Castiglione delle Stiviere, Rodolfo: misrule and death, 44–46; mentioned, 42, 43
Gonzaga of Guastalla, Cesare, 55, 234
Gonzaga of Guastalla, Cesare II, 234
Gonzaga of Guastalla, Ferrante, 3, 10, 25, 32, 234
Gonzaga of Guastalla, Ferrante II (duke): death, 239; mentioned, 32, 232, 234, 235
Gonzaga of Novellara, Alfonso, 229
Gonzaga of Novellara, Barbara Borromeo, supports Jesuits, 25
Gonzaga of Novellara, Camillo, supports Jesuits, 25
Gonzaga of Novellara, Isabella: death, 239; marriage, 229–30
Gonzaga of Solferino, Orazio, 45
Gorzoni, Giuseppe, S.J.: describes closing of university, 245–46; mentioned, 32
Gregory XIV (pope), 109
Gregory XV (pope), 76–77
Guastalla, principality of, 3

Habsburg, Barbara (duchess of Ferrara), supports Jesuits, 26–27
Habsburg, Catherine, 14
Habsburg, Don Diego, 43
Habsburg, Giovanna (grand duchess of Tuscany): humiliated, 28; supports Jesuits, 27
Habsburg, Maria (empress), 43
Hadrian (emperor), 161
Hartmann, Johann, 180
Harvey, William, 142, 190
Heberden, William, 190
Helena, St., 73
Henry IV (king), 182
Hermes Trismegistis, 131
Hippocrates, 140, 185
Holy Roman Empire, 234
Horace, 199

Ignatius Loyola, St., 15, 47
Immortality of the soul debate, 205–08
Index of Prohibited Books: bans Paracelsian works, 135–36; mentioned, 98, 196
Innocent IX (pope), 109
*In sacrosancta beati Petri* (papal bull), 174
Ippoliti family, 3
Irnerius, 119
Isocrates, *To Demonicus*, 50
Italian universities: compared to northern universities, 15–16; curricular freedom and lack of structure, 224–25; teach little theology, 209–10

James I (king): and conciliarism, 112; goals, 105; mentioned, 101, 107, 108, 114
Jehoshaphat (king), 159
Jesuit *Constitutions*, 15
Jesuit curriculum and teaching: attempts to enter Italian universities, 14–22; attitude toward Averroes, 206–08; biblical studies, 213–15; careers of Jesuit teachers, 216–17; casuistry, 211–13; compared with lay universities, 198–215, 223–25; and Copernicus, 200; criticized, 217–18, 221; debate on textbooks, 219–21; do not teach astrology, 201; probabilism, 213; response to criticism, 221–23; theology, 211; and Thomism, 210–11; view of university education, 224
Jesuit Province of Venice: boundaries, 52; helps Mantuan Jesuits, 240; holds congregation, 66
Jesuits: and University of Catania, 19–20; and University of Ingolstadt, 15; and University of Macerata, 20–21; and University of Messina, 15, 16; and University of Padua, 21–22; and University of Paris, 15; and University of Parma, 22–23; University of Rome, 15; and University of Turin, 16–19
Jesuits, at Novellara, 25–26
Jesuits of Mantua: agreement with Ferdinando Gonzaga, 76–79; agreement with Guglielmo Gonzaga, 29–31; college established, 31–33; die in plague, 246–47; island, 7; and Jews, 33, 35; and Marta legacy, 244–45; oppose taxing contado, 157; rebuild school, 247–48; school, 49–51; suppressed, 248; teach philosophy, 52–53; and war, 237–40, 246
Jesuit teaching in University of Mantua: Aristotle, 203–04; biblical studies, 214; casuistry, 213; ethics, 202; Gilbert of Poitiers, 203; humanities, 199–200; *Isogage* of Porphyry, 203; logic, 203–04; mathematics, 200–01; metaphysics, 209; natural philosophy, 208; theology, 209, 211
Jews: and the Gonzaga, 7; and Jesuits, 33, 35; in Mantovano, 7; in sack of Mantua, 239
Jonson, Ben, 196

Kepler, Johann, 59
Kimhi, David, 215
Knitwear guild, opposes tax for university, 155
Knitwear industry, does not recover, 240

Laínez, Diego, S.J.: Ercole Gonzaga, 24–25; mentioned, 15
La Rochelle, 235
Lateran Palace, 73
Lendinara, 246
Leo X (pope), 161
Libavius, Andreas, 131n
Lipsius, Justus, 195
Loreto (shrine), 44
Lorraine, Henry of (duke), 63
Lucedio, Santa Maria di (monastery), 76
Ludovisi, Ludovico (cardinal), 141–42
Luigi Gonzaga, St.: beatification, 46–48; canonization, 48; and Jesuits of Mantua, 48; life, 41–45; protector of Mantua and the Gonzaga, 74; mentioned, 24, 53
Luzzara, given to duke of Guastalla, 239–40

# Index

Machiavelli, Niccolò, 196
Macolo, Giacomo, teaches chemical medicine, 181
Magati, Cesare, 135n
Magini, Giovanni Antonio: scholarship and teacher of Gonzaga princes, 59–60, 61, 65; mentioned, 56, 138
Maldonado, Juan, S.J., 214–15
Malpighi, Marcello, 191
Mancini, Domenico, 195
Manfredini, Francesco, S.J.: biography, 252; mentioned, 151, 152, 217
Mantegna, 231
Mantovano: economy, 5; knitwear industry, 5; population, 6, 240; slow economic recovery, 240; mentioned, 1, 3
Mantua (city): ghetto, 7; Hebrew press, 6; knitwear, 3–5; location, 1; plague, 237–38; population, 6, 238, 240; press, 58; sacked, 238–39; under siege, 237–38; textile industry, 3–5
Mantua, duchy of: becomes part of Italy, 249; conquered by Napoleon, 249; incorporated into Austrian empire, 248
Mantua, State Archive, 249
Mantuan Senate, 241
Manzoni, Alessandro, *I promessi sposi*, 238
Marbais, Nicolas de, 113n
Mariani, Andrea: leaves Mantua, 246; mentioned, 146, 167, 175
Marie de Médicis (queen), 43, 103
Marino, Giambattista, 72
Marta, Giacomo Antonio: advises James I, 104–05; advises on University of Mantua, 149; burial, 245; *Compilatio totius iuris*, 118–21; and conciliarism, 111–12; *Consilia*, 193–95; criticizes Paul V, 109–11; *Decisionum . . . Collegii Pisani*, 89–92; delivers inaugural oration, 159–61; doctorate questioned, 114–17; early life and works, 84–88; and Ferdinando Gonzaga, 122–23, 159, 161; hears sample lecture, 154; imprisoned, 242–43; and Jesuits, 123, 161; leaves goods to Jesuits, 244–45;

location of tomb unknown, 249; not a Protestant, 114; organizes law instruction, 152; recruited to Mantua, 122–26; at Roman Curia, 87–88; salary, 101, 117, 121, 124, 166; and Sarpi, 99–100; spies for James I, 101–08; *Supplicatio*, 108–14, 121; testament, 244; *Tractatus de clausulis*, 117–18; *Tractatus de iurisdictione*, 92–98, 112, 113, 243; at University of Padua, 100–01, 103, 117; at University of Pavia, 121–22; at University of Pisa, 88; wants council of Greek bishops, 107–08; writes *consilium* for Ferrante II, 242–43; mentioned, 174, 175
Marta, Giulio Camillo: obtains degree, 174; teaches, 174; mentioned, 193
Matthias (emperor), 69, 112
*Mechanics*, attributed to Aristotle, 60, 200
Medici, Cosimo de', 161
Medici, Cosimo I de' (grand duke), 195
Medici, Cosimo II de' (grand duke), 67, 69, 129
Medici, Ferdinando I de' (grand duke): oversees Ferdinando Gonzaga's studies, 61–62; mentioned, 116
Medici, Francesco I de' (grand duke), 28
Medici, Lorenzo il Magnifico de', 56
Medina, Bartolemé, 213
Megli, Lorenzo, S.J., biography, 252
Micanzio, Fulgenzio, 107
Michelangelo, 231
Mincio River, 1
Minor orders, 65n
Mithridate, 182
Mithridates VI, 182
Moletti, Giuseppe, 56
Monferrato, duchy of: acquired by Gonzaga, 9–11, 13–14; awarded to Piedmont-Savoy, 248; economy, 11; income from, 13; part given to Piedmont-Savoy, 239; mentioned, 105
Montecchio, Sebastiano, 100
Monte di San Giorgio, 244
Monteverdi, Claudio: *La favola di Orfeo*, 149; at Gonzaga court, 14

Morando, Antonio, S.J.: biography, 252; mentioned, 152, 217
Moscatelli, Cesare, S.J., biography, 252–53
Moses, 159
Müller, Philip, *Miracula chymica*, 138–39
Murano, 231
Muret, Marc'Antoine, 195

Natta, Giovanni Francesco, S.J., biography, 253
Natural history, at Mantua, 176
Negri Ciriaco, Francesco: answers Marta, 242; witnesses testament of Vincenzo II, 241; writes for Gonzaga-Nevers, 240–41
Nepotism, 109
Nicholas V (pope), 161
Noceto, Giovanni Battista, S.J., biography, 253
Novellara, county of, 3

Oborski, Stanislaus, S.J., 46
Osanna, Francesco, ducal printer, 33, 58
Osanna Press, destroyed in sack, 239
Otto II (emperor), 105
Ovid, *Tristia*, 51
Oxford University, 180

Pacifico Gymnasio Mantuano. See University of Mantua
Padua, 4
Paleologo, Bonifacio (marquis), 10
Paleologo, Gian Giorgio (marquis), 10
Paleologo, Guglielmo IX (marquis), 9
Paleologo, Maria, 9, 10
Paleologo family, 9–10, 11, 13
Paleologus. See Paleologo
Pallavicino, Ottavio (cardinal), 93
Palperia, Giacomo Francesco: complains, 153; teaches medicine and medical botany, 177–78
*Pandects* professorship, 167
Pappazoni, Flaminio, 67
Paracelsian medicine: not influential in Italy, 134–36; at University of Mantua, 178–84; mentioned, 131, 133–34, 183

Paracelsus: Ferdinando Gonzaga wishes to read works, 63; life and works, 131, 133
Parenti, Luca, S.J.: biography, 217; mentioned, 253
Parmigianino, Il, 231
Paul III (pope), 15, 76, 195
Paul V: criticized, 109, 111–12; death, 121; denies annulment, 230; mentioned, 51, 73, 93, 99
Peaceful University of Mantua. See University of Mantua
Peace of Cateau-Cambrésis, 10
Pedro de Fonseca, S.J., *Institutionum dialecticarum*, 203, 220
Pellegrino, Marco Antonio, 100
Peña, Francisco, 88
Perera, Benedetto, S.J., on Averroes, 206
Peter, St., 96
Peter Canisius, St., 43
Petrazzini, Giovanni, 147–48; trial lecture, 153–54
Phillip IV (king), 242
Piazzoni, Rocco: syndic of university, 149; wants head tax, 155, 157–58; mentioned, 152, 165
Piedmont-Savoy: name explained, 2n; mentioned, 13, 105, 235
Pius II (pope), 161
Pius IV (pope), 55
Pius V (pope), 27
Plague, 237–39
*Plenitudo potestatis*, 118
Polanco, Juan Alfonso de, S.J., 25
Poliziano, Angelo, 56
Pomponazzi, Pietro: on the immortality of the soul, 206, 207, 208; mentioned, 61, 84
Po River, 11
Porzio, Simone, 84
Possevino, Antonio (the elder), S.J.: funeral oration, 39; on immortality of the soul, 207; persuades Guglielmo Gonzaga, 29–30, 33; mentioned, 196
Possevino, Antonio (the younger): biog-

raphy and teaching Tasso, 196–97; cured by Bartoletti, 187
Possevino, Giovanni Battista, 196
Prophyry, *Isagoge*, 203, 204
Ptolemy, 60
Public Academy of Mantua, 79–82, 151
Public anatomy, 179

Quercentanus. *See* Du Chesne, Joseph

Ramboldoni da Feltre, Vittorino, 56
Raphael, 231
Rashi (Rabbi Solomon Ben Isaac), 215
*Ratio studiorum*: and Aristotle, 202; and Averroes, 207–08; and biblical studies, 215; conception of education, 199; and logic, 203; and mathematics, 200; and natural philosophy, 204–05; and theology, 210; mentioned, 49, 50, 51, 198, 220, 224
Rattazzi, Giacomo Filippo, 153
Reggiolo, given to duke of Guastalla, 239–40
Remond, François, S.J.: biography, 253; death, 247
Republic of Venice, provides assistance, 237
Rhazes, *Liber Almansoris*, 139
Rho, Alessandro da, 91, 92, 120
Ricci, Matteo, S.J., 20
Richelieu (cardinal), invades Piedmont-Savoy and Monferrato, 235–36
Riformatori dello Studio di Padova, 115, 142
Ripa, Ercole, 241
Ripa, Silvestro, 172
Rivière, Lazare, 190
Robert Bellarmine, St. (cardinal): *Disputationes*, 211; mentioned, 97, 104, 113, 216, 224
Roman Rota, 118, 120
Rossano, Francesco, S.J., biography, 253–54
Rubens, Peter Paul: in Mantua, 39, 41; mentioned, 249
Rudolf II (emperor), 11, 43, 228

Ruffinelli, Venturino, 58
Rufus, Quintus Curtius, *History of Alexander the Great*, 199
Ruini, Carlo, 120

Sabbioneta, duchy of, 3; Hebrew press, 6
Sack of Mantua, 238–39
Sacrobosco, Johannes de, *De sphaera*, 200
Sagliero, Ottavio, 145–47
Sallust, *Bellum Iugurthinum*, 51
Salmerón, Alfonso, S.J.: protects Marta, 84; mentioned, 126, 144
San Pietro (cathedral), 158
San Salvatore (church), 31, 33
San Salvatore Monferrato (town), 177
Sant'Agnese (Augustinian monastery), 54–55
Santissima Trinità (Jesuit church): construction, 35–39; deconsecration and fire, 249; Marta buried in, 244
Santorio, Santorio, 118
Sarpi, Paolo: theologian to Guglielmo Gonzaga, 27; mentioned, 99–100, 102, 107
Sarro (king), 161
Savoia, Carlo Emanuele I (duke): death, 239; invades Monferrato, 68; presses demands, 235; sides with France, 236; mentioned, 104, 105, 228
Savoia, Emanuele Filiberto (duke): and Jesuits, 16–18; mentioned, 2, 13
Savoia, Vittorio Amedeo I (duke), 239
Savoia family, 2n, 10
Scala Sancta (Holy Stairs), 73
Scioppio, Gaspare: criticizes Possevino's book, 197; negotiates for Ferdinando, 71n
Seneca, 199
Senesi, Alessandro, 140
Septuagint (Greek text of the Bible), 215
Serugo, Vincenzo, S.J.: biography, 254; mentioned, 151, 217
Severinus, Peter, 181
Sigismund I of Luxemburg (emperor): grants university charter, 54; mentioned, 1, 158

Silvatico, Bartolomeo, 145
Silvatico, Benedetto, 145
Simonetta, Alessandro, S.J.: biography, 254; mentioned, 217
Simony, 109
Sixtus V (pope): criticized, 109; mentioned, 73
Soardi, Vincenzo Agnelli (bishop), 158
Soares, Cipriano, *De arte rhetorica*, 33, 50, 220
Society of Jesus. *See* Jesuits
Soldati, Giorgio, S.J., 37
Solferino, 43
Sommaja, Girolamo da, 130n
Soncini, Fausto, 166–67
Spain: attacks Piedmont-Savoy, 104; enters war, 235–36; mentioned, 234
Spiritual Exercises of Ignatius Loyola: and Ferdinando Gonzaga, 59, 74; mentioned, 44
Stanislaus Kostka, S.J., St., 46, 47
Striggi, Alessandro: death, 239; final preparations for university, 152; gives privileges to German students, 173; justifies sale of paintings, 231; searches for professors, 144–45; threatens Isabella of Novellara, 230; and university finances, 155; writes libretti for Monteverdi, 149, 151; mentioned, 77, 123, 148, 191, 233, 245
Stuart, Henry, 103
Suárez, Francisco, S.J., 211, 224
Sundials, 81, 200
Synclitico, Alessandro, 145

Tacitus, Cornelius: life and popularity, 195–96; mentioned, 175
Tagliacozzi, Gaspare, 57
Tasso, Torquato, *Gerusalemme Liberata*, 58
Telesio, Bernardino, 86
Terence, not taught by Jesuits, 199
Tesauro, Antonio, 120
Themistius, 203
Theriac, 182
Thomas Aquinas, St.: and casuistry, 213; *Summa theologica*, 210; mentioned, 202, 220
Tintoretto, 231
Titian, 231
Tonti, Michelangelo (cardinal), 102
Torto, Matteo, S.J., biography, 254
Treaty of Cheraso, 239
Treaty of Ratisbon, 239
Trezzi, Giacomo Filippo, S.J., biography, 254
Tristano, Giovanni, S.J., 35–36

Union of Halle, 105
United Provinces of the Netherlands, 105
University of Alcalá de Henares, 45
University of Bologna: and chemistry, 181; compared with University of Mantua, 172, 173, 208; tax, 154; teaches little theology, 210; mentioned, 128
University of Catania: and Jesuits, 19–20; tax, 154
University of Ferrara, and chemistry, 181
University of Graz, 204
University of Ingolstadt: and Jesuits, 15, 217–18; mentioned, 60–61
University of Leiden, 180
University of Louvain, 180
University of Macerata, and Jesuits, 20–21
University of Mantua: agreement with Jesuits, 78–79; beadles, 165; begins, 158–59; botanical garden, 162, 176–78; building, 153, 161–62; calendar, 162; closes, 245–46; compared with other universities, 165, 166, 167; differences over medical doctorates, 225; expenses, 166–69; final preparations, 149, 151–54; financing, 154–58; first mentioned, 74; German students, 172–73; harassment of Jesuits, 226; inaugural oration, 159–61; Jesuit teaching, 198–215; Jesuit teaching begins, 79–82; matriculation, 152–53; metaphysics professorship, 151–52; name, 158; proclamation of, 149; professorships, 162–64, 166–69; professors of law, 192–93;

# Index

professors of medicine, 175–76; reasons for, 75; rights of students, 194–95; rolls, 163–64, 168–69; student nations, 171–72; students, 170–74; summation, 250; syndic, 165; Tacitus professorship, 195–97

University of Marburg, professorship of chemistry, 180

University of Messina, and Jesuits, 15–16

University of Montpellier, 180

University of Padua, 166; against papal jurisdiction, 243–44; calendar, 162n; compared to University of Mantua, 173; few lectures, 223; German students, 172; head tax, 157; and Jesuits, 21–22; matriculation forms, 152; students criticize Jesuits, 217–18; taxes, 154

University of Paris, 15, 180

University of Parma: and Jesuits, 22–23; teaches casuistry, 210; mentioned, 202

University of Pavia: and chemistry, 181; mentioned, 121–22

University of Perugia, 167

University of Pisa: teaches chemical medicine, 181; mentioned, 166

University of Rome: and chemistry, 181; compared to University of Mantua, 208; tax, 154; mentioned, 15, 115, 116, 166, 187

University of Salamanca, 242

University of Siena: and chemistry, 181; compared to University of Mantua, 173

University of Turin: and Jesuits, 16–19; tax, 154

University of Vienna, 219

Urban VIII (pope): debates Ferdinando Gonzaga, 67; supports Gonzaga-Nevers, 239; mentioned, 77, 109, 241

Valier, Agostino (cardinal), 31
Valois, Elizabeth, 41
Varoli, Costanzo, 129
Venetian interdict, 51–52, 93, 95, 111
Venetian Senate, 21
Venice, Republic of, 105
Verasio, Giovanni Domenico, searches for professors, 146, 147
Verona, 4
Vesalius, Andreas, 129, 140, 191
Vesling, Johann: *Syntagma anatomicum*, 191; at University of Mantua, 172–73, 191; at University of Padua, 191–92
Vialardi, Fausto, distiller, 178, 179
Villa Fabrico, Jesuit property, 78–79
Virgil, *Aeneid*, 50, 199
Visdomini, Francesco, 102–03
Vitelleschi, Muzio, S.J., 77, 106
Vulgate (Bible), 214, 215
Vulpio, Francesco, S.J., 254

Wotton, Henry, Sir, 107–08

Zabarella, Giacomo, 21
Zamberti, Carlo, S.J., 254
Zocchi, Claudio, 148
Zucchi, Emilio, S.J., biography, 254